THE INTERNAL DEBTS
OF THE UNITED STATES

TWENTIETH CENTURY FUND, INC.

This study has been made under the auspices of the Twentieth Century Fund, Inc., founded by Edward A. Filene, President of William Filene's Sons Company of Boston, Massachusetts.

———

———

11 WEST 42ND STREET

NEW YORK CITY

THE INTERNAL DEBTS
of the UNITED STATES

EDITED BY
EVANS CLARK
Director, Twentieth Century Fund, Inc.

ASSISTED BY
GEORGE B. GALLOWAY

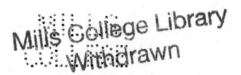
PUBLISHED FOR
TWENTIETH CENTURY FUND, INC.

THE MACMILLAN COMPANY
NEW YORK   1933

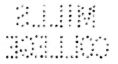

THE CONTRIBUTORS

The following are the contributors to this volume with the subjects of their special interest.

FRIEDA BAIRD
Formerly of The Brookings Institution
Farm Mortgage Debts

JOHN BAUER
Director, American Public Utilities Bureau
Public Utility Debts

EVANS CLARK
Director, Twentieth Century Fund
The Nation's Total Debts

WILFRED ELDRED
Economist, National Transportation Committee
The Railroad Debt

GEORGE B. GALLOWAY
Twentieth Century Fund
The Debts of the Federal Government
and Financial Corporations

WYLIE KILPATRICK
Institute for Government Research, The Brookings Institution
State and Local Debts

GARDINER C. MEANS
Columbia University
The Debts of Industrial Corporations and Banks

VICTORIA J. PEDERSON
Columbia University
Urban Mortgage Debts

FRANKLIN W. RYAN
Vice President and Economist, Van Strum Financial Service
Short-Term Debts

v

THE CONSULTANTS

The following acted as advisers in the preparation of this volume and reviewed the findings without, however, assuming personal responsibility for them.

LEONARD P. AYRES
Vice President, Cleveland Trust Company
The Debts of Banks

JAMES C. BONBRIGHT
Professor of Economics, Columbia University
Public Utility Debts

PHILIP H. CORNICK
Institute of Public Administration
State and Local Debts

CHARLES G. EDWARDS
President, New York Real Estate Securities Exchange
Urban Mortgage Debts

CHARLES O. HARDY
Economist, The Brookings Institution
The Debts of Railroads and Banks

CLARENCE HEER
Professor of Economics, University of North Carolina
State and Local Debts

LEON HENDERSON
Director, Division of Remedial Loans, Russell Sage Foundation
Short-Term Personal and Household Debts

HARLEY L. LUTZ
Professor of Political Science, Princeton University
State and Local Debts

EDWIN G. NOURSE
Director, Institute of Economics, The Brookings Institution
Farm Mortgage Debts

LAURENCE H. SLOAN
Vice President, Standard Statistics Company
The Debts of Industrial Corporations

CONTENTS

	PAGE
PREFACE	XV
CHAP. ONE. THE NATION'S TOTAL INTERNAL DEBTS	3
CHAP. TWO. FARM MORTGAGE DEBTS	24
1. Summary	24
2. The Facts	24
3. Recommendations	25
CHAP. THREE. URBAN MORTGAGE DEBTS	63
1. Summary	63
2. The Facts	63
3. Recommendations	64
CHAP. FOUR. THE RAILROAD DEBT	92
1. Summary	92
2. The Facts	92
3. Recommendations	93
CHAP. FIVE. PUBLIC UTILITY DEBTS	140
1. Summary	140
2. The Facts	140
3. Recommendations	142
CHAP. SIX. THE DEBTS OF INDUSTRIAL CORPORATIONS	171
1. Summary	171
2. The Facts	171
3. Recommendations	173
CHAP. SEVEN. THE DEBTS OF FINANCIAL CORPORATIONS	204
CHAP. EIGHT. THE DEBT OF THE UNITED STATES GOVERNMENT	211
1. Summary	211
2. The Facts	211
3. Recommendations	212
CHAP. NINE. THE DEBTS OF STATE AND LOCAL GOVERNMENTS	254
1. Summary	254
2. The Facts	254
3. Recommendations	255

	PAGE
CHAP. TEN. SHORT-TERM BUSINESS DEBTS	291
CHAP. ELEVEN. SHORT-TERM PERSONAL AND HOUSEHOLD DEBTS	302
CHAP. TWELVE. BANK DEBTS	326
1. Summary	326
2. The Facts	326
3. Recommendations	327
CHAP. THIRTEEN. GENERAL RECOMMENDATIONS	385
1. Approaches to the Debt Problem	386
2. Measures of Immediate Relief	388
3. Measures of Permanent Protection	398

APPENDICES

I. Farm Loans and Mortgage Refinancing through the Federal Land Bank System	409
II. Sources of Data on Public Utilities	415
III. Reservations by Authors of Chapter Thirteen	424
Index	427

TABLES

		PAGE
1.	Amount and Percentage Distribution of Long-Term Debts by Class and Year	10
2.	Rates of Change in Long-Term Debts by Class	11
3.	Long-Term Debts, Population, Prices, Wealth and Income	13
4.	Changes in Long-Term Debts, Population, Prices, Wealth and Income	14
5.	Basic Data on Farm Mortgage Debts	28
6.	Farm Mortgage Debt Outstanding 1910–1930	29
7.	Farm Mortgage Indebtedness According to Type of Tenure	29
8.	Ratio of Mortgaged Debt to Value of Farms Mortgaged	34
9.	Number of Farms Changing Ownership 1928–1932	36
10.	Delinquent Instalments 1928–1932	36
11.	Length of Term of Farm Mortgage Loans	37
12.	Holders of Farm Mortgages	40
13.	Ratio of Real Estate Acquirements to Mortgage Loans	42
14.	Real Estate Holdings 1928–1932	43
15.	Foreclosures Pending 1928–1932	44
16.	Extent of Relief Resulting from Waiving of Principal Payments	48
17.	Extent of Relief Granted by Reducing Interest Rates, etc.	49
18.	Loans by Federal Land Banks	51
19.	Basic Data on Urban Mortgage Debts	66
20.	Trend of National Income, Urban Population, Building and Building Costs	67
21.	Growth of National Income, Building and Urban Population	67
22.	Urban Real Estate Loans Held by Building and Loan Associations	69
23.	Non-Farm Mortgages Held by Life Insurance Companies	70
24.	Estimated Loans on Non-Farm Mortgages and Real Estate Held by Banking Institutions	71
25.	Estimate of Volume of Real Estate Securities Outstanding 1913–1931	74
26.	Guaranteed Mortgages and Certificates Outstanding, New York City	75
27.	Guaranteed Mortgages and Certificates Outstanding Not Duplicated in Previous Tables	76
28.	Estimated Urban Real Estate Mortgage Debt Outstanding 1913–1931	76

PAGE

29. Percentage of Total Urban Real Estate Mortgage Debt Held by Each Agency — 79
30. Relationship of Urban Real Estate Mortgage Debt to Total Assets, by Agencies — 79
31. Trend of Residential Rents — 83
32. Railroad Debts in Relation to Capitalization, Investments and Income 1913–1931 — 96
33. Percentages Changes in Railroad Debts in Relation to Capitalization, Investments and Income 1913–1931 — 97
34. Railroad Debts in Relation to Railway Traffic, Revenues, Expenses, National Wealth and Income 1913–1931 — 98
35. Percentage Changes in Railroad Debts in Relation to Railway Traffic, Revenues, Expenses, National Wealth and Income 1913–1931 — 99
36. Relationship of Railway Funded Debt to Total Railway Capitalization 1890–1931 — 114
37. Public Utility Debts, Capitalization and Investment — 143
38. Basic Data on Debts of Public Utilities — 144
39. Basic Data on Debts of Specific Utility Industries — 146
40. The Development of the Electrical Industry 1912–1931 — 149
41. The Development of Electric Railways 1912–1931 — 152
42. Price and Value of Public Utility Bonds — 154
43. Debts of Industrial Corporations — 175
44. Income of Industrial Corporations — 179
45. Relation of Debts to Assets of Industrial Corporations — 182
46. Debts and Assets of Major Industrial Groups in 1929 — 185
47. Debts and Assets of Manufacturing Industries in 1929 — 186
48. Industrial Debt by Major Divisions — 188
49. Debts of Large Industrial Corporations — 193
50. Debts of Smaller Industrial Corporations — 194
51. Commercial Failures 1928–1932 — 196
52. Commercial Failures, Quarterly Record 1931 and 1932 — 199
53. Debts of Financial Corporations 1929 and 1930 — 206
54. Growth of Reserves of Life Insurance Companies — 206
55. Total Volume of Real Estate Bonds Outstanding — 207
56. Investment Trust Financing — 207
57. Funded Debts of Investment Trusts — 208
58. Long-Term Debts of Financial Companies — 209
59. Long-Term Debts of Financial Corporations — 210
60. Basic Data on Federal Government Debts — 214
61. Public Debt, January 31, 1933, Classified by Character — 216
62. Preliminary Statement of the Public Debt, January 31, 1933 — 219
63. Issues of Interest Bearing Securities of the United States — 221
64. Maturities of Interest-Bearing Securities of the United States — 222

PAGE

65. Annual United States Surpluses or Deficits 1920–1934   222

66. Public Debt Retirements by Source 1919–1932   227

67. Total Outstanding Interest-Bearing Securities of the United States Government 1930   232

68. Domestic and Government Bond Prices and Yields 1929–1933   233

69. United States Loans and Investments Subject to Capitalized Segregation   244

70. Basic Data on State and Local Debts   258

71. State and Local Net Debt 1840–1932   258

72. Percentage Increase in State and Local Debts 1922–1932   259

73. Taxable Wealth in Relation to Population and Debts 1850–1932   263

74. Relative Debt Burdens 1922 and 1932   264

75. Amount of Increase in Ratios of State and Local Debts to Income 1922–1932   264

76. The Trend of Taxes 1922–1931   265

77. Short-Term Business Debts in the United States 1931 and 1932   296

78. Estimated Total of Loans by Brokers to Their Customers   299

79. Short-Term Debts in the United States   301

80. Statistics of Leading American Industries   305

81. Short-Term Indebtedness for Household Purposes in the United States 1931 and 1932   307

82. Estimated Volume and Amounts Outstanding of Loans by Small Loan Agencies 1932   312

83. Estimated Volume and Amounts Outstanding of Loans by Small Loan Agencies 1931   314

84. Bank Debt in the United States Exclusive of the Debt of the Federal Reserve Banks, June 30, 1932   329

85. Debt of All Banks in the United States, Distributed by Type of Bank, June 30, 1932   330

86. Debt of All Banks in the United States Except Savings Banks, Distributed by Relation to Federal Reserve System, June 30, 1932   331

87. Geographical Distribution of Banks and Bank Debt in the United States Including Alaska and Insular Possessions   332

88. Debt of National Banks Classified According to Size of Capital Stock, December 31, 1931   334

89. Changes in Debt of All Banks 1913–1932   335

90. Growth in Debt of All Banks in the United States, Demand and Time Deposits by Type of Bank 1913–1932   337

91. Growth in Debt of Commercial Banks, Distributed in Relation to Federal Reserve System   340

92. Increase in Deposits 1922–1929   342

                                                                                PAGE
93. National Banks, Distribution of Earning Assets   347
94. Bank Suspensions   348
95. Bank Suspensions by Size of Town or City   349
96. Loss of Clear Reserves to Member Banks of Federal Reserve
        System, September 16, 1931–February 29, 1932   369
97. Distribution of Utility Bond Capitalization by Yield at the end
        of 1932   418
98. Distribution of Bond Capitalization of Operating Companies,
        Mainly Gas and Electric, by Yield at the end of 1932   419
99. Distribution of Telephone and Telegraph Bond Capitalization
        by Yield at end of 1932   420
100. Distribution of Utility Company Bonds by Yield and Number
        of Times Fixed Charges are Estimated as Earned in 1932   422

CHARTS

		PAGE
1.	Percentage Distribution of Long-Term Debts	6
2.	Growth of Long-Term Debts by Class and Year	8
3.	Relation of National Wealth to Debts	9
4.	Relation of National Income to Debt Service	12
5.	Comparative Changes since 1913 in Debt Service, Production and Prices	15
6.	Changes in Agricultural Income, Land Values and Mortgage Debt and Fixed Charges on Farm Property	31
7.	A Comparison of Farm Prices and Prices Paid by Farmers	33
8.	Money Income of Industrial Workers and Farm Income	62
9.	Total Urban Mortgage Debt and Estimated Total Value of Urban Real Estate 1913–1931	77
10.	Percentage Distribution of Urban Mortgage Debt by Various Agencies 1913–1931	80
11.	Total Assets and Urban Mortgage Debts by Agency 1913–1931	81
12.	Railway Capitalization, Property Investment and Funded Debt at the End of Each Year, 1890–1932	110
13.	Leading Income Account Items, Steam Railways of the United States, by Years, 1890–1932	111
14.	Net Railway Operating Income, Interest on Funded Debt, and Net Income After Charges in Relation to Operating Revenues 1890–1932	112
15.	Volume of Traffic, Average Freight and Passenger Unit Revenue, and Ratio of Interest Cost to Traffic Units 1890–1932	124
16.	Public Utility Debts and Finances 1912–1931	150
17.	Percentage Changes in Public Utility Debts and Finances 1912–1931	151
18.	Relation of Net Corporate Income to Interest Charges 1920–1931	178
19.	Relation of Debts to Assets of Industrial Corporations	181
20.	Division of Long-Term Indebtedness between Major Industrial Groups 1930	184
21.	Long-Term Debts and Assets of Major Industrial Groups 1926–1930	187
22.	Credit Condition of Large and Small Corporations	192
23.	The Trend of Commercial Failures 1928–1932	198
24.	Prices of Industrial Bonds 1929–1932	201
25.	The Federal Debt in Relation to National Wealth and Income	215

PAGE

26. State and Local Debts in Relation to Tax Receipts, and National
Wealth and Income   257
27. Index of Change in Commercial Bank Deposits 1875–1928   339
28. Clear Reserves in Banking System and Major Factors in Change   364
29. Ratio of Clear Reserves to Legal Reserve Requirement   366
30. Percentage Distribution of Clear Reserves in Banking System
1929–1932   367
31. Changes in Total Deposits and in Borrowed Reserves or Excess of Clear Reserve over Legal Reserve Requirement, New York and Chicago Banks   372
32. Changes in Total Deposits and in Borrowed Reserves or Excess of Clear Reserves over Legal Reserve Requirement, City and Country Reserve Banks   373

PREFACE

DOMESTIC long-term debts have been a dominant problem of the latter months of the great depression, as they always must be in periods of continued low levels of corporate and individual earnings. A vast fixed and rigid structure of indebtedness has been imposed upon a foundation of national wealth and income which have subsequently suffered a drastic decline. During the years preceding the collapse of 1929 the American people, both as corporations and individuals, contracted debts, payable many years thereafter and bearing an unchanging rate of interest, on the basis of pre-depression assets and income. These debts were incurred in the confident expectation that both values and income would continue to increase with the years. Precisely the opposite development, of course, actually occurred. Values shrunk to a shadow of boom-year levels, and incomes, both corporate and individual, either vanished altogether or were deeply cut—because of continuing low prices, unemployment or wage and salary reductions, and industrial inactivity.

Fixed Debts and Reduced Incomes

Urban and farm mortgage loans written in boom-time terms, railroad and corporation bonds floated in the bull market or in the relative stability of pre-war economy, government securities marketed when assessed values were at, or approaching, the peak and taxable income was at high levels—most of them are still outstanding. Both the principal to be repaid and the interest rate remain practically unchanged. But the income of the people of the United States out of which these debts must be met has been cut in half. Industrial production at the beginning of 1933 was 50 per cent of 1929 levels; factory employment 41 per cent below; wholesale commodity prices 37 per cent lower; and farm prices are less than 50 per cent of what they were in 1929.

During the first months of the depression the issue was not acute. Debt obligations, where current income was insufficient, were met out of surplus and savings accounts—and recovery was momentarily expected even by those in high places. Had business activity returned and prices risen within a year or two, the issue would to a large degree have automatically solved itself. But prices sagged still further with the years and industrial activity registered new lows. With the depletion of reserves and savings, with confidence in immediate recovery at a low ebb, the strain of fixed debt upon shrinking income rapidly increased until it became a national issue in the latter part of 1932.

The Scope of the Study

Recognizing the importance of this problem the Twentieth Century Fund has made a canvass of the amount of indebtedness of the various classes of debtors in the United States in relation to their "capacity to pay," the results of which are included in this volume. The study has not been confined merely to a statement and analysis of the facts. Its object has been not only to disclose, as precisely as possible, the location and extent of existing strains between debts and incomes, but to suggest ways in which the strains can be eliminated or eased.

It compares the long-term debt burden, in *toto* and by specific classes of debts, with the amount of indebtedness outstanding at four crucial periods: (1) before the World War (1912, 1913, or 1914), (2) in a post-war depression year (1921 or 1922), (3) at the peak of prosperity in 1929 and (4) at the end of 1932 or beginning of 1933. It further compares the debt structure at these times with contemporaneous changes in population, production, commodity prices, wealth, and income, both by groups and for the nation at large. It also shows the relation between the debt and wealth of the several groups, on the one hand, and the relation between the debt charge and the income of borrowers, on the other. And, finally, it contains specific recommendations for easing the strains of existing debts and for preventing these difficulties in the future.

A brief survey of short-term debts in the United States is also included. Most short-term obligations are not subject to the strains of long-term debts because they are more readily adjustable to changes in income and prices. One class of them, however—the debt of banks to their depositors—has proven to be a crucial element in the entire economic situation. Furthermore a general review of short-term debts is useful to give perspective to the picture of internal indebtedness as a whole.

A Cooperative Venture

Because of the urgency of the situation and the necessity of quick action, the Twentieth Century Fund adopted a cooperative plan in carrying on the investigation. Eight well-qualified research experts were retained by the Fund in January, 1933, to make a canvass of the facts, and to suggest remedial action, in the eleven major segments of the problem with which they were most familiar. The first drafts of the reports of each of these experts were in hand within six weeks thereafter and were then submitted to the critical review of one or more leading authorities in each field. Insofar as time has allowed, the original manuscripts were revised in the light of the criticisms of these authorities. Those who reviewed the findings, however, have not assumed responsibility for them or for the recommendations of the contributors. The reports, with a chapter combining the facts in each field into estimates of the internal debt and income of the nation as a whole, are all included in this volume.

The urgency of the situation did not allow for extended original research. The purpose of the Fund has been to assemble the facts where they were available, to make the most informed guesses at them where they were not, and to piece all this material together in a broad picture of the debt structure and the support upon which it now rests, to reveal its serious weaknesses, and to suggest ways in which it may be buttressed. As a piece of economic research the value of this study has been limited by the necessities of time. It may be of real service, however, not only as a summary of what is known in this field but also in disclosing the lack of knowledge and pointing to the specific areas in which further investigation is urgently called for.

The several chapters were written and revised before April 1st. They do not, therefore, take account of subsequent events. In making this study it has been exceedingly difficult to keep pace with the swift changes in economic and political affairs.

Conclusions

Certain broad conclusions stand out of the findings. They are of the utmost importance to an understanding of the present debt situation and in the formulation of policies to meet it.

1. The present long-term internal indebtedness of the United States is approximately $134 billion.

2. There is no positive evidence of an intolerable debt burden upon our economy as a whole, assuming even a moderate improvement in general business conditions.

3. Contrary to popular impression debts bear with widely varying weight upon the nation's economic life. Railroad bonds and farm mortgage loans, as a group, for example, are far less adequately supported by income and assets than industrial and public utility bonds which are, on the whole, relatively sound.

4. Even within each area the variation in existing strains is great. For example, 58 per cent of American farms have no mortgage indebtedness at all and of the 42 per cent on which loans are outstanding, two-thirds now in difficulty are located in 11 of the north central states. The debts of electric light and power operating companies constitute no real problem at the present rate level, while electric railways as a group present an acute situation.

5. The facts alone suggest that blanket remedies, applying to all debts alike, would be ill-advised. Where conditions vary to such extreme degrees, the same treatment for all cases has obvious disadvantages and even dangers.

6. Each of the eight experts considering remedies in his own particular area of the whole problem, and without consultation with the others, has opposed measures which apply indiscriminately to all debtors and creditors in the special field with which he has been concerned.

7. Both the facts themselves and the unanimous opinion of those who have contributed to the study support the broad conclusion that adjustments should be made between individual debtors and creditors where the burden of payments is too heavy to be met at current income levels; but that machinery be set up by government agencies, suitable to conditions in each class of debt and geographical region, which will facilitate such adjustments in the best interests of debtors and creditors alike and prevent unnecessary receiverships and foreclosures.

8. While the difficulties of agricultural debtors are due primarily to a disproportionate decline in the prices received for farm products the strain upon debtors in other fields has come as much, if not more, from a decline of industrial activity.

9. These facts suggest that a marked increase of industrial activity,

even at low price levels, would ease the strains upon most debtors, although the effect would be least marked in the case of the relatively small proportion who are farmers.

10. The greatly disproportionate increase in long-term debts in relation to national wealth and income which occurred between 1921 and 1929, however, raises the question as to whether many debtors did not incur unwarranted long-term liabilities in those years which will be difficult, if not impossible, to support even with a general pick-up of business.

11. Even though economic recovery would not solve all our troubles measures which make for better business conditions in general would ease enough strains to be looked upon as debt remedies of the first importance.

The Long Future

These conclusions apply to debts which have already been incurred, but they also raise serious questions for the long future. Unless our economy is to be freed of reductions of income in the years to come the existence of any fixed, long-term debt obligations will cause recurring difficulties which will also aggravate the fluctuations themselves. Conversely the fewer and the less rigid are long-term obligations the easier will be the adjustments to income and price changes and the less drastic the changes will be. It would, of course, be far preferable so to stabilize our economy as to eliminate wide fluctuations in prices and business activity. Measures designed to accomplish this end are, therefore, to be included in remedies for future debt strains. But this sort of general stabilization cannot be accomplished at once and in the meantime policies for regulating new debts are urgently called for.

A searching inquiry is in order as to the economic wisdom of continuing to finance our economy, at least in so large a volume, through bonds, mortgage loans and other obligations payable in unchanging amounts over a long stretch of time. The same question should be directed toward the practice of meeting long-term maturities with the issuance of other long-term obligations. Refunding such as this has, of course, been especially prevalent in the railroad field. The possibility should also be explored of incorporating a provision in debt agreements themselves that payments of principal and interest be adjusted if necessary to some recognized index of the national income or of commodity prices.

Some way must be found to keep the various parts of our economic machine in a state of equal flexibility and balance. Elasticity in any one direction must be met with a proportionate change in every other. Any moving part which meets with rigidity in another sets up strains and friction—as current events described in this volume amply demonstrate. The contributors to this volume have themselves joined in making certain suggestions in Chapter Thirteen which, it is hoped, may prove useful in the formulation and application of policies to reduce present and future debt strains.

In presenting this volume the editor wishes to express his deep appreciation and that of the Trustees of the Twentieth Century Fund to those who coöperated in its preparation. They have rendered a genuine public service, some of them at great personal sacrifice.

EVANS CLARK

TWENTIETH CENTURY FUND, INC.
11 West 42nd Street
New York City
May 15, 1933.

THE INTERNAL DEBTS
OF THE UNITED STATES

Chapter One

THE NATION'S TOTAL INTERNAL DEBTS

T HE nation's internal debts are of two principal kinds: short and long-term, roughly divided into those payable within a year and over a period of years. It is obvious that it is long-term debts which cause most of the difficulty during hard times. Short-term obligations are far more readily adjusted to changes in income and price levels and, as a matter of fact, have been drastically liquidated during the depression. It is with long-term debts that this study is chiefly concerned.

These obligations can be divided into three main classes, given in the order of their size: corporation, real estate and government. Corporate debts make up very roughly about one-half of the national total, and may be further divided into those of financial institutions such as life insurance companies, those of railroads and other public utilities, and those of industrial concerns. They are mostly in the form of bonds and notes, although the paid-up values of insurance policies are also included. Real estate debts, representing about one-quarter of the total, are largely in the form of mortgage loans, although in the cities mortgage bonds have become popular in recent years. The remaining one-quarter of our internal debts are government obligations.

Debtors and Creditors

In considering the situation, however, it should be carefully observed that the nation's internal debts are also the nation's credits. Every promise of an American to pay is an assurance that another American is to receive payment. Also, strictly speaking, internal debts are not a drain upon the nation's income as a whole. As a matter of fact, the statistics of the national income include, among their many items, interest received upon these very debts. The internal debt problem is entirely a matter of adjustment between Americans who owe money and those to whom it is owed.

But here again the picture is not as clear as might at first be supposed. Contrary to the popular assumption it is impossible to segregate debtors from creditors. There is no "debtor class" any more than there is a "creditor class" in the United States. Most of us are both at the same time. We are creditors in relation to our bank which owes us the money we deposited, to the corporation whose bonds we hold and to our insurance company which owes us the paid-up value of our policies. We are debtors to the holder of the mortgage on our house, to the company that finances the purchase of our car or piano and to the bank from which we have borrowed to tide over some personal or business emergency.

The nation's chief debtors are not individuals at all but insurance companies, banks, railroads and industrial corporations. If one were to buttonhole the first thousand people one met on a New York street corner and to ask each one whether he was more of a debtor than a creditor one might well find creditorship to predominate. Even the farmer, who is looked upon as the nation's most militant debtor is also often a creditor as well—especially to the insurance company and bank. Farmers themselves also hold 14 per cent of the mortgages of, and are creditors to, other farmers.

If any generalizations about debtors and creditors are possible at all it is probably true that in terms of dollars the majority of debtors are corporations and the majority of creditors are individuals. As will be seen later on, the corporate nature of so many debtors complicates the debt problem for the very simple reason that adjustments of obligations between individuals are far easier than when one or both parties are incorporated institutions.

A careful who's who of debtors and creditors generates a conclusion which stands out of the debt problem wherever one attacks it: simple, blanket remedies will not bring satisfactory results. It would be so easy if the American people could be divided into two classes, the poor hard-pressed debtors on the one hand and the rich hard-hearted creditors on the other. We could then, as Senator Thomas so naïvely suggested in the Senate recently, legislate the transfer of purchasing power from individual creditors to individual debtors—and still leave enough for the creditors' needs.

The Sum Total of Our Debts

The sum total of all the long-term debts now outstanding as estimated by the contributors to this study is approximately $134 billion. There are $126.8 billion out of this total for which statistics are available covering the various kinds of debts and running back to pre-war years. Of the debts so reported 26 per cent are government obligations and 74 per cent are private. Government debts are not far from evenly divided. Of the total of $33 billion, $14 billion are federal obligations and $19 billion are those of state and local units. Loans on urban real estate are the next largest single class of long-term debt. Over $27 billion of obligations of this sort are reported outstanding—or 22 per cent of the known total. Including second mortgage loans the total is probably as much as $35 billion. Next in point of size are the long-term debts of financial institutions—the paid-up value of life insurance policies, bonds of investment trusts and loan agencies, etc.—which probably amount to about $22 billion or 17 per cent of the total.

In sharp contrast to the amount of newspaper notice and government solicitude given to farm mortgage loans, they are the least important in point of size. They represent less than 7 per cent of the nation's long-term debts—less than $9 billion out of $126.8 billion. Railroad debts account for 11 per cent ($14 billion) of the reported total, while public utility and industrial debts are each about 8 per cent ($10 billion).

Chart 1 on page 6 shows the relative size of the various classes of debts.

Growth of the Debt Structure

The most striking fact about these debts today compared with previous years is their enormous growth. The grand estimated total of $134 billion represents an increase of $96 billion from the pre-war figure, which was $38 billion for the same categories of long-term debt. Of this increase, $37 billion came before the post-war depression (1921–22), $51 billion more came between 1921–22 and 1929, and $8 billion developed during the current depression. In other words, long-term debts about doubled between 1913–14 and 1921–22; increased about 68 per cent more between 1921–22 and 1929; and expanded a further 6 per cent in the past four years, so that for every $1.00 of debts we carried before the war we carry $3.53 today.

A comparison of the various classes of long-term debts as reported ($126.8 billion) today with the pre-war period shows that railroad

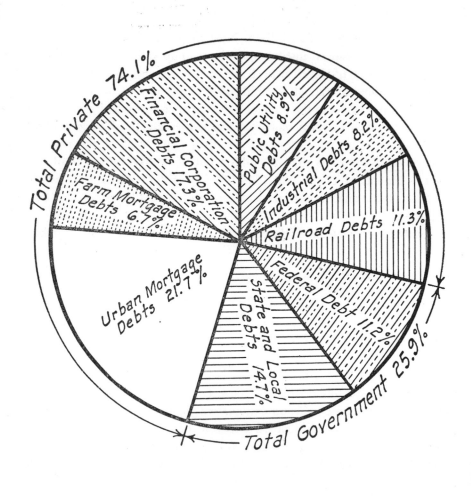

CHART 1

PERCENTAGE DISTRIBUTION OF
LONG-TERM DEBT BY CLASS
1933

Total Private 74.1%

Financial Corporation
Debts 17.3%

Public Utility
Debts 8.9%

Industrial Debts 8.2%

Farm Mortgage
Debts 6.7%

Railroad Debts 11.3%

Urban Mortgage
Debts 21.7%

Federal Debt 11.2%

State and Local
Debts 14.7%

Total Government 25.9%

debts bulk far less large in the picture now than they did then. In 1913–14 these obligations amounted to 31 per cent of the total compared with 11 per cent today. The federal debt was insignificant before the war—2 per cent. Now it has grown to 11 per cent. Urban mortgage loans have also increased in relative importance—from 14 to 22 per cent of the total. The relative size of the other classes has remained comparatively constant, except financial corporations, whose debts increased from 11 to 17 per cent of the reported total.

Table 1 on page 10 gives the size of the various debts in detail and Table 2 on page 11 gives the percentages of their change from period to period. Chart 2 on page 8 shows these changes in graphic form.

The rapid growth of urban mortgages from $5 billion to over $27 billion and of federal obligations from less than $1 billion to $14 billion are the most striking changes. The debts of financial institutions also showed a marked growth—443 per cent. Railroad obligations were notable for the relative slowness of their increase—28 per cent.

Debts in Relation to Assets and Income

By themselves, however, these figures have very little meaning. The important matter is not the size, or even the growth, of these or any other debts but their relation to the income and assets of the debtors over the years. A debt of $100,000 means nothing for a public utility company with assets in the hundred millions and earnings many times the carrying charges, but the same debt for a small retail store would be fantastic.

We can get a rough range on the validity of our national debts by comparing them with the national wealth, which is, in a way, the security on which they are based—even though the nation's assets as a whole are not actually put up as security for the payment of its debtors' obligations. Judged in terms of our national wealth we are now mortgaged up to about 45 per cent on our long-term debts. In other words, the total of these obligations is a little less than one-half of the nation's assets.

Chart 3, page 9, shows the growth of the debt structure in relation to the national wealth.

The size of our debts in comparison with our wealth is not as alarming as has been commonly presumed; but it is more menacing when

debts bulk far less large in the picture now than they did then. In
1913-14 these obligations amounted to 31 per cent of the total compared with 11 per cent whad by federal debt accounting at before
the war. 2 per cent. Now their growth is 11 per cent. Urban mortgage
loans have also increased in relative importance from 12 to 23 per
cent of the total. The relative importance of other classes has remained
comparatively constant, except minor exceptions, whose changes are
covered from 11 to 13 per cent of the reported total.

To show on page 10 gives the size of the various debts in 1913 and
Table 2 on page 11 gives the percentage of that change from period
to period. Chart 2 on page 8 shows these changes in graphic form.

The rapid growth of urban mortgages from $8 billion to over $21
billion and of federal obligations from less than $1 billion to $15 billion
are the most striking changes. The tables at urban mortgage also
recorded a growth of 12 per cent. Railroad obligations have
decreased...

Relation to Money and Income

The financial...

CHART 2

Growth of Long-Term Debts
by Class and Year

1913-1933

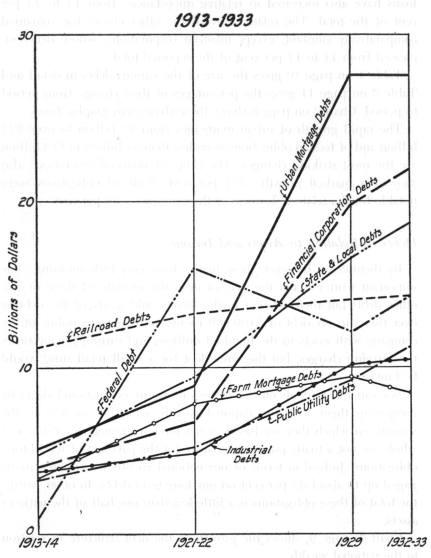

CHART 3

RELATION OF NATIONAL WEALTH TO INTERNAL DEBTS
1913-1933

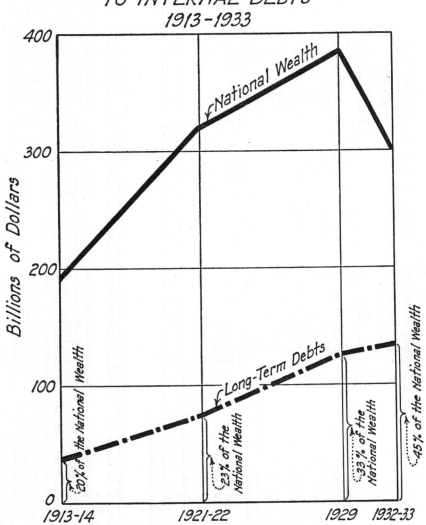

TABLE 1

AMOUNT AND PERCENTAGE DISTRIBUTION OF LONG-TERM DEBTS BY CLASS AND YEAR

(Amounts in Millions of Dollars)

Class	Latest Available Year		1929		Post-War Depression Year		Pre-War Year	
	Amount	Per Cent of Total	Amount	Per Cent of Total	Amount	Per Cent of Total	Amount	Per Cent of Total
1. Farm mortgage debts	$8,500	6.7	$9,469(a)	8.0	$7,858(d)	10.9	$3,320	9.1
2. Urban mortgage debts	27,554(f)	21.7	27,616	23.2	8,968	12.4	5,151	14.1
3. Railroad debts	14,264	11.3	14,065	11.8	13,216	18.3	11,186	30.7
4. Public utility debts	11,225(g)	8.9	9,251	7.8	5,249(b)	7.3	3,294(b)	9.0
5. Industrial debts	10,450	8.2	10,170	8.5	4,820	6.7	3,738	10.3
6. Financial debts(c)	21,919	17.3	19,767	16.6	6,740	9.3	4,040	11.1
7. Federal debt	14,237	11.2	12,155	10.2	15,965	22.1	968	2.1
8. State and local debts	18,685	14.7	16,556	13.9	9,420	13.0	4,751	13.6
Total reported debt	$126,834	100.0	$119,049	100.0	$72,236	100.0	$36,448	100.0
Total estimated debt(h)	$134,280	.....	$126,433	.....	$75,158	.....	$37,989	.....

(a) 1928.
(b) Excluding manufactured gas companies.
(c) Including for 1929 and 1930 the bonded debt and mortgages of all financial corporations submitting balance sheets with income tax returns to the U. S. Treasury Department, except real estate bonds which are included in urban mortgage debts, and the net reserves of life insurance companies for each year.
(d) 1920.
(e) 1910.
(f) Total mortgage holdings of all institutions and individuals estimated at $35,000 million as of December 31, 1931.
(g) Inclusion of the funded debt of holding companies brings the aggregate funded debt of the utility systems to $14,000 million as of December 31, 1931.
(h) Including total reported debt plus adjustments to make final totals for all years comparable. The following adjustments have been made to obtain the total estimated debt in Table 1. The item "urban mortgage debts" has been increased 27 per cent in each year to take account of second mortgages, individual holdings, etc., not available and therefore not included in the reported figure for this item. Cf. Chapter III, p. 78. The "financial debt" item has been increased in the pre-war and post-war depression years to take account of the debt of holding companies not available for those years and therefore not included in the reported figures for railroad and public utility borrowers. In the pre-war year holding company debt has been estimated at $150 million, and in the post-war depression year at $500 million. The "financial debt" item for 1929 and the latest available year includes holding company debt. These adjustments have been made to correct omissions in the reported debt figures referred to and to avoid error in the grand total. They have been based on known figures and assumed relationships. Though these adjustments are subject to wide error, such error tends to disappear in the final totals.

TABLE 2

RATES OF CHANGE IN LONG-TERM DEBTS BY CLASS

(Changes in Percentages)

Class	1921–22 over 1913–14	1929 over 1913–14	1929 over 1921–22	1933 over 1929	1933 over 1913–14
1. Farm mortgage debts..............	137	185	20.5	−10.2	156
2. Urban mortgage debts.............	74	436	208	− 0.2	435
3. Railroad debts....................	18	26	6	1	28
4. Public utility debts...............	59	181	76	21	241
5. Industrial debts..................	29	172	111	2	179
6. Financial debts...................	67	389	193	11	443
7. Federal debt.....................	1549	1154	−24	17	1371
8. State and local debts.............	98	248	76	13	293

compared with previous years. Before the war, for example, the ratio was 20 per cent. In other words, we are twice as heavily in debt in relation to our wealth now as we were before the war. The value of these figures, however, is vitiated by the impossibility in times like these of placing an accurate valuation on any kind of property—particularly real estate for which there is practically no market at all.

A better test of the validity of the nation's debts is to compare the debt service with the national income. While the nation's wealth is not actually pledged as collateral for the debts of its inhabitants payments on the interest and principal do come out of the national income—or at least out of that part of the total income which goes to the debtors and which varies, from year to year, very much as does the income as a whole.

The figures show that the carrying charges on our long-term obligations last year (1932) were equal to 20 per cent of the total national income compared with 6 per cent before the war. In other words, out of every $100 we now receive from wages, salaries, dividends, interest, profits and rent we must pay $20 in charges on money we have borrowed while in 1913–14 we were obliged to pay only $6. By this test our debt burdens are over three times as heavy now as they were before the war. Chart 4, page 12, shows the relation between debt service and national income since 1913–14.

That our debt burdens weigh on us so much more now than before can hardly be said to be news—even though we have not known the precise amount of the added weight. The figures do reveal, however,

[1] The debt service figures used in this study include interest charges on all debts but amortization payments only in fields where they have been available—i.e. railroad and government debts.

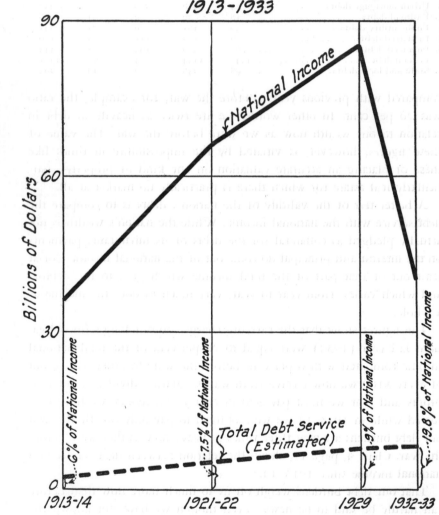

CHART 4

RELATION OF NATIONAL INCOME
TO DEBT SERVICE
1913–1933

National Income

Billions of Dollars

Total Debt Service
(Estimated)

.6% of National Income

7.5% of National Income

.9% of National Income

19.8% of National Income

90

60

30

0

1913-14   1921-22   1929 1932-33

some dramatic evidence of how and when it happened, which is of the greatest value in planning for relief. They show that we went into debt in relation to income and assets much more rapidly between 1921 and 1929 than we did before; but that, in spite of this over-extension, we should probably not be in serious difficulty now were it not for slow business and low prices. In other words, we are in trouble now partly because we over-borrowed in the boom years and partly because general business conditions since then have drastically reduced our income.

Pre-War and Post-War Debts

The proof of this statement lies in the varying courses of indebtedness, national wealth and income over the past 20 years. From the pre-war period of 1913–14 to 1921 American long-term debts increased 97 per cent—from $38 to $75 billion. This growth, taken by itself, seems enormous. To have doubled our load of debts in seven years—

TABLE 3

LONG-TERM DEBTS, POPULATION, PRODUCTION, PRICES, WEALTH AND INCOME

(Dollars and Population in Millions)

	Pre-War Year (1913–14)	Post-War Depression Year (1921)	Peak Boom Year (1929)	Latest Available Year (1932–33)
1. Long-term debts................	$38,000	$75,000	$126,000	$134,000
2. Population of U. S.(a)..........	98	110	121	125
3. Index of industrial production (F.R.B.) (1923–25 average = 100)	..	85	119	64
4. Wholesale commodity price index (B.L.S.) (1926 = 100)..........	68	97	95	65
5. National wealth(b)..............	$192,000	$321,000	$385,000	$300,000
6. National income(c)..............	$36,000	$66,000	$85,000	$40,000
7. Total debt service(d)............	$2,143	$4,953	$7,642	$7,910
8. Per capita debt (in hundreds).....	$387.76	$681.82	$1,041.32	$1,072.00
9. Per cent of national wealth represented by debts..............	19.7	23.4	32.7	44.7
10. Per cent of national income represented by debt service.........	6.0	7.0	9.0	19.8

(a) Taking 1914, 1922, 1929, and 1933.
(b) Taking census figure for 1922, estimates of National Industrial Conference Board for 1914 and 1929, and Leonard Ayres' estimate for 1932.
(c) W. I. King's estimates for 1914 and 1921. Estimates of National Industrial Conference Board for 1929 and 1932.
(d) Known debt service comprises farm mortgage interest payments, accrued interest on funded debt plus amortization and sinking fund charges on the railroad debt, public utility interest charges excluding manufactured gas in the pre-war and post-war depression years, and interest charges on the gross public debts plus public debt retirements. Interest charges on urban mortgages, industrial and financial debts are rough estimates based on an assumed average annual interest rate of 6 per cent.

the carrying charges more than doubled—was an unprecedented performance. But the increased load did not represent very much of an increased burden because it was supported by an expansion of assets and earnings almost as prodigious. In the same period the national income grew 83 per cent and the national wealth expanded 67 per cent. In other words, while we piled up our debts rapidly between 1914 and 1922 we had earned so much more money with which to pay them in 1922 than we had had in 1914 that we did not feel any great strain —even in the worst days of the depression of '21.

Tables 3 and 4 on pages 13 and 14 give the detailed figures of the amount and percentages of change of long-term debts and carrying charges in relation to national wealth and income, and to production

TABLE 4

CHANGES IN LONG-TERM DEBTS, POPULATION, PRICES, WEALTH, AND INCOME

(Changes in Percentages)

	Change 1921–22 over 1913–14	Change 1922 over 1913–14	Change 1929 over 1921–22	Change 1933 over 1929	Change 1933 over 1913–14
1. Long-term debts...........	97	232	68	6	253
2. Population of U. S.(k)......	12.2	23.5	10.0	3.3	27.6
3. Index of industrial production (F.R.B.)................	....	....	77.6(a)	−49.6(b)	....
4. Wholesale commodity price index (B.L.S.)...........	42.6(c)	39.7	− 2.1(h)	−36.8(d)	−11.8(e)
5. National wealth(l)..........	67.2(i)	100	20.0(j)	−22.1(f)	56.2(f)
6. National income(g).........	83.3	137	28.8	−52.9	11.1
7. Total debt service(m).......	131	257	54.3	3.5	269
8. Per capita debt............	75.8	168.6	52.7	2.9	176.3

(a) 1929 over 1921.
(b) December, 1932, over 1929.
(c) 1922 over 1914.
(d) February, 1933, over 1929.
(e) February, 1933, over 1914.
(f) Taking Colonel Ayres' estimate of $300 billion for 1932.
(g) W. I. King's estimates for 1914 and 1921.   Estimates of National Industrial Conference Board for 1929 and 1932.
(h) 1929 over 1922.
(i) 1922 over 1914.
(j) 1929 over 1922.
(k) Taking 1914, 1922, 1929, and 1933.
(l) Taking census figure for 1922 and estimates of National Industrial Conference Board for 1914 and 1929.
(m) Total debt service comprises farm mortgage interest payments, accrued interest on funded debt plus amortization and sinking fund charges on the railroad debt, public utility interest charges excluding manufactured gas in the pre-war and post-war depression years, and interest charges on the gross public debt plus public debt retirements. Interest charges on urban mortgages, industrial and financial debts are rough estimates based on an assumed average annual interest rate of 6 per cent.

CHART 5

COMPARATIVE CHANGES SINCE 1913 IN DEBT SERVICE, INCOME, PRODUCTION, AND PRICES
(Expressed in Index Numbers)
1913-1933

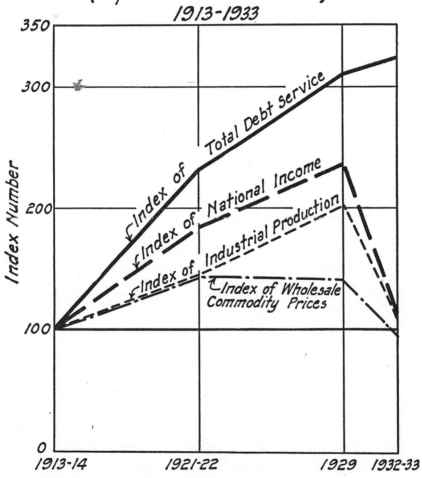

and commodity prices. Chart 5, page 15, shows in graphic form the relative changes in these indices since pre-war days.

By all odds the most important factor in the debt increase of the war and post-war years was public finance. The federal government borrowed heavily to pay the expenses of military and naval operations in 1917 and 1918. Its long-term obligations grew 1,549 per cent from 1914 to 1922—from less than $1 billion to almost $16 billion. If we exclude these from the picture we find that our private and local government borrowings in this period were actually very conservative—an increase of only 60 per cent in debt compared with the 83 per cent increase in wealth and the 67 per cent growth of national income. The only two classes of debts which showed a larger increase than our national economic development were farm mortgage loans which went up 137 per cent, and state and local debts which grew 98 per cent.

The Expansion of 1921–1929

But the picture is completely different for the period of 1922 to 1929. That these seven years were the "new era" of economic madness the figures amply demonstrate. We piled up our debts almost three times as fast as our wealth and income increased. Long-term obligations went from $75 to $126 billion, an increase of 68 per cent, while our wealth expanded only 20 per cent, from $321 to $385 billion, and our income increased but 29 per cent—from $66 to $85 billion.

While we liquidated almost $4 billion of federal long-term obligations in these seven years we took on $55 billion in other fields—an increase of over 93 per cent. If we exclude United States Government obligations we find the almost incredible fact that we shouldered debts during this period over four times as fast as we added to our wealth and well over three times as rapidly as our income expanded. Even if we assume that the debt policies of pre-war years were sound—an assumption which some would challenge—our performance in the post-war boom was almost beyond belief.

The greatest expansion came in urban real estate. Loans on city property were actually increased three-fold in these seven years—from $8.9 to $27.6 millions. It may be said in mitigation that these were years of an unprecedented expansion in real estate construction and values—a growth that even outstripped that in other areas of our economic life. But the facts do not entirely excuse the performance. The value of residential contracts awarded in 1929, which accounted for almost two-thirds of the total, was only twice as great as in 1921 and commercial contracts rose 140 per cent in value while urban mortgage debts went up 208 per cent.

The long-term obligations of financial and industrial corporations also showed an expansion in these fantastic years far out of line even with the general average. For example, investment trusts which were born in the United States in the '20's and multiplied greatly in the bull market added $384 million in bonds to the nation's long-term debts while the paid-up value of life insurance policies—in reality a long-term debt—more than doubled and instalment finance companies had accumulated long-term obligations of $135 million by the time the boom had reached its peak. All together financial corporations increased debts of this sort almost three-fold in the period of 1921–29.

Industrial corporations expanded their long-term commitments by 111 per cent during these years—from $4.8 billion to $10.2 billion. Those were the days when even the coolest heads were turned by the prevailing illusion of indefinite and unbroken expansion for American business. But, after all, balance sheets and the income statements did nourish the phantasy. The net income of all industrial corporations reporting to the United States Government started with a minus quantity in the depression of 1921 and reached $5.5 billion in 1929—an increase which is impossible even to express in percentages. The value of their real estate, buildings and equipment increased almost $3 billion from 1926 to 1931 alone.

Most of the debt expansion among industrial corporations occurred in retail trade, the service industries and manufacturing—at least for the years 1928–30 for which detailed figures are available. Mining and quarrying showed a slight liquidation of long-term obligations while the increase of debts in the field of construction was not so much out of line with assets and income. Bonds and mortgage indebtedness of retail trade concerns, for example, showed an increase of 117 per cent in these four years alone while their tangible assets increased only 17 per cent in value. Long-term debts of hotel and other service corporations also doubled during the same time, although assets were only half as much again. Because debts of manufacturing concerns make up more than half of those of all industrial corporations put together their expansion of $1.5 billion from 1920 to 1930, even though relatively small in terms of percentages—about 33 per cent—had a marked effect on the total.

Of all classes of debtors the railroads increased their borrowings the least during the years of the boom—only 6 per cent. But they had saddled themselves with a burden of long-term obligations equal to more than half their total capitalization as far back as 1890, and at no time since 1921 had the percentage been less than 58. Other public utility operating companies as a whole extended their long-term obligations in the period of 1921–29 by 76 per cent, but at least in the fields of electricity, gas and telephones this expansion was supported to a considerable extent by increases in income and assets. Interest charges of electric companies, for example, grew 146 per cent but their income increased almost 90 per cent and assets over 140 per cent. Farmers, like the railroads, had increased their long-term debts more before than during the boom years of 1921–29—an expansion of only 21 per cent in that period compared with 137 per cent during the seven years previous.

Boom-Time Debt Policies

Using the pre-war period as "normal" there can be no question that in relation to assets and income the nation as a whole plunged far more heavily into debt in 1922–29 than it had been accustomed to in previous years. That the federal government, the railroads and the farmers were exceptions to this rule sets the action of the other debtors in even more striking perspective. It is interesting, even though academic, to speculate on the wisdom of this policy. The indefinite expansion of American business was the easy assumption upon which this greatly increased debt had been erected. But 1928–29 levels were highly abnormal and should not have been expected to continue. American business had always contracted after every previous expansion. The seriousness of the mistake in assuming the contrary is obvious enough to us now.

Whether or not continued prosperity would have supported the debt vagaries of the bull market, good business did not in fact continue. The sensational contraction of the national income which has since taken place has seriously undermined the debt structure's support—at least where it has carried the heaviest loads. How much the difficulties of the present are due to overloading and how much to this weakened underpinning is impossible to state in general terms.

As a matter of fact any genuinely detached study of the debt problem discloses the pitfalls that lurk in generalities. Totals and averages hide as much as they reveal—with debts as with any other facts, and the more inclusive they are the more treacherous do they become. When we begin to speak of "national debt" and "national income" we become almost meaningless. After all, we do not pay debts as a nation or even as a class or group of debtors, but as individuals—personal or corporate. The statement, for example, that the charges on the nation's internal debts today are three times as great as before the war, while the national income is very little more, gives the impression that those of this or that specific group of debtors are also three times as great.

Debt Strains Vary Widely

As a matter of fact, however, such is emphatically not the case. Both the debt burden and its support vary in the most extreme degree, not only as between the various classes of debts but also within each class. As a group the electric light and power operating companies, telephone and gas companies are free of any serious difficulties even in this fourth year of the depression. Public utility rates have not been materially reduced and the demand for service has not gone as low as the demand for many commodities. Interest and principal can still be met out of earnings without much strain. But the public utility holding companies and the street railways are at the opposite extreme. As much as 20 per cent of the bonds of street railways are now in default while 11 per cent of the holding company debt is in the same straits.

The farm mortgage situation is another case in point. From the amount of attention the farm debtors have managed to capture and from the over-all statistics of their debts one would imagine that all farmers were borne down by a crushing load of obligations that cannot be carried without general and immediate relief. The facts are, however, that about 60 per cent of American farms have no debts on them at all and that of the 40 per cent which are mortgaged almost two-thirds are located in the North Central States.

To say that a relatively small proportion of farmers are in trouble and to place most of them in a restricted area is not, of course, to minimize the difficulties of those who are in debt. In these particular states one-fifth of the farms are mortgaged over 75 per cent of their value, while last year half of the transfers of farm property in Iowa and the Dakotas were through foreclosures and bankruptcy sales.

Urban real estate is not only responsible for debts three times the size of those of agriculture but a far larger proportion of them are in trouble. Farm debts represent 25 per cent of farm values for the country as a whole, but urban mortgages are now approximately 45 per cent of city property values. Just as city property owners plunged into debt at a greater rate than other borrowers in boom years so now are they in trouble proportionate to their folly. It is estimated that almost two-thirds of urban mortgagors are now unable to make the payments specified on their bonds.

The nation's railroads also disclose a specially high proportion of debt strains as a class. But here, too, generalities are often deceptive. While railroads are indebted up to half their value, while 10 per cent of them by mileage are now actually in receivership, and while about one-quarter of their debt is now in default, or only saved from it by emergency credit, most of the defaulted issues are "junior" bonds. Relatively few of the underlying issues are in difficulty and these are the securities which are held by insurance companies, banks and educational institutions. Almost half of all railroad bonds are held by such institutions. Again this is not to minimize the seriousness of the railroad debt problem. Last year only 15 per cent of the roads earned enough to pay interest on their bonds, and other fixed charges. Even in 1931 the figures show that railroad income had declined 88 per cent below the average of the preceding four years.

Corporations Relatively Secure

The debts of corporations and government agencies disclose a relatively low index of strain—as a whole. The credit of the Federal Government is still unimpaired in spite of the current deficit of $1.4 billion and a per capita debt of $173 compared with $12 in 1914. But even this load is less than the $209 per capita we carried in 1922. With public debt generalizations, however, exceptions must also be noted. While total tax collections of all state and local governments put together in 1932 were almost five times the entire carrying charges on their debts no less than 1,120 local public units had defaulted in their bond obligations up to February of this year. Among the chief causes of local defaults have been the mounting tide of tax delinquency, inability to fund floating debts, the failure of banks in which public funds have been deposited and increased expenditures for emergency relief.

Compared with property values the debts of industrial corporations are the most adequately secured of any private obligations, representing as they do only one-fifth of tangible assets. But corporate income has dropped further than that of any other single class of debtors. While corporate long-term debts have increased as a whole 2 per cent since 1929 corporate income, as a whole, turned into a deficit in 1931. The credit position of industrial corporations, especially the large companies, was so good in 1929, however, that they have managed to support their debts relatively well. Also, judged by the record of failures, which have declined steadily since the middle of last year, the burdens have been eased in recent months. The recovery of the better quality of industrial bonds which in March 1933 were only 18 per cent below the peak of 1929 is a striking index of the relatively sound position of these industries.

So much for the facts. When the pieces of the puzzle are put together they make a picture of far greater lights—if not shadows—than has been commonly supposed. It can truthfully be said that there is no evidence of an intolerable debt burden upon all parts of our economic life, assuming even a moderate recovery—even though parts of it, here and there, are now clearly insupportable under present business conditions. These weakest spots must be dealt with for they present a serious barrier to economic recovery. Not only must we ease the strains of the debts we have already incurred; but, if we are to avoid trouble we must formulate basic policies for incurring new debts which will better insure us against future defaults. The contributors to this study have made specific suggestions for the relief of existing debt strains, each in his own field, and they have all cooperated in suggesting general policies, both in respect to present and future debts, in Chapter Thirteen.

The Nation's Short-Term Debts

Although the debt problem today centers chiefly in long-term obligations, the short-term debt structure also deserves attention as part of the same general problem. The distinction between short-term and long-term debts is not always easy to determine. By short-term debt we mean, as a rule, debt maturing within a year or less of the date of issue, and variously described as current, temporary, or floating, while long-term debt is spoken of as fixed, permanent, or funded. There is a third category—intermediate debt—meaning debt maturing in three, four or five years. United States treasury notes, which run for not to exceed five years, though redeemable at a shorter interval, are an example of intermediate debt. In this study all intermediate items are treated as short-term obligations. The distinction between short-term and long-term debt becomes obscure in cases where, as in certain American cities, the repeated renewal of floating obligations renders them, in effect, lasting liabilities.

Chapters Ten and Eleven by Dr. Franklin W. Ryan describe the short-term debts outstanding in the United States at the end of 1913, 1921, 1929, 1931 and 1932, including business and personal and household obligations. Dr. Ryan places the total short-term debt burden on December 31, 1931, at $112.4 billion and at the end of 1932 at $103.6 billion. If his estimates are approximately correct the total short-term debt exceeded the long-term debt in 1929, is more than three-quarters of the present long-term debt total, and is 44 per cent of all outstanding indebtedness, current and fixed.

Dr. Ryan avoids actual duplication of debts in his estimate, not counting the same loan more than once, but he includes all separate credit advances, even of the same money, where each loan involves the incurrence of new debt.[2] If A deposits $100 in a bank, and the bank lends the $100 to B, two debts have been incurred; the bank's debt to A, and B's debt to the bank. The same $100 has been used twice as a credit advance and must be counted twice in the short-term debt total. Similarly, when B repays the bank and A withdraws his deposit, $100 wipes out $200 in the total of current debt.

Most forms of short-term debt have experienced drastic deflation in recent years. During 1932 short-term cash loans declined half a billion dollars, open account debts dropped 700 million dollars, and instalment debts also decreased at an equal pace. On the other hand, life insurance policy loans have expanded enormously. Meanwhile, however, all short-term personal and household debts showed a net increase of about half a billion dollars. These debts occupy an important place

[2] See Chapter X, p. 293, for a description of his procedure.

in the current debt structure, for upon the solvency of each family unit depend the stability and health of our social life. Individual and household debts were 12 per cent of all short-term debts in December 1931, and 14 per cent a year later.

A large volume of short-term obligations will probably never be paid. These include frozen deposits in unsound banks, some bank and life insurance policy loans, some debts of closed banks and bankrupt corporations to the Reconstruction Finance Corporation, and the floating debt of various cities. Two present tendencies are combining to reduce the current debt outstanding: (1) the efforts of families, individuals, and small business concerns to keep solvent by balancing their budgets and living well within their incomes, and (2) the charging off of uncollectible debts due to retailers from individuals and families. To these should be added the efforts of banks to reduce their commercial loans and investments so as to improve their liquidity.

Bank Debts

Bank debt constitutes the largest single category of all types of indebtedness—long or short. It is also the most important and perhaps the most sensitive element in our economy. The place of bank debt in the United States is described by Dr. Gardiner C. Means in Chapter Twelve. He reports the total amount outstanding in June, 1932, the latest date for which complete figures are available, as $47 billion, and analyzes the composition, character, and status of these obligations. Then he traces the changes in bank debt over the last twenty years and discusses their significance. Particular attention is paid to the developments of the last three years—the growing number of bank failures, the changing character of bank portfolios, the tremendous liquidation of 1931–32, the rôle of bank reserves, and the disastrous struggle for "clear" reserves in which $7,500 millions of deposits were destroyed.

In the chapters that follow the various contributors to the study have discussed each particular field of indebtedness in detail.

Chapter Two

FARM MORTGAGE DEBTS

Summary

The Facts

THE present mortgage debt on farm properties is about $8.5 billion or 25 per cent of the value of *all* farm land and buildings or about 40 per cent of the value of all *mortgaged* farms. This mortgage debt is concentrated on 42 per cent of all farms, of which 60 per cent are located in the following eleven north central states: Ohio, Indiana, Illinois, Michigan, Wisconsin, Missouri, North Dakota, South Dakota, Nebraska, and Montana. Nearly 60 per cent of the nation's farms, however, are entirely free of mortgage debt (p. 27).

Farm mortgage debt doubled between 1910 and 1920 but this increase was seemingly justified by a rapid increase in land values. In 1933, however, the debt remained two and one-half times greater than in 1910 while in the areas where mortgage indebtedness is heaviest, land values were approximately 20 per cent below the 1913 level and gross farm income had declined by one-half (p. 29).

In 1932, for the country as a whole, nearly 16 per cent of all mortgaged farms were encumbered for more than 75 per cent of their value. The proportion rises to from 18 to 22 per cent in the north central states. Since these ratios of debt to values were calculated land values have continued to decline rapidly, so the number of farms indebted for more than 75 per cent of their value may be considerably higher (p. 34).

Land mortgage interest amounts to more than $500 million annually and in 1932 farm property taxes were $629 million. Together these items consume at least one-third of the annual gross income from farms compared with an average of 19 per cent for the previous ten years. Moreover interest and taxes must be paid from *cash* and not *gross* income (p. 28).

The problem of renewals of maturing mortgages is also very acute since more than one-fourth of all farm mortgages are drawn to mature in four years or less. Sources of funds for refinancing these maturing obligations have practically disappeared since mortgage institutions find it difficult to float their securities at the present time (p. 36).

Foreclosures on farm property have increased in an alarming degree. In 1928 forced sales of farm property because of foreclosure or bankruptcy made up 27 per cent of the total number of transfers while in 1932 they had increased to 37 per cent. In North Dakota, South Dakota, and Iowa the proportion was over 50 per cent (p. 35).

Farm mortgage holdings are widely distributed. In 1928 life insurance companies were the largest holders of farm mortgages with 23 per cent of the total outstanding. Individuals other than farmers held 15 per cent and farmers held 14 per cent. The Federal Land Banks and Joint Stock Land Banks together held 19 per cent and commercial banks 11 per cent, while mortgage companies held 10 per cent. Since 1928 life insurance holdings of farm mortgages have declined, the Federal Land Banks now hold a somewhat larger proportion of the total, while commercial banks have been rapidly reducing their holdings (p. 40).

Recommendations

No single scheme for the readjustment of farm mortgage indebtedness can be devised since all farmers are not equally hard-pressed to meet their obligations. However, the various phases of the problem must be attacked simultaneously if a minimum of injustice and hardship is to be inflicted on both debtors and creditors. Unusual leniency in a few cases may increase the pressure to collect in full in other instances (p. 45).

Any program of farm mortgage relief should be formulated and administered with the following classes of farmers clearly in mind:

a. The 60 per cent who are free of mortgage debt.

b. Farmers whose mortgage debt is quite moderate (not more than 25 per cent of the value of their property) and who can meet their interest and amortization payments.

c. Those moderately indebted but temporarily embarrassed in meeting current payments and requiring loans to keep their mortgage debt in good standing.

d. Those who might work out of their difficulties if they could refund their debts on more lenient terms which would relieve them of immediate danger of foreclosure.

e. Those hopelessly insolvent and who can carry on only if their debts are revised downward.

Probably one-fourth of the mortgaged farmers in the United States are in the last two classes—"d" and "e"—and in need of refinancing of their debts on more favorable terms or a downward revision of their debts if they are to retain title to their property (p. 46).

At the short session of Congress amendments to the Farm Loan Act were passed which increased the loan facilities of the Federal Land Banks. They are now authorized to make loans for the refinancing indebtedness previously incurred; they may postpone the payment of any regular instalment; and they are now permitted to issue consolidated bonds in lieu of bond issues of individual banks (p. 47).

A substantial increase in the loan resources of the Federal Land Banks is essential if they are to assume a larger responsibility for taking over loans that mature and must be renewed. Probably $500 million annually for a period of several years would enable them to take over all loans that could qualify under the present law. These funds should be supplied by the purchase of Land Bank Bonds by the United States Treasury until such time as the banks can sell bonds to the investing public (p. 50).

A new division in the Federal Farm Loan Bureau or an emergency mortgage corporation with resources between $300 and $500 million should be organized and financed by advances from the treasury to refund outstanding indebtedness at moderate rates on the security of first or second mortgages. Such action—if it did not bring the total mortgage debt above 75 per cent of the value of the property—would not expose the government to unusual losses (p. 56).

For debtors in class "e" who are hopelessly insolvent a drastic scaling down of the principal amount of their debts is essential and machinery should be set up to facilitate these adjustments providing for voluntary settlements outside of court jurisdiction and with the participation of representatives of the federal farm financing agencies (p. 57).

Inflationary measures do not promise any advantage to the farmer unless they result in stimulating business activity and increasing employment. Inflationary schemes will not necessarily eliminate the disparity between the prices of agricultural commodities and the prices of products the farmer must buy and it is unlikely that the inflation of domestic credit or currency will have any marked effect upon the prices of staple farm commodities which are determined by world markets (p. 60).

NOTE.—Since this chapter was written Congress has enacted legislation to meet the farm mortgage situation. The provisions of this act are explained in Appendix, I.

1. THE FACTS [1]

ACTIVE resistance on the part of farmers to the enforcement of legal claims against their mortgaged property has been one of the most dramatic aspects of the present farm mortgage situation. Many insurance companies are now refraining from foreclosure suits except in cases of abandonment; the Comptroller of the Currency has instructed receivers of national banks to pursue a lenient policy in liquidating farm mortgage loans; in a few instances judges have refused to order forced sales of land; tax sales are being postponed in many sections; and in a number of states mediation committees have been appointed to facilitate negotiations between farm debtors and their creditors.

Some observers regard these extra-legal proceedings as justifiable measures designed to extricate farmers from an unbearable economic situation. Others see in the limitations upon creditors' rights and the intimidation of prospective purchasers of foreclosed property a threat to the security of all contracts and a sacrifice of the claims of creditors without regard to the ability of debtors to meet their obligations. Although it is socially desirable to enable farmers to retain their property whenever possible, the rights of creditors cannot be ignored. A survey of recent changes in the farm mortgage situation will afford a basis for appraising the numerous proposals for adjusting the conflicting claims of farm debtors and their creditors.

The mortgage debt in the United States is concentrated on 42 per cent of all farms and in 1930 amounted to $9,241 million, in contrast to a mortgage debt of only 3,320 millions in 1910. Since 1930 numerous foreclosures and the reduction in size of new and renewal loans have reduced the total mortgage debt to an estimated amount of $8,500 millions as of January 1, 1933. Nearly 60 per cent of this debt is concentrated in the east north central and west north central states which include Ohio, Indiana, Illinois, Michigan, Wisconsin, Minnesota, Iowa, Missouri, North and South Dakota, Nebraska, and Kansas. It is in these states primarily that irate farmers have resorted to direct action to prevent mortgagees from exercising their legal rights. The accompanying tables show the distribution of mortgage indebtedness by geographical divisions and types of farm tenure.

---

[1] Table 5 summarizes the basic data used in this chapter.

TABLE 5

BASIC DATA ON FARM MORTGAGE DEBTS

(Dollars in Millions)

	1932	1930	1928	1920	1910
1. Total farm mortgage debt	$8,500	$9,241	$9,469	$7,858	$3,320
2. Total short-term debt(a)	3,500				
3. Gross farm debt (1, 2)	12,000				
4. Mortgage interest payments	510	540	563	545	210
5. Taxes on all farm property(b)	629	777	766	452	268
6. Total fixed charges (4, 5)	1,139	1,317	1,329	997	478
7. Gross income from farm production	5,240	9,406	11,741	13,566	6,643
8. Ratio, gross income from farm production to mortgage interest payments	9.7%	5.8%	4.8%	4.0%	3.2%
9. Gross income from mortgaged farms(c)	2,384				
10. Ratio, gross income from mortgaged farms to mortgage interest payments	21.3%				
11. Mortgage debt per capita of farm population		$303.53		$248.56	$276.99
12. Total value of farm property(d)		57,246		77,924	40,991
13. Total value of lands and buildings(e)	34,244	44,248	47,927	61,315	35,974
14. Ratio, mortgage debt to value of all farms(f)	24.8%	20.9%	21.0%	11.8%	9.5%
15. Total value of mortgaged farms:(g) (a) Owner operated farms	7,977	10,308	12,087	13,776	6,330
16. Ratio, debt to value of mortgaged farms: (a) Owner operated farms(h)		39.6%	46.0%	29.1%	27.3%
17. Percentage, farm income for all industries(i)		7.6%	9.6%	16.1%	17.3%
18. Percentage, value of farm property of national wealth	17.4%			15.9%	17.7%
19. Index of farm prices (average for year)(j)	57	117	139	205	103

(a) Short-term debt includes bank loans, merchant credit, and open book accounts, some of which is non-interest bearing. This estimate is a rough approximation of the total.

(b) Includes personal property and real estate taxes.

(c) It is estimated that 45.5 per cent of all farm acreage is mortgaged. This same proportion of gross income is assigned as gross income from mortgaged farms.

(d) Includes land and buildings, farm dwellings, farm implements, machinery, and domestic animals.

(e) Census data. Data are from *The Farm Real Estate Situation, 1931–32*, United States Department of Agriculture, Circular No. 261, p. 16. The real estate index for March 15, 1932, was used in estimating the value for 1932.

(f) Data for 1910, 1920, and 1928 are from David L. Wickens, "Farm-Mortgage Credit," *United States Department of Agriculture, Technical Bulletin No. 288*, p. 50. For 1930 and 1932 the ratios are an estimate based upon the estimated value of lands and buildings, and farm mortgage indebtedness. For 1932 an estimate was made using the real estate index for 1932, applied to the value of owner-operated farms. Census data are used for census years.

(g) Data are available only for owner-operated farms in 1930.

(h) Census data are used for census years. The 1928 figure is taken from *Technical Bulletin No. 288*, United States Department of Agriculture, p. 51.

(i) Figures are for realized income exclusive of imputed income. Data for 1910 and 1920 are from W. I. King *The National Income and Its Purchasing Power*. For the years 1928 and 1930 figures are confidential estimates based on W. I. King's study.

(j) Data from *The Agricultural Situation*, March 1, 1933. Although the average for 1932 was 57, farm prices had dropped to 52 in December, 1932, and were at 49 in February, 1933.

TABLE 6

FARM MORTGAGE DEBT OUTSTANDING JANUARY 1, 1910, 1928, 1930(*a*)

(In Thousands of Dollars)

Geographical Division	1910	1920	1928	1930
New England	$76,110	$120,860	$122,494	$144,744
Middle Atlantic	281,530	396,640	376,614	478,554
East North Central	794,950	1,591,420	1,950,126	1,890,811
West North Central	1,296,080	3,199,690	4,056,187	3,605,280
South Atlantic	141,250	347,470	491,896	508,927
East South Central	123,560	320,100	381,497	365,609
West South Central	291,210	703,680	901,252	904,940
Mountain	113,710	544,550	496,551	546,000
Pacific	202,070	633,290	691,909	796,525
United States	$3,320,470	$7,857,700	$9,468,526	$9,241,390

TABLE 7

FARM MORTGAGE INDEBTEDNESS ACCORDING TO TYPE OF TENURE(*a*)

(In Thousands of Dollars)

Tenure	1920	1928	1930
Owner operated	$5,314,150	$5,560,017	$5,185,399
Tenant	2,185,480	3,644,009	3,671,677
Manager-farms	350,070	264,500	384,314
Total	$7,857,700	$9,468,526	$9,241,390

(*a*) Data are from David L. Wickens, "Farm-Mortgage Credit," *United States Department of Agriculture, Technical Bulletin No. 288*, pp. 3-4, 15.

The fact that in January 1933 the farm mortgage debt was nearly two and one-half times the debt in 1910 is significant only in terms of the factors which affect the ability of producers to carry this increased burden of debt. The value of the land pledged to secure the loan, and the available income for the payment of interest and amortization instalments are the criteria commonly accepted to determine the amount that can be safely loaned on farm property. Unfortunately, the mortgage debt continued to expand long after land values and farm income showed marked declines.

The farm mortgage debt more than doubled between 1910 and 1920, but this increase was seemingly justified by the steady increase in land values throughout the decade. By 1920, however, land values had reached their peak and since that date have declined continuously. In 1932, land values for the country as a whole were 11 per cent below the 1913 figures, a drop of 17 per cent from the level of the preceding year. In the north central states, where the mortgage debt is most burdensome, land values are more than 20 per cent below the 1913 level.[2]

Farm Debt Versus Gross Income from Mortgaged Farms

Gross income from production advanced to its highest point in 1919 when it amounted to approximately $17 billion. In 1931 it had declined to $6,920 million, while for 1932 the Bureau of Agricultural Economics estimated that gross income will be $5,240 million, or only 77.5 per cent of the 1910–14 average. If it is assumed that mortgaged farms claim the same proportion of gross income that their acreage forms of the total acreage, and that they bear a similar proportion of all farm taxes, then in 1932 interest on mortgages and taxes claim 33.4 per cent of the gross farm income.[3] The Farm Loan Board's estimate is somewhat higher. It finds "that taxes and land mortgage interest consumed in the aggregate 36 per cent of the gross income from mortgaged farms in 1932, as compared with an average of 19 per cent for the previous ten years.[4] Moreover, gross income includes the value of commodities consumed in farm households, while interest and taxes can be paid only from cash income.[5] The changes in land values, gross income from agricultural production and mortgage debt for the period 1909–1932 and changes in farm mortgage interest and taxes on farm property for the same period are shown in the two sections of Chart 6 on the next page.

The decline in farm incomes is not attributable to any pronounced decrease in production, for the volume of net agricultural production has remained quite steady during the past decade. Farm prices at the close of 1932, however, were approximately one-half the 1913 level and one-quarter of the 1920 level, while the price of commodities the farmers purchase remained 6 per cent above pre-war prices. In other words, mortgagors, as a group, are now attempting to carry obligations two and one-half times the amount carried in 1910, but their crops and livestock bring them only 50 per cent of the pre-war prices. The

---

[2] *The Farm Real Estate Situation, 1931–32,* Circular No. 261, United States Department of Agriculture, pp. 7–8.

[3] The Bureau of Agricultural Economics estimates that 45.5 per cent of the farm acreage is mortgaged.

[4] *Annual Report of the Federal Farm Loan Board,* 1932.

[5] Final figures are not yet available for cash income for 1932 but it is unlikely that it will exceed $4,250,000,000. In 1929, cash income was estimated to be $10,146,720,000.

CHART 6

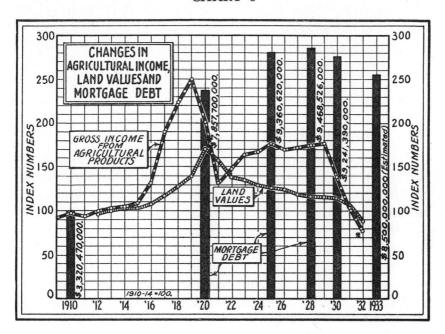

CHANGES IN AGRICULTURAL INCOME, LAND VALUES AND MORTGAGE DEBT

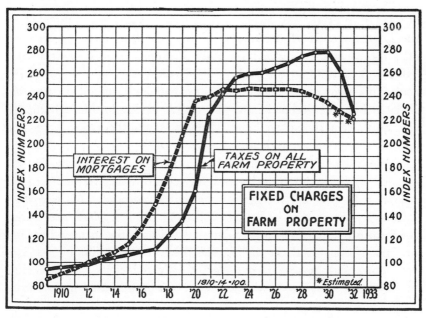

FIXED CHARGES ON FARM PROPERTY

great disparity between the prices for agricultural products and the prices which farmers must pay for commodities they purchase is shown in Chart 7, which compares the annual average of farm prices with the average of prices paid by farmers for the period 1910–1932.[6] With this shrinkage in income, defaults on the part of a large number of mortgagors are inevitable.

Debts in Relation to Values

Conservative creditors ordinarily do not advance more than 50 per cent of the appraised value of farm land, plus some allowance for permanent improvements. Consequently, the decline in land values without a proportionate liquidation of indebtedness leaves a large number of loans inadequately secured when tested by the value of the underlying property. Needless to say, the value of farm property as security for loans is largely illusory when the market for farm real estate is as completely demoralized as it is at present. Nevertheless, the ratio of debt to the market value of the farm is one indication of the present status of the loans.

The ratio of mortgage debt to the value of the farms was reported at census dates for all owner-operated farms and was estimated by the Department of Agriculture for other dates. In 1910 owner-operated farms were mortgaged for only 27.3 per cent of their market value and in 1920, at the peak of land prices, the ratio was 29.1 per cent. This ratio of debt to land values had increased to 46 per cent in 1928 but had declined in 1930 to 39.6 per cent, although for the east north central and west north central states the ratios were 45.0 and 43.4 per cent respectively.

These ratios of debt to land values would seem to indicate that the owner's equity in his property is sufficient to insure the safety of his loan if a 50 per cent margin is regarded as adequate. At least three factors, however, must be kept in mind. In the first place, the market for farm property is thoroughly demoralized with the increased volume of forced sales. And, in the second place, these ratios are averages and many farmers are more heavily indebted than these averages indicate. And, finally, our data for land values are based in part upon

---

[6] The index number of farm prices had fallen to 49 in February 1933 and the ratio between prices received by farmers to prices paid for commodities purchased was 47.

CHART 7

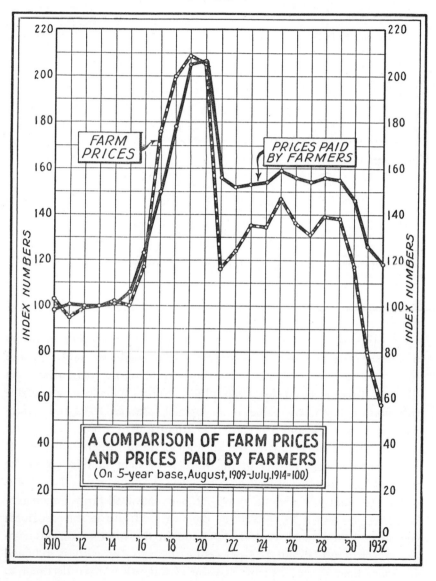

FARM
PRICES

PRICES PAID
BY FARMERS

INDEX NUMBERS

INDEX NUMBERS

A COMPARISON OF FARM PRICES
AND PRICES PAID BY FARMERS
(On 5-year base, August, 1909-July, 1914=100)

TABLE 8

RATIO OF MORTGAGED DEBT TO VALUE OF FARMS MORTGAGED, JANUARY 1, 1932, BY
GEOGRAPHICAL DIVISIONS, AND COMPARISON WITH 1931 AND 1928
FOR THE UNITED STATES AS A WHOLE(a)

Geographic Division	0.1 to 25 Per Cent	26 to 50 Per Cent	51 to 75 Per Cent	76 to 100 Per Cent	Over 100 Per Cent
New England................	32.4	38.5	25.0	2.7	1.4
Middle Atlantic.............	26.9	41.1	21.2	8.3	2.5
East North Central..........	21.5	38.3	22.7	12.3	5.2
West North Central.........	20.3	33.8	23.6	14.7	7.6
South Atlantic..............	29.0	37.0	18.3	11.8	3.9
East South Central..........	31.2	36.0	17.5	10.5	4.8
West South Central.........	27.9	41.4	20.0	7.6	3.1
Mountain...................	27.6	42.1	20.4	6.6	3.3
Pacific.....................	33.8	42.3	15.3	5.0	3.6
United States, 1932..........	25.4	37.9	21.0	10.7	5.0
1931..........	25.0	37.3	22.0	10.5	5.2
1928..........	25.3	39.0	23.5	7.8	4.4

Distribution by Tenure

Farms operated by:					
Owners.....................	24.7	37.7	20.9	11.4	5.3
Tenants and managers........	27.1	38.5	21.2	9.0	4.2

(a) Data are from *U. S. Department of Agriculture Office of Information Press Service*,
a mimeographed release, Sept. 28, 1932.

the judgment of the farmers themselves and may be subject to some
error.[7]

The proportion of farms that are mortgaged for amounts in excess
of the sum that conservative lending agencies would willingly advance
is a more satisfactory measure of the portion of the debt that is in
distress. Table 8 shows by geographical divisions the percentage distribution of debt to the value of mortgaged farms in 1932 and a comparison with 1928 and 1931 for the country as a whole. The lower
section of the table compares the position of farm owners with tenants
and managers with respect to the burden of debt in relation to the
value of the farm.

For the country as a whole, nearly 16 per cent of all farms are encumbered for more than 75 per cent of their value. Loans in the east north
central and west north central states are in the most precarious condition, for here 17.5 and 22.3 per cent of the farm property is indebted
for more than 75 per cent of its value. Land values have declined so

[7] Figures for actual sales check very closely with the estimated value of farm
real estate.

precipitously since these ratios were computed that the conditions are considerably worse than these figures indicate.[8] Another disturbing feature is that farmers who operate their own land are more deeply indebted than are farm owners whose property is operated by tenants or managers. Consequently, the foreclosures which are inevitable often result in physical dispossession, as well as loss of title to property.

Foreclosures and Delinquent Payments

The extent of foreclosures is apparent from an analysis of the methods by which property has changed ownership during the last five years. The number of farms per 1,000 changing ownership in the years 1928–32 and the method of transfer are shown in Table 9.

Foreclosure and bankruptcy sales increased from 26.6 per cent of the total transfers in 1928 to 37 per cent in 1932. If tax sales are included, the involuntary transfers of farm property comprised 54.5 per cent of the total transfers in 1932. If the record for individual states is examined, the showing is even more distressing. In North Dakota, South Dakota, and Iowa, more than half the total transfers were through foreclosure sales or bankruptcy proceedings. Moreover, forced sales have not declined in number during the past year.

The delinquencies on amortization instalments as reported by the Federal Land Banks and the Joint Stock Land Banks are evidence not only of the financial difficulties of the farmers but of the collection problems confronting lending agencies which in turn have obligations to their bondholders, policy holders, or depositors. In 1931 instalments delinquent for 90 days and over were five times the amount in 1928 and for 1932 they were nearly double the amount for the preceding year. The extent of such delinquencies during the past five years for the Federal Land Banks and the Joint Stock Land Banks is shown in Table 10.

The seriousness of these delinquencies is even more apparent when the situation of individual banks is examined. For instance, the Federal Land Bank of Wichita reports that at the close of 1932, 44 per cent of its amortized loans in number were delinquent as to payment of matured instalments and 30 per cent of its real estate sales contracts

[8] From March 15, 1931 to March 15, 1932 the index of farm real estate dropped from 106 to 89 and undoubtedly has declined further in the past year.

TABLE 9

NUMBER OF FARMS CHANGING OWNERSHIP, 1928–1932
AND METHODS OF TRANSFER(a)

Method of Transfer	1928		1929		1930		1931		1932	
	Number per 1000	As Percentage of Total Transfers	Number per 1000	As Percentage of Total Transfers	Number per 1000	As Percentage of Total Transfers	Number per 1000	As Percentage of Total Transfers	Number per 1000	As Percentage of Total Transfers
Voluntary sale and trade	26.3	39.8	23.5	40.5	23.7	38.6	19.0	30.7	16.2	21.1
Forced sales:										
a. Foreclosure of mortgage, bankruptcy, etc.	17.6	26.6	14.8	25.5	15.7	25.5	18.7	30.2	28.4	37.0
b. Delinquent taxes	5.2	7.9	4.7	8.1	5.1	8.3	7.4	12.0	13.3	17.4
All other transfers	16.9	25.7	15.0	25.9	17.0	27.6	16.8	27.1	18.8	24.5
Total	66.0	100.0	58.0	100.0	61.5	100.0	61.9	100.0	76.7	100.0

(a) Data are from *The Farm Real Estate Situation, 1931–32*, Circular No. 261, United States Department of Agriculture, pp. 37–40. The data refer to the twelve months ended March 15.

TABLE 10

DELINQUENT INSTALMENTS, 1928–1932(a)

I. Federal Land Banks

December 31	Total Delinquencies(b)	Accounts Delinquent 90 Days and Over
1928	$ 4,017,243	$ 1,541,870
1929	4,664,512	1,873,042
1930	7,637,494	2,967,580
1931	16,854,623	8,377,831
1932	44,379,976(c)	13,017,350

II. Joint Stock Land Banks

1928	$ 1,915,461	$ 997,977
1929	1,917,434	1,033,298
1930	3,338,362	1,780,460
1931	7,480,603	4,275,371
1932	12,593,791	9,374,663

(a) Data are from *Annual Reports of the Federal Farm Loan Board*.
(b) Partial payments have been deducted from the total.
(c) The extensions which were made from the $25,000,000 Congressional appropriation of January 23, 1932, are included with delinquencies for they represent obligations not met at maturity.

were likewise delinquent in payments.[9] A similar condition undoubtedly exists in the case of other mortgage holders, although comparable data are not available.

Another difficulty facing farm mortgagors is the necessity to renew their loans at a time when the sources of funds for such refinancing have disappeared. A majority of farm mortgages, except those of the

[9] Seventy-second Cong., 2 sess., *Refinancing Past-Due Obligations on Farms and Homes,* Hearings before Subcommittee of Senate Committee on Banking and Currency, Testimony of John Field, president, Wichita Federal Land Bank, p. 194.

Federal and Joint Stock Land Banks which are drawn on an amortized basis, mature in five years, although the average period of indebtedness for mortgaged property is approximately 30 years.[10] In 1924, 17 per cent of the farm mortgage loans were drawn for one year and an additional 12 per cent matured in two to four years. Only 13 per cent of all loans were drawn for a period of more than 30 years. Table 11, which shows the length of term of farm mortgage loans in 1924, suggests the magnitude of the problem of refinancing maturing farm mortgage obligations.

TABLE 11

LENGTH OF TERM OF FARM MORTGAGE LOANS(a)

As of January 1, 1924

Agency	Average Term Years	Percentage of Loans For:				
		1 Year, Per Cent	2 to 4 Years, Per Cent	5 Years, Per Cent	10 to 30 Years, Per Cent	Over 30 Years, Per Cent
Insurance companies.........	5.6	4.4	13.3	64.8	17.1	
Federal Land Banks.........	33.0	....	....	....	....	100.0
Joint Stock Land Banks......	33.0	....	....	....	....	100.0
Commercial banks..........	2.6	52.1	19.9	26.7	1.3	
Mortgage companies.........	6.2	.3	2.8	74.5	22.4	
Other sources.............	4.7	20.1	13.5	53.6	12.8	
All Agencies............	8.5	17.5	11.5	46.5	11.1	13.2

(a) Data are from David L. Wickens, Farm-Mortgage Credit, *United States Department of Agriculture, Technical Bulletin No. 288*, p. 77.

The practice of amortizing loans over a longer period of years is being extended gradually, but this change in policy affords no relief to debtors who are faced with the immediate necessity of renewing their loans at a time when mortgage companies are unable to sell their securities and commercial banks and individual lenders are unwilling to invest in farm mortgages.

The Burden of Farm Debts

The persistent and extraordinary decline in farm prices at the same time that interest charges and taxes have fallen only slightly below their peak of 1929 is of course the most serious threat to the continued good standing of many loans. Borrowers who have succeeded thus far

[10] David L. Wickens, "Mortgage Credit Use Requires Close Study of Long-Term Factors," *United States Department of Agriculture Year Book*, 1932, p. 511.

in maintaining their regular payments are in imminent danger of defaulting unless agricultural prices improve. The severity of the strain is emphasized by Mr. Englund of the Bureau of Agricultural Economics, who finds that farmers whose property is mortgaged at more than three-fourths of its value would need all their gross income to meet interest on their mortgages and to pay taxes and that "even with the most drastic retrenchment in cash expenditures for production and living on the farm, a large number of farmers find it utterly impossible under present conditions to pay debt charges and taxes." [11] If farmers cannot pay these obligations in full, the question naturally arises as to what portion of them creditors can expect to collect.

Any estimate of the amount of mortgage indebtedness that agriculture could carry under the present level of farm prices is subject to very serious errors. Variations in crop yields, in local tax burdens, and in the sources from which farm income is derived make it difficult to estimate a reasonable burden for any particular locality. Any estimate for the entire country becomes quite meaningless when you are unable to specify the land on which the mortgage is assumed to rest.[12] It is possible, however, to illustrate the extent to which mortgage indebtedness has outstripped the income-producing capacity of farms during the past few years and how much the mortgage debt must be reduced if it is adjusted to present farm incomes.

Debts, Taxes and Prices

The gross income from agricultural production affords a basis for comparing the relative burden of fixed charges at different dates. Since

[11] Eric Englund, Assistant Chief of the United States Bureau of Agricultural Economics, "Farm Mortgages: A Pressing National Issue," *New York Times,* Feb. 8, 1933.

[12] Studies have been made at Iowa State Agricultural College in an effort to determine the mortgage burden per acre that Iowa land can carry. A letter to the writer from W. G. Murray describes their approach to the problem as follows: It is estimated that the 45 per cent of Iowa land that is mortgaged has an average mortgage debt of $70. Cash rents for the coming year in Iowa will range between $3.00 and $4.00 per acre. Taxes on the mortgaged land average $1.50 an acre, which leaves only $1.50 to $2.50 an acre for interest payments. This means that for the coming year Iowa land can only carry from $25 to $40 an acre in mortgage debt.

This computation assumes an interest rate of 6 per cent, which is probably too high for Iowa mortgages. The calculation suggests that Iowa farmers can pay interest on a mortgage debt of not more than from 40 to 60 per cent of the existing indebtedness. However, taxes are being reduced and obviously the revaluation of debts cannot be made on the basis of one year's income and that a year of severe depression, although it is true that the inability to meet payments for one year may mean the loss of title to the farm.

the amount of land under mortgage changes slowly, it can be assumed that the same portion of the total farm acreage was mortgaged January 1, 1933 as was mortgaged January 1, 1928. The Bureau of Agricultural Economics estimates that 45.5 per cent of the farm acreage in the United States is mortgaged. In the following calculation the writer assumes that mortgaged farms obtain the proportion of the gross income that their acreage forms of the total acreage and that they bear their proportionate share of the total farm real estate taxes.[13]

In 1928 when farm mortgage indebtedness was at its peak, gross income from agricultural production attributable to mortgaged farms was $5,342 million and real estate taxes on this acreage amounted to $280 million.[14] By 1932 estimated gross income from such farms had declined to $2,384 million and their real estate taxes were only $230 million. Consequently, if the mortgage debt was to be no more burdensome in 1932 than in 1928 it should amount to only $4,029 million instead of the $8,500 million estimated for January 1, 1933, since there has been no appreciable decline in mortgage interest rates during this period. This would seem to call for a reduction of 52.5 per cent in the present farm mortgage indebtedness. Of course, there is no convincing evidence that the mortgage debt in 1928 was not unduly onerous. Calculations of this character are not particularly illuminating, however, for the mortgage problem cannot be dealt with as a total sum of indebtedness but only as it affects individual farmer debtors and their creditors.

But before discussing the numerous proposals for readjusting farm mortgage indebtedness to meet changed conditions, it is well to note who are the farmers' creditors and to determine what has been their attitude and policies in the present crisis.

The Farmers' Creditors

Farm mortgages are widely distributed among financial institutions who in turn have obligations to policy holders, bond holders, or depositors; individuals who have invested their savings in farm mortgages;

[13] Probably mortgaged farms account for a larger proportion of the gross income from agricultural production and pay a larger share of farm real estate taxes than their acreage would suggest, for it is the more valuable farm lands that carry the heaviest mortgage debt.

[14] Farm real estate taxes are used in this calculation rather than taxes on all farm property.

and farmers who have accepted mortgages in part settlement for property sold. The annual mortgage interest payment of more than half a billion dollars which the farmers owe cannot be postponed or arbitrarily reduced without seriously disturbing the affairs of these groups who have invested in farm mortgages. The distribution of farm mortgage holdings as estimated by the Bureau of Agricultural Economics was as follows on January 1, 1928.

TABLE 12

HOLDERS OF FARM MORTGAGES

	Amount	As Percentage of Total
Life insurance companies........	$2,164,000,000	22.9
Federal Land Banks............	1,146,000,000(a)	12.1
Commercial banks.............	1,020,000,000	10.8
Mortgage companies............	988,000,000	10.4
Joint Stock Land Banks.........	667,000,000	7.0
Retired farmers.................	1,006,000,000	10.6
Active farmers.................	339,000,000	3.6
Other individuals...............	1,453,000,000	15.4
Other agencies.................	685,000,000	7.2
	$9,468,000,000	100.0

(a) The loans placed in Puerto Rico have been omitted so the total does not agree with the total loans outstanding Dec. 31, 1927 as reported by the Federal Farm Loan Board.

Some shifts have occurred in this distribution during the past few years. The Federal Land Banks have been the most active lending agencies during this time and at the close of 1932 they held $1,128 million of farm mortgage loans or 13.3 per cent of the estimated amount then outstanding. The unusual demand for policy loans as well as the number of foreclosures has reduced the farm mortgage investments of insurance companies. Consequently at the close of 1932, insurance companies held approximately $1,819 million in farm mortgages or 21.4 per cent of the amount outstanding.[15] Joint Stock Land Banks in recent years have closed practically no new loans, and at the close of 1932 had only $413 million loans outstanding.[16] National banks show a decline in farm real estate loans of approximately $20 million

[15] This figure is based upon the estimate of farm real estate loans for 52 life insurance companies which represent 91.6 per cent of all companies in the United States. See *Proceedings of the Twenty-sixth Annual Convention of the Association of Life Insurance Presidents*, p. 109.
[16] The three Joint Stock Land Banks which are in receivership are not included in this amount. Data are from *Statements of Condition of Federal Land Banks, Joint Stock Land Banks, Federal Intermediate Credit Banks, Dec. 31, 1932*, United States Treasury Department, Federal Farm Loan Bureau.

since 1928. Of course, the heaviest liquidation has been on the part of banks that have failed. Data are not available to show the extent of the decline in mortgage loans held by all commercial banks, but figures for member banks show a decline of $88 million in farm mortgage loans in the last five years, a decline of 20 per cent.

Loans on farm real estate make up a comparatively small portion of the total investments of life insurance companies and of the loans and discounts of commercial banks. Life insurance companies reduced their holdings of farm mortgages from 10.9 per cent of their total investments December 31, 1930 to 8.8 per cent as of December 31, 1932.[17] If their holdings of farm real estate were included, however, their total investment in farm property would not show a marked decline.

Loans on farm real estate on June 30, 1932 made up only 2.9 per cent of the loans and discounts of national banks and 3.1 per cent of those of state commercial banks.[18] Despite the fact that farm mortgages comprise a relatively small portion of the total investments of these financial institutions, the safety of their mortgage loans is a matter of serious concern to them. Many institutional holders of farm mortgages as well as individual mortgagees have been obliged to take legal action to protect their investments when borrowers have been unable to meet their interest payments.

Policies Toward Delinquent Debtors

Adequate data are not available to reveal the policies of all lending agencies in the event mortgagors do not maintain their regular payments, but the increased real estate holdings of the most important lenders indicate the extent to which they have taken over farm property to protect their interests. An exhibit was offered at hearings before a subcommittee of the Senate Committee on Banking and Currency showing the ratio of the real estate owned December 31, 1931 to the mortgage loans outstanding on the same date for life insurance companies, Federal Land Banks, and Joint Stock Land Banks. Real estate owned, however, reflects the policy of the lending agencies in respect to the disposition of farms as well as foreclosure policies. A better indicator

---

[17] *Proceedings of the Twenty-Sixth Annual Convention of the Association of Life Insurance Presidents*, p. 108.
[18] *Annual Report of the Comptroller of the Currency*, 1932, p. 44.

of foreclosure policy is the ratio of real estate acquirements during the year to mortgage loans outstanding. Both ratios for 1931 are given in Table 13 for the three lending agencies.

TABLE 13

RATIO OF REAL ESTATE ACQUIREMENTS TO MORTGAGE LOANS(a)

Lending Agency	Percentage Ratios of Real Estate Acquirements in 1931 to Loans Outstanding at Beginning of Year		Real Estate Owned as a Percentage of Mortgage Loans Outstanding
	Number of Loans	Amount	
Life Insurance Companies.........	2.4	3.2	11.3
Federal Land Banks(b).............	1.4	1.9	8.7
Joint Stock Land Banks(c).........	2.8	3.9	4.8

(a) Data were submitted by C. B. Jennett, vice president, First Joint Stock Land Bank, Chicago, 72 Cong., 2 sess., Hearings before Subcommittee of Senate Committee on Banking and Currency, *Refinancing of Past-Due Obligations on Farms and Homes*. Real estate owned includes real estate sales contracts but apparently does not include real estate held subject to redemption unless the period of redemption has already expired.

(b) Data were compiled from annual reports submitted to the Superintendent of Insurance, District of Columbia, by 20 companies holding approximately 84 per cent in amount of the total farm mortgage loans of all life insurance companies in the United States.

(c) Data were compiled from reports of 47 Joint Stock Land Banks in operation on Dec. 31, 1931. Three banks in receivership and in voluntary liquidation on that date, and two which began operations during 1931 are excluded.

In spite of the vigorous agitation against foreclosures, the real estate holdings of mortgagees continued to mount throughout 1932. At the close of 1932 Federal Land Banks had acquired outright or held subject to redemption 18,503 farms and Joint Stock Land Banks, exclusive of three large banks in receivership, held 6,406 farms on the same date. In a short period of five years the investment in farm real estate for the twelve Federal Land Banks has increased from $35,392,454 to $112,731,350—an increase of more than 200 per cent. Similarly, the real estate holdings of Joint Stock Land Banks increased from $23,889,127 in 1928 to $63,729,701, an increase of 152 per cent. The real estate holdings of the Joint Stock Land Banks in receivership would increase this total materially. The extent to which the Federal and Joint Stock Land Banks have become farm owners and the relation of their land holdings to their mortgage loans is shown in Table 14.

TABLE 14

Real Estate Holdings, 1928–1932(a)

As of December 31

I. Federal Land Banks

	1928	1929	1930	1931	1932
		(Dollars in Thousands)			
Owned outright	$20,101	$23,287	$29,541	$39,465	$57,896
Held subject to redemption	6,377	6,230	7,456	13,735	25,492
Real Estate sales contracts, and purchase money mortgages	8,915	15,108	19,474	24,682	29,343
Total	$35,393	$44,605	$56,471	$77,882	$112,731
As percentage of 1928	100	126	160	221	319
As percentage of net mortgage loans outstanding December 31	3.0	3.7	4.7	6.7	10.0

II. Joint Stock Land Banks

	1928	1929	1930	1931	1932
Owned outright	$12,892	$19,065	$24,821	$37,668	$39,325
Held subject to redemption	5,271	6,008	5,204	10,925	13,169
Real Estate sales contracts, and purchase money mortgages	5,726	9,148	12,620	13,752	11,236
Total	$23,889	$34,221	$42,645	$63,345	$63,730
As percentage of 1928	100	143	179	261	267
As percentage of net mortgage loans outstanding December 31	3.9	5.8	7.7	11.9	15.4

III. Number of Farms Held, 1928–1932(a)

As of December 31

	1928	1929	1930	1931	1932
Federal Land Banks	6,010	6,641	8,532	12,543	18,503
Joint Stock Land Banks	1,401	2,133	2,801	4,958	6,406(b)

(a) Data are from the *Annual Reports of the Federal Farm Loan Board*.
(b) Three large banks placed in receivership in 1932 are omitted.

Complete data are not available in respect to foreclosure proceedings in 1932 but the foreclosure suits pending at the close of the year by the Federal Land Banks involved 4,423 farmers and represented an unpaid principal of nearly 20 million dollars. At the same date foreclosures were pending upon 2,593 loans of the Joint Stock Land Banks (exclusive of the three in receivership) involving approximately the same amount. The rapid increase in the number of foreclosure suits instituted by the Federal and Joint Stock Land Banks is revealed in Table 15.

Obviously, if the lending agencies which confine their investments exclusively to first mortgage loans find it necessary to take over property at the rate these figures indicate, loan agencies whose equities are much smaller would be under even greater pressure.

TABLE 15

FORECLOSURES PENDING, 1928–1932(a)

December 31	Federal Land Banks			Joint Stock Land Banks		
	Number	Unpaid Principal	As Percentage of 1928	Number	Unpaid Principal	As Percentage of 1928
1928	1,523	$4,659,495	100	529	$5,174,683	100
1929	1,921	6,311,447	135	691	5,391,400	104
1930	2,402	8,655,477	186	1,076	8,820,700	170
1931	4,014	16,093,488	345	2,342	20,388,400	394
1932	4,423	19,974,980	429	2,593	19,725,823	381(b)

(a) Data are from the *Annual Reports of the Federal Farm Loan Board.*
(b) Three large banks placed in receivership in 1932 are not included.

The sympathy of the public is quite often aroused by impending foreclosure suits, but without discrimination between the cases in which legal action is practically forced upon the mortgagees and instances in which a more lenient policy might be followed without endangering the creditors' interests. Many farmers are so hopelessly in debt that they abandon their farms rather than continue the struggle. Merchants and other local creditors who are often the only source of further credit are on the ground and frequently claim all available income from current production without leaving the farmer sufficient to pay his taxes or mortgage interest. Holders of chattel mortgages may foreclose and leave the farmer without adequate working capital to operate his farm. If the action of other creditors make it impossible for the farmer to meet his mortgage obligations, any leniency which the mortgagee shows redounds to the benefit of other creditors rather than assists the farmer.

The Federal Farm Loan Board insists that the policy of the Federal Land Banks and Joint Stock Land Banks has not been unduly harsh. In response to a Senate resolution, the Board describes the foreclosure policies of these banks as follows:

In cases of delinquency, it is their policy to consider each case on its individual merits and to institute foreclosure proceedings only when investigation discloses that a borrower is not a capable farmer, is not making a real effort to meet his obligation to the full extent of his capacity to pay, and is not likely to succeed if given a reasonable opportunity, or when there are other factors making it necessary to take action in the vital interests of the bank.[19]

[19] *Annual Report of the Federal Farm Loan Board,* 1931, p. 7.

The policy of the Federal Land Bank of Wichita as expressed by its president is to avoid foreclosures so long as the farmer pays the bank out of his crop receipts the amount it would receive if it had title to the farm and rented it to a tenant. This amount may well be less than the instalment due on the mortgage but presumably it is as much as the bank would realize if it took title to the property. On the other hand, if the farmer gives chattel mortgages on his entire production without providing for taxes or making certain that the mortgagee receives at least a landlord's share, then the mortgage holder has no alternative except to foreclose.[20]

The issue, however, is not whether individual creditors are as lenient as conditions will permit or whether each debtor is straining every effort to meet his obligations. The real issue is that an increasing number of farmers cannot meet their obligations at present prices and that some readjustment is inevitable. The wide assortment of proposals to accomplish this objective is evidence of the interest in this problem but also adds to the difficulty of choosing a line of action and prompt action is imperative.

2. RECOMMENDATIONS

No single scheme for the readjustment of mortgage indebtedness can be devised, for all farmers are not equally hard pressed to meet their obligations. Moreover, it must be remembered that 60 per cent of all farms are entirely free of mortgage debt.[21] Legislation to relieve the debt burden of the other 40 per cent must be carefully drawn if the social cost is not to be unnecessarily high. If the sacrifices demanded of creditors further embarrass our financial institutions or result in the loss of individual savings, the attendant hardships will largely offset the advantages accruing to farm debtors. It must also be recalled that many farmers hold mortgages from which they expect to derive an income.[22] And finally, farmers are taxpayers and any ill-conceived plan

[20] Section 14 of the Federal Farm Loan Act was amended recently to forbid Federal Land Banks to accept any security other than Federal Land Bank stock or mortgages on farm real estate. Consequently, the Land Banks cannot protect their loans by accepting chattel mortgages or crop liens as additional collateral and it may be necessary for them to take more prompt action in the case of default than would otherwise be necessary. Public No. 430, 72 Cong., Sec. 5, Approved Mar. 4, 1933.

[21] This figure is based on 1930 census for owner-operated farms and Bureau of Agricultural Economics studies of farms or other tenures. See David L. Wickens, "Long-Term Farm Credit in a Depression," *Journal of Farm Economics,* October 1932.

[22] Retired and active farmers together held 13.9 per cent of all farm mortgages in 1928.

for the revaluation of farm indebtedness might involve the federal and state governments in considerable expense which is ultimately borne by all taxpayers.

Farm mortgagors, for the purpose of this discussion, may be broadly classified into the following groups: First are the farmers whose mortgage debt represents only a small fraction of the value of their property and who are in no immediate danger of defaulting on their obligations even with the diminished farm receipts of 1932. These farmers are having a difficult time, but they are not the primary concern of Congress and state legislatures at the present moment.

A second group includes farmers who, under more prosperous conditions, would be regarded as quite moderately indebted but who are temporarily unable to meet their interest payments, taxes, and operating costs from their reduced incomes. Furthermore, the breakdown of the commercial banking system in agricultural areas precludes further short-term borrowing to tide them over this period of abnormally low prices. In a third class are those producers who might work out of their present financial difficulties if they could refund their outstanding obligations on terms that would relieve them of any immediate danger of foreclosure. A fourth group comprises those hopelessly insolvent farmers who can carry on only if they obtain a substantial revision downward of their debts. And finally, in addition to those farmers who are having difficulty in meeting their interest and amortization payments are those mortgagors who face the problem of obtaining renewals of their maturing loans.

It is impossible to define accurately the boundaries of these several groups or to estimate the numbers falling within each. Broadly speaking, it can be assumed that farmers indebted for not more than 25 per cent of the value of their property would normally fall in the first group and require no governmental aid in the present emergency, other than is given through strengthening the Federal Farm Loan system and extending the services of the Federal Land Banks.[23] However, approximately one-fourth of all farmers in the United States, or a million and a half, might reasonably be expected to seek aid under the numerous financial measures now under consideration by Congress.

[23] To be sure, those farmers are having a serious time and as soon as the bond market improves sufficiently to enable Federal Land Banks to refund their outstanding bonds at lower interest rates, every effort should be made to pass on to present borrowers the saving in the form of dividends on their stock in national farm loan associations or in lower interest rates and to extend their loan services to other eligible applicants.

Mortgage Relief Legislation

Legislative measures to aid farm mortgagors are of three general types. First, amendments to the Federal Farm Loan Act to extend and liberalize the services of the Federal Land Banks, to enable them to pursue more lenient collection policies, and to refrain from exerting further pressure on the farm real estate market by immediate sale of foreclosed lands. Second, there are emergency measures that are avowedly of a temporary nature designed to halt foreclosures until Congress has had an opportunity to enact a comprehensive scheme of debt reform. And, third, there is legislation establishing machinery, and outlining procedures and policies to be followed in securing a permanent settlement of the farm mortgage problem.

The legislative jam in the short session of Congress made it quite impossible to enact a comprehensive program of farm mortgage relief. Legislation was confined to an act to amend the Federal Farm Loan system and an amendment to the Federal Bankruptcy law to facilitate composition settlements with the farmers' creditors without formal bankruptcy proceedings. The special session of Congress was left with the task of enacting more far-reaching farm mortgage relief legislation.

The amendments to the Federal Farm Loan Act which have been enacted are designed to extend the services of the Federal Land Banks and to offer relief to borrowers without impairing the financial stability of these institutions.[24] In the first place, the Federal Land Banks are authorized to loan directly to farmers in communities where national farm loan associations are not functioning effectively or where no association has been formed. Under this provision farmers can be accommodated without the necessity of the endorsement of a local association.

A second section of the act extends the purposes for which the Federal Land Banks may make loans. Loans are permitted for the purpose of refinancing indebtedness incurred prior to January 1, 1933 and to provide the owner of the mortgaged farm with funds for general agricultural purposes. In this way borrowers whose mortgages are now less than the maximum amount permitted by law can refund their floating debt and obtain working capital at the mortgage interest rate which is normally lower than short-term interest rates. Furthermore, payments can be extended over a longer period of time.

[24] Public No. 430, 72 Cong. Certain sections modify the provisions for the collateral security of Federal Land Bank bonds which may tend to reduce the security behind them unless the provisions are carefully administered.

Another section of the act authorized the Federal Land Banks at any time during the next five years to defer the collection of any unpaid instalment for a period not to exceed ten years.[25] In addition to waiving the payment of instalments for a time, the banks, with the approval of the Federal Farm Loan Board, can arrange an amortization plan which will extinguish the unpaid balance of any mortgage in a period of time not more than forty years after the date of the agreement.[26] As a result of such readjustment, the semi-annual payments on loans would be materially reduced. The extent of the reductions effected by these provisions would depend upon the rate of interest on the loan, the length of time it had been in force, and the interest rate prevailing at the time the new amortization plan goes into effect. Table 16 indicates

TABLE 16

EXTENT OF RELIEF RESULTING FROM WAIVING OF PRINCIPAL PAYMENTS ON LOANS OF
$10,000 AT 5.5 PER CENT INTEREST WHICH ARE REPAYABLE IN $34\frac{1}{2}$ YEARS(a)

Age of Loan	Number of Instalments Paid	Total Amount of Next Semi-Annual Instalment	Interest Portion of Next Instalment	Principal Portion of Next Instalment	
				Amount	Per Cent of Total Instalment
5	10	$325	$259.42	$65.58	20.2
10	20	325	238.98	86.02	26.5
15	30	325	212.17	112.83	34.7

(a) Data are from the Statistical Division of the Federal Farm Loan Bureau.

the reduction in semi-annual payments which would be effected if a borrower secured a waiver of the payment of only the principal amount on a 5½ per cent $10,000 loan which is drawn to mature in thirty-four and one-half years.

If a loan has been in force ten years, the waiver of payments on the

[25] The deferment of these payments does not affect the eligibility of loans as security for farm loan bonds. These postponed |payments are to be repaid in 10 annual or 20 semi-annual instalments and are payable at the time each succeeding instalment is due. Postponed instalments bear simple interest at the same rate as the mortgage. Taxes, liens, etc., paid by the mortgagee become part of the mortgage debt and all bear interest at the same rate as the mortgage.

[26] These loans may be deposited as collateral for Federal Land Bank bonds to an amount equal to the principal of the original loan remaining unpaid at the date the new amortization plan goes into effect.

principal sum reduces the semi-annual instalments by 26.5 per cent. If, at the end of a few years, the unpaid balance of the loan is amortized over a period of 40 years at a lower interest rate than the loan formerly carried, the regular semi-annual payments are materially reduced. The relief which a farm debtor would obtain from a postponement of the principal payments on his loan for three years followed by the amortization of the unpaid balance over a period of 40 years is shown in Table 17.

TABLE 17

EXTENT OF RELIEF GRANTED BY REDUCING INTEREST RATES TO 4½ PER CENT, WAIVING PRINCIPAL PAYMENTS FOR 3 YEARS, AND AMORTIZING THE BALANCE ON A 40-YEAR BASIS, IN THE CASE OF LONG-TERM, SEMI-ANNUAL $10,000 LOANS OF VARIOUS AGES(a)

(5.5 Per Cent Loan, Repayable in 34½ Years)

Age of Loan (Years)	Original Semi-Annual Instalment	Unpaid Balance	Interest Only 4.5 Per Cent		New Instalment to Amortize in 40 Years	
			Amount	Percentage of Reduction from Original Instalment	Amount	Percentage of Reduction from Original Instalment
5	$325	$9,433.36	$212.25	34.7	$255.30	21.4
10	325	8,690.12	195.53	39.8	235.19	27.6
15	325	7,715.25	173.59	46.6	208.80	35.8

(a) Data were prepared by R. C. Engberg, statistician of the Federal Farm Loan Bureau. They were submitted by C. B. Jennett, vice president, First Joint Stock Land Bank, Chicago, 72nd Cong., 2nd Sess. Hearings before Subcommittee of Senate Committee on Banking and Currency, *The Refinancing of Past-Due Obligations on Farms and Homes*, p. 108.

Further relief is afforded farm mortgagors by the provision for extensions and for new loans by the Federal Farm Land Banks. No additional capital was voted these banks in the short session of Congress but the amendment provides that the balance of the $125 million appropriated January 23, 1932 for the purpose of strengthening their capital structure must be used either for extending maturing instalments or for making new loans. Originally $25 million was allocated for the purpose of enabling the banks to extend the time for maturing instalments, and by the close of 1932 the Federal Land Banks had granted extensions to approximately 93,000 borrowers. The balance of $100 million has been used in the following manner:

Purpose	*Amount*
For purchase and retirement of Federal Land Bank bonds (a)	$14,628,991
To pay bond interest..............................	6,683,471
For other purposes (b)............................	9,404,649
Total expended.........................	30,717,112
Balance (in securities and cash)............	69,282,888
Total amount.........................	$100,000,000

(a) Columbia, New Orleans, St. Paul, and Spokane Banks found it desirable to use a portion of the amount allocated to them to repurchase their own bonds at a discount and thus increase the security underlying the volume outstanding.

(b) Includes funds used for the retirement of the Spokane participation certificates, for new loans, and for other purposes.

Under the amended act the unexpended balance of slightly more than $69 million must be used exclusively for the extension of delinquent instalments or for new loans.

Another section of the amendment permits Federal Land Banks to carry real estate as an asset for a period of five years at its normal value but not in excess of the amount of the bank's investment in the property at the time it is acquired. This permission will undoubtedly remove the pressure upon the banks to dispose of their real estate holdings immediately and thus will relieve the farm real estate market of the depressing influence of distress sales. However, lending agencies are not desirous of operating parcels of land, so it is to be expected that they will dispose of their farm holdings as rapidly as they can sell for a price that will enable them to avoid losses.

Need for Increased Resources of Federal Land Banks

A substantial increase in the loan resources of the Federal Land Banks is essential if they are to pursue lenient policies in respect to borrowers and to furnish the maximum assistance in the present emergency. Loans made by the Federal Land Banks in 1932, although by no means negligible, were only slightly more than one-quarter the volume placed in 1928, as is shown in the table below.[27]

The Federal Land Banks must obtain additional funds if they are to be in a position to take over maturing obligations now held by lending agencies which are unable or unwilling to renew them, or if they are

[27] Data are from the *Annual Reports of the Federal Farm Loan Board.*

TABLE 18

LOANS BY FEDERAL LAND BANKS

	Number of Loans Closed	Amount	As Percentage of 1928
1928	26,988	$102,236,400	100.0
1929	17,132	64,252,500	62.8
1930	12,572	47,971,000	46.9
1931	10,898	42,015,300	40.1
1932	7,208	27,569,800	27.6

to give a larger number of farmer-borrowers the benefit of their lower rates. Their sources of funds are current income from maturing instalments, invested capital, and the proceeds from the sale of Federal Land Bank bonds. The present state of the bond market precludes any public sale of securities at satisfactory prices so this source of funds is temporarily not available. Current receipts have declined and the unexpended balance of the $125 million previously appropriated is not sufficient to meet the demands which may reasonably be placed upon the Federal Land Banks.

The volume of farm mortgage loans which must be renewed or refinanced by other lending agencies amounts to approximately a billion and a quarter or a billion and a half dollars annually.[28] What proportion of this amount would be acceptable by the Federal Land Banks it is impossible to determine accurately. The Federal Land Banks can only accommodate farmers operating their own farms, which means that less than 60 per cent of the loans maturing each year would be eligible business for the Federal Land Banks. Of the farms operated by their owners, nearly 40 per cent are encumbered for amounts in excess of 50 per cent of their value which makes them ineligible under the present law.[29] Probably not more than $450 million of the mortgage loans which must be renewed each year could be accepted by the Federal Land Banks, and of this amount a large portion would undoubtedly be rejected as undesirable credit risks. If the loan resources of the Federal Land Banks were increased sufficiently to give them half a million dollars annually for the next three years they could certainly accommodate all eligible applicants who are obliged to renew their loans during this period. Although the restriction of loans to farm

[28] See David L. Wickens, "Farm-Mortgage Credit," *U. S. Department of Agriculture, Technical Bulletin No. 288*, p. 77.

[29] Loans of the Federal Land Banks may not exceed 50 per cent of the value of the real estate plus 20 per cent of the value of permanent improvements.

owners who operate their farms and the conservative loan policy which they are required to observe make it impossible for the Federal Land Banks to take over many of the existing farm mortgages, nevertheless a substantial increase in their resources would enable them to give a large number of farmer borrowers the benefit of lower interest rates.

The present bond market, however, makes it impossible for the Federal Land Banks to sell their securities in the open market. Consequently it will be necessary for the United States Treasury to purchase bonds to supply the necessary funds for refinancing maturing mortgages until such time as Land Bank bonds can be sold to the investing public at reasonable rates. One of the recent amendments to the Farm Loan Act which provides for the issue of consolidated bonds in lieu of bonds of the individual banks may hasten the time when their securities can be sold to the general public. Probably consolidated bonds can be marketed more readily and possibly at lower rates than bonds of the individual banks and hence this amendment is a necessary step in a refunding program which the Federal Farm Loan system will undoubtedly undertake as soon as the bond market improves.[30]

Measures to Prevent Foreclosures

These provisions to extend and liberalize the Federal Farm Loan Act are highly desirable but they are insufficient to meet the existing emergency. Farmers are demanding legislation which will prevent foreclosures and assist them in retaining their property. Discussions of various measures to accomplish these purposes occupied much of the time of the House and Senate Banking and Currency Committees during the closing weeks of the Seventy-Second Session of Congress and continue to absorb the attention of the present session.

A moratorium on interest and amortization payments with a postponement of foreclosures for several years is frequently proposed as a temporary expedient.[31] The postponement of interest payments as well

[30] The Federal Land Banks are jointly liable for all bond issues, but the fact that a few banks have experienced heavy losses has made it difficult to float their bonds.

[31] Governor Bryan of Nebraska has issued a proclamation asking all holders of mortgages on farms and homes to withhold foreclosure proceedings until a board of conciliation appointed by him completes its organization and the Legislature has an opportunity to pass a mortgage moratorium. *U. S. Daily,* Feb. 16, 1933.

The Fletcher-Steagall Bill, Public No. 430, 72 Cong., permits the Federal Land Banks to postpone the payment of maturing instalment but applications for such postponements must be approved by the directors of the Land Bank involved.

as amounts due on the principal sum and the suspension of the rights of creditors to foreclose are practical only if it is certain that agricultural prices will advance sufficiently during a comparatively short time to permit a majority of mortgagors to resume payments. Otherwise, the non-payment of interest due threatens the solvency of creditors without giving any assurance that they will not be required ultimately to revise their claims. Meanwhile, if taxes remain unpaid, creditors not only forego their current income, but preferred claims accumulate which jeopardize their investments. The suspension of foreclosures without providing for the payment of interest and taxes offers indiscriminate relief to all debtors without regard to their necessities and without adequate safeguards for creditors' interests.[32]

More equitable proposals to avoid foreclosures provide a source of loans to enable farmers to meet their current payments of interest and taxes. Such loans are advocated only if the farmers' total indebtedness is of such proportions that they have a fair opportunity to work out of their financial difficulties. Loans for the purpose of meeting interest and taxes can be made either after the payments are past due for a specified length of time or at the time they fall due. Such advances may be made directly to the mortgagee who in turn must offer evidence to show that taxes have been paid, or they may be made in the first instance to the mortgagor for the exclusive purpose of paying taxes and interest.[33] Legislation for this purpose is admittedly of an emergency and temporary character but it would afford farmer debtors a breathing spell and enable them to keep their loans in good standing.[34]

The administration of loans for the purposes of meeting current payments of interest and taxes would be simplified if advances were made to creditors rather than to the farmers directly for the number of transactions would be enormously reduced. Moreover, loans to mortgagees

[32] 72 Cong., 2 sess., *Refinancing Past-Due Obligations on Farms and Homes,* Hearings before Subcommittee of Senate Committee on Banking and Currency, Testimony of John Field, president of the Wichita Federal Land Bank, Feb. 4, 1933.
[33] S. 5639, 72 Cong., 2 sess., would authorize the Reconstruction Finance Corporation through the regional agricultural credit corporations to make loans at interest rate of 4 per cent to *mortgagees* for the payment of delinquent taxes, and defaulted interest and taxes. No loan is to be made unless the mortgagor has attempted to meet his obligations and is in default six months.
H. R. 14565, 72 Cong., 2 sess., Title II proposes to make advances to *farmers and stockmen* for the purpose of paying interest or amortization instalments on first farm mortgage loans or for the payment of real estate taxes. Loans are limited to a sum required to pay interest and taxes for two years, bear interest at 5 per cent, and have a maturity not to exceed ten years.
[34] See Senate Report, No. 1220, which accompanies S. 5639.

would ordinarily be secured by more satisfactory collateral than could be offered by the individual farmer. However, a bill introduced in the House which proposed to loan directly to farmers provided that the mortgagee must agree, in consideration of the cash payment he otherwise would not receive, to add the amount of the loan to the principal of the first mortgage.[35]

Loans to borrowers to enable them to meet their interest and taxes promise more assistance to the farmers than do loans to the mortgagees for the same purpose. Individual holders of mortgages or even commercial banks will hesitate to borrow funds to enable their farmer debtors to keep their loans in good standing, if in return, they must bind themselves not to foreclose the loans for a definite length of time.[36] Even now there is a limited cash market for farm lands at prices that are above the present income producing value of the property and mortgagees will be reluctant to agree to borrow funds for the benefit of their debtors and to forego opportunities of disposing of the land.[37]

Objections to Loans

Serious objections can be raised to all proposals to advance funds for the purpose of meeting interest and principal payments or to pay taxes. Obviously a substantial increase in farm mortgage indebtedness which such loans contemplate is not wholly desirable. However, if loans are restricted to farmers whose total mortgage debt, together with these loans, would not exceed 50 per cent of the present value of their property, the debt would not exceed an amount which mortgage agencies ordinarily regard as conservative and on which future payments could be maintained if agricultural prices show even a modest improvement.

Another criticism of this method of assisting the farmers is based upon the belief that federal funds should not be made available to

[35] H. R. 14565, 72 Cong., Title II, Sec. 10. The bill also requires that the mortgagor must first ask his creditor to extend the time of payment for the interest and to pay the taxes. If the creditor refuses, then the farmer may apply for a loan.
[36] H. R. 14565 would provide that in the event any mortgage loan is foreclosed, any loss sustained through the resale of the property shall be shared by the Reconstruction Finance Corporation (which advanced the loan to the borrower) in proportion to the ratio which the loan bears to the total principal amount of the loan foreclosed.
[37] 72 Cong., 2 sess., *Refinancing Past-Due Obligations on Farms and Homes*, Hearings before Subcommittee of Senate Committee on Banking and Currency, Testimony of C. B. Jennett, vice-president, First Trust Joint Stock Land Bank, Chicago.

enable them to meet taxes levied by state and local governments. There is a widespread belief that local taxes bear too heavily upon farm real estate. If tax burdens are not fairly distributed, the solution for the problem is a reallocation of taxes and not loans from the Reconstruction Finance Corporation or some other federal source.[38] The gravity of the present emergency is, however, a justification for the use of federal funds for such purposes. Nevertheless, such loans should not weaken the movements for needed tax reforms.

Refunding of Debts

Many farmers do not require further loans but instead desire assistance in securing some readjustment of their existing indebtedness. In short, machinery must be created, funds provided, and procedure outlined which will enable farmers: (a) to refund their existing indebtedness on more favorable terms as to repayment and at lower interest rates; (b) to negotiate settlements with their creditors which will scale down their obligations to amounts commensurate with their ability to pay. These two propositions are not mutually exclusive, for if existing loans can be refunded at lower interest rates and the time of payment extended, the result is to effect a substantial reduction of the annual or semi-annual payments although the principal amount remains the same.

Plans to refund existing debts contemplate a more extensive use of mortgage credit in furnishing working capital, paying off short-term obligations, meeting tax payments and past due interest rather than concentrate on securing abnormally low interest rates. However, it would seem that loans for such purposes need not bear more than $4\frac{1}{2}$ or 5 per cent interest if government funds are made available either through the Federal Farm Loan system or the Reconstruction Finance Corporation.

The refinancing of outstanding indebtedness will frequently require loans in excess of amounts which would be regarded as safe under more normal circumstances. However, the present conditions seem to warrant the use of government funds in carrying these more hazardous loans in an effort to prevent wholesale dispossessions. Frequently, it is the action of junior lien holders or even unsecured creditors which forces

[38] A similar argument is raised in the case of the Reconstruction Finance Corporation's loans to railroads which are in part for the payment of taxes.

first mortgage holders to foreclose in order to protect their prior lien.[39] If outstanding obligations could be refunded on the security of either a first or second mortgage at moderate rates with payments extended over ten years, many farmers now facing foreclosure or bankruptcy would have a reasonable chance to retain their property.

A separate division of the Federal Farm Loan system or an independent emergency mortgage corporation could be organized to handle these refunding operations which involve loans in excess of the amounts which the Federal Land Banks are permitted to advance.[40] In either case it would be necessary for the federal treasury to advance the capital. If it is assumed that all farmers whose present mortgage debt ranges from 40 to 60 per cent of the value of their property could refund their floating debt and obtain necessary working capital without bringing their total mortgage debt beyond 65 or 75 per cent of the present value of their property, these loans would not expose the government to unusual losses. It is difficult to estimate what proportion of farmers would apply for such loans and quite uncertain how many would be regarded as acceptable credit risks, but probably a mortgage corporation with loan resources between $300 and $500 million would be required.[41]

If the Federal Farm Loan system is entrusted with the administration of these more hazardous loans, this division of its operations must be entirely separate from the regular loan business of the Federal Land Banks. Loans on which the owner's equity is only 25 or 35 per cent are not acceptable collateral for bonds to be sold in the investment market. As repayments are made and the margin of safety on these loans is increased, they could be taken over by the Federal Land Banks. But meanwhile no emergency financing should be permitted to create any doubts in the minds of the public as to the high character of Federal Land Bank bonds.

[39] The *Annual Report of the Federal Farm Loan Board, 1932*, states that "The difficulties of many farmer-borrowers have been increased by the existence of heavy junior liens and chattel mortgages. In many cases creditors other than those holding the first mortgages on the land have taken over the borrowers' equipment and livestock, making it impossible for them to continue their farming operations and forcing many abandonments and foreclosures."

[40] The Federal Land Banks are authorized to loan not in excess of 50 per cent of the value of the real estate plus 20 per cent of the value of the fixed improvements.

[41] S. 5515, 72 Cong., 2 sess., introduced by Senator Robinson provides for an Emergency Agricultural Refinance Corporation with a capital of 1 billion dollars, but this amount seems excessive now that the Federal Land Banks can make loans for the purpose of refunding indebtedness incurred prior to January 1, 1933 and for general agricultural purposes.

Additional loans for the payment of interest and taxes or the refunding of debts already incurred will not meet the requirements of many mortgagors who are facing foreclosure and possibly dispossession. A large number are either insolvent or cannot meet their obligations as they mature unless agricultural prices advance more rapidly and to a greater degree than is anticipated by even the most optimistic observers. A drastic scaling down of their debts is inevitable. Probably a substantial portion of borrowers whose mortgage debt exceeds 75 per cent of the value of their property fall in this group.[42] If their unsecured obligations are included, their debts undoubtedly wipe out most, if not all, of their remaining property.

Readjustment Procedure

Debt settlements which involve more lenient terms of payment or an actual writing down of the principal sum may be accomplished in one of two ways. A composition settlement can be worked out under the supervision of an appointee of a bankruptcy court. Second, a voluntary plan for readjusting debts can be drawn up with the assistance of mediators or debt-counselors appointed and paid by the federal government and acceptable to both debtor and creditor. In either case the object is to effect a final disposition of the claims against the farmer without disturbing him in the possession of his farm.

The amendment to the Federal Bankruptcy Act enacted during the short session of Congress provides a method by which agricultural debtors can negotiate composition or extension settlements with their creditors.[43] The act authorizes courts of bankruptcy to appoint referees to be known as conciliation commissioners upon the petition of at least 15 farmers within any county who certify that they intend to file petitions under this section. The conciliation commissioner must be a resident of the county and familiar with agricultural conditions, but he must not be engaged in "the farm mortgage business, the business of financing farmers, or transactions in agricultural commodities or the business of marketing or dealing in agricultural commodities, or of furnishing agricultural supplies."

The chief advantage of applying for a composition settlement or an extension of time of payment from the point of view of the farmer is

[42] See Table 2.
[43] Public No. 420, 72 Cong., Sec. 75, Agricultural Compositions and Extensions, approved Mar. 3, 1933.

that such a petition automatically stays any action for debt until the court acts upon his petition. A settlement cannot be confirmed by the court, however, until (1) it has been accepted in writing by a majority in number of all creditors whose claims have been allowed, including secured creditors whose claims are affected, which number shall represent a majority in amount of such claims, and (2) the money or security necessary to pay all debts which have priority unless waived, and in case of a composition, the consideration to be paid by the farmer to his creditors has been deposited in such place as shall be designated by and subject to the order of the court.

Another section of the act provides that the settlement may extend the time of payment of either secured or unsecured debts and may provide for priority of payments between secured and unsecured creditors during the period of extension. Although the court's approval of a composition settlement or an extension arrangement makes it binding upon the farmer and his creditor the act provides that "such composition or extension shall not reduce the amount of nor impair the lien of any secured creditor, but shall affect only the time and method of its liquidation." These restrictions limit the usefulness of this method of readjusting mortgage indebtedness, for in most instances the first mortgage holder would be in a position as one of the largest creditors to prevent any settlement that required a scaling down of his claim.

The Case for Voluntary Settlements

The creation of machinery to facilitate voluntary debt settlements outside the jurisdiction of the courts seems a more hopeful approach to the problem of debt adjustments. Farmers are notoriously opposed to bankruptcy proceedings and they may be reluctant to seek a composition settlement or an extension of time under the supervision of a court officer even though this method offers relief from an intolerable situation. Moreover as the amendment is drawn, it appears that conciliation commissioners are more likely to have legal training rather than experience in granting credit or in appraising the value of farm property for agricultural purposes.

A bill introduced at the short session of Congress which provides for the voluntary readjustment of farm mortgage debt offers a feasible scheme for handling the problem.[44] In general, the plan is for the

[44] H. R. 14565, 72 Cong., 2 sess.

Secretary of Agriculture to set up farm mortgage adjustment districts throughout the country and appoint debt adjustment counselors to act as mediators in effecting adjustments between farmer debtors and their creditors.[45] These mediators or debt adjusters might be appointed in consultation with the Federal Farm Loan Board and with the officers of the emergency mortgage corporation or the regional agricultural credit corporations if these latter agencies are authorized to make advances to farmers on more liberal terms than the Federal Land Banks.

The advantages of having these financial institutions participate in the administration of any plan of voluntary debt adjustment are obvious. In some instances debt settlements can be consummated only if a new loan can be negotiated and the proceeds used to pay off existing creditors in accordance with the settlement agreed upon. The maximum loan which the farmer could obtain would represent the maximum cash settlement he could offer his creditors. With this sum as a guide in the negotiations, an agreement could be reached in a minimum of time. Unsecured creditors are unlikely to demand unreasonable concessions if the alternative is a foreclosure sale at which their entire claims are certain to be wiped out or a settlement under the supervision of a court of bankruptcy, since secured creditors are protected against any writing down of their claims. Even first mortgage holders can afford to accept a smaller cash sum and avoid the expense and possible greater loss by taking over the property.[46]

Summary of Remedies Proposed

Briefly, the essential features of any thoroughgoing scheme to effect a solution of the farm mortgage problem can be summarized as follows: (1) An increase in the resources of the Federal Land Banks to enable them to take over a larger portion of the farm mortgage debt at the lower interest rates these banks have been able to maintain; (2) a source of loans to enable farmers who are quite moderately indebted to pay their interest, amortization instalments, and taxes;

[45] Farmers can file petitions under Sec. 74 of the Act which applies to individual debtors. Practically the same relief is provided and procedure outlined as under Sec. 75 except for the appointment of conciliation commissioners if 15 farmers indicate an intention to file petitions under the Act.

[46] If there continues to be a speculative cash market for farm lands, creditors—particularly secured creditors—are unlikely to agree to a settlement that requires any substantial sacrifice. However, many of the farms most heavily indebted would not sell readily and creditors may have no choice except to write down their claims.

(3) an emergency refinancing mortgage corporation capitalized by federal funds to refund existing indebtedness. The loans should bear the current interest rate but a total mortgage debt equal to 65 or 75 per cent of the value of the property might be approved. If the administration of the loans is placed under the Department of Agriculture, the exact percentage of the value of the property that might be advanced could be left to the discretion of the officers entrusted with formulating loan policies; (4) administrative machinery to facilitate prompt and equitable agreements between creditors and (a) farmers who require more lenient terms in order to pay out their obligations in full and (b) farmers who are hopelessly insolvent and whose debts must be written down.

The various phases of the farm mortgage problem must be attacked simultaneously if a minimum of injustice and hardship is to be inflicted upon both debtors and creditors. Unusual leniency in a few cases may increase the pressure to collect in full in other instances. Moreover the farm mortgage problem is one that affects the prosperity of the entire agricultural industry and it must be approached from the point of view of the industry itself as well as with a maximum regard for the rights of the debtors and creditors immediately involved. Such a problem cannot be handled piecemeal, and under a wide variety of auspices. Otherwise, the inevitable delays would postpone the recovery of agriculture, and the uncertainties in respect to the extent of the readjustments that are inevitable would impair the status of even the highest grade farm mortgage securities.

Inflation and Mortgage Debts

Inflationary measures are frequently suggested as a way of reducing the burden of mortgage indebtedness. Obviously farmers' fixed obligations can be discharged more readily if the prices of agricultural products advance while their debts are unaffected. But whether inflationary measures are a satisfactory method of relieving farmers of their present excessive burden of mortgage debt depends in part upon the effect of such measures upon non-agricultural prices.

The present disparity between the prices farmers receive for their products and the prices they pay for commodities used in production and consumed in the household accentuates the farmers' debt problems. If this disparity continues, a portion of any gain from higher prices for agricultural products is offset by increased costs of production and living.[47]

A second consideration in judging the efficacy of inflation as a remedy is whether the overproduction of certain staple commodities would not leave the prices comparatively unaffected by the measures adopted. The prices of wheat and cotton, particularly the former, are determined largely in world markets and they would respond slowly if at all to the inflation of domestic credit or currency. Moreover the accumulation of surplus stocks of both cotton and wheat and the inability thus far to curtail production make it highly problematical whether inflationary measures would raise the prices of these commodities to the extent anticipated.

And finally, the efficacy of particular inflationary measures in affording permanent relief to the farm mortgagor depends primarily upon their effect upon economic activity. The major factor in the price decline of agricultural commodities consumed primarily in the domestic market is the sharp contraction of consumers' purchasing power during recent years. In fact, the Bureau of Agricultural Economics finds a striking correspondence between the decline of food prices, particularly since 1929, and the reduction in payrolls. The accompanying chart which compares farm income with the money income of industrial workers emphasizes the importance of the recovery of business activity.

Clearly the restoration of consumer purchasing power is essential before a marked improvement in agricultural prices can be expected. Unless inflationary measures can be devised which have as their chief objective the stimulation of business activity and an increase in industrial employment, they are unlikely to afford the necessary relief to the farmers in their present distress.

[47] Ordinarily the prices of raw materials respond more quickly than the prices of finished, semi-finished goods, or wages to price raising influences, but the prices of certain agricultural products are more influenced by world conditions than are manufactured products or labor which are protected by tariffs and immigration restrictions.

CHART 8

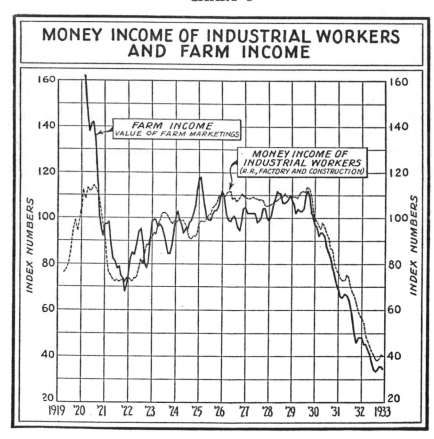

MONEY INCOME OF INDUSTRIAL WORKERS
AND FARM INCOME

FARM INCOME
VALUE OF FARM MARKETINGS

MONEY INCOME OF
INDUSTRIAL WORKERS
(R.R., FACTORY AND CONSTRUCTION)

Chapter Three

URBAN MORTGAGE DEBTS

SMALL CAPS text: SUMMARY

The Facts

THE total long-term indebtedness represented by urban mortgages and real estate securities in the United States was as of Dec. 31, 1931 approximately $35 billion.

Of this total $27.6 billion—or 82 per cent—is allocated as follows: building and loan associations 24.5 per cent, life insurance companies 19.5 per cent, mutual savings banks 18.5 per cent, other banks 12.5 per cent, title and mortgage companies 7.8 per cent and real estate bond houses 17.2 per cent (p. 79).

Urban mortgages make up roughly 86 per cent of the total assets of building and loan associations, 49 per cent of the assets of savings banks, 28 per cent of the assets of life insurance companies, and 6 per cent of those banks other than savings institutions (p. 79).

The total amount of this kind of debt has not varied appreciably since the boom year of 1929—a decrease of only one-half of one per cent has taken place since then (p. 66).

The value of the property which secures these debts, however, is estimated to be only 60 per cent of the 1929 value.

Furthermore, the income of urban real estate borrowers, out of which the debt charges must be paid, have been drastically reduced. The income of individuals has decreased almost 50 per cent since 1929, while rents have fallen 40 to 50 per cent, and vacancies have increased to 25 per cent (p. 83).

On the other hand, the costs of operating real estate have not decreased sufficiently to offset the fall in income. Interest charges, amortization and taxes, which make up 55 per cent of these costs, have not been appreciably reduced. Maintenance and repairs and wages (making up 45 per cent of operating costs) are the only items which have come down, but not sufficiently to affect the total to any substantial degree (p. 84).

Although defaults on payments by debtors are widespread, foreclosures in many cases are not being forced. Mortgagees apparently realize that it is neither economical nor desirable to foreclose where the owner is an honest and competent manager and is cooperating with them in making the necessary adjustments—reducing or postponing interest payments, waiving amortization, and extending maturities (p. 84).

RECOMMENDATIONS

Any blanket legislative action to reduce interest charges or to scale down the principal of urban real estate debts is undesirable, because:

a. Legal difficulties and legislative delays would retard action;
b. Many properties can afford to pay the debt charges now;
c. Reductions would not be sufficient in many other cases.

Remedies should be discriminatory rather than general. Even though individual reduction of debt charges tends to penalize good management, the results equalize the burden more expediently (p. 87).

The burdens of debtors could be substantially relieved by the reduction of taxes and assessments made possible by the elimination of waste and unnecessary expenditure in government (pp. 88–9).

The following kinds of adjustments should be made voluntarily by agreement between creditors and debtors:

a. Reasonable extension of maturities;
b. Waiving of amortization payments where the property is not earning sufficient income to meet them;
c. Reduction of interest rates to levels comparable to current earning capacity (p. 91).

Funds should be provided at low interest rates to refinance property.

Central agencies should be established suitable to the particular needs of each locality to act as intermediaries between mortgagors and mortgagees when the two parties cannot agree.

Legislation should be passed prohibiting foreclosures unless approved by such adjustment agencies.

These recommendations are short-run relief measures only. Unless they are combined with a more comprehensive economic policy aimed at a general revival of business activities the present difficulties will persist (p. 91).

1. The Facts [1]

THE excellent record for safety heretofore enjoyed by urban mortgage real estate bonds now seems to be threatened with defaults and foreclosures. During the past few months many plans have been proposed and discussed to correct the situation and consequently bring real estate values back to approximately their former level. Before discussing plans for readjustment and proposed remedies, it will be helpful to grasp the facts of the situation and in particular to understand first, the importance of the building industry; second, the source of funds which finance construction; third, the effect of the decline in business activity upon revenue of property, and especially the factors that enter into the cost of operating the properties which secure the mortgage; fourth, the extent of foreclosures; and fifth, the current situation in the realty market. With this background we can undertake a discussion of the more important plans for readjustment, and make some general recommendations with respect to the mortgage problem.

Building, with an aggregate volume of approximately ten to twelve billion dollars during the peak year 1928, constitutes one of the three largest industries in the United States. Not only is building one of the key industries of the country, but no other industry can compare with it in the range of economic activities and number of communities that feel its stimulus. When building is active, employment is given to one group after another of skilled or semi-skilled workers, and to professional men such as architects and engineers; every contract for an apartment or large office building sets up a demand for innumerable types of raw materials whose manufacture in turn puts thousands of laborers to work. Business is also given to the railroads and other agencies which transport the materials. Few industries can, therefore, fail to be affected in some manner by increased activity in the building field.

The great increase in aggregate construction during the period 1922–1928 led to an overproduction of certain types of buildings, notably the expensive apartments, apartment hotels, and large office buildings. The extent to which overproduction has occurred is indicated to some degree by Tables 20 and 21 which compare the rate of growth of building, especially residential and commercial, with national income and urban population.

[1] Table 19 summarizes the basic data used in this chapter.

TABLE 19

BASIC DATA ON URBAN MORTGAGE DEBTS

(Dollars in millions)

	1931 Amount	1931 Per Cent Change	1929 Amount	1929 Per Cent Change	1921 Amount	1921 Per Cent Change	1913 Amount	1913 Per Cent Change
1. Total long-term debt(a)	$27,554	—.5	$27,616	208	$8,968	74	$5,151	
2. Percentage distribution of debt by agency:								
a. Building and loan associations		24.5		26.6		28.4		21.9
b. Life insurance companies		19.5		18.0		14.2		17.5
c. Mutual savings banks		18.5		17.8		26.0		32.9
d. Other banks		12.5		13.8		20.8		22.2
e. Real estate bonds		17.2		16.9		5.4		2.9
f. Title and mortgage guarantee companies		7.8		6.9		5.2		2.6
3. Percentage, debt of assets by agency:								
a. Building and loan associations	86		89		92		92	
b. Life insurance companies	28		30		17		19	
c. Mutual savings banks	49		52		40		42	
d. Other banks	6		7		5		5	
4. Debt per capita of urban population	382	—6	407	154	160	43	112	
5. Estimated total value of urban real estate	61,300	17	73,700	14	64,600	64	39,300	
6. Ratio, mortgage debt to value of urban real estate	2.2		3.7		7.2		7.6	
7. Index of residential rents	142		154		159		100	
8. Urban population, in millions	72	6	68	21	56	22	46	
9. Index of urban population	156		148		122		100	
10. Index of building costs:								
a. For brick, wood, and frame	180		214		216		100	
b. For brick, steel, and frame	167		197		201		100	
11. Residential contracts awarded	738	—57	1,736	98	878	104	430	
12. Commercial contracts awarded	279	—66	829	145	338	87	181	

(a) Exclusive of unavailable data.   Grand total debt estimated to be about $35,000 million in 1931.

TABLE 20

TREND OF NATIONAL INCOME, URBAN POPULATION, BUILDING, AND BUILDING COSTS

Year	National Income(a)	Urban Population(b)	Residential Contracts Awarded(c)	Commercial Contracts Awarded(c)	Building Costs(d) (1913=100)	
		(000,000 omitted)			A	B
1913	$34,400	46	$430	$181	100	100
1921	54,600	56	878	338	216	201
1929	85,200	68	1,736	829	214	197
1930	70,700	69	986	565	208	191
1931	52,700	70	738	279	180	167
1932	40,000	72	245	109	157	150

(a) National Industrial Conference Board.
(b) U. S. Bureau of the Census. Estimates are made for inter-census years.
(c) F. W. Dodge Corporation. For 27 states only.
(d) American Appraisal Company. (A) For brick, wood and frame; the total comprises about 50 per cent of the aggregate type residential building. (B) For brick, steel and frame; the total represents about 50 per cent of residential and 50 per cent of commercial building.

TABLE 21

GROWTH OF NATIONAL INCOME, BUILDING, AND URBAN POPULATION

(1913=100)

Year	National Income(a)	Residential Contracts Awarded(b)	Commercial Contracts Awarded(b)	Urban Population(c)
		In 1913 Dollars		
1913	100	100	100	100
1921	94	98	93	122
1929	155	196	232	148
1930	134	115	162	150
1931	110	99	92	152
1932	...	37	40	156

(a) National Industrial Conference Board.
(b) Adjusted to 1913 dollars; Residential Contracts Awarded were divided by the average of the two indexes of Building Costs as given in Table 20; Commercial Contracts Awarded were divided by Building Cost Index B of Table 20.
(c) See Table 20 for basic data.

From 1913 to 1921 there was a slight decrease in national income and in both types of building, whereas population increased about 22 per cent. During the next eight years, however, residential building increased approximately twice as fast and commercial building almost three times as fast as national income. This rapid growth in building reflects the demands based on a rising standard of living, for larger and more comfortable homes, apartments and offices. It also reflects the prompt action on the part of builders and speculators not only to satisfy this demand, but to create a desire in the residential field for more luxury by erecting dwellings of a more and more expensive type, the result being an overproduction of high rental apartments and apartment hotels; in the case of office buildings the aim of the sponsor was to construct the tallest and most modernistic skyscraper in the world; this was true particularly in New York City. Since 1929, however, building activity in these two fields has shown a drastic decline, the 1932 figure for contracts awarded being almost 50 per cent below the 1913 level.

Source of Funds Which Finance Construction

Urban mortgages and real estate bonds are secured almost entirely by lien on residential and commercial buildings.[2] The following section will therefore confine itself to an analysis of the realty market which furnishes the funds for the financing of residential and commercial buildings.

This market is a very complex and relatively unorganized one. Although the ordinary investment banking machinery has been used in the raising of capital for construction expenditures in the public utility, railroad, industrial and municipal fields, it is only recently that it has functioned to any important degree in the urban mortgage and real estate field. In this latter field the standards of practice are more varied than in the former, the costs are higher, and the securities enjoy a less active market. On the margin of this market is a so-called "lunatic fringe" of irresponsibility characterized by more or less unsound lending practices and excessive costs. Aside from or between the market in which the investment banking machinery has been fully developed, and the market in which this same machinery has only lately begun to function, are a series of financial institutions, such as the building and loan associations, life insurance companies, mutual savings banks, etc., which supply capital for building purposes directly. These agencies, operating under varying degrees of public regulation, have for the most part very conservative standards, and supply huge amounts of capital for certain types of building at reasonable rates.

The statistics in regard to the funds supplied in the realty market are known to be inadequate and in many instances relatively unreliable. This section of the chapter will, in so far as the data permit, attempt

---

[2] Residential building, which includes individual homes, apartments, apartment hotels, etc., comprised during the peak year 1928 about 42 per cent of the total value of building, while commercial building which is mainly office buildings comprised about 13 per cent of the total value of building.

to give a picture of the urban mortgage and real estate debt outstanding. Where the statistics are known to be either inadequate or unreliable, an estimate accompanied by a detailed explanation of the method used will be given.

Building and Loan Associations

The building and loan associations are probably of greatest importance in the urban mortgage credit field, playing a dominant part in the financing of small individual homes and small apartment buildings. In some states these associations have made second as well as first mortgage loans and have been active in the financing of small commercial buildings. Loans are usually made for periods of from 3 to 10 years, the member repaying his loan in monthly instalments which include principal and interest. In 1929 the urban mortgages held by these agencies totalled $7,791 million, having more than doubled between 1913 and 1921 and having nearly tripled between 1921 and 1929; since 1929, however, they have shown a steady though slight decline, as indicated in Table 22.

TABLE 22

URBAN REAL ESTATE LOANS HELD BY BUILDING AND LOAN ASSOCIATIONS(a)

(Millions of Dollars)

1913.........	$1,148(b)	1930.........	$7,760
1921.........	2,659	1931.........	7,210
1929.........	7,791		

(a) U. S. Building and Loan League, as of December 31.
(b) Estimated on the basis of the average relationship existing, during the years when data were available, between mortgages outstanding and total assets.

Life Insurance Companies

Second in importance are the life insurance companies with a total of over $5 billion of urban mortgages in 1929, an amount representing approximately 29 per cent of their total assets. These companies usually limit their loans to 50 or 60 per cent of the appraised value of a property, lend almost exclusively on individual homes, apartments, and business properties (although occasional hotel loans are made) and require 2 to 5 per cent amortization of their mortgages which usually run from 3 to 15 years.

As indicated by Table 23, the amount of non-farm mortgages held increased slowly between 1913 and 1921 but nearly quadrupled between

1921 and 1929. In the earlier period they increased less rapidly than mortgages held by building and loan associations, but in the latter period the respective rates of growth were reversed. Since 1929 the total of non-farm mortgages held by life insurance companies increased 9 per cent, whereas those of the building and loan associations decreased about 7 per cent. This decline was probably due somewhat to the increased number of failures of building and loan associations.

TABLE 23

NON-FARM MORTGAGES HELD BY LIFE INSURANCE COMPANIES(a)

(Millions of Dollars)

1913..........	$ 919	1930..........	$5,564
1921..........	1,326	1931..........	5,730
1929..........	5,241		

(a) The data available for the companies reporting to the Association of Life Insurance Presidents are as of December 31 and are comparatively reliable and accurate. The companies reporting to the Association cover from 92.6 per cent to 96.8 per cent of the total assets of all life insurance companies in the United States. In making an estimate of urban mortgage loans outstanding for all life insurance companies, we assumed that the percentage relationship between the urban mortgages held by the companies reporting and the urban mortgages held by the total number of companies is the same as that which existed during the year between the assets of the reporting companies and the assets of the total number of companies.

Banking Institutions

Statistics for loans on urban real estate mortgages made by banking institutions are less adequate than the first two categories considered. The information on this score is derived from the "Annual Report of the Comptroller of the Currency," and the data are as of June 30, of each year. Prior to 1916 the Comptroller compiled real estate loan statistics from individual reports of the different classes of banks throughout the country. Since 1916 he has received individual reports from national banks only and has compiled the statistics of other classes of banks from the reports of the various state banking departments. Inasmuch as all the state banking reports do not always segregate urban real estate loans from other loans, sometimes including them under the general classification of "Unclassified Loans" and sometimes under "Farm Loans," it has been necessary to make estimates for non-farm real estate loans for the years when they were not segregated by all the states. Details as to the method of estimating these loans on non-farm real estate and mortgages are explained in a footnote accompanying Table 24.

Mutual Savings Banks

The mutual savings banks, which had made loans on urban mortgage real estate amounting to over $5 billion in 1929, rank first in importance among the banks, and third among the financial institutions which supply capital directly to the building industry. Except in the case of the large New York City savings banks, which finance many large office and apartment buildings, these loans are usually made for small homes, apartments, and business properties in the immediate vicinity of the bank. The mortgages generally run for 3 to 5 years, though one-year loans are not uncommon. Amortization is usually not required and extensions or renewals, sometimes for smaller amounts than the original loan, are usual in normal times. These institutions play a particularly important role in New York state where the law permits them to invest up to 70 per cent of their total assets in real estate mortgages.

Other Types of Banks

The statistics for other important types of banking institutions,[3] which lend their funds on non-farm real estate and mortgages, are attended with the possibility of some error due to the inconsistency and the inadequacy of the classification of loans. Estimates for this type of loan have been made on the basis of a careful study of lending policies not only in the various geographical divisions reported but also of the states within these divisions. The following table shows the trend of loans on non-farm mortgages and real estate held by the various banking institutions.

TABLE 24

ESTIMATED LOANS ON NON-FARM MORTGAGES AND REAL ESTATE HELD BY BANKING INSTITUTIONS(a)

(Millions of Dollars)

Year	Mutual Savings Banks(b)	National Banks(c)	Loan and Trust Cos.(d)	State Banks(e)	Stock Savings Banks(f)	Private Banks(g)	Total All Banks(h)
1913	$1,731	$64	$478	$284	$338	$11	$2,906
1921	2,439	119	479	796	543	7	4,383
1929	5,221	1,104	1,354	1,016	562	7	9,264
1930	5,306	1,176	1,274	959	514	7	9,236
1931	5,446	1,281	1,222	811	370	5	9,135

(a) These estimates as of June 30, although attended by the possibility of error, are more nearly correct than the figures reported under "Loans on Non-Farm Mortgages and Real Estate" in the report to the Comptroller of the Currency.

[3] Except National Banks.

(*b*) In the Comptroller's report urban real estate loans made by mutual savings banks, when not segregated, are usually included under the general classification of "Unclassified Loans" or "Other Loans"; in some instances they are included with "Farm Loans." In computing the estimate a study was made not only of the reports of the geographical divisions but also of the states within these divisions, and it was found that during the years when loans were classified the non-farm mortgage loans averaged for the country as a whole about 90 per cent of the total of all loans and discounts.

(*c*) Data for national banks are as reported by the Comptroller of the Currency.

(*d*) The data regarding non-farm mortgage loans made by loan and trust companies are relatively complete and therefore the estimates are more likely to be attended with less possibility of error. The figures for 1913 and 1921 are as reported. For the years 1929–1931 a number of states reported non-farm mortgage loans together with farm loans or vice versa; farm loans in these states during preceding years when these two types of loans were segregated comprised only about one per cent of total real estate loans. The estimate for non-farm mortgage loans in these states was therefore made on the assumption that they comprised 99 per cent of total real estate loans.

(*e*) The statistics for total loans made by state (commercial) banks are usually reported as a lump sum under the classification of "Unclassified Loans." Data pertaining to the loans on non-farm mortgages and real estate were studied for the years during which they were segregated, and it was found expedient to use different methods of estimation for the various geographical groups. The loans made by the middle western group comprise the largest part of non-farm mortgage loans of all state banks; in studying the data available it was found that in 1915 when loans were segregated that non-farm mortgage loans for all states comprised about 46 per cent of total real estate and mortgage loans, and farm loans about 54 per cent. During the years 1929–1931 inclusive, all states in the middle western group with the exception of Wisconsin reported non-farm mortgage loans, together with farm loans. Wisconsin segregated the real estate loans, and the proportion between farm and non-farm to the real estate loans was approximately 55 per cent and 45 per cent respectively. Thus, assuming that lending practices are relatively similar among the states within a group, loans on non-farm mortgages were estimated on this basis. For 1921 the loans for the whole group were reported under "Unclassified Loans." In 1915 non-farm mortgage loans made by this group comprised about 13 per cent of the total of all loans and discounts in the group; thus for 1921 this rate of 13 per cent of total loans and discounts was used in computing the estimate.

The non-farm mortgage loans made by the southern group comprise about 18 per cent of the total loans made by all state banks. These data are reported by all states in the group, with the exception of Texas, under "Unclassified Loans." Non-farm mortgage loans made by Texas amounted to about 10 per cent of the total of all loans and discounts. This percentage relationship was also approximately correct in 1915. Assuming that for the group as a whole lending policies were relatively uniform among the states within a group, the estimate for loans on non-farm mortgage and real estate made by the southern group was computed by taking 10 per cent of the total loans and discounts for the group as a whole.

The loans on non-farm mortgages made by the eastern group were segregated in 1913, 1921 and 1931. In 1929 and 1930 loans in the New York district were reported together with loans on farm mortgages; since loans on non-farm mortgages in this district comprised 85 per cent of the real estate loans in 1931 this percentage was used to estimate loans on non-farm mortgages for New York state in 1929 and 1930.

(*f*) The data for non-farm mortgage loans made by stock savings banks for the years 1913, 1929, 1930 and 1931 are as reported. For 1921 a correction was necessary because California, which includes the figures for the savings departments of the departmental banks, was not included in the report of the Comptroller of the Currency. During the years when California did report to the Comptroller, it was found that this type of loan comprised about 97 per cent of non-farm mortgage loans made by all states. Therefore, the correction for 1921 was made on the assumption that this percentage relationship was valid for 1921.

(*g*) Data for loans on non-farm mortgages made by private banks comprising only an infinitesimal amount of the total are as reported to the Comptroller of the Currency.

(*h*) None of these data include the item "Real Estate Owned other than Banking House."

From 1913 to 1921 practically all of the banking institutions, which in 1931 were the largest lenders on real estate, about doubled their urban mortgage and real estate loans; loan and trust companies, however, showed practically no increase in this type of loan. During the next eight years the increase in these loans was slightly more than two times, except in the case of urban mortgage loans made by national banks, where the increase was 10 times. Since 1929 mutual savings banks and national banks, which are the two largest lenders among the banking institutions, increased their loans on urban real estate, the former slightly less and the later somewhat greater than the increase in urban mortgages held by life insurance companies. Non-farm loans by other banking institutions followed the downward trend from 1929 to 1931, as shown by building and loan associations, the percentage decrease however being greater in the case of the former institutions.

Real Estate Bond Houses

During recent years there has been a tremendous growth in the number of urban mortgages and real estate bonds offered to the investing public by realty companies. Up to 1925 or 1926 the bulk of such "real estate bonds" were sold by a group of specialized "real estate houses"; since 1925, however, the ordinary investment dealers of the country, members of the Investment Bankers Association and normally underwriters and distributors of public utility, railroad, and industrial securities, began to play an increasingly important part in the distribution of real estate securities.

Information on the volume of real estate bonds outstanding is scanty. None of the statistical series available purporting to show the annual volume of real estate securities offered publicly by real estate bond houses and investment dealers is entirely satisfactory. The difficulty of compiling such data is very great, as the only sources of information at the present time are the announcements or advertisements in the daily newspapers and the financial and real estate journals, etc. The only statistics available covering a long period are those of the *Commercial and Financial Chronicle*; these figures, however, are unfortunately far from complete.

Comparison of these data with those published by a private real estate financing organization seems to show that the *Chronicle's* statistics are relatively incomplete. This latter series is about 25 per cent higher than the *Chronicle's* figures and it purports to cover only "long term real estate bonds, notes, collateral trust obligations, and land trust certificates publicly advertised or announced"; even in this field its coverage is admittedly incomplete. This series dates back only to 1926 and is therefore of relatively little use for comparative purposes with earlier years. Neither one of these includes the issues which are offered "over the counter" or which for one reason or another are not publicly announced through the channels ordinarily followed by the compilers of these statistics. They also contain some duplication with the figures already reported for various types of financial institutions, as some of the latter buy portions of the real estate bond issues which are offered to the public by investment dealers.

Any estimate as to the total volume of such credit outstanding based on the available data is likely to contain some error. Mr. W. C. Clarke, formerly of S. W. Straus and Company, made an estimate of this volume of credit as follows: he assumed that there were about $300 million of such issues outstanding in 1919;[4] then, by assuming that amortization and redemption averaged 5 per cent through 1923 and 4 per cent from 1924 to date, and after adding 40 per cent to the *Chronicle's* figures for new capital offered each year, he was able to arrive at an estimate for total real estate bonds outstanding. The following table gives the results obtained by this method.

TABLE 25

ESTIMATE OF VOLUME OF REAL ESTATE SECURITIES OUTSTANDING, 1913–1931
(Millions of Dollars)

1913	$ 150	1930	$5,040
1921	502	1931	5,017
1929	4,918		

Title and Mortgage Guarantee Companies

The title and mortgage guarantee companies are another type of agency which acts as an intermediary in supplying capital to finance urban buildings. Unlike the institutions previously mentioned which supply capital for building, and which hold the mortgages in their respective portfolios, the title and guarantee companies guaranty the mortgages as to principal and interest and then sell them to individuals, banks, trustee estates, charitable and other institutions.

[4] It is interesting to note that C. E. Parsons in a somewhat similar estimate assumes a volume of $500 million outstanding at the end of 1920. See *Quarterly Journal of Economics,* March, 1931, p. 100.

The title and guarantee companies play a particularly important role in the New York metropolitan area. Current publications regarding the realty situation estimate the total amount of guaranteed mortgages and certificates outstanding as of December 31, 1932, at approximately $3 billion, of which $2.5 billion is held by five of the largest title and guarantee companies in the city.

It is interesting to note from Table 26, which shows the trend of the total amount of guaranteed mortgages held by the four largest title and guarantee companies in New York City, that, although in 1913 the two largest title companies were not engaged in a mortgage guarantee business, they had as of December 31, 1931, a total of almost one and three-quarter billion dollars of such mortgages outstanding. This growth clearly reflects the popularity that this type of security has enjoyed during the past decade among investors.

TABLE 26

GUARANTEED MORTGAGES AND CERTIFICATES OUTSTANDING(a)
NEW YORK CITY

(Millions of Dollars)

	1913	1921	1929	1930	1931
Bond and Mortgage Guarantee Co....$	o	$258	$776	$862	$921
New York Title and Mortgage Co....	o	60	639	703	729
Lawyers Title and Guarantee........	.3	38	200	219	224
Lawyers Mortgage Co..............	138.0	134	395	420	435
Total.......................$	138.3	$490	$2,010	$2,204	$2,309

(a) Source:

   1913, 1921—Annual Report of New York State Superintendent of Insurance.
   1929 to 1931—Companies' Annual Reports.

It should be noted in regard to the above data that a considerable portion of these guaranteed mortgages is sold to other financial institutions and another portion are publicly advertised in the New York papers, so that only a moderate percentage of their issues would escape inclusion in the reports already discussed. On the basis of the distribution among individuals and institutions of the guaranteed mortgages and certificates outstanding, as reported by one of the large title and guarantee companies, it would seem safe to assume that about 20 per cent of the total guaranteed mortgages and certificates outstanding were not duplicated in our previous estimate.

TABLE 27

GUARANTEED MORTGAGES AND CERTIFICATES OUTSTANDING
NOT DUPLICATED IN PREVIOUS TABLES

NEW YORK CITY

(Millions of Dollars)

1913	1921	1929	1930	1931
$28	$98	$402	$440	$462

Preliminary Summary of Debt

Table 28 and Chart 9 present the aggregate urban mortgage and real estate debt so far covered in this chapter. It includes only mortgage debt that is (1) held by institutions and (2) that is issued or guaranteed by real estate houses or institutions. It does, however, cover the bulk of all urban mortgage and real estate debt outstanding in the United States.

TABLE 28

ESTIMATED URBAN REAL ESTATE MORTGAGE DEBT OUTSTANDING IN U. S.(a)

(Millions of Dollars)

	1913	1921	1929	1930	1931
Building and Loan Associations(b)	$1,148	$2,659	$7,791	$7,760	$7,210
Life Insurance Cos.(c)	919	1,326	5,241	5,564	5,730
Mutual Savings Banks(d)	1,731	2,439	5,221	5,306	5,446
Other Banks(e)	1,175	1,944	4,043	3,930	3,689
Real Estate Bonds(f)	150	502	4,918	5,040	5,017
Title and Mortgage Guarantee Cos.(g)	28	98	402	440	462
Total	$5,151	$8,968	$27,616	$28,040	$27,554

(a) As of December 31.
(b) See Table 22.   (d) See Table 24.   (f) See Table 25.
(c) See Table 23.   (e) See Table 24.   (g) See Table 27.

As far as the data in Table 28 cover urban mortgage and real estate debt outstanding, the figures indicate an increase of about 75 per cent from 1913 to 1921 and of approximately 208 per cent during the following eight-year period. Since 1929 all of the agencies showed a steady increase in urban mortgages and real estate securities held, with the exception of building and loan associations, and banks other than mutual savings and national banks. The total real estate debt outstanding, however, showed a decrease of about 0.5 per cent during this same period.

Data not Included in Estimate of Total Urban Mortgages and Real Estate Securities

The figures given above, while they cover all the fields for which data for real estate debt are reported or can be estimated with any reasonable

CHART 9

Total Urban Mortgage Debt
and Estimated Total Value
of Urban Real Estate
1913–1921–1929–1931

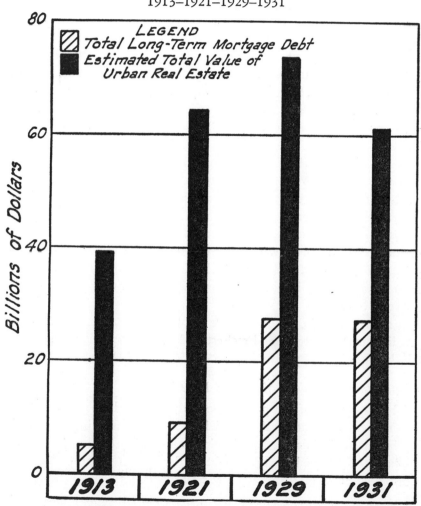

degree of accuracy, are by no means complete. They do not, for instance, include real estate mortgage holdings of local mortgage companies, fire and casualty insurance companies, educational and religious institutions, foundations, trustee estates and individual investors—except to the extent that such mortgage securities are purchased from investment dealers, real estate bond houses, title and mortgage guarantee companies, etc. Although individual mortgages bought directly by individual investors are known to be of a large volume, especially in the middle west, there are no data available. This is also the case in regard to the mortgage investments of trust companies for their legal and discretionary trust funds.

No account has, moreover, been taken of the aggregate amount of second mortgages outstanding, except to the slight extent that they are included in the holdings of building and loan associations and in the series of real estate bonds publicly offered. Specific data in this field are impossible to obtain. The market is highly unorganized and, with the exception of two or three corporations which are attempting to organize the purchase and sale of second mortgages on a national scale, it is in the hands of individuals or small concerns who operate under no restrictions except possibly under the formal features of the usury laws, and who publish no information as to their activities. In the absence of specific data, any estimate of the total volume of such credit would have to be a guess. An estimate of this aggregate has been made by Dr. Franklin W. Ryan [5] who places this figure of amount of second mortgages outstanding at $2 billion.

It seems plausible, in view of the comment just made, that the outstanding urban mortgage and real estate debt, if complete data were obtainable, would be approximately $35 billion [6] as of December 31, 1931.

Distribution of Urban Mortgage Debt

The importance of this part of the study is not only in its estimate of the urban mortgage and real estate debt as a separate item in the make-up of the total debt burden, but also in its indication of the significance of the real estate and mortgage debt burden upon the various agencies which hold urban mortgage and real estate securities.

[5] *Journal of Business of the University of Chicago,* October, 1930.
[6] This is a very rough estimate. It was made on the assumption that second mortgage urban debt amounted to $2 billion and the urban real estate and mortgage debt held by individuals, trustees, educational and charitable institutions, fire and casualty insurance companies, etc., amounted to about $5.5 billion. These two figures were added to the total estimate as given in Table 27.

Tables 29 and 30 and Charts 10 and 11 summarize not only the percentage of total urban mortgage debt that is held by each agency, but also the percentage of total assets which is invested in urban mortgages and real estate by each important agency.

TABLE 29

PERCENTAGE OF TOTAL URBAN REAL ESTATE MORTGAGE DEBT
HELD BY EACH AGENCY(a)

(Per Cent)

	1913	1921	1929	1930	1931
Building and Loan Associations	21.9	28.4	26.6	26.0	24.5
Life Insurance Cos.	17.5	14.2	18.0	18.7	19.5
Mutual Savings Banks.	32.9	26.0	17.8	17.8	18.5
Other Banks.	22.2	20.8	13.8	13.2	12.5
Real Estate Bonds.	2.9	5.4	16.9	16.9	17.2
Title and Mortgage Guarantee Cos.(2). . .	2.6	5.2	6.9	7.4	7.8
Total.	100.0	100.0	100.0	100.0	100.0

(a) See Table 28 for basic data.

TABLE 30

RELATIONSHIP OF URBAN REAL ESTATE MORTGAGE DEBT
TO TOTAL ASSETS, BY AGENCIES(a)

(Approximate Per Cent)

	1913	1921	1929	1930	1931
Building and Loan Associations	92	92	89	88	86
Life Insurance Cos.	19	17	30	29	28
Mutual Savings Banks.	42	40	52	52	49
Other Banks.	5	5	7	6	6

(a) In estimating the percentages the data for Guaranteed Mortgages as given in Table 26 were used instead of 20 per cent of this figure.

The per cent of the total urban mortgage debt held by each type of agency since 1913 has varied relatively little in the case of both building and loan associations and life insurance companies. The former group, however, although it has slightly increased its share of the total urban mortgage debt, has tended to reduce the ratio of its urban mortgage debt to its total assets, whereas the latter has increased both its share of the total debt and also, to a much greater extent, the ratio of urban mortgages held to total assets. All types of banks have shown a rather marked decrease in the percentage of the urban debt carried by them, whereas the ratio of their loans on urban real estate and mortgages to total assets has shown a slight increase. In the case of both real estate bonds issued and of mortgages issued by title and mortgage guarantee companies, the

CHART 10

Percentage Distribution of Urban Mortgage Debt by Various Agencies 1913–1921–1929–1931

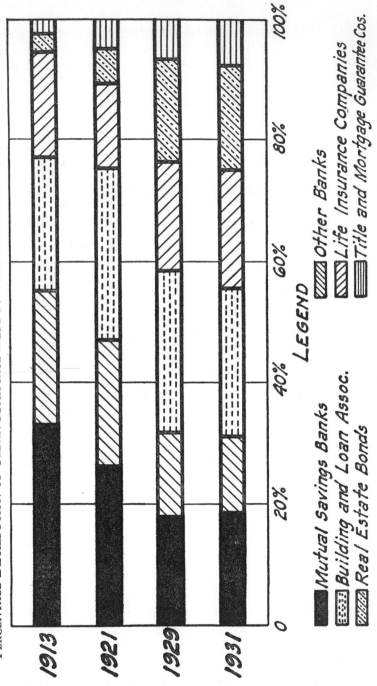

LEGEND

Mutual Savings Banks   Other Banks

Building and Loan Assoc.   Life Insurance Companies

Real Estate Bonds   Title and Mortgage Guarantee Cos.

CHART 11

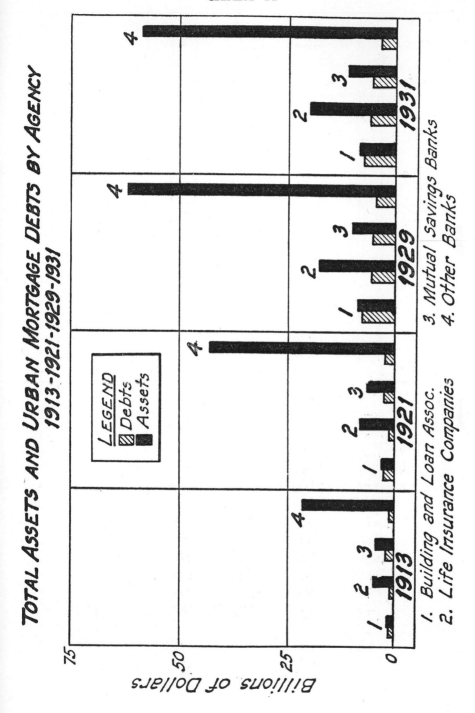

TOTAL ASSETS AND URBAN MORTGAGE DEBTS BY AGENCY
1913-1921-1929-1931

LEGEND
Debts
Assets

1. Building and Loan Assoc.
2. Life Insurance Companies
3. Mutual Savings Banks
4. Other Banks

1913   1921   1929   1931

Billions of Dollars
75   50   25   0

increase in their ratio of urban mortgage debt to total urban mortgage debt outstanding has increased very greatly. This has been commented upon in a previous paragraph.

As one would expect, the building and loan associations have most of their assets invested in urban mortgages, and carry the largest part of the total urban mortgage debt. Mutual savings banks, with about half of their total assets (in New York state nearly three-quarters of total assets) and life insurance companies, with about one-third of their assets invested in urban mortgages and real estate, each holds about one-fifth of the total urban debt. Other banks hold about one-eighth of the total urban debt, and have only about 6 per cent of their total assets so invested.

Effect of the Decline in Business Activity Upon the Realty Market

The realty market is neither an isolated one, nor one that functions without being influenced to a greater or lesser degree by the heights and depths of prosperity and depression. It is, in fact, a market whose very stability is not only dependent upon but also very sensitive to the fluctuations of business activity. This close relationship between business activity and the realty market is clearly reflected through the factors which determine the value and stability of a realty security.

Sources of Income of Realty Securing a Mortgage

The value and stability of a real estate bond or mortgage are based upon the ability of the underlying property to earn sufficient gross revenue to meet total charges consisting of operating and maintenance charges, interest, amortization, taxes, etc. This ability directly depends upon business conditions. When business activity is low, wage incomes are reduced due both to wage rate cuts and to part-time work and unemployment. An increasing number of vacancies occur not only in the better type of apartments and apartment hotels, due to doubling up of families and a shifting to the cheaper and older types of apartments, but also in the new skyscraper office buildings due to a decline in individual businesses and a general exodus to cheaper quarters.

The two factors, income and number of vacancies, which are closely related to business activity, determine the revenue of the property. In the case of the individual home, the former only is important and depends upon the income of the owner. During the past few years the incomes of individuals, which for the most part consist of wages,[7] have been reduced about 50 per cent from 1929 levels, and in many cases income has ceased altogether due to unemployment. This reduction in earning power not only directly affects the real estate issues and mortgages secured by individual homes, but also indirectly affects the revenue earned by other types of residential buildings through the inability of tenants to pay rent. Some attempt on the part of the landlords has already been made to adjust residential rents to present incomes and to prevent the increasing rate of vacancies. Table 31 reflects the general trend of residential rents, particularly for wage earners in the lower income groups.

TABLE 31

TREND OF RESIDENTIAL RENTS(a)

(1913 = 100)

1913	100	1930	150
1921	159	1931	142
1929	154	1932	127

(a) U. S. Bureau of Labor Statistics.   Dates are as of June of each year.

The figures show about a 17 per cent reduction from June, 1929, to June, 1932; during the latter part of 1932, however, rents were drastically reduced in order to decrease the number of vacancies, and thus to enable the properties to earn enough to cover at least taxes, interest, and amortization. The extent to which rentals have been reduced during 1932–33 is indicated by a testimony given by Mr. D. Elliman before the Hofstadter Commission in which he stated that rents have fallen 40 to 50 per cent and vacancies have increased to 25 per cent.[8]

A somewhat similar situation prevails among the commercial type of buildings. Rents of office buildings and stores have been voluntarily reduced in many cases by the owner at the expiration of a lease. In some cases, however, where the lease did not expire for a period of years and the corporate tenant is now unable to meet the high rental which was contracted for during a period of increasing business activity, the corporate tenant has gone into bankruptcy, and under a new name has continued business in the same place but with a reduced amount of rent.

The decline in the revenue of property, due to the reduction in indi-

[7] See W. I. King, *National Income and Its Purchasing Power* (1930), p. 80.
[8] The normal figure for vacancies is 10 per cent.

vidual incomes and rentals, and also to the increased amount of unemployment and the larger number of vacancies, would seem to indicate that a reduction in total charges upon property must take place.

Factors Affecting Cost of Operating Mortgaged Property

The factors entering into the cost of operating the property which secure the mortgage are, first, the cost of maintenance and running the property; second, interest; third, amortization; and fourth, taxes. These have been estimated to comprise roughly the following percentages of total revenue:[9] maintenance and repairs 10 per cent, wages 35 per cent, taxes 25 per cent, and interest and amortization 30 per cent. Of course, these percentages would vary with each type of building depending upon the use of the building, the number of people employed to run the building, etc.: however, the above percentages are only average allocations. In the case of the first two factors there have been some reductions, but not sufficient to affect the total.[10] In the case of interest and taxes, which together comprise about 55 per cent of the total operating charges, there had been practically no change up to December 31, 1932 in New York City. In other cities, however, there have been some attempts to reduce taxes as is shown in a later section. During the past year there has been a great deal of agitation, especially in New York City, for a reduction in both interest rates and taxes, and some favorable results have been obtained. This phase of the subject will be discussed later.

Extent of Foreclosures

The reduced incomes and rentals resulting in non-payment of taxes, interest, and amortization, have greatly increased the number of foreclosures. Although there are no definite data available in regard to this number, one estimate has been made to the effect that about 60 per cent of the urban real estate bonds outstanding are in difficulty.[11] This estimate does not seem unduly high when it is realized that individual incomes have fallen about 50 per cent, unemployment has increased to alarming numbers, rentals in a relatively large number of cases have declined about 40 to 50 per cent, while fixed charges of operating a

[9] This estimate was made by S. R. Firestone of Pease and Elliman.
[10] Mr. Firestone estimated that this type of wage had been reduced about 12 per cent.
[11] Investment Bankers Association, Report of Real Estate Securities Committee, November, 1931, p. 130.

building have remained practically constant, and vacancies in apartments, hotels, and offices have greatly increased. Be it noted, according to this estimate, that 60 per cent of urban real estate securities are in more or less distress, but have not actually all been foreclosed. This estimate would seem to indicate that, although defaults were occurring, foreclosures in many cases were not being forced upon the mortgagors.

This circumstance may be explained in part as follows: In the beginning of a business depression the mortgagee usually brings foreclosure proceedings on the property as soon as there has been a default. This action is extremely expensive and involves a large and unnecessary loss to both mortgagee and mortgagor. As the depression progresses, however, the individual mortgagees and large lending agencies and institutions begin to realize that it is neither economical nor desirable to foreclose upon the property which is held by an owner who is an honest and competent manager, but rather to allow the present owner to continue to hold title to and operate the property. Instead of foreclosing, a large number of mortgagees are now cooperating with the mortgagors and making necessary adjustments such as reducing or postponing interest, waiving amortization, and extending the term of the maturing mortgages or real estate bonds.

In various cities some mechanism has been set up to prevent foreclosures, either by securing the cooperation of the mortgagee and thus arriving at some equitable adjustment, or by obtaining funds to refinance the property. Although these agencies have been relatively successful in forestalling a great many foreclosures purely by persuasive and logical means, nevertheless it would be beneficial and would facilitate matters if some legislative measures were enacted whereby no foreclosure proceedings could be brought against any property unless approved by these agencies. A foreclosure would be expedient under the following cases: (1) when the mortgagor was found incompetent and was not likely to succeed in making the property earn enough to meet its obligations, even if given a reasonable opportunity, and (2) when there were specific factors entering in which made it necessary to take such action in the vital interests of the mortgagee.

The Realty Market and Current Values

Several years ago the Real Estate Securities Exchange was founded for the purpose of establishing a regular organized realty market where real estate securities and mortgages could be traded in, and where investors could obtain correct information in regard to the earning capacity of the property securing the real estate bond or mortgage. The bulk of the trading in this type of security, however, has not as yet found its way to this market, and is still being done "over the counter." Quotations of real estate securities from this latter source are very difficult to obtain even in prosperous times when trading is active. This, together with the fact that at present first mortgage holders have practically stopped trying to sell their holdings because of the terrific losses that would have to be taken, and with the general feeling of uncertainty prevailing, has made it almost impossible to get any quotation of realty securities which would be significant of their true value.

Another way to obtain the value of an urban mortgage or real estate security is to capitalize the earnings of the property securing the mortgage. Data, however, in regard to earning power of any particular piece of property are almost impossible to obtain. Thus this method of discovering the current value of real estate bonds and mortgages is of little help. The only indication of current values of realty securities that we have is that present property values are estimated to be, on the average, about 40 per cent below 1929 levels. This means that the value back of both the equity holders and the second mortgage holders has been eliminated in the case of properties on which first mortgages have been issued up to 60 per cent [12] of assessed value.

2. RECOMMENDATIONS

In an earlier section of this chapter it was shown that mortgage interest, amortization charges, and taxes comprise on the average about 55 per cent of the total operating expenses of a building. It was also suggested that, if there was to be any easing of the realty market, it would have to come about through a readjustment of these factors to current earning capacity. The plans and recommendations that have been suggested by various economists, realty experts, and others regarding this readjustment will now be considered.

Adjusting Amortization and Interest Charges

Through no fault of the individual home owner or landlord, property is now in most cases unable to earn enough income to meet present

[12] This percentage has been considered conservative by realty authorities.

amortization or interest charges. If these obligations are not met, the mortgagee can force a foreclosure, thereby disposing of the property not only at a great financial loss to himself but also to the mortgagor. It has been previously remarked in this chapter that, as a business depression continues, a great number of mortgagees begin to realize the waste of foreclosures, and therefore attempt to make some readjustment with the mortgagor, which involves some sacrifice for a temporary period of time on the part of the former, but which does not in any way affect the principal amount of the mortgage. This is precisely the case at the present time, and a number of the large mortgage holders have already taken steps to deal with the problem of adjusting amortization and interest charges. The problem of the former is a relatively simple one, being settled in a very large number of cases by waiving amortization until such time as the property is back on a normal earning basis.

The problem of interest is somewhat more complex and difficult to handle. This circumstance is due to some extent to the fact that a number of mortgagees are entirely or partially dependent upon interest for their income, and any threatened curtailment in their mode of living through a reduction in interest and therefore income will arouse their hostility; for this reason it is often rather difficult to secure any immediate cooperation from the mortgagee, who has first to be convinced that unless he puts his own interest aside and cooperates he is likely to suffer a loss of principal. Another factor that tends to make this situation difficult is the method to use in reducing the interest rate.

Blanket versus Discriminatory Reduction of Interest Rates

In order to force all mortgagees to take a cut in interest rates, some legislative measure would seem to be necessary. The trouble involved, especially regarding the legal technicalities and long delays which attend the passage of our laws, does not seem warranted at the present time. Furthermore, there are many properties that are earning their current interest charges and can, therefore, afford to pay them. If a reduction to, say, 4 per cent in all interest rates were to be enforced, it would place an unjust burden on the large holders of urban mortgages for the following reason: a reduction to 4 per cent, while helping a great number of people, would not relieve the situation in those cases where the property was not earning that much, and, therefore, a further reduction or even indefinite postponement might be necessary; thus the entire burden of the differential between the 4 per cent top rate of interest allowed by law and the lower rates enforced by necessity, would be borne by the mortgagee. While discriminatory reduction of interest rates would, in effect, penalize good management and efficiency, nevertheless this latter method of reducing interest rates to levels comparable with the earning capacity of the property in question would, in general, be more expedient.

Lightening Tax Burden on Real Estate

That form of wealth which is the greatest sufferer from mismanagement and waste in municipal government is real estate. As the expenses of these local governments, which derive more than two-thirds of their revenue from taxes on property, mount, an increasing burden is placed upon real estate. Thus, in order to reduce taxes, one of two alternatives may be used: either the municipalities must adjust their expenses to their income by elimination of waste and unnecessary expenditure, or new sources of revenue must be found. The first of these alternatives seems to be not only the most expedient but also the quickest way to reduce taxes. An effort to bring about a reduction in the 1933 budget in New York City was made during the last year by the Citizens Budget Committee; the result has been a reduction of $112 million from the tax levy of the 1932 budget. The Committee estimated that this reduction would lighten the total property or real estate tax levy by about $88 million.

Another method of reducing taxes is by lowering the assessed value of property. For the first time in the history of New York City the total assessed valuation of real estate showed a decrease of $1.2 billion from 1932 to 1933. Lower assessments together with a smaller budget should result in a marked cut in the tax levy and so materially aid the current realty situation.

The extent to which assessments and property taxes have been reduced in other cities may be gleaned from a recent study [13] of tax burdens in 277 cities, where it was found that, for the most part, there was a definite trend in 1932 toward lower taxes in at least 115 cities and possibly more. To quote from this study:

"For 149 cities in which reduced valuations were reported for 1932, it is found that 66 cities increased, 61 reduced, and 22 reported no change from

[13] "Tax Burden Lightens," by C. E. Rightor. *National Municipal Review,* December, 1932, pp. 686–697.

their 1931 rates. Thus in 61 cities a reduced tax levy is assured, because both the rate and valuation are lower than last year. In 22 cities a reduced levy also is assured, because the rate is unchanged and the valuation is lower than in 1931. In the remaining 66 cities, the reduction in assessed valuation has been partially or wholly offset by increased taxes.

"For 67 cities in which assessed valuation reported for 1932 were unchanged from the preceding year, it is found that 23 cities increased, 32 decreased, 12 reported no change, from the rates for 1931. This indicates a reduced tax levy in 32 cities." [14]

The writer of the above article points out that, in interpreting the decline in tax levies as shown by the 115 cities, it must be remembered that, although assessments have been lowered, they have not in many cases been reduced in proportion with the decline of actual real estate market values. With continued economy in municipal government expenditures and lowered assessment values, further decline in real estate property tax levies to levels comparable with current conditions may be hoped for.

Scaling Down of Principal of the Mortgage

In many circles the opinion has been expressed that, in order to put the realty market back on a sound basis, the principal or par value of the mortgage or real estate security should be scaled down to conform with present-day property values. The effect of this action on our leading financial institutions such as banks, life insurance companies, etc., which are the principal holders of these obligations, would be rather drastic. To see clearly what would happen and to what extent these institutions would be affected by such action, let us examine briefly what would take place in the case of the mutual savings banks.

The mutual savings banks of the country have invested about one-half of their total assets in urban real estate and mortgages. The funds that were used to purchase these mortgages represent the savings of individuals who were entirely confident when they deposited their money that they could withdraw on demand or on short notice the identical number of dollars, no matter what the tempo of business activity was. Their trust that their deposits would remain fully intact was their compensation for the low interest return they received. If mortgage debt were scaled down to conform with present-day property values, total assets of the mutual savings banks would be drastically decreased, and the depositor

[14] *Ibid.*, pp. 684–685.

would not be able to withdraw the same number of dollars that he had previously put in.

To this argument it is replied that he will be able to withdraw the same amount of purchasing power; but this assertion is not entirely true because many of these individuals deposited their money either years ago, when the purchasing power of the dollar was equal to or even greater than that of today, or deposited it during the past two years. Moreover, before a measure to scale down mortgages or all debts could be passed, there would be a great deal of discussion, controversy, and delay; in the interim depositors, policyholders of life insurance companies, and others would probably try to get their money as soon as possible; the immediate consequences of such action are obvious.

Creation of Central Agencies to Relieve Realty

The type of central agency that might be set up in any city will depend upon the particular needs of that locality. As an example of what may be done along this line the following brief summary of the work which is being done by the agencies that have been established in Chicago and Philadelphia is presented.

In Chicago the trust companies have organized a corporation which will advance funds on master certificates of sale or will buy first mortgages on distressed property. The loans are to be used to pay back taxes, reasonable attorneys' fees, costs, etc. The period of the loan is 3 years, it is limited to 30 per cent of the present income value of the property, and the income must be sufficient to liquidate the loan in five years. These loans, classified as "A" loans, are acceptable as security by trust companies and life insurance companies and are rediscountable with the Reconstruction Finance Corporation.

In Philadelphia a Joint Welfare Committee of the Philadelphia Real Estate Board functions as the central mechanism which is aiding that city to solve its real estate problems, especially in connection with individual homes. This committee, which was appointed by the president of the Philadelphia Real Estate Board and the president of the Pennsylvania League of Building and Loan Associations, consists of realtors and building and loan men who receive no remuneration for their services. The main aim of this committee is to prevent foreclosures and to help check demoralization of property values by obtaining the cooperation of mortgage holders.

Recommendations and Conclusions

For immediate relief in the urban real estate and mortgage field the following measures are recommended:

1. Reasonable extensions of time for maturing obligations by mortgagees.

2. Waiving of amortization charges in cases where the property is not earning sufficient revenue to meet these charges.

3. Reduction of interest rates in individual cases only. Amount to be decided by the present earning capacity of the property.

4. Provision of funds at low interest rates to refinance property.

5. Establishment of a central mechanism, suitable to the particular needs of the location, which will act as an intermediary between mortgagor and mortgagee when these two parties cannot agree. Legislation to prevent foreclosures unless approved by the above-mentioned central mechanism.

6. Stricter economy in municipal government expenditures so as to reduce property taxes.

The above recommendations are to be viewed as short-run relief measures only, and unless they are combined with a more comprehensive economic policy aimed at a general renewal of business activity, the problem will persist and further measures of a drastic nature may be necessary.

Chapter Four

THE RAILROAD DEBT

SUMMARY

The Facts

THE long-term indebtedness of railroads is very large—$13.3 billion or almost one-half of the book value of the properties (p. 101).

Almost one-half (40 per cent) of all outstanding railroad bonds are held by insurance companies, savings banks, educational and charitable institutions—hence their stability is of crucial social importance (p. 95).

More than ten per cent of the railroads (by mileage) are now in receivership and about one-quarter of their total funded debt is either in default or saved therefrom by emergency credit advances (p. 97).

Most of the defaulted issues, however, are junior bonds—refunding issues, income bonds, miscellaneous debentures, etc. Relatively few of the underlying liens which constitute the investments of fiduciary institutions are in default or likely to be "under any conceivable debacle of railway revenues" (p. 97).

Railroad bonds as a whole (652 issues) have at March 1, 1933, depreciated 45 per cent below par compared with a 21 per cent depreciation of all American listed bonds. Better grade railroad issues, however, have depreciated only about 25 per cent, while junior issues have dropped over 60 per cent (p. 134).

The net income, after paying interest on bonds, of Class I roads (92 per cent of the total by mileage) shrank from an average of $584 million in 1926–1930 to $75 million in 1931—a decline of 88 per cent (p. 102).

Railroads have to meet not only an interest payment of $580 million a year on bonds, but also repayments to bondholders on account of maturities averaging about $262 million a year (p. 102).

Railroad net income in 1932 before paying interest on bonds was only about $500 million, while the debt charges alone were approximately $600 million (p. 106).

Of 167 Class I roads 75, or almost one-half, failed to earn enough in 1931 to pay interest on their bonds and other fixed charges, and 112, or 67 per cent, failed to do so in 1932. Because there has been practically no market for new security issues, interest has been paid only by drawing on cash balances or through further borrowing from banks and government agencies (pp. 102–106).

The Reconstruction Finance Corporation had authorized loans to railroads of $337 million (as of February 2) and the Railroad Credit Corporation had advanced $52 million—thus avoiding a general epidemic of receiverships (p. 105).

The years 1933 and 1934 promise to be even more critical than 1932. While bond maturities in 1933 are $100 million less than last year the outlook for revenues is poor, unless a general business improvement brings an increase in traffic. Although the emergency rate increases of 1931 have been extended to the end of September, 1933, considerable pressure is being exerted for a general downward revision of the entire rate structure (p. 107).

The railroads have, however, already drastically reduced operating costs largely through reduced wage and maintenance of way expenses (p. 108).

Prior to 1910 railroad net income after fixed charges was sufficient to support a market for stock issues. With the subsequent decline of net income, however, increasing reliance for new capital has had to be placed on bonds. The result has been a constant growth of fixed interest charges which, in times of low traffic and competition with other forms of transportation, threatens the solvency of the roads (pp. 109–116).

The expansion of long-term debt was based upon the assumption, now challenged by the facts, that railroads were an "adolescent" industry in a rapidly expanding nation (p. 117).

Recommendations

The problem of the present and future is to determine the amount of debt which can safely be carried by the railroads in view of probable earnings, but it is almost impossible to establish a basis for sound capital structures at the present moment because of the different circumstances of different roads and rapidly changing general economic conditions (pp. 117–118).

The makeshift capitalization of deficits through loans from the Reconstruction Finance Corporation and the Railroad Credit Corporation cannot be continued indefinitely (pp. 117–118).

Any plan must be *flexible,* discriminating between the ultimately sound and the hopelessly insolvent roads. A clear-cut national policy is needed which would develop basic criteria of soundness to be used by some administrative tribunal such as the Interstate Commerce Commission in authorizing or refusing financial assistance by the government or other agencies (pp. 118, 125).

The reduction of operating costs is as essential as the readjustment of fixed charges in relieving the strain of debts. Competitive wastes must be drastically cut—duplication of facilities, circuitous haulage, uneconomical mileage, etc. Future traffic can probably be handled economically with only 75 per cent of the present mileage and equipment (pp. 127–130).

Motor vehicle transportation has made difficult any predictions of further railroad traffic and has made rate reductions an essential to the future maintenance of traffic (p. 126).

Large economies might reasonably be expected to follow a policy of enforced regional consolidation rather than present policies of "unification" based upon "traditional methods of competition" (p. 136).

Because of the growing participation in railroad finance by the Reconstruction Finance Corporation, the present is an opportune time to scrutinize critically the financial set-up of every applicant for loans. The administration's "Emergency Railroad Transportation Act," now pending in Congress, undertakes to exert definite pressure in the direction of compelling a revision of capital structures by weak railroads (pp. 136–138).

Roads applying for assistance should be required to bring their capital structures into line with demonstrated capacity to meet their carrying charges. Certain properties, and in some cases whole lines of railways, must be liquidated—with or without more liberal bankruptcy laws (p. 137).

As suggested elements in the national policy of assisting distressed railways through the current emergency, it is recommended that financial aid be withheld from those carriers which in such a "test period" as 1923 to 1929 either: (1) failed to cover their fixed charges by a reasonable margin of safety, or (2) permitted their fixed charges to expand much more rapidly than their operating revenues. Such carriers should be required to undergo reorganization, unless it is reasonably certain that their distressed condition is due to factors not directly associated with their previous financing (p. 138).

As integral phases of a permanent policy governing railroad debts it is recommended that:

(a) funded debt should be reduced as railway property is retired, abandoned, or withdrawn from public use;

(b) existing railway debts be amortized to a figure representing not to exceed 50 per cent of total capitalization;

(c) new bond issues (other than refunding) be made self-liquidating through provision for amortization;

(d) public policies be modified so as to build up stockholder interest to not less than 50 per cent of total railway capitalization (p. 139).

1. THE FACTS [1]

(a) INTRODUCTION

R AILROAD bonds, representing substantially one-half of the total
property investment in rail facilities, have traditionally been regarded as among the prime investment securities of American fiduciary
institutions. More than 40 per cent of the outstanding railway bonds are
held by insurance companies, savings banks, educational and charitable
institutions, and philanthropic foundations. They also constitute an important part of the portfolios of commercial banks, ranking next to government bonds as a part of the secondary reserves of these institutions
for the protection of their deposit liabilities, the greater part of which
are payable on demand. It is this unique importance of railway senior
securities in the investment program and liquid assets of the key financial institutions of the country, and the prime necessity of their ready
marketability at prices reasonably close to their par values, which invest
the existing problem of railroad debt with peculiar significance.

These investments have, within the past two years, suffered their most
severe shock in a generation. Not since the long-drawn-out depression
of the eighteen-nineties has the fundamental security of so large a proportion of railway bonds been brought into question. For practically
the first time in their history the American railways have experienced
a three-year decline in traffic, revenues, and net earnings. Within that
short period their revenues have been substantially cut in half. Never
before had railway gross earnings or total freight traffic failed to make
at least some recovery after two years of shrinkage, and only once before
in the whole period from 1890 to 1929 did freight revenues and tonnage decline for two successive years. Entirely aside from the steady
and continuous loss of passenger patronage over the past decade—a
phenomenon which everyone has observed but whose implications few
have realized—it is obvious that the sudden reversal of railway fortunes
during the past three years has created a crisis of major proportions.
The failure of many roads to earn their operating expenses in these
years, to say nothing of covering their interest charges, has resulted in
a drastic depreciation in the quoted prices of all except the very highest
grades of railway bonds. This situation made it impossible to liquidate,

---

[1] See Tables 32 to 35 inclusive for summaries of the data used in this chapter.

TABLE 32

RAILROAD DEBTS IN RELATION TO CAPITALIZATION, INVESTMENT, AND INCOME, 1913–1931(a)

(Amounts in Millions of Dollars)

	1931	1929	1921	1913
1. Total railway capitalization(b)	$24,344	$23,983	$22,292	$19,796(c)
2. Total funded debt(b)	14,264	14,065	13,065	11,186(c)
Per cent of total capitalization	58.6	58.6	59.2	56.5
3. Investment in road and equipment	23,574	23,295	19,092	16,261
4. Funded debt actually outstanding	12,739	12,459	11,358	10,365(c)
Per cent of investment in road and equipment	55.3	53.9	6.16	63.8
5. Net railway capitalization(d)	18,941	18,680	17,083	15,366(c)
6. Net railway funded debt(d)	11,830	11,467	10,409	9,526(c)
Per cent of net capitalization	62.5	61.4	60.9	62.0
7. Railway corporate surplus	4,993	5,472	3,104	1,999(c)
Ratio funded debt actually outstanding to corporate surplus	2.55	2.28	3.66	5.18
8. Railway short-term debt(e)	252	78	393	
9. Total railway debt actually outstanding (4+8)	12,981	12,537	11,751	10,365
10. Railway operating revenues	4,246	6,373	5,633	3,193(c)
Ratio funded debt actually outstanding to operating revenues	3.05	1.96	2.02	3.24
11. Interest accrued on funded debt	592.9	580.8	529.4	434.8(c)
Per cent of operating revenues	14.0	9.1	9.4	13.6
12. Interest accrued on short-term debt(b)	17.8	12.7	42.7	23.0
13. Amortization and sinking fund charges(b)	9.7	16.0	12.1	15.1
14. Total debt service (11+12+13)—approximate	620	610	584	473
15. Net railway operating income before interest charges	528.2	1,262.6	601.1	805.3(g)
Ratio to total debt service	0.85	2.07	1.03	1.70

(a) Data are for years ending December 31, except in 1913, where the fiscal year ending June 30 is used, and include Class I, Class II, and Class III railways and their non-operating subsidiaries, unless otherwise stated, but exclude switching and terminal companies.

(b) Includes securities "nominally issued," and "nominally outstanding," as well as those actually outstanding.

(c) Class I and Class II railways and their non-operating subsidiaries.

(d) Total outstanding (items 1 and 2) less railway securities owned by railways.

(e) Class I roads and their non-operating subsidiaries.

(f) Class I railways only.

(g) Class I and Class II railways.

except at ruinously deflated prices, the holdings of banks and insurance companies during the financial crisis of 1931–32, and was indeed one of the principal factors contributing to their difficulties. In order to preserve the technical solvency of many of these institutions it became necessary to resort to extra-legal subterfuges in valuing their security portfolios and to suspend temporarily the provisions of state laws governing the eligibility of railway bonds for savings bank investments. Railway credit in these circumstances practically disappeared and the railways themselves became the first to take advantage of the emergency

TABLE 33

RAILROAD DEBTS IN RELATION TO CAPITALIZATION, INVESTMENT, AND INCOME, 1913–1931(a)

(Percentage Changes Over Successive Periods)

	1929–31	1921–29	1913–21	1913–31
1. Total railway capitalization(b)	1.3	7.3	12.5	23.0
2. Total railway funded debt(b)	1.2	6.2	18.4	27.2
3. Investment in road and equipment	1.0	22.0	17.4	44.8
4. Funded debt actually outstanding	2.3	9.6	9.8	23.0
5. Net railway capitalization(c)	1.4	9.4	11.1	23.3
6. Net railway funded debt(c)	3.2	10.0	9.3	24.2
7. Railway corporate surplus	−8.8	76.0	55.1	150.0
8. Railway short-term debt(d)	223.0	−80.2	....	....
9. Total railway debt actually outstanding (4+8)	3.4	6.8	(13.6)	(250.0)
10. Railway operating revenues	−33.4	13.2	76.4	32.9
11. Interest accrued on short-term debt	2.0	10.0	22.0	36.4
12. Interest accrued on short-term debt(e)	40.0	−70.3	86.0	−22.6
13. Amortization and sinking fund charges(e)	−39.4	32.2	−19.8	−35.8
14. Total debt service (11+12+13)—approximate	1.8	4.2	23.6	31.0
15. Net railway operating income before interest charges	−58.3	110.4	−25.2	−34.4

(a) Data are for years ending December 31, except in 1913, where the fiscal year ending June 30 is used, and include Class I, Class II, and Class III railways and their non-operating subsidiaries, unless otherwise stated, but exclude switching and terminal companies.

(b) Includes securities "nominally issued," and "nominally outstanding," as well as those actually outstanding.

(c) Total outstanding (items 1 and 2) less railway securities owned by railways.

(d) Class I roads and their non-operating subsidiaries.

(e) Class I railways only.

credit facilities provided early in 1932 by the national government through the establishment of the Reconstruction Finance Corporation.

The current position, then, is that a substantial proportion of the railway mileage of the country is essentially bankrupt and is saved from becoming technically so only by the government's exercise of emergency remedies, assisted in some cases by the efforts of banking interests, and by the mutual protective association known as the Railroad Credit Corporation. Actual insolvencies, resulting from default on capital obligations or fixed interest payments during the four years 1929 to 1932, included thirty-nine railroad companies representing about seven per cent of the total amount of railway securities in the hands of the public and nearly one-tenth of the total railway mileage.

This whole situation obviously gives rise to a number of highly intricate problems, towards the solution of which the community is anxiously trying to find its way. The purpose of this chapter is to

TABLE 34

RAILROAD DEBTS IN RELATION TO RAILWAY TRAFFIC, REVENUES, EXPENSES, NATIONAL
WEALTH AND INCOME, 1913–1931(a)

(Dollars in Millions)

	1931	1929	1921	1913
1. Revenue freight carried 1 mile, monthly				
average, millions of tons...........	25,923	37,516	25,794	25,144
Per cent of average for 1923–25......	76.1	110.1	75.8	73.8
2. Passengers carried 1 mile, monthly				
average, millions..`.`...............	1,828	2,597	3,142	2,889
Per cent of average for 1923–25.....	59.3	84.3	102.1	93.9
3. Index of industrial production, per cent				
of average for 1923–25 (F.R.B.).....	81	119	67	....
4. Revenues and expenses, Class I railways				
1. Operating revenues, monthly avge.	$349.0	523.3	459.7	253.6
2. Freight revenues, monthly avge...	270.7	401.3	325.9	178.3
3. Passenger revenues, monthly avge.	45.9	72.7	96.0	56.6
4. Operating expenses, monthly avge.	268.6	375.5	380.2	175.8
5. Estimated national income(b).........	$52,700	$85,200	$63,371	$35,723
Per cent railway operating revenues				
of estimated national income......	7.9	7.4	8.7	8.5
Per cent net railway operating income				
of estimated national income.....	1.0	1.5	0.9	2.3
6. Estimated total national wealth(c)....	$329,700 (1930)	$361,800	$317,200	$192,500
7. Railway assets, book value(d).........	$24,292	$24,302	$20,197	$17,041
Per cent of estimated total national				
wealth........................	7.4	6.7	6.4	8.8
8. Estimated total U. S. funded debt.....	$112,364	$99,282	$65,496	$32,408
Per cent railway outstanding funded				
debt of estimated U. S. total funded				
debt.............................	12.7	14.2	20.2	34.5
9. Population of U. S., millions.........	124.0	121.5	108.2	96.5
10. Average freight revenue per ton mile				
(mills)........................	10.62	10.88	12.94	7.29
11. Average freight revenue index (calcu-				
lated on same base as price index) ..	94.5	96.5	115.0	64.6
12. Wholesale commodity price index (BLS)	60.4	95.3	96.7	68.1

(a) See corresponding footnote to Table 32.
(b) National Bureau of Economic Research estimates for 1913 and 1921. National
Industrial Conference Board estimates for 1929 and 1931.
(c) National Industrial Conference Board estimates. *N.I.C.B. Bulletin*, Feb. 20, 1932.
(d) Investment in road and equipment, less accrued depreciation, plus cash, and
materials and supplies. "Cash" and "materials and supplies" in 1913 are for Class I
and Class II railways and their non-operating subsidiaries; in the other years "cash"
is for Class I roads and their non-operating subsidiaries only.

present, in as clear and straightforward a manner as the complex nature
of the subject will permit, the basic facts which are essential for the
formulation of intelligent judgments with respect to the several issues
involved. The immediately following paragraphs are intended to give
an outline summary of the "argument" as it is developed in the remainder of the chapter.

TABLE 35

RAILROAD DEBTS IN RELATION TO RAILWAY TRAFFIC, REVENUES, EXPENSES, NATIONAL HEALTH AND INCOME, 1913–1931(a)

(Percentage Changes Over Successive Periods)

	1929–31	1921–29	1913–21	1913–31
1. Revenue freight carried 1 mile, monthly average, millions of tons.............	−30.8	45.3	2.8	3.0
2. Passengers carried 1 mile, monthly average, millions......................	−29.6	−17.3	8.7	−36.7
3. Index of industrial production (F. R. B.).	−31.9	77.6		
4. Revenues and expenses, Class I railways:				
1. Operating revenues, monthly average	−33.2	13.9	81.0	37.7
2. Freight " " "	−32.4	23.1	82.6	52.0
3. Passenger " " "	−36.8	−24.2	69.7	−19.0
4. Operating expenses " "	−28.5	−1.0	116.2	53.0
5. Estimated national income(b)..........	−38.1	34.4	77.4	47.5
6. Estimated total national wealth(c)......	−8.9	10.4	64.8	71.3
7. Railway assets, book value(d)..........	......	20.2	18.3	42.8
8. Estimated total U. S. funded debt.......	13.2	50.1	102.1	246.7
9. Population of U. S....................	2.0	12.3	12.1	28.5
10. Average freight revenue per ton mile (mills)............................	−2.0	−16.0	78.0	46.0
11. Average freight revenue index (calculated on same base as price index).........	−2.1	−16.1	78.0	46.3
12. Wholesale commodity price index (B L S)	−26.1	−1.5	27.3	−11.3

(a) See corresponding footnote to Table 32.
(b) See footnotes, Table 34.
(c) See footnotes, Table 34.
(d) See footnotes, Table 34.

Summary of the Argument

Any worthwhile consideration of the railway debt problem must start from the premise of distinguishing as clearly as possible between what may be called the immediate and emergency aspects of the situation, and the long run or permanent aspects. This distinction is particularly pertinent at the present moment, when in addition to the general influences affecting all business the railways are confronted with special problems arising from the rapid development of competing forms of transport, some of which are partly subsidized at public expense and are to a large degree unrestrained by regulation or control. This competitive situation is aggravated by the lack of any clearly defined public policy with respect to the transportation system as a whole. It is a time not only of low levels of production and business volume, and lowered standards of competition, but also a time of "low economic visibility." The analysis of the railway debt problem, therefore, must point out as clearly as may be those elements in the situation which are peculiarly of a temporary or emergency nature, and having cleared the ground, so to speak, proceed to the consideration of what is essentially permanent and lasting.

The first part of this discussion begins then with a brief statement of the relation between railway funded debt and the total railway property investment at the end of 1931, and traces the course of railway finances during the critical years, 1931 and 1932. The increasing seriousness of the railway financial problem during those years is developed in some detail and a brief account given of the activities of the Railroad Credit Corporation and the Reconstruction Finance Corporation in preventing a general epidemic of railway receiverships which, but for their existence, would surely have ensued.

This hasty summary of the events of 1931 and 1932 is followed by a discussion of the place of debt in American railway finance and its gradually increasing importance in proportion to the total railway capitalization. Some attempt is made to explain why borrowed funds have come to occupy so large a place in railway capital structures, and to point out the dangers to which this condition exposes both borrower and lender. In the case of the railway enterprise there are certain economic characteristics, as well as certain political influences, which have resulted in a disproportionately high relation between the burden of debt and fixed charges, on the one hand, and total investment and earning power, on the other. The statistical record of operating and financial data for the period from 1890 to date is examined in order to find whether any significant trends can be detected which indicate improvement in these relationships or the reverse. The general conclusion is reached that, while the aggregate totals and averages do not indicate any importantly growing disparity between railway investment and debt, or between total traffic, revenue, earning power, and fixed charges, such general aggregates and averages conceal a fairly large number of individual cases in which the relationship is anything but a sound one. These cases obviously call for thoroughgoing remedial action, since the mere fact of their existence tends to undermine the whole basis of sound railway credit.

The proper adjustment of debt and interest charges to railway earning power is far from being the whole story, however. It would be in the highest degree unfortunate to permit a mere redistribution of railway equities between bondholder and stockholder to lull the community into the belief that anything more than a beginning had been made. Drastic revision of railway operating methods and indeed of the whole organization of the railway system may be the ultimate price of solvency. Incident to such revision sacrifices will have to be accepted all around, by security holders, by railway labor, by the general public. Much of the existing railway plant is obsolete or out-moded or is rapidly being made so by continuous improvements in other methods of transport, by shifts in population and industry, and by changes in methods of doing business. Obsolescent lines and needlessly duplicating facilities must be abandoned and written off; operating methods will have to be refined and adapted more closely to the requirements of a changing economic world; jobs will have to be sacrificed; communities which cannot or will not support existing lines of railway must be reconciled to surrender some part of those facilities or to accept drastically curtailed service. The future of railway transportation, in other words, and its continuous adaptation and integration with other agencies of transport, must be envisaged as the ultimate criterion by which to judge the soundness of the railway debt structure. It is the only standpoint from which a statesmanlike approach can be made to any aspect of "the railway problem."

(b) THE CURRENT EMERGENCY IN RAILWAY FINANCE

The total investment in "road and equipment" of the American steam railways, taken as a whole, amounted at the end of 1931 to some $27 billion. Against this property investment the railways had actually outstanding a total funded debt amounting to $13.3 billion—or practically one-half the book value of their property.[2] At the end of that year 45 railways, large and small, representing about five per cent of the total railway mileage of the country, were in receivership.[3] At the end of 1932 the proportion of the railway mileage in receivership had increased to approximately 10 per cent of the total.

The ten Class I roads [4] placed in receivership during the three years,

[2] The totals for the two items mentioned vary somewhat in different statements according to the classifications of roads included. The above figures are taken from the Interstate Commerce Commission's annual, *Statistics of Railways in the United States,* 1931, Statements 17 and 54-F, and are inclusive of all classes of steam railways reporting to the Commission. For details see Tables 32 to 36, pp. 96 to 114.

[3] *Ibid.,* Statement No. 6.

[4] Class I railways are those having annual operating revenues above $1 million. They operate about 92 per cent of the total railway mileage and earn over 98 per cent of the total railway revenues of the country.

1930, 1931 and 1932, operate some 18,000 miles of line and had a total funded debt at the end of 1931 of approximately $795 million. Not all this debt is in default, of course, but the figure named gives some indication of the magnitude of the problem presented by the roads whose difficulties were so acute that receivership could not be avoided even with the marshalling of governmental and inter-railway assistance, as exemplified in the Reconstruction Finance Corporation and the Railroad Credit Corporation.[5]

Decline in Operating Revenues and Net Income, 1929–1932

The total operating revenues of the railways of the country, regarded as a single system with intercorporate payments eliminated, shrank from a peak figure of $6,619 million in 1926 to $4,317 million in 1931.[6] The total income left after paying operating expenses, taxes, and miscellaneous equipment rentals reached its maximum in 1929, with a total of $1,484 million.[7] By 1931 this figure had fallen to $728 million. Out of this $728 million had to come miscellaneous deductions in the nature of "fixed" charges amounting to about $73 million, and interest on funded debt, $580 million, leaving for stockholders' equity, other than railway intercorporate holdings, a net income of $75 million for the year. This figure compares with an annual average of $584 million during the five years 1926 to 1930.[8] Of the 167 largest railway systems comprising the group officially styled "Class I" roads—those having annual operating revenues above $1 million—not less than 75 failed to cover their fixed charges in 1931.[9] These roads not only had nothing left from gross earnings for their stockholders' equity, but were able to pay their bonded interest and guaranteed lease rentals only by drawing upon their cash balances or by resorting to the expedient of bank loans.

The Problem of Maturities

This was far from being the whole story, however. Of the huge total of some $13 billion of outstanding railway debt, a certain proportion

[5] The number of railway bond issues in default in 1931 was 30, with an aggregate par value of $213,228,000; for 1932 the defaulting issues numbered 37, with a value of $201,738,580.

[6] The annual average for the five years, 1926 to 1930, was $6,244 million. *Statistics of Railways in the United States,* 1931, p. S-54.

[7] The average for the five years, 1926 to 1930, was $1,330 million. *Ibid., loc. cit.*

[8] *Ibid.,* 1931, p. S-54.

[9] "Fixed charges" include rents for leased roads, miscellaneous rents, interest on funded and unfunded debt, and discount amortization.

matures every year—some indeed every month. In some cases these maturities are very large. For the railways as a whole in recent years the total volume of funded obligations falling due has averaged somewhere between $250 and $275 million annually. In 1931 the amount of such maturities was approximately $270 million. Ordinarily the maturing obligations of a railroad are paid off by the creation of new debt, that is to say, by "refunding," either on a short term or a long time basis. A considerable volume of such refinancing was in fact arranged by the railroads in the early months of 1931. As the year advanced, however, and the outlook for railway earnings became increasingly unfavorable it proved to be progressively more difficult to float new security issues and a considerable number of roads became heavily indebted to banks for short-term loans, the proceeds of which were used to take up maturities.[10]

Creation of Railroad Credit Corporation

It was primarily to help in meeting the problem of fixed interest payments that the Railroad Credit Corporation was established late in 1931. This institution was set up by the railroads for the purpose of making available to needy but solvent carriers the fund growing out of the emergency increase in certain freight rates authorized by the Interstate Commerce Commission in October of that year.[11] In its original decision upon the application of the railways for a general increase of 15 per cent in freight rates in order to protect railway credit, the Commission had authorized comparatively small increases in specified rates, coupled with the proviso that the revenues from such increases be marshalled into a general pool and earmarked for the exclusive benefit of those roads threatened with the necessity of defaulting on their fixed interest charges. To this proposal the railways demurred, alleging various legal and practical objections, and requested the Commission to sanction a substitute plan under which the proceeds of the increased rates would be pooled, as before, but *loaned* instead of given outright to the carriers in distress. To this petition the Commission gave a qualified assent. While it explicitly refrained from approving or disapproving the arrangements made by the railroads for the administration

[10] The volume of railway bank loans probably more than doubled in 1931; the "loans and bills payable" of the Class I roads increased from $115 million at the end of 1930 to nearly $246 million a year later. See *Statistics of Railways in the United States*, 1930, 1931, Statement No. 42.

[11] *Fifteen Per Cent Case, 1931; Ex Parte* No. 103, 178 I.C.C., 539, October 16, 1931.

of these funds, the Commission relieved them from the necessity of pooling the "surcharges," but indicated that it relied upon them to apply the resulting funds in aid of financially weak railroads.[12] In accordance with this understanding, the carriers proceeded to organize their plan for marshalling and distributing the increased revenues.[13]

During 1932 the Railroad Credit Corporation collected from its participating members, which include substantially all the interstate railways except those in receivership or in default upon their fixed interest obligations, approximately $52 million.[14] Some $48 million of this amount was loaned out again to those roads which needed assistance in meeting their fixed interest charges that would otherwise have been defaulted, but no loans were made to carriers already in default or in receivership. The amount realized from the emergency rate increases proved to be materially less than had been anticipated, however, and the effectiveness of the Railroad Credit Corporation's activities in relieving the financial burdens of the necessitous carriers was correspondingly reduced.[15] Moreover, the Credit Corporation did not undertake to assist in the refinancing of maturing funded obligations. This situation resulted in increased pressure from roads facing such maturities upon the funds of the Reconstruction Finance Corporation.

Loans from Reconstruction Finance Corporation

The Reconstruction Finance Corporation was set up in consequence of emergency legislation [16] at the beginning of February, 1932. Among its primary functions is the making of loans to railroads and railroad receivers to enable them to meet their maturing obligations and fixed charges. Such loans are required by law to be "fully and adequately secured," and must first receive the approval, in each case, of the Interstate Commerce Commission.[17] Railroads were indeed among the first

[12] *Ibid.*, 179 I.C.C., 215, December 5, 1931.

[13] See *46th Annual Report,* Interstate Commerce Commission, 1932, pp. 11–12.

[14] Monthly financial statements, Railroad Credit Corporation, 1932–33.

[15] It was originally estimated that the "surcharges" would yield between $100 and $150 million for the year 1932. They actually produced for the Class I roads only about $62 million. Even so, they represented approximately 20 per cent of the net railway operating income of these carriers for the first nine months of 1932.

[16] The Reconstruction Finance Corporation Act was approved January 22, 1932.

[17] *Reconstruction Finance Corporation Act;* section 5. ". . . the corporation may . . . make loans to aid in the temporary financing of railroads and railways engaged in interstate commerce . . . when in the opinion of the board of directors of the corporation such railroads or railways are unable to obtain funds upon reasonable terms through banking channels or from the general public and the corporation will be adequately secured;" . . . See also *46th Annual Report,* Interstate Commerce Commission, 1932, pp. 12–15.

applicants for such governmental assistance. From the date of its organization, February 2, 1932, up to the end of the year the Reconstruction Finance Corporation had received the approval of the Interstate Commerce Commission upon applications from 71 railways for a total of approximately $352 million of loans.[18] Of this amount the Finance Corporation had authorized loans aggregating about $337 million, of which some $284 million had actually been advanced, while of the latter amount nearly $12 million had been repaid, leaving about $272 million outstanding at the end of the year.[19]

Of the total amount of loans to railways authorized by the Reconstruction Finance Corporation during 1932, slightly over one-half was for the purpose of retiring bonds and other maturing funded obligations or for meeting interest on funded debt.[20] About 16 per cent was for the repayment of bank loans and other temporary advances which had been made in anticipation of the enactment of this emergency legislation, while nearly one-third was for the payment of taxes, wages, materials, etc., and for new construction, rehabilitation, and the building or repair of equipment. These latter items were designated "work loans" and were intended to enable the continuance of improvements or construction works to which the applicant carriers were committed and to aid in providing employment.[21]

As security for loans from the Reconstruction Finance Corporation the borrowing railroads or their receivers were required to pledge whatever acceptable collateral they had available. The rapid exhaustion of such collateral necessitated the authorization by the Interstate Commerce Commission of additional evidences of debt which could be pledged as loan security. According to unofficial but probably reliable reports, the total volume of such authorizations, including those pledged for loans from private sources and from the Railroad Credit Corporation, during

[18] Standard Statistics Co., Inc., *Standard Railroad Securities*, Vol. 20, No. 6, January 14, 1933.

[19] Press release No. 371, Reconstruction Finance Corporation, January 23, 1933.

[20] Advances by the Reconstruction Finance Corporation to aid in taking up maturing funded obligations were conditioned in practically all cases upon the requirement of concessions from the holders of such securities. Where payment could not be made in accordance with the terms of the indentures, even with the Corporation's assistance, the usual procedure was to accompany an offer of part cash with a plan to extend the unpaid balance for such periods as the security holders could be induced to agree to. In at least one case a complete revision of a railroad's capital structure was insisted upon by the Interstate Commerce Commission as a condition to its approval for a loan to repay maturing funded debt. See page 120 below.

[21] *Ibid.;* see also *46th Annual Report,* Interstate Commerce Commission, 1932, pp. 13–14.

the year 1932, amounted to more than $1,188 million, of which $1,082 million represented mortgage bonds.[22] To some extent of course these new evidences of debt were offset by maturing obligations retired, although information is not yet available to permit an exact statement of the net increase in total railway obligations, including those actually, as well as those nominally, outstanding.[23] The total amount of railway borrowing from all sources, including private bank loans, during the year 1932 was, however, in excess of $600 million.

Traffic, Revenue, Income and Maturities in 1932

From a traffic and revenue point of view, the year 1932 proved to be even worse than 1931. Freight traffic handled by the Class I roads was nearly 24 per cent below the 1931 volume, and over 38 per cent under the figure for 1930, while passenger traffic was the smallest for any year since 1900.[24] Gross and net earnings continued to shrink until the final quarter of the year. Out of 167 Class I roads, not less than 112 failed to cover their fixed charges while 59 did not even earn their operating expenses and taxes, but reported operating deficits before interest and other fixed charges.[25] An estimate based upon the returns for these 167 roads, which operate about 92 per cent of the total railway mileage of the country, indicates that the net total railway income for 1932, out of which interest on funded debt and other fixed charges had to be met, was probably substantially below $500 million, while the debt charge alone had increased to somewhere around $600 million.[26] On the other hand, the volume of funded obligations falling

[22] Associated Press dispatch, January 18, 1933. See also *46th Annual Report*, Interstate Commerce Commission, 1932, pp. 44–46.

[23] According to the *Annual Report* of the Commission, out of some 605 millions of new securities and notes *actually issued* during the year ending October 31, 1932, approximately 401 millions were issued in exchange for, or to pay, extend, renew, or refund other outstanding securities or notes. This was in addition to the authorization by the Commission of 829 millions of securities "for pledge."

[24] Bureau of Railway Economics, press release, February 8, 1933.

[25] Bureau of Railway Economics, *Monthly Report, Series No. 280, Railway Revenues and Expenses,* December, 1932. See also *Moody's Investment Survey,* Vol. 25, No. 14, p. 2472, February 16, 1933.

[26] The 167 Class I roads reporting to the Bureau of Railway Economics show the following results for 1932:

Total operating revenues,	$3,162 million
Total operating expenses,	2,429 "
Taxes,	279 "
Net railway operating income,	334 "

See *Monthly Report, Series No. 280,* Bureau of Railway Economics, *Railway Revenues and Expenses,* December, 1932.

due in 1932 were nearly $100 million less than in the previous year, and to this extent, at least, the pressure upon railway finances was relaxed. None the less, as was pointed out at the beginning of this section, the proportion of the total railway mileage in receivership had doubled between the beginning and the end of the year.

Prospects for 1933 and 1934

The years 1933 and 1934 promise to be even more critical for American railway finance than the two years through which the carriers have just passed. Roughly $667 million of funded debt obligations mature during the next two years, while the outlook for traffic and revenues remains distinctly uncertain, not to say unpromising.

The *passenger business* has almost reached the vanishing point on many lines of railway and has become unprofitable in the aggregate on perhaps a majority of all the roads. Even in 1930 for the Class I roads, taken as a whole, the estimated expenses apportioned to the passenger service represented $1.01 for each dollar of passenger revenue. For 1931 the excess had grown to nearly 11 per cent.[27] Over large sections of the country indeed the probable returns from the passenger service were distinctly worse than indicated by these general averages. In the Southern District, for example, in 1931 the apportioned expense of conducting passenger service was 35 per cent above the passenger service revenues while in the Western District the excess was over 23 per cent.[28]

As to *freight* revenue to be expected in 1933, this depends obviously upon the state of general business activity. No guess will be hazarded at this point as to how the total physical volume of freight movement to be expected during the current year will compare with that for the year just closed. The results for the first quarter were distinctly disappointing and the outlook for the remainder of the year remains uncertain. The rate situation is none too reassuring. As a consequence of

[27] *Statistics of Railways in the United States,* 1931; p. S-57.
[28] These ratios of "apportioned" expense to revenue for the passenger service are not to be taken as indicating that the railroads as a whole would be better off without any passenger business. They may on the other hand indicate the need for critical scrutiny of all preventable wastes and the elimination of duplicating and unnecessary services. While the passenger revenues may not contribute in all cases to railway net earnings they do, on many roads, help appreciably in paying for such joint costs as maintenance of way and structures, much of which would go on whether the passenger service were operated or not.

petitions from the carriers the emergency increases or "surcharges," which were sanctioned in October, 1931, and were to have expired in March of this year, have been extended by the Commission to the end of September. On the other hand, petitions were presented to the Commission in January by several important groups of shippers calling for a general and substantial reduction of freight rates on a number of basic commodities, including in particular coal, lumber, and farm products. Acting on its own initiative the Commission has broadened the range of this latter proceeding and is now actively canvassing the whole situation with respect to the basic level of freight rates in relation to the general price level and the business situation. There is evidence that a substantial volume of opinion both among business men and economists supports the view that a thorough-going revision of the railroad rate structure is essential as one of the first steps to permanent business recovery.[29]

Attempts to Reduce Operating Expenses

Very vigorous efforts were made by the carriers to reduce their operating expenses during 1932, with a substantial measure of success. Between the years 1929 and 1932 approximately 600,000 railway employees out of an aggregate number of 1,661,000 were dismissed or "laid off." In January, 1932, the railway managements succeeded in persuading their remaining employees, or those of them included in the organized unions, to accept a general 10 per cent reduction in basic standards of pay. By mutual consent this arrangement has been extended to October 31, 1933. The greater part of this drastic reduction in number of employees was enforced by the decline of revenues incident to curtailed volume of freight and passenger movement. Much of it, however, reflected the sharp reduction which railway management was able to effect in outlays for maintenance, particularly maintenance of way. These reductions in maintenance costs have probably been pushed to the extreme limits consistent with adequate standards of efficiency and safety, and it is not to be expected that current low costs of maintenance can be continued indefinitely.

It is undoubtedly true that any significant upturn in general business, with resulting increased volume of railway traffic, will enable the

[29] See p. 126 below.

THE RAILROAD DEBT 109

roads to save a much larger than usual fraction of their gross revenue
for net. This is because railway operating expenses do not rise as rapidly as revenues when both start from a level already low. Such a result,
however, can be only temporary at best, since deferred maintenance
will ultimately, and perhaps soon, have to be made good and a certain
proportion of the dismissed or laid off employees reinstated, although
it seems fairly obvious that a considerably smaller number of people
can look to the railroads for their livelihood during the next few years
than was the case during the decade ending in 1930.

(c) THE PLACE OF DEBT IN RAILWAY FINANCE

For upwards of at least forty years, since the official record has been
available, American railways have usually financed their new capital
requirements much more largely through borrowing than from the sale
of stock. Partly because of the general unwillingness of investors to
participate in the earnings of the industry on any other basis, partly
because of the relatively favorable terms on which mortgage money
could be obtained, and partly because of ingrained habit, American
railway finance has traditionally depended on the bond buyer to supply
the major part of its new investment funds. In consequence the formal
"capital structure" of the railway system, taken as a whole, is heavily
weighted with funded debt as against share capital, in a ratio which
tends to approximate 55 to 60 per cent for bonds and 40 to 45 per cent
for stock.

Growing Use of Borrowed Funds

In the early days of American railroad development there was a
much more general use of share capital, and bonds were sold only as
a means of supplementing the stock subscriptions of local supporters of
this new form of land transport. With the rapid extension of rail lines
into undeveloped territory, however, particularly during the period following the Civil War, and the realization of the need for a more substantial type of physical construction, it became necessary to draw more
heavily upon investment funds from the larger capital markets, both at
home and abroad. In consequence, borrowed money began to assume
rapidly increasing importance in railway capitalization, until by 1890,
at about which time the first official figures issued by the Interstate

CHART 12

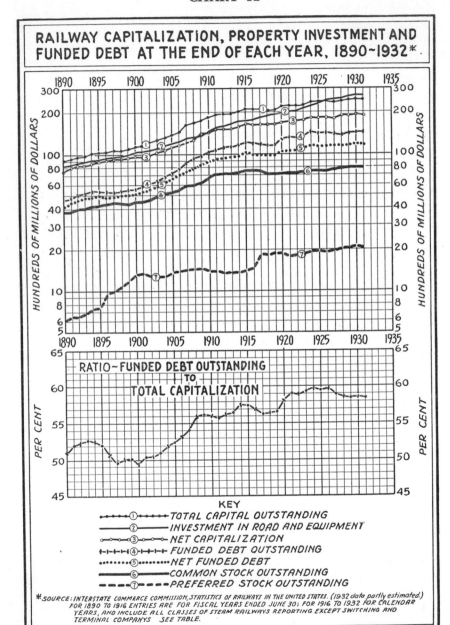

RAILWAY CAPITALIZATION, PROPERTY INVESTMENT AND FUNDED DEBT AT THE END OF EACH YEAR, 1890~1932*

RATIO~FUNDED DEBT OUTSTANDING TO TOTAL CAPITALIZATION

KEY

- ①· TOTAL CAPITAL OUTSTANDING
- ② INVESTMENT IN ROAD AND EQUIPMENT
- ③ NET CAPITALIZATION
- ④ FUNDED DEBT OUTSTANDING
- ⑤ NET FUNDED DEBT
- ⑥ COMMON STOCK OUTSTANDING
- ⑦ PREFERRED STOCK OUTSTANDING

*SOURCE: INTERSTATE COMMERCE COMMISSION, STATISTICS OF RAILWAYS IN THE UNITED STATES. (1932 data partly estimated.) FOR 1890 TO 1916 ENTRIES ARE FOR FISCAL YEARS ENDED JUNE 30; FOR 1916 TO 1932 FOR CALENDAR YEARS, AND INCLUDE ALL CLASSES OF STEAM RAILWAYS REPORTING EXCEPT SWITCHING AND TERMINAL COMPANYS   SEE TABLE.

CHART 13

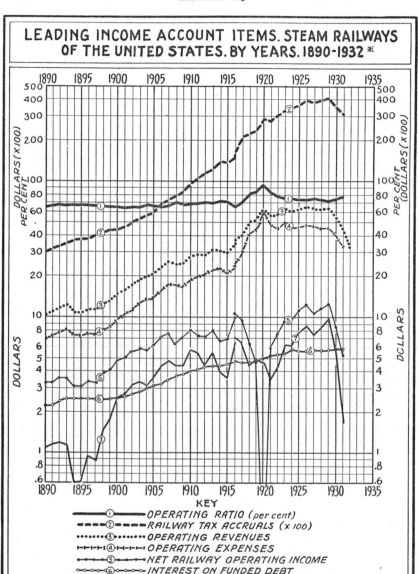

LEADING INCOME ACCOUNT ITEMS. STEAM RAILWAYS OF THE UNITED STATES. BY YEARS. 1890-1932 *

KEY

———①———OPERATING RATIO (per cent)
- - - -②- - - -RAILWAY TAX ACCRUALS (x 100)
·······③·······OPERATING REVENUES
⊢⊢⊢④⊢⊢⊢OPERATING EXPENSES
—·—·—⑤—·—·—NET RAILWAY OPERATING INCOME
○—○—○⑥○—○—○INTEREST ON FUNDED DEBT
———⑦———NET INCOME AFTER CHARGES

*SOURCE: INTERSTATE COMMERCE COMMISSION, STATISTICS OF RAILWAYS IN THE UNITED STATES (1932 data partly estimated) FOR 1899 TO 1916 ENTRIES ARE FOR FISCAL YEARS ENDED JUNE 30; FOR 1916 TO 1932 FOR CALENDAR YEARS, AND INCLUDE ALL CLASSES OF STEAM RAILWAYS REPORTING EXCEPT SWITCHING AND TERMINAL COMPANIES.   SEE TABLE

CHART 14

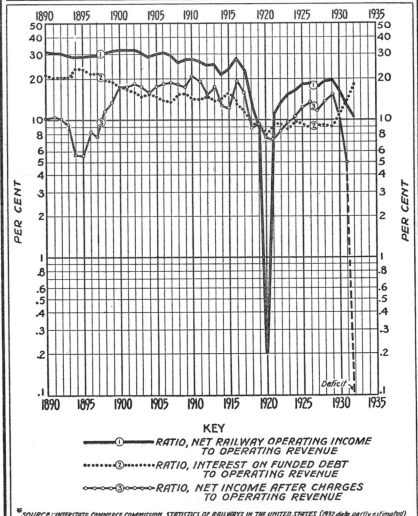

NET RAILWAY OPERATING INCOME. INTEREST ON FUNDED DEBT. AND NET INCOME AFTER CHARGES IN RELATION TO OPERATING REVENUES. 1890-1932*

KEY

————①———— RATIO, NET RAILWAY OPERATING INCOME TO OPERATING REVENUE

••••••②•••••• RATIO, INTEREST ON FUNDED DEBT TO OPERATING REVENUE

⊶⊶③⊶⊶ RATIO, NET INCOME AFTER CHARGES TO OPERATING REVENUE

*SOURCE: INTERSTATE COMMERCE COMMISSION, STATISTICS OF RAILWAYS IN THE UNITED STATES (1932 data partly estimated) FOR 1890 TO 1916 ENTRIES ARE FOR FISCAL YEARS, ENDED JUNE 30: FOR 1916 TO 1932 FOR CALENDAR YEARS, AND INCLUDE ALL CLASSES OF STEAM RAILWAYS REPORTING EXCEPT SWITCHING AND TERMINAL COMPANIES. SEE TABLE.

Commerce Commission became available, the ratio of funded debt to total capitalization of the American railway system as a whole had risen to approximately half the total. At no time since the year 1900 has this ratio, taking the railways as a whole, been below 50 per cent and since the year 1921 it has consistently been above 58 per cent of the total volume of railway securities outstanding.[30]

Among the numerous factors which have contributed to this condition perhaps the most fundamental is the narrowing "spread" between railway gross earnings and the net income available to pay dividends and for reinvestment in the property. Up to about the year 1910, net income, that is, what is left from railway gross revenues after paying operating expenses, taxes, rentals, and interest charges, was increasing at least as rapidly as railway gross revenues, while the ratio of net income to the stockholders' equity in the railroad property investment was rising at a very much faster rate.[31] This would probably be true even after making allowance for the depressed level of earnings in the "nineties," and for the circumstance that property book values were somewhat overstated in the earlier period, at least in comparison with later years. Be that as it may, the fact is that the increasingly favorable returns from the stockholders' viewpoint, and the rapidly rising proportion of railway stock upon which dividends were actually paid—the proportion rose from about 36 per cent of the total in 1896–1900 to about 66 per cent of the total in 1906–1910—enabled the railways to float large additional issues of stock.[32] Common stock outstanding rose from $4,522 million in 1900 to $6,710 million in 1910, an increase of some 48 per cent, while in the whole period from 1910 to 1931 the additional increase has been only $1,321 million, or less than 20

[30] These ratios are based upon the total volume of railway securities, including those "nominally issued," "nominally outstanding," and "actually outstanding." If the comparison were limited to the actually outstanding securities, as distinguished from those still held by the issuing company, pledged, or reacquired and not cancelled or retired, the ratios would in general be somewhat lower but only to the extent of 2 or 3 per cent. On the other hand, it should be noted that of the railway "net capitalization," that is, securities outstanding in the hands of the public, as distinguished from those held by other railroads, funded debt constitutes a relatively higher proportion than is true for the gross issues including intercorporate railway holdings. In other words, railways hold relatively more of each other's stocks than of bonds. See Tables 32 and 36.

[31] Stockholders' equity, as here used, means the total railway investment in road and equipment less funded debt. See Charts 13 and 14 and pp. 111–112.

[32] See Charts 12 and 14.

TABLE 36

RELATIONSHIP OF RAILWAY FUNDED DEBT TO TOTAL RAILWAY CAPITALIZATION(a)
1890–1909

Year Ended June 30	(1) Total Railway Capital Outstanding	(2) Net Railway Capitalization (c)	(3) Funded Debt Outstanding	(4) Railway Bonds Owned by Railways (b)	(5) Net Railway Funded Debt (c)	(6) Ratio Col. 3 to Col. 1	(7) Ratio Col. 5 to Col. 2
	Millions of Dollars					Per Cent	Per Cent
1890	$8,984	$7,577	$4,575	$433	$4,132	50.9	54.5
91	9,291	8,008	4,840	338	4,502	52.1	56.2
92	9,686	8,295	5,053	327	4,726	52.2	57.0
93	9,895	8,332	5,226	427	4,798	52.8	57.6
94	10,191	8,647	5,357	415	4,941	52.6	57.2
1895	10,347	8,900	5,385	396	4,990	52.1	56.0
96	10,567	9,066	5,340	400	4,940	50.6	54.5
97	10,635	9,168	5,270	404	4,866	49.6	53.1
98	10,819	9,297	5,430	370	5,060	50.1	54.5
99	11,034	9,432	5,519	394	5,125	50.2	54.4
1900	11,491	9,548	5,645	473	5,172	49.1	54.2
01	11,688	9,483	5,882	469	5,413	50.4	57.1
02	12,134	9,926	6,110	498	5,612	50.4	56.5
03	12,600	10,282	6,444	520	5,924	51.1	57.6
04	13,213	10,712	6,873	558	6,315	52.0	59.0
1905	13,805	11,167	7,251	568	6,683	52.5	59.9
06	14,570	11,672	7,767	641	7,126	53.2	61.1
07	16,082	......	8,725	...	.....	54.2	
08	16,768	12,834	9,394	...	.....	56.0	
09	17,488	13,914	9,802	...	.....	56.1	

(a) *Statistics of Railways in the United States*, 1926, Statement No. 53. Includes Class I, Class II, and Class III steam railways, except where otherwise noted, and from 1890 to 1907 includes also switching and terminal companies.

(b) Covers only mortgage bonds, 1890 to 1906, inclusive.

(c) Amounts outstanding in the hands of the public, excluding railways' holdings of each others' securities.

per cent.[33] In other words railway credit was relatively high in the first decade of the century and the railways could in general easily raise additional capital by the sale of stock for cash. Funded debt was of course also increasing, having nearly doubled between 1900 and 1910,[34] but it kept on rising through the whole subsequent period to a figure nearly 40 per cent greater in 1931 than in 1910.

This growing discrepancy between the respective roles of share capital and borrowed funds during the period following 1910 is one of the

[33] The comparison has been confined to common stock for the reason that preferred stock issues have arisen very largely as an incident to railway reorganizations rather than as a means of attracting new investment capital. See Chart 12, p. 110. It might also be added that no small part of the increase in common stock outstanding in more recent years is accounted for by the conversion of bonds rather than the sale of stock for cash.

[34] The figures are: $5,645 million in 1900 and $10,303 million in 1910. See Table 32, p. 96, and Chart 12, p. 110.

TABLE 36—*Continued*

RELATIONSHIP OF RAILWAY FUNDED DEBT TO TOTAL RAILWAY CAPITALIZATION(*a*)
1910–1931

Year	(1) Total Railway Capital Outstanding(*b*)	(2) Net Railway Capitalization (*c*)	(3) Funded Debt Outstanding (*b*)	(4) Railway Bonds Owned by Railways	(5) Net Railway Funded Debt (*c*)	(6) —Ratio— Col. 3 to Col. 1 Per Cent	(7) Col. 5 to Col. 2 Per Cent
			Millions of Dollars				
1910	$18,417	$14,376	$10,303	$1,486	$8,817	56.0	61.3
11	19,209	15,044	10,738	1,569	9,169	55.7	60.9
12	19,753	15,126	11,130	1,801	9,329	56.2	61.7
13(*d*)	19,796	15,366	11,186	1,660	9,526	56.5	62.0
14(*d*)	20,247	15,759	11,567	1,849	9,718	57.6	61.7
1915	21,128	16,308	12,133	1,951	10,182	57.5	62.4
16	21,092	16,336	12,033	2,012	10,021	57.0	61.3
16	21,049	16,333	12,000	2,084	9,916	57.0	60.7
17	21,249	16,402	11,947	2,128	9,819	56.2	59.9
18	20,785	16,454	11,730	2,008	9,722	56.5	59.1
19	20,950	16,550	11,859	2,086	9,773	56.6	59.1
1920	21,891	16,994	12,778	2,490	10,288	58.2	60.5
21	22,292	17,083	13,216	2,807	10,409	59.2	60.9
22	22,290	17,280	13,149	2,621	10,528	59.0	60.9
23	22,839	17,810	13,589	2,626	10,963	59.4	61.6
24	23,636	18,202	14,162	2,766	11,396	59.8	62.6
1925	23,644	18,191	14,105	2,800	11,305	59.6	62.1
26	23,677	18,234	14,192	2,788	11,404	59.8	62.5
27	23,614	18,137	13,952	2,571	11,381	59.0	62.8
28	23,747	18,511	13,904	2,477	11,427	58.7	61.7
29	23,983	18,680	14,065	2,598	11,467	58.6	61.4
1930	24,331	19,066	14,249	2,369	11,880	58.6	62.3
31	24,344	18,941	14,264	2,434	11,830	58.6	62.5

(*a*) Compiled from Interstate Commerce Commission, *Statistics of Railways in the United States*, 1931; Statement No. 53. Includes Class I, Class II, and Class III steam railways and their lessors, and excludes switching and terminal companies unless otherwise noted. For 1910 to 1916 the data are for fiscal years ending June 30; for 1916 to 1931 for calendar years.

(*b*) The figures in these columns include actually outstanding, nominally issued, and nominally outstanding securities. The figures for actually outstanding total capital, and actually outstanding funded debt, at the end of 1931, were: $22,747,228,619 and $12,738,815,233, respectively, indicating a ratio of debt of 56.1 per cent. See *Statistics of Railways in the United States*, 1931; Statement No. 17.

(*c*) Amounts outstanding in the hands of the public, excluding railways' holdings of each others' securities.

(*d*) Class I and Class II railways and their non-operating subsidiaries.

outstanding features of contemporary railway finance. It rests fundamentally upon the relative unattractiveness of railway equities as compared with other types of equity investments, and reflects the increasing handicaps with which railway share ownership has had to contend in recent years in comparison with the situation during the first decade of the century. The favorable trend in the ratio of net income to stockholders' equity which had characterized that decade was abruptly reversed after 1910 and experienced a sharp decline during the eleven years ending with 1921. While there was some improvement during the twenties, the average return for the eight years, 1922 to 1929, was below 8 per cent as contrasted with nearly 10 per cent for the eight years culminating in 1910.

It is this relatively unfavorable showing from the stockholders' standpoint and the remoteness or complete absence of any speculative appeal resulting from the profit stimulus that has forced the railways increasingly to resort to the practice of financing their current capital requirements by borrowing.[35] That this is a highly dangerous policy the events of the past two or three years have made abundantly clear. The steady and persistent growth of funded debt with its resultant burden of interest charges, approaching $600 million annually in recent years, constitutes a serious threat to railway solvency at times when current revenues are sharply curtailed. The very fact that the margin between operating revenues and operating expenses plus taxes is so narrow prevents the setting up of adequate reserves to equalize the results of good years and poor years. The situation is doubly complicated by the necessity of meeting maturities of funded obligations which fall due in good times and bad times alike. It may well be questioned whether any business carrying a volume of debt substantially in excess of its owners' equity can hope to be permanently successful unless it enjoys some monopoly privilege or is in a position to benefit from a rapidly increasing public demand for its product or service.

Historic Basis of American Railway Financial Policy

It is this latter qualification, perhaps, which supplies the clue to American railway financial policy and gives it a certain measure of justification. Railway management in this country has traditionally looked to the growth of the country to validate the investment in railway facilities. There is no need to call attention to the obvious cases of constructing railway lines too far in advance of any demonstrated or even probable economic need for them, or of competitive overbuilding by rival railway managements or financial promoters. Aside from such

[35] (or by requiring the stockholder to forego dividends through the practice of reinvesting current surplus earnings *in the property* rather than in forms readily available for conversion into dividends at the inevitable "rainy day.")

instances of imprudent or even reckless investment, which were all too numerous, it is not too much to say that railway funded debt has in many cases been expanded out of all relation to stockholders' investment, in the frank expectation that the growth of the territory served would ultimately validate the bonds and even make the total investment good. It is such reasoning as this which explains and attempts to justify the policy of not retiring railway bonds when they fall due but of refunding them, virtually perpetuating the debt regardless of changes which may have occurred in the meantime. So long as the region or industries served continued to grow and the need for railway services continued to increase, the policy was not indeed, in general, an unwise one. It was predicated, in short, on the assumption that the railway industry or the railroad in question was an expanding, "adolescent" industry or enterprise.

Once the stage of economic maturity is reached, however, or the railway begins to lose any significant part of the public patronage upon which its continued success depends, the situation as to what constitutes a sound capital structure becomes radically different. It may be suspected that many railway managements, bankers, investors and others, have failed adequately to consider the changing fortunes of the railway industry in the light of recent economic changes and have continued to act on the assumption that the procedures appropriate to a stage of industrial development and expansion are equally suitable to a stage of relatively settled maturity. It is high time that this entire situation be examined from the standpoint of *what is* the really sound policy in view of the rapidly changing status of the railway industry in the economic and social life of the country.

(d) ADJUSTMENT OF DEBT AND INTEREST CHARGES TO RAILWAY EARNING POWER

Whatever the wisdom or unwisdom of railway financial policies in the past, the practical question which confronts railway managements, their bankers, the investing public, and the national treasury at the present moment, is to determine what amount of debt and fixed interest charges can safely be carried by the individual roads in view of the current and future outlook for railway earnings. It is becoming increasingly evident that the temporary and makeshift policy of capitalizing deficits through loans from the Reconstruction Finance Corporation or the Railroad Credit Corporation cannot be continued indefinitely. Some rational plan must be adopted which will discriminate more effectively between the ultimately sound and the hopelessly insolvent cases than the policy of drift and hope which has marked the past year of governmental "assistance" to needy railroads. It should also be apparent that in the formulation of any such plan the watchword must be *flexibility*. No single rule or formula can be laid down which is equally applicable, without more or less modification in detail, to the scores of individual situations. Vague generalizations as to horizontal scaling down of fixed charges are especially to be avoided. Each railway has its own specific problem which may differ in material respects from those of others. Such individual cases require individual prescriptions. The type of remedy appropriate to one situation is often not suitable or effective in another. Within the general policy of adjusting the burden of fixed charges to the reasonable expectancy of earning power of the individual road there must be a considerable margin of flexibility in detail.

Revision of Operating Methods

This proposal is not intended to beg the whole question of the relation of interest charges to railway revenues. It is not suggested for a moment that interest charges are to be regarded as the only flexible element in the situation, or that the apparent need for an adjustment of interest charges, with or without a scaling down of debt, is put forward as a shield behind which railway management is to be relieved of the responsibility and necessity of reducing operating costs. The relation of interest charges to operating revenues is not, on the whole, an unsound one; as a matter of fact it has been rather consistently improving, regarding the railways as an aggregate, over the whole period from 1894 to 1929.[36] The crux of the problem lies rather in the unsound relation of operating expenses and taxes to revenues, with a consequent declining ratio of net railway operating income in relation to total earnings. It is this relatively smaller net operating income, out of which funded debt charges must come before anything is left for the stockholder, which gives to fixed charges their apparently dominating importance in the financial picture.

[36] See Charts 14 and 15, pp. 112 and 124.

It would be a serious mistake, in other words, to fasten attention exclusively upon the "burden of fixed charges" and thus disregard the need for putting pressure upon railway management to reduce operating costs. This does not necessarily mean wage cuts, undermaintenance, or other ways of economizing which may be of doubtful advantage in the end. It does mean the most critical scrutiny of current methods of conducting the railway business, however, and the ruthless elimination of certain competitive practices which are eating the substance of the railway security owner and subjecting the general public to unnecessarily high costs and charges for railway service.

Fortunately, in this respect, the railway stockholder and the general public have a common interest and should be able to exert a concerted pressure, which need not be directed against the bondholder's interest as such. The bondholder is as vitally interested in the ability of the railways to cover their fixed charges with a reasonable margin of safety as the stockholder is concerned to receive dividends. Otherwise his investment remains essentially precarious and is exposed to the hazards of default and forced reorganization whenever net operating income falls below a certain minimum relation to fixed charges. All parties concerned, in other words, have a mutuality of interest, not a set of separate and opposing interests.

The Public Interest in Railway Finance

The general public interest in securing its necessary railway services at the basic minimum of cost consistent with the maintenance of an efficient and adequate transportation system is powerfully reenforced at the present moment by the circumstance that some $300 million of public funds, more or less, have been advanced to necessitous railroads during the past year under the urgent plea of preventing an epidemic of railway receiverships which might have seriously unsettled the whole financial structure of the country. It is now beginning to be realized that this policy was adopted a bit too precipitately, perhaps, or at least entered upon without sufficient thought being given to its implications. The requirement of more rigorous qualifying conditions as to past record and future prospects might have drawn the line more sharply between the roads to be helped and those denied help.[37] In the case of

---

[37] The Railroad Credit Corporation, it may be remembered, did not undertake to assist roads already in receivership or those whose insolvency would not be prevented by the temporary expedient of a loan. See above, p. 103.

at least one important carrier receivership was not avoided, in fact, even after the grant of a substantial advance, which itself was conditioned upon the requirement by the Interstate Commerce Commission that the road in question scale down its burden of fixed charges.[38] It might have been better, perhaps, to have acknowledged the fact, at the outset, that certain railways were hopelessly involved by unsound capital structures and maturing obligations, and to have frankly permitted these roads to go through the purging process of receivership and reorganization.

Disadvantages of Receiverships

Receiverships under present legal conditions, however, are not well adapted to public service operations. As the Interstate Commerce Commission very aptly puts the situation in its *Annual Report* for 1932:

" . . . The process not only makes the continuation of adequate service difficult, but imposes on the public and the security holders losses and expenses which frequently are very burdensome and should be unnecessary. The receivership of a railroad corporation ordinarily extends over a period of years, and in most cases results in the foreclosure of mortgages and sale of the property. Seldom is such a sale one in the ordinary sense. It usually consists of bidding in by a committee representing some class or classes of security holders with a view to reorganization. The reorganization normally consists of the acceptance by security holders of new securities in the property. To arrange reorganization, managers, usually banking concerns, are employed at large expense. Committees representing various classes of security holders are created to represent particular interests in the property. Counsel for such committees, counsel for the reorganization managers, counsel for the receivers, counsel for trustees, trustees, the receivers themselves, and other officials, have to be paid out of the property or at the expense of the security holders. In many cases members of the various committees also require payment out of the assets available. Litigation between interests claiming priorities of one sort or another is widespread and expensive. It, too, is usually made a charge on the property."

"The result is," the Commission continues, "that security holders are deprived of a return on their investments for varying periods that may, and usually do, extend into years. Much of the delay, expense, and difficulty involved in a receivership and reorganization is due to the opportunity afforded, under our present laws, for a minority, no matter how small, to make trouble without regard to the interests of the property as a whole."[39]

[38] The St. Louis-San Francisco Railway. The Missouri Pacific Railroad, after receiving several advances of public funds, aggregating $23,134,800 declared itself insolvent in April, 1933.
[39] *46th Annual Report,* Interstate Commerce Commission, 1932; pp. 15–16.

New Reorganization Procedure

It was primarily to correct this unsatisfactory legal situation that an entirely new procedure was incorporated in the revised Federal Bankruptcy Act providing for railway reorganization without receivership.[40] The new act clothes the Interstate Commerce Commission with large powers designed to prevent or control some of the practices just enumerated and promises to expedite materially the procedure of reorganization and to reduce its cost. Whether it will be as effective, however, as its sponsors hope, in protecting more adequately the equities of the different classes of investors in railway securities is questioned by some students of finance. If it should, as these observers fear, result in merely aggravating and perpetuating some of the inequities involved in the present system, the consequences could not fail to be hurtful to railway credit through their destructive effect upon the confidence of investors in the good faith of the indentures supposed to be drawn for their protection. Further comment is perhaps better deferred until the working of the revised procedure has been put to actual test. At the present writing some half dozen railroads have signified their intention of taking advantage of its provisions in order to effect a reorganization of their financial structure.[41]

Whatever the ultimate outcome of individual reorganizations in effecting a redistribution of railway earnings as between the different equity holders, the basic problem remains one of improving the earning power of the really permanent and solvent roads so that a larger fraction of operating revenues can be carried to net operating income. It cannot be too strongly emphasized that it is only from such enhancement in earning power that any permanent or lasting improvement can be expected in the position of either the bondholder or the stockholder. Lacking such improvement, most of the weaker roads will drift inevitably into government ownership, or will have to undergo reorganization at the cost of excessive sacrifices by security holders, without any real prospect of remedying the fundamental economic weakness in the situation of the roads.

[40] H.R. 14,359, Section 77. *Reorganization of Railroads Engaged in Interstate Commerce.* Public No. 420, 72nd Congress. Approved, March 3, 1933.

[41] An excellent discussion of railway reorganization procedure, both critical and constructive, by Dr. C. O. Hardy, will be found in *The American Transportation Problem,* H. G. Moulton and Associates (1933), pp. 321–360.

Conclusions as to Reduction of Debt Charges Necessarily Tentative

To the question how far the present debt burden of the railways needs to be scaled down in order to restore a sound relationship between current prices, earnings, and fixed charges, no certain answer can be given. The preceding discussion has pointed out that it is exceedingly unsafe to generalize on this question; each situation is a problem in itself, and general statements are likely to be misleading and positively harmful. Furthermore, so many elements enter into the question, and their relative importance varies so greatly from one situation to another and from time to time, that conclusions necessarily have to be tentative and contingent. *Much* depends upon the relative improvement in general business and volume of traffic, upon the degree of success of the railways in securing their "normal" share of a general increase in volume of freight haulage, upon the level of rates and charges on which that volume is handled, upon the basic level of wages and other costs of operation, upon the weight of taxes, national and local, upon the vigor with which railway managements attack the problem of competitive wastes, duplication of services, and uneconomic practices, and their relative success in reducing them; to say nothing of such fundamental questions as the possibility of large economies in operation which might reasonably be expected to follow from a policy of enforced regional consolidation, as contrasted with the present vague and tentative steps towards system "unification" based upon the ideal of maintaining the full force and effect of traditional methods of competition. The range and variety of forces that influence the net outcome are so numerous and their incidence so uncertain, as to make exceedingly hazardous any attempt to estimate the weight of fixed charges appropriate to the railway industry under present conditions.

(e) PREREQUISITES FOR RECOVERY OF RAILWAY CREDIT

The question, then, of the ability of the railways as a whole, or of individual roads, to sustain any given volume of funded debt and of fixed interest charges, goes back to the basic issue of revenues and expenses. Stated thus baldly, the proposition smacks of a truism. The essential points to bear in mind, however, are: (1) that railway revenues can be expected to return to "normal" only with a return of general business to a normal level, whatever that may be; and (2) that out of such normal revenues the railways must, through increased efficiency of operation and the reduction of competitive wastes save a larger fraction for the respective equities represented in railway capital investment than they have done in recent years. These two theses call for brief discussion which, incidentally, may serve to show how intimately they are associated.

Competition in Transportation and Changing Business Methods

Lasting improvement in railway revenues will depend not only upon basic recovery in national and international economic activity, but is likely to be increasingly influenced by the rapidly changing methods of doing business which have become a matter of common observation during the last decade. Those changes can be summed up in the statement that American business is to a considerable degree changing from a wholesale to a retail basis. As a consequence the public generally has relatively less need than at an earlier stage of economic development for the wholesale type of transportation service, and that is what American railroads essentially provide. Over the past 16 or 17 years there has occurred a very definite slackening in the rate of growth of the volume of business which the railroads are called upon to perform.[42] At the same time there has been a corresponding increase in the public use of highway transport based upon the motor vehicle, as well as an extraordinary development of pipe-line transportation of petroleum products and natural gas, and an increasingly wide distribution of electric power from modern central stations by long-distance transmission lines. All of these tend to reduce the need for railway transport. As the Interstate Commerce Commission pointed out in its report on "Coordination of Motor Transportation" in 1931:

"The motor truck has been one of the greatest contributing factors to these changes. There is now large distribution of products by manufacturers direct to retailers and jobbers. Merchants now hold inventories at a minimum as stocks can be quickly replenished by motor truck—in many instances over night. The rapid expansion of chain store systems has been made possible to a large extent by the motor truck. Small towns, even though provided with rail facilities, now obtain a considerable portion of goods for retail distribution by motor truck service from jobbing centers. Retail dealers are able to operate with smaller stocks of goods. The amount of capital invested is less

[42] See Chart 15.

CHART 15

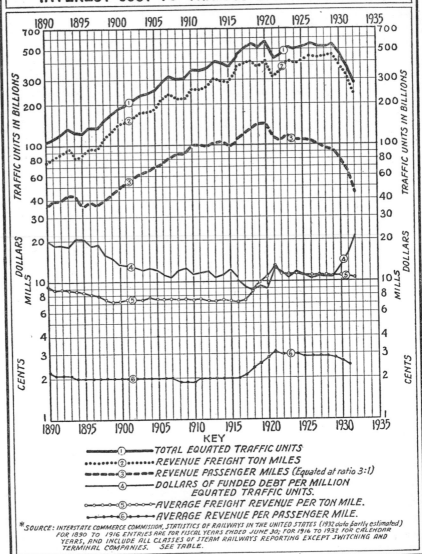

VOLUME OF TRAFFIC. AVERAGE FREIGHT AND
PASSENGER UNIT REVENUE. AND RATIO OF
INTEREST COST TO TRAFFIC UNITS. 1890-1932*

KEY

①————TOTAL EQUATED TRAFFIC UNITS.
②••••••REVENUE FREIGHT TON MILES
③——REVENUE PASSENGER MILES (Equated at ratio 3:1)
④————DOLLARS OF FUNDED DEBT PER MILLION
           EQUATED TRAFFIC UNITS.
⑤—○—○—AVERAGE FREIGHT REVENUE PER TON MILE.
⑥•—•—•AVERAGE REVENUE PER PASSENGER MILE.

*SOURCE: INTERSTATE COMMERCE COMMISSION, STATISTICS OF RAILWAYS IN THE UNITED STATES (1932 data partly estimated)
FOR 1890 TO 1916 ENTRIES ARE FOR FISCAL YEARS ENDED JUNE 30; FOR 1916 TO 1932 FOR CALENDAR
YEARS, AND INCLUDE ALL CLASSES OF STEAM RAILWAYS REPORTING EXCEPT SWITCHING AND
TERMINAL COMPANIES. SEE TABLE.

and consumers are provided with fresher goods. In the past two or three years trucks have made decided inroads into railroad carload traffic.[43]

While the fraction of the nation's freight haulage represented by motor trucks was estimated by the Commission to be only 6 per cent of the total in 1929, there are indications that it has increased materially during the past two or three years. This was perhaps to have been expected as an incident to the current economic depression. As the Commission said in October, 1931, in disposing of the application of the railroads for a general 15 per cent advance in freight rates:

"Movement by truck is a new form of competition which has been developing with great rapidity. It has been principally effective on a less-than-carload traffic, and relatively short hauls of such commodities as livestock, cotton, cement, sand and gravel, gasoline, fruits and vegetables, and general merchandise; but it is continually extending to more and more traffic, and for longer distances, as trucks and trailers are enlarged and highways improved. At present it is aided by prevailing low prices for gasoline and rubber and the oversupply of labor. In addition to rates, advantages which it offers to the shipper are in rapid and flexible service, store-door receipt and delivery, the transportation at carload rates of much smaller lots than are possible by railroad, and elimination of costly railroad packing requirements. The carriers introduced evidence to show that it would be feasible for the trucks to divert only a comparatively small amount of additional tonnage, even if rates were increased. But without exaggerating the menace of this form of competition, we are convinced that the carriers have under-rated it, and that its possibilities are materially greater than they are prepared to concede." [44]

Need of Clearer Public Policies for a Balanced Transport System

Whatever the ultimate outcome of railway and motor vehicle competition, it is evident that the very fact of this competition, and more particularly the general lack of any clearly defined public policies with respect to determining the rules or "umpiring" the game, leaves the whole question of the future of railway traffic very much in the air. It would obviously be impracticable to hazard any estimate as to the probable future volume of railway freight traffic and revenues until there has been some clarification, at least, of public policies with respect both to motor vehicle freight transportation and to railway regulation. At the present moment public policies are highly uncertain in both fields,

[43] Interstate Commerce Commission, No. 23,400, *Coordination of Motor Transportation*, 182 I.C.C., 263
[44] *Fifteen Per Cent Case, 1931, Ex Parte No. 103;* 178 I.C.C. 539; p. 574.

with some indication perhaps of a tendency to bring highway commercial transport under somewhat more strict regulation and control, and to relax somewhat the rigidity of administrative control over railway rates and traffic practices. Whether the efforts of the national administration to effect a better integration of transport agencies through the establishment of a federal "coordinator" will result in a real clarification of public policies, it is, of course, too early to predict.

Rate Reductions Necessary for Permanent Railway Stability

Basic to any relative gain by the railways as against their highway competitor in the struggle for public patronage is the necessity of constant adjustment of freight and passenger rates downward to conform to the movement of the general price level. In this respect the railways appear to be standing in their own light. Railway freight and passenger rates are well above pre-war levels, while the whole structure of commodity prices is substantially back to the 1913 basis. It may well be doubted whether the railways can expect to attract much competitive traffic until they are prepared to make some concessions in rates. The time-honored inducement to buy is price, and while reductions in freight rates might not be immediately effective in stimulating business recovery, they would at least afford relief at an important point and might well help pave the way for a general improvement in business. It is significant in this connection to note that the Commission remarks in its last annual report that to a considerable extent the railroads were unable to maintain the emergency rates of 1931 at even the slightly increased level which the Commission had approved. Indeed, as the Commission goes on to point out, "In recent months there has been a veritable flood of such reductions," [45] which were made necessary chiefly by motor truck or water carrier competition. All of which would seem to point to the obvious moral that the railways must be prepared to bring their basic rates and charges into line with the fundamental changes which have occurred in the general level of prices and wages. Certainly there appears to be little basis for belief that any significant improvement in railway credit is to be expected from a policy of pressing for higher rates.

Internal and External Economies

Not only must the railroads adjust their rates and services to an increasingly critical and sensitive public demand which can pick and

[45] *46th Annual Report,* Interstate Commerce Commission, 1932, p. 10.

choose between rival agencies of transportation, but if they are to achieve permanent solvency they will have to effect major economies in operating methods. They cannot hope to enlist the permanent support of any widespread or substantial stockholder interest and thus save themselves from becoming a charge on the public revenues, to be operated as job-providing agencies, unless they can save a larger fraction of their gross revenues for "net" than they have done in recent years. At no time during the last decade has the ratio of net railway operating income to operating revenues approximated the levels of the first decade of the century when railway credit stood high. The relation of interest charges to operating revenues, on the other hand, has rather consistently improved, taking the roads as a whole, over the entire period from 1893 to 1929. It cannot be fairly maintained, therefore, that the relatively low proportion of operating revenues remaining for stockholders' equity, averaging about 11 per cent during the decade 1921–1930 as against about 18 per cent for the years 1901–1910, is something for which the burden of interest charges can, *per se,* be held responsible.[46] The effective causes explaining this marked difference must be sought elsewhere.

Where, then, does the responsibility lie? Some observers point to taxes, some to the rigidity of railway wages, some to the high costs of excessive railway competition. Each of these factors has an obvious bearing on the problem, and all alike should be brought under the most critical scrutiny. There are certain essential differences between them, however, which should be pointed out, since they are not all equally susceptible to control by those who are responsible for railway management policies.

Taxes, obviously, are practically outside the domain of management control. They are imposed by external authority and their amount depends primarily upon the exigencies of public finance, with little regard, at least in the local jurisdictions, to the current profitableness of the railway enterprise. Of much the same nature are the so-called "unproductive" expenditures which are necessitated by public requirements for safety and service, such as outlays for the protection or elimination of grade crossings, certain types of signaling, "full crew" laws, the expenses incident to filing of tariffs, accounting and statistical reports, etc.

Wages, while not as inflexible as taxes, are likewise substantially beyond the control of railway management, although there is a consid-

[46] See Charts 13 and 14, pp. 111 and 112.

erable zone within which wage rates are subject to negotiation. Fundamentally, however, the wages of railway labor are responsive to broad movements in the general price level and to the pervasive influence of changes in the cost of living. The great bulk of the railway employees are compactly organized into a relatively small number of inclusive nation-wide unions or "brotherhoods." This fact, and their relatively large numbers—upwards of a million individuals—together with the essential nature of railway service to the public, gives them a bargaining power and a political influence beyond that of any other large group of wage earners in American industry. As a practical matter these conditions have to be accepted by railway management and dealt with as part and parcel of the general enonomic situation.

Quite different, however, is the situation with respect to the basic principles of internal railway organization and operation, and with respect to competitive railway policies and practices. These are matters peculiarly within the competence and control of railway management and in this field management should be held responsible for results, not only from the standpoint of private business administration but also from the standpoint of adequate public service at reasonable rates.

The Balance Sheet of Railway Management

What, then, is to be said for the basic efficiency of American railway management in the discharge of these peculiarly managerial functions? An appraisal of the degree of its success or failure in this field may supply the essential perspective from which to view the problem of railway debt in its larger aspects and perhaps indicate the direction where permanent improvement must be sought. Obviously, no more than a hasty summary can be attempted here and the following comments are offered with full appreciation of their limited and partial character.

Full credit must be given, in the first place, to the noteworthy record for steadily increasing operating efficiency established by American railway management during the decade following the return of the roads to private management in 1920. Huge sums were spent upon improvements in the railway physical plant, both in roadway and structures and in equipment. The gross capital expenditures of the Class I railways for these purposes in the ten years ending in 1931 aggregated over seven and one-half billion dollars.[47] These outlays have been made for the de-

[47] Statement by Dr. J. H. Parmelee, Director, Bureau of Railway Economics, relating to railway pensions, before sub-committee of the Senate Interstate Commerce Committee, Jan. 10, 1933.

velopment of yards and terminals, multiple tracking, installation of larger and more powerful equipment, heavier rail and ballast, drainage, strengthening of bridges, enlargement of tunnels, track elevation and elimination of grade crossings, electrification, improved signaling, and the like. The benefits of this enormous new capital investment have been reflected in the complete elimination of the car shortages with which the shipping public formerly had to contend, and in steadily higher standards of railway service. It has also contributed materially to the reduction of the railway "operating ratio," that is, the relation between operating expenses and operating revenues, from a peak figure of 94.4 per cent in 1920 to 71.8 per cent in 1929.[48]

Granting the fullest measure of credit, however, for these splendid results in the details of service and in the physical efficiency of mechanical operation, there remains a large area in which the results are not so impressive. This area concerns more particularly the relationships of the railways to the general public and to each other, as contrasted with the more restricted field of internal organization and administration. Here is involved the whole range of controversial subjects included under the designation "competitive wastes." Unnecessary duplication of facilities and services, needlessly expensive freight and passenger terminals, competitive solicitation of traffic, circuitous haulage of freight in order to secure the greater fraction of the joint rate that goes to the road performing the long haul, the maintenance of thousands of miles of thin traffic branch lines of doubtful value to the parent road, the unnecessary and wasteful hauling of empty freight cars beyond any conceivable justification in order to avoid *"per diem"* charges or to earn them at the expense of other roads—all these are instances of the sort of thing which collectively go far to explain why the ratio of net railway operating income to operating revenues falls so far short of what the public has a right to expect.[49]

There is no use to talk about "scaling down" funded debt and fixed charges while these traditional methods of conducting the nation's railway service are allowed to go unchallenged. It is suggested that so long as this "legacy from the past" is permitted to dominate the thinking and the policies of the men who run the railroads, there can be no permanent relief from a burden of rates and charges utterly out of line with the general price level. Nor, for that matter, can anything more

---

[48] See Chart 13, p. 111.
[49] See, for example, *Ex Parte No 109, Duplication of Produce Terminals*, 188 I.C.C., 323, October 11, 1932.

than a temporary respite be gained from any scheme of scaling down fixed charges unless it is backed up with positive action for real economy. Standing alone, it would merely widen, for a time, the range within which this type of competition could continue, until the process of attrition resulted in another crisis, with a renewed demand for "scaling down" capital charges, at the expense of the investors who supply the funds.

Potential Economies

Not even an approximate estimate can be made by anyone not intimately familiar with the details of railway administration as to the potential savings which might accrue from the elimination or reduction of the kinds of competitive wastes just enumerated. No less an authority, however, than Mr. L. F. Loree, president of the Delaware & Hudson Railroad Corporation, testified before the Senate Finance Committee on February 18, 1933, to the effect that about $400 million a year could be saved by reduction of unnecessary passenger service alone. Mr. Loree also urged the elimination of duplicating and obsolete facilities and thin traffic branch lines as a means of preventing unwarranted drains on railway revenues.[50]

2. RECOMMENDATIONS

Measures proposed for the correction or relief of the railroad debt problem fall into two general classes: (1) those aimed to relieve the immediately existing situation, and (2) those looking to the more distant future. While it is impracticable to draw any hard-and-fast line of demarcation between these two aspects of the problem, since so large a proportion of railroad debt is of long standing and has a relatively distant maturity, something may be gained by differentiating them in the following discussion.

Proposals for Meeting the Existing Emergency

The activities of the Railroad Credit Corporation and of the Reconstruction Finance Corporation in assisting distressed railways have already been indicated.[51] The extension of new loans by the former of

[50] Associated Press dispatch, Washington, Feb. 18, 1933.
[51] See pp. 104–105, above.

these agencies is to cease after May 31, 1933, and its further activities will be confined to the collection and liquidation of loans outstanding after that date. The national government, which has now advanced the railroads some $300 million through the Reconstruction Finance Corporation,[52] must soon face the question as to how much further the current policy of emergency assistance to railways in the general interest of preventing receiverships is to be carried. The urgency of need for such aid in order to avoid the necessity of financial reorganization has been relaxed by the enactment of the revised bankruptcy statute permitting a greatly simplified procedure of railway reorganization without the expense and delay of receivership.[53] Extensive reorganizations might result in a considerable scaling down of fixed charges, and thus enable certain water-logged roads to carry on after a period of government assistance, pending a general revival of business activity. The chief obstacle, from the standpoint of equity to all concerned, is the practical difficulty of determining a fair basis of recapitalization during a period of depressed earnings and low business activity. Current revenues will not support the debt structure of more than a handful of roads. On the other hand there are obvious limits to the indefinite continuance of a policy of capitalizing deficits, nor should the government be called upon to make good for all and sundry such deficits in current earnings in order that bondholders may continue to receive their income unimpaired.

What is needed is agreement upon the fundamentals of a sound national policy, and the establishment of certain basic criteria which can be applied by some administrative tribunal, such as the Interstate Commerce Commission, to each individual railway. The distressed roads come before that tribunal automatically, whether seeking assistance from the government or from outside agencies. The very fact that the national government's hand is already so deep in the pockets of these carriers gives it a strategic power to dictate terms and to insist as a matter of common decency that they get their houses in order. It is greatly to be hoped that at least the elements of a general solution can be formulated by the Administration and Congress before the situation becomes much worse. Existing policies are not adequate, even regarded from a

[52] Up to April 22, 1933, cash advances to railroads by the Reconstruction Finance Corporation were $335,809,572, and repayments were $20,278,174 (Press release, *A.P.* April 30, 1933).

[53] See p. 121 above.

purely "emergency" viewpoint, and the critical condition into which the finances of many railroads are rapidly drifting indicates the imperative need of a basic overhauling of the situation, not merely in its financial aspects, but also from the broader standpoint of maintaining an adequate national transportation system.[54]

Defaults, Loans, and Receiverships

In order to help visualize the magnitude of the problem, it may be well to point out that the aggregate of railway bonds and notes in default of interest or principal increased by $363 million during the two years, 1931 and 1932, to approximately $424 million on January 1 of this year.[55] By April 15, the figure had risen to $818 million; since that date there has been a further substantial increase. Advances by the Railroad Credit Corporation and the Reconstruction Finance Corporation during 1932 in order to meet interest charges were approximately $120 million.[56] At an assumed average interest rate of $4\frac{1}{2}$ per cent, this latter figure would indicate a total of approximately $2,700 million additional which were saved from default. A total, therefore, of somewhere around $3 to $3\frac{1}{2}$ billion, or, say, between 20 and 25 per cent of the total outstanding funded issues of American railways at the present time are either in default, or saved therefrom by the emergency aid of the credit arrangements established in part for that specific purpose.

In addition to eleven Class I railways in receivership at the beginning of this year, there are about as many others whose plight is so desperate that it is scarcely to be expected that they can survive another twelve months without seeking similar relief or undergoing a drastic reorganization of their capital structures. Most of these latter roads are hopelessly involved and could probably not be saved from the inevitable scaling down of fixed charges even with the utmost conceivable upswing of traffic and earnings. Practically all of them had to be helped by the Reconstruction Finance Corporation in meeting their fixed interest charges in 1932 and most of them in meeting their bond or equipment trust maturities; some even had to borrow in order to pay taxes and current operating expenses. Their total income before fixed charges

[54] See below, page 136 ff.
[55] As compiled by Dow, Jones & Co., Inc.
[56] See above, p. 105.

in 1932 was about $34 million against fixed charges amounting to $102 million. Against this somber background of last year's results these dozen carriers have to look forward to some $66 million of funded obligations falling due in 1933.[57]

Bond Maturities, 1933–1936

The total volume of bonds of various kinds and equipment obligations of the Class I railways falling due over the next four years, from 1933 to 1936, aggregates approximately one and one-quarter billion dollars, or nearly one-eighth of their total outstanding long-term debt. Here is revealed one of the fundamental weaknesses of the traditional method of financing preponderantly through borrowing, namely, the danger to which such financing exposes the borrower when a large volume of maturities falls due at a time inconvenient to repay or refund. It is this precariousness of the position, as much as a high proportion of fixed charges, that constitutes a major hazard, both to the borrower and to the lender. Should default occur in meeting such maturities, receivership, with its attendant sacrifices all around, is the almost inevitable result.[58] The maturities to be met in 1933 and 1934 aggregate about $666 million, indicating a rate nearly $90 million in excess of the ten-year average over the period, 1931–1940.

Security of the Existing Railway Debt

It would scarcely be worth while to attempt an estimate of the total amount of railway debt whose security is above suspicion or to guess at the proportion which is inadequately secured, since the situation is so rapidly changing and is subject to so many diverse influences. The facts just cited give some general indication of the gravity of the situation. In order to preserve a balanced perspective, however, it should be noted that relatively few of the *underlying* liens are likely to be defaulted under any conceivable debacle of railway revenues. It is primarily these underlying liens that constitute the investments of fiduciary institutions, such as savings banks and insurance companies. Much the greater part of *these* investments are amply secured, since they represent

[57] The Missouri Pacific Railroad placed itself in the hands of the federal court at the end of March, 1933, owing to its inability to meet fixed interest charges and maturing funded obligations.
[58] See Editorial Research Reports, *Railroad Receiverships and Reorganizations* (Edward T. Paxton), Vol. I, 1933, Number 2, pp. 29–31.

a prior charge on earnings, ranking next after taxes, and against them are pledged the more important traffic lines and terminals of the issuing roads. The equipment issues are also rated high; until the present depression, in fact, there had scarcely ever been a default on an equipment obligation. The weak issues are in general the "junior" bonds, including the so-called overlying and refunding issues, the income bonds, on which interest is contingent on earnings, and the miscellany of debentures, mixed, and "collateral" pledges. It is this complex and heterogeneous mass of issues, ranging all the way from underlying first mortgages to highly contingent income bonds, that constitutes one of the serious problems of American railway finance. It would be well if some of this heritage of flotsam and jetsam from previous mergers, reorganizations, and more or less speculative financing, could be cleaned up once for all.[59]

Value and Yield of Rail Bonds

The sentiment of the market as to the fundamental security of rail bonds in general is best reflected, perhaps, in the aggregate stock market valuation of the 652 issues listed on the New York Stock Exchange. At March 1, 1933, these issues with a total par value of $10,533,743,366 were valued, at their then current quotations, at only $5,762,170,933. The difference between the two figures indicates an average depreciation of more than 45 per cent, which compares with less than 21 per cent for all American listed bonds at that date.[60]

Another way of expressing the market valuation is by means of an index of yields. On this basis representative rail bonds ordinarily rank next to municipals with respect to low yield, and take precedence over the utilities and industrials. This relationship was maintained, for example, over the six and one-half years from 1925 to the middle of 1931, with a general tendency during that period for all classes of bonds, including the rails, to show progressively lower yields, reflecting higher credit. Since about the third quarter of 1931, however, the yield on representative rail bonds has shot upward to a point over 30 per cent above its then level and has lost its preferred position over the utilities.

---

[59] Some idea of the relative deterioration in investment status of railway bonds incident to the current depression may be gained from the fact that in 1926 approximately three-fourths of all the rail bonds listed on the New York Stock Exchange were rated by Moody's Investors Service as "high grade" (i.e. "Aaa" or "Aa"), while in March of 1933 less than 50 per cent qualified for that rating.

[60] *New York Stock Exchange Bulletin*, Vol. IV, No. 3, March, 1933, pp. 8–9.

In June, 1932, indeed, the yield on 15 representative rail bonds, which had varied only slightly from 4½ per cent during the period from 1925 to 1931, reached a figure of 6.83 per cent. Since that date there has been some recovery, but the yield at March 1, 1933, was still nearly 6 per cent.[61]

These figures are for the better grade securities. The relative depreciation of lower grade (not necessarily the lowest grade) rail bonds since 1930 is well illustrated by the chart of bond prices published each week by the *New York Herald Tribune*. Starting from a level above 98 at the beginning of 1931, the average price of five second-grade rail bonds, representative of "junior" or overlying issues, sank to below 50 in December of that year. These bonds fluctuated in 1932 through an average range of more than 30 points and closed the year at about 36. By the end of the first week in May of 1933 they had recovered to above 50.[62] The *Herald Tribune's* ten "high grade" rails exhibited similar, though much less extreme fluctuations, and at the closing prices of May 6, 1933, were quoted at an average price of about 77 as against about 98 at the end of July, 1931, just before the railways and security owners launched their "drive" for a general 15 per cent advance in freight rates.

Conditions of Further Federal Aid

As an indication of a procedure which might prove useful in determining *which* railways should be given further government assistance without the necessity of revamping their capital structure, and *which* should be required to revise their financial set-up, the following suggestions are offered for what they may be worth. They are based on the underlying principle that the maintenance of an adequate national transportation system should not be handicapped by the consideration of keeping alive outmoded and obsolescent lines of railway, or burdened by the necessity of earning returns upon unnecessary and duplicating facilities. There must be a drastic reduction in the total cost of operating the railways, taken as a whole, else there can be no adjustment of railway rates to the changed level of prices and wages, and this latter adjustment is fundamental to any permanent scheme for restoring the

[61] *Ibid.*, p. 12, data based on Standard Statistics Co., Inc. yields.
[62] See Chart, *Price Trend of Bond Averages Since 1931, New York Herald Tribune,* May 8, 1933.

railways to health and sanity. There can be little doubt that with the improvements in operating efficiency that characterized the decade, 1921 to 1930, any volume of traffic which the railways can reasonably expect to secure in the next few years, and probably in the next decade, can be handled economically and efficiently with not to exceed 75 per cent of the mileage and equipment now being maintained. There is no way to cut costs except by resolutely cutting out the things that do not pay and ceasing to spend money on them.

It has been suggested [63] that no permanent improvement in the situation can be expected from a reorganization of railway capital structures, with or without a liberalization of the bankruptcy laws, unless such financial revamping is accompanied by the actual removal of excess railway mileage and the integration of the remaining lines into really efficient systems, coordinating rail and highway transport. The recent report of the National Transportation Committee goes even further and urges as a matter "vital to the public welfare" that railway consolidations should be hastened, by government compulsion, if necessary, with a view to the creation of a single efficient system, rather than maintaining competing systems, for each natural trade area.[64] Whatever the ultimate policy to be followed in this respect, it seems reasonably certain that some railway properties, in certain cases whole lines of railway, must be liquidated before the question of debt reduction has any real significance. The question of capital structure, after all, is one between the railway bondholder and the stockholder, not between the bondholder and the public.[65]

From the public viewpoint, however, as represented by the national government's growing participation in railway finance through the functioning of the Reconstruction Finance Corporation, the present is an opportune moment to scrutinize critically the capital set-up of every railway coming to the government for financial assistance. Under existing law, public funds may not be loaned to railroads or their receivers without securing the approval of the Interstate Commerce Commission. This requirement gives that tribunal a certain amount of bargaining power with respect to compelling temporary revisions in existing capital struc-

[63] By a close student of railway affairs and a former officer of the United States Railroad Administration.
[64] *Report of the National Transportation Committee*, Feb. 13, 1933; p. 11.
[65] See Harold G. Moulton and Associates, *The American Transportation Problem*, 1933, Part III, Chapter XIII, Railroad Capitalization.

tures. Such control promises to be considerably augmented by the provision of the Administration's "Emergency Railroad Transportation
Act" which prohibits the approval of loans unless there is reasonable
prospect that the carrier in question "can without reorganization survive
the existing economic depression and provide for its capital needs thereafter." [66] The adoption of some such restriction would of course put
definite pressure upon necessitous railroads to reorganize their financial
structures under the terms of the recently amended bankruptcy act [67]
providing for reorganization without receivership.

It is a sound rule of railway finance that funded debt should not
be permitted to expand at a more rapid rate, taking one year with another, than the growth of operating revenues. It is suggested that this
principle might well be made one of the "yardsticks" by which to determine whether in individual cases certain carriers have permitted their
funded debt and burden of fixed charges to "run away" from their
reasonable expectancy of business. While no exhaustive survey of the
situation has been made from this point of view, a cursory examination
of railway debt and operating revenues for the ten-year period from
1921 to 1930 indicates that no small proportion of the roads that are
in trouble have in fact permitted their funded debt and fixed charges
to outrun their operating revenues. Instances of unwise investments,
promising enough, perhaps, at the time when they were undertaken,
will occur to anyone who is familiar with the recent financial history
of American railways, particularly among the western and southern
roads, though the eastern "trunk" lines are also not without their glaring
examples. In some cases, it should be said in extenuation, public authority must assume at least some share of responsibility both for encouraging or even requiring, unwise constructions or extensions, and for setting
up uneconomic subsidized competition, notably on some of the interior
waterways, and in the waterborne coastwise traffic.

Another sound principle of railway finance, as exemplified in the various statutory regulations governing the "legality" of railway bonds for
fiduciary investment, is the requirement of a defined minimum coverage
or "margin of safety" by which fixed charges must be earned in order that
a given security may qualify as eligible for investment. The New York
law governing savings bank investments, for example, requires a 50

[66] Emergency Railroad Transportation Act, 1933, Section 13.
[67] See pages 119–121 above.

per cent margin of safety maintained consecutively for five out of six years. It is believed that some such yardstick, more generous to the railroad perhaps, but based upon the same underlying philosophy, might well be applied to the carriers coming to the Reconstruction Finance Corporation for financial assistance. Those roads, in other words, which had been "skating on thin ice" during the years of general business expansion, say from 1923 to 1929—with appropriate modification for individual regions—should as a matter of prudent finance be required to bring their capital structures into line with demonstrated net earning capacity. Such a requirement is appropriate, surely, as a condition for continued public assistance.

It is not suggested that either of these two criteria could be applied literally or without qualification to every instance likely to arise, but they do indicate, at least in a general way, a line of approach to the problem which is believed to promise substantial results in achieving the main objective—economy and efficiency in railway operation through whatever methods are likely to be effective to that end.

(2) *Recommendations for Permanent Debt Policies*

Considerable hardihood may be assumed to characterize anyone who would venture to suggest a permanent program for railway debt at such a time as the present. In view of existing uncertainties as to the nature and degree of economic recovery, the ultimate transportation "set-up" in this country, and indeed the survival of the competitive regime in the field of railway transportation, any suggestions for a permanent policy are necessarily tentative. Frankly recognizing these limitations the following recommendations are offered, more as indicating the general direction in which railway financial policy should aim than as a statement of immediately attainable objectives. They assume the maintenance of substantially the present degree of private ownership and management control, although adaptable to a considerable extension of the principle of direct public intervention in the fields of finance and operation. The basic viewpoint underlying them is that everything possible should be done to reduce outstanding railway debts to a proportion more nearly in accordance with probable net earning power—not at a period of "normal" business activity but at a time of definitely subnormal public demand for railway service.

To this end the following recommendations are offered without further comment:

(1) To the extent that obsolete or unnecessary railway properties are retired, abandoned or withdrawn from public use, they should be written off from the property investment accounts and appropriate reductions made in the funded debts outstanding against these properties.

(2) Definite provision should be made for the amortization of existing railway debt to a proportion not to exceed 50 per cent of total capitalization, including a reasonable capitalization of fixed leases, guaranteed dividends, etc. under supervision of appropriate public authority.

(3) All future issues of railway bonds to provide new capital—i.e. issues other than those for refunding maturing obligations—should carry definite provision for amortization over a period not to exceed the probable economic life and usefulness of the capital assets to be acquired. Refunding issues should be handled in a way similar to that suggested for amortization of existing debt.

(4) Pressure should be exerted, as far as practicable, to require the maintenance of a ratio of at least 50 per cent stockholder interest in the total capitalization of all important railroads, as above (No. 2) defined. Public policies of rate regulation and control of maximum earnings of the railways should be modified to take account of the necessity of attracting a reasonable investment of stockholder funds in railway properties.

Chapter Five

PUBLIC UTILITY DEBTS

SUMMARY

The Facts

THE nation's long-term public utility debts amount to $11.2 billion (1932) exclusive of those of holding companies which add over $2 billion, making a total of about $14 billion (p. 143).

The book value of public utility plant investment (1932) is $25 billion (p. 143).

The long-term debts are, therefore, a little less than one-half the book value of the tangible assets.

Of the various groups of utilities street railways have the highest ratio of debts to plant investment—60 per cent, and telephones the lowest—27 per cent. That of electric companies is 47 per cent (p. 148).

Plant values, however, have been written up far in excess of actual cost investment (p. 148).

The interest charges are $578 million a year as of 1932 compared with net earnings prior to interest charges of $1,333,000,000 (p. 144).

The long-term debts of the electric industry have grown from $1.1 billion in 1912 to $5.8 billion in 1931, but plant values have expanded in almost exact proportion and earnings have kept even with increased interest charges—even since 1929 (p. 149).

The debt of the industry is as well protected today, under existing unreduced rate levels, as it was in 1912 (p. 152).

The condition of electric railways, however, is very different. Their long-term debts increased about 40 per cent 1912–1932, while the book value of their plant decreased 12 per cent. Their interest charges increased 27 per cent, while their net earnings declined 34 per cent (p. 153).

Street railways have suffered through automotive competition and the difficulty in adjusting fares to rising costs after the war (p. 153).

The debt of the industry is in a precarious condition—20 per cent was in actual default at the beginning of 1932—and a large part of its debt will have to be stripped off if street railways are to continue to be an important factor in urban transportation (p. 154).

The long-term debts of the telephone industry are well-secured. The total increased 250 per cent from 1912 to 1932 and interest charges increased 320 per cent. Net earnings, however, grew 375 per cent in the same period and have not been less than three times interest requirements at any time (Table, p. 146).

The debts of the manufactured gas industry also are relatively less well-secured and are large in proportion to plant investment values. The funded debt grew from $661 to $826 million between 1929 and 1932—an increase of 25 per cent, while plant investment expanded only from $861 to $906 million—an increase of 5 per cent; and net earnings grew 3 per cent (from $134 to $138 million) while interest charges increased 13 per cent (from $45 to $51 million). Even for the year 1931, however, net earnings were 2.7 times interest charges (Table, p. 147).

On the whole, except for street railways, the long-term debt of public utility operating companies is well secured from the standpoint of earnings. On the basis of present and prospective conditions most of the companies will be able to bear their interest burdens without serious financial handicap (p. 154).

Market quotations of public utility operating company bonds (except those of street railways) are generally regarded as well secured: gas and electric company bonds average $95 at the current market; those of communication companies, $98, and those of water and central heating concerns, $102; but traction companies' bonds average only $51 (p. 154).

Public utility holding company debt, in striking contrast to that of operating companies, is very poorly secured. An analysis of such securities quoted at the end of 1932 shows that less than one-half of one per cent have the yield of first class investments (5 per cent) while 67 per cent yield over 9 per cent and 11 per cent are in default (pp. 156–58).

The debts of all public utilities should be considered in the light of rate reductions which have not yet been made but are sure to come, unless general prices turn sharply upward (pp. 158–59).

Because rates are regulated by government commissions, however, the processes of which take time, there is a far greater lag between rate changes and the general price level than in competitive business and reductions will not come quickly (pp. 159–60).

If the "reproduction cost" theory of rate-making, which the companies espoused during the period of high prices, were applied today many otherwise sound companies would be insolvent; but the companies are now stressing the "actual cost" theory and commissions are not likely to force rate reductions beyond the limits of solvency (pp. 161–62).

Furthermore, rate reductions, if coupled with reductions in operating costs, would be more likely to bring increased than decreased net earnings, because of large potential untapped volume of sales (p. 162).

Recommendations

There is no general formula which can be applied to adjust those few utility debts—mostly of street railway and holding companies— which are insupportable (p. 165).

With a few holders of a single debt voluntary adjustments are practical, but with large companies like utilities whose debts are widely held, receiverships are unavoidable; but receiverships have no really serious public consequences (pp. 165–66).

Receivership procedure, however, should be simplified (p. 167).

Because of the increasing fluctuations of prices under present economic conditions public utilities should rely for their financing far less on rigid long-term debts, and more upon capital stock issues. Limits should be set to the assumption of further funded debts (p. 168).

Furthermore, if bonds are issued, or previous issues refunded, they should be subjected to systematic amortization as a part of government regulation and by suitable mandatory state legislation (pp. 169–70).

---

1. THE FACTS [1]

THIS chapter is devoted to the long-term or funded debt of public utilities. It sets out the amounts, their relation to total capitalization, to total investment in physical properties, and to the development of the industries. It considers the status of the debt in connection with the present economic depression, business recovery, and the special public problems created by the probable price level under which readjustment will take place. It discusses, particularly, the public aspects and, as far as practicable, formulates a program for future control of public utility debt issues.

The industries included as public utilities are electric light and power companies, gas companies, street railways, telephone, telegraph and water companies. The discussion is concerned primarily with operating companies, but also brings into consideration the holding companies,

[1] Tables 38 and 39 give the basic data used in this chapter.

and the entire financial structure associated with public utility organization and management.

The aggregate long-term public utility debt comes to about $11,225 million. This compares with approximately $22,905 million of total capitalization (including capital stock), and with $25,405 million of plant investment as represented by the book figures of the companies.[2] These are operating company figures and do not include the superstructures of the holding companies and other affiliated concerns above the realm of direct operation. As of December 31, 1931, the long-term debt, total capitalization, and plant investment were as follows for the different utility groups: [3]

TABLE 37

PUBLIC UTILITY DEBTS, CAPITALIZATION, AND INVESTMENT

(In Millions)

	Total Funded Debt	Total Capitalization	Total Plant Investment
Electric companies..............	$5,800	$11,600	$12,300
Electric railways................	2,480	4,205	4,100
Telephone companies............	1,400	4,100	5,200
Gas companies.................	1,035	2,165	2,630
Telegraph companies............	160	335	575
Water companies...............	350	500	600
Total....................	$11,225	$22,905	$25,405

In addition, there are also the holding company figures, which represent an additional debt of about $2,500 million. The aggregate funded debt of the utility systems—operating and holding companies—comes to a maximum of $14,000 million.[4]

The above figures not only present the magnitude of long term debt for the different classes of public utilities, but also indicate the relative proportion of debt in the financial structure. While there is great variation between individual companies, the figures furnish a comprehensive picture for each utility and show the differences between the several industries.

[2] Non-par stock is included at stated value, while plant investment is gross, without deduction for accrued depreciation.

[3] The source of these figures and the method of compilation are explained in Appendix II as are all other calculations made for this study.

[4] These are long term debts representing generally fixed investments in the public service. In addition, there are short term or current debts. But the burden of these involves an analysis of current assets, including debts receivable; and no adequate or even approximately satisfactory analysis could be made within the limits of our study.

TABLE 38

BASIC DATA ON PUBLIC UTILITY DEBTS

AMOUNTS

	1931	1929	1922	1912
		(Dollars in Millions)		
Total funded debt(a)	$10,506	$9,251	$5,249	$3,294
Excluding manufactured gas	9,680	8,589		
Total interest charges(b)	578	513	339	174
Excluding manufactured gas	527	468		
Total net earnings prior to interest charges	1,333	1,348	692	355
Excluding manufactured gas	1,195	1,214		
Total capitalization(a)	21,637	19,085	9,853	6,477
Excluding manufactured gas	19,905	17,562		
Total plant investment(a)(c)	23,703	21,281	11,484	7,777
Excluding manufactured gas	21,600	19,315		
Services:				
Number of telephones (thousands)	19,690	20,068	14,347	8,730
Kilowatt-hours generated (thousands)	85,575,307	99,084,428	40,291,536	11,569,110
Revenue car miles (thousands)	1,929,000	2,131,000	2,124,523	1,921,000
Cubic feet of gas sold (millions)	511,100			

RATIOS

	1931	1929	1922	1912
		(Per Cent)		
Total capitalization to plant investment	91.3	89.7	85.8	83.3
Excluding manufactured gas	92.2	90.9		
Funded debt to total capitalization	48.6	48.5	53.3	50.9
Excluding manufactured gas	48.6	48.9		
Net earnings to plant investment	5.6	6.3	6.0	4.6
Excluding manufactured gas	5.5	6.3		
Net earnings to total capitalization	6.2	7.1	7.0	5.5
Excluding manufactured gas	6.0	6.9		
Net earnings to interest requirements (times)	2.31	2.63	2.04	2.04
Excluding manufactured gas	2.27	2.60		

PERCENTAGE CHANGES DURING PERIOD

	1931 over 1929	1929 over 1922	1922 over 1912	1931 over 1922	1931 over 1912	1929 over 1912
Total funded debt	13.6	63.6	59.4	84.4	193.9	160.7
Excluding manufactured gas	12.7					
Total interest charges	12.6	38.0	94.4	55.4	202.1	168.2
Excluding manufactured gas	D 1.1					
Total net earnings prior to interest charges	D 1.6	75.4	94.9	72.7	236.6	242.0
Excluding manufactured gas	13.4					
Total capitalization	13.3	78.2	52.1	102.0	207.3	171.1
Excluding manufactured gas	11.4					
Total plant investment	11.8	68.2	47.7	88.1	177.7	148.4
Excluding manufactured gas						
Services:						
Number of telephones	D 1.9	39.9	64.3	37.2	125.5	129.9
Kilowatt-hours generated	D 5.0	123.6	248.3	112.4	639.7	678.7
Revenue car miles	D 9.5	0.3	10.6	D 9.2	0.4	10.9
Cubic feet of gas sold	D 2.5	49.7	96.4	46.0	186.8	194.1

NOTE: The data tabulated above are aggregates of figures for telephone, electric light and power, electric railway, and manufactured gas companies. For 1922 and 1912, however, no financial data were available in the manufactured gas industry, and hence, where comparable ratios were desired for the entire period, the figures for the gas industry were excluded also from 1929 and 1931.

(a) After an adjustment for manufactured gas, for which a complete set-up could not be obtained, to include the entire industry, and after the inclusion also of telegraph and water companies, the total funded debt, total capitalization and total plant investment amount, respectively, to $11,225 and $23,880 and $25,405 million on December 31, 1931, as shown in the text. See Appendix.

(b) In the past, practically no provisions have been made for debt amortization.

(c) Without deduction for accrued depreciation.

D = Decrease.

TABLE 39

BASIC DATA ON DEBTS OF SPECIFIC UTILITY INDUSTRIES

(Figures in Thousands)

	1912	1922	1929	1931
TELEPHONES:				
Number of telephones(a)	8,730	14,347	20,068	19,690
Plant investment, book figures, gross(b)	$1,081,433	$2,134,545	$4,515,474	$5,200,000
Capitalization, stock	561,707	886,985	2,378,060	2,700,000
funded debt	387,123	709,492	1,234,340	1,400,000
Total	$948,830	$1,596,477	$3,612,400	$4,100,000
Net earnings prior to interest charges	72,233	142,582	367,400	342,700
Interest	20,907	45,918	75,700	85,900
Ratios: Total capitalization to plant investment	87.7%	74.8%	80.0%	78.8%
Funded debt to total capitalization	40.8%	44.4%	34.2%	34.1%
Net earnings to plant investment	6.7%	6.7%	8.1%	6.6%
Net earnings to total capitalization	7.6%	8.9%	10.2%	8.4%
Net earnings to interest requirements (times)	3.45	3.11	4.85	3.99
ELECTRIC LIGHT AND POWER:				
Kilowatt-hours generated(a)	11,569,110	40,291,536	99,084,428	85,575,307
Plant investment, book figures, gross(b)	$2,098,613	$4,290,325	$10,800,000	$12,300,000
Capitalization, stock	841,745	1,928,669	5,075,000	5,800,000
funded debt	1,084,444	2,039,786	5,075,000	5,800,000
Total	$1,926,189	$3,968,455	$10,150,000	$11,600,000
Net earnings prior to interest charges	109,780	336,361	714,000	724,000
Interest	48,385	137,674	269,000	307,000
Ratios: Total capitalization to plant investment	91.8%	92.5%	94.0%	94.3%
Funded debt to total capitalization	56.3%	51.4%	50.0%	50.0%
Net earnings to plant investment	5.2%	7.8%	6.6%	5.9%
Net earnings to total capitalization	5.7%	8.5%	7.0%	6.2%
Net earnings to interest requirements (times)	2.27	2.44	2.65	2.36

	1912	1922	1929	1931
ELECTRIC RAILWAYS:				
Revenue car miles(a)	1,921,620	2,124,523	2,131,000	1,929,000
Plant investment, book figures, gross(b)	$4,596,503	$5,058,762	$4,000,000	$4,100,000
Capitalization, stock	1,779,490	1,788,197	1,520,000	1,725,000
funded debt	1,822,716	2,500,046	2,280,000	2,480,000
Total	$3,602,206	$4,288,243	$3,800,000	$4,205,000
Net earnings prior to interest charges	173,222	212,694	132,500	128,500
Interest	105,082	155,506	123,100	133,900
Ratios: Total capitalization to plant investment	78.4%	84.8%	95.0%	102.6%
Funded debt to total capitalization	50.6%	58.3%	60.0%	59.0%
Net earnings to plant investment	3.8%	4.2%	3.3%	3.1%
Net earnings to total capitalization	4.8%	5.0%	3.5%	3.0%
Net earnings to interest requirements (times)	1.65	1.37	1.08	0.96
MANUFACTURED GAS:				(c)
M cubic feet of gas sold(a)(d)	......	......	524,100	511,100
Plant investment, book figures, gross(b)	......	......	$1,965,282	$2,103,000
Capitalization, stock	......	......	861,387	906,000
funded debt	......	......	661,443	826,000
Total	......	......	$1,522,830	$1,732,000
Net earnings prior to interest charges	......	......	134,345	137,600
Interest	......	......	45,094	50,900
Ratios: Total capitalization to plant investment	......	......	77.5%	82.4%
Funded debt to total capitalization	......	......	43.4%	47.7%
Net earnings to plant investment	......	......	6.8%	6.5%
Net earnings to total capitalization	......	......	8.8%	7.9%
Net earnings to interest requirements (times)	......	......	2.98	2.70

(a) The units indicating growth in the utility services over the period are not in all cases for the companies for which the detailed financial data are shown; they usually cover a broader segment, if not 100 per cent of the industry, while the financial set-up in most cases was not obtainable for the entire field.

(b) That is, without deduction of accrued depreciation.

(c) The figures shown here are approximately 20 per cent lower than the ones given in the text, because a complete set-up could not be obtained for the entire industry.

(d) The corresponding amounts for the years 1912 and 1922 were 178,229,000 and 350,000,000 M c.i. ft, respectively.

Debt and Total Investment

For all the utilities the debt constitutes about 49 per cent of the total capitalization, and 44 per cent of the plant investment. For the electric companies, the corresponding ratios are 50 per cent and 47 per cent. The street railways have the highest ratios—59 per cent and 60 per cent; and the telephones the lowest—34 per cent and 27 per cent. The ratios of debt to the total capitalization and plant investment furnish one indication of the relative security of the debt in the several industries. But in making such comparisons, the fact must be kept in mind that the figures for debt constitute absolute obligations, while those for capital stock and plant investment may be materially at variance with the real magnitude that they are intended to represent. Neither the capital stock nor the plant investment, as stated, represents a like amount of cash capital outlay for the public service. Each has been subject to irregular accounting and inflation.

In many instances, the plant investment has been "written up" above the actual monetary investment in properties. This has been brought about in three ways. First, by revaluation of properties and increasing the book figures accordingly. Second, by purchasing existing properties from other companies at a greater price than the actual installation cost, and then entering the purchase price under plant investment. Third, by failing to write off properties as they were retired or became useless for the public service.

The extent of the "write-ups" is conjectural. That the aggregate is considerable has been shown by the Federal Trade Commission's investigation of the electric companies. The total may reach two or three billion dollars for all the utilities.[5] There is also depreciation to be considered. The overstatement in plant investment mostly reflects also corresponding overcapitalization in stock outstanding. The real ratios of debt to total capitalization and plant investment, on a strict cost basis, are therefore considerably higher than shown by the nominal figures.

The huge volume of debt is particularly significant because of the important position occupied by the utilities in our industrial and social organization. It must be regarded from the standpoint of the many thousands of individual and institutional investors, as well as the con-

[5] These figures are merely experienced guesses. They come respectively to 9 per cent and 13 per cent of the stated book costs. In his own experience, the author has found 30 per cent write-ups in the case of large properties brought together piece-meal through successive purchases. A ten per cent average looks rather modest.

sumers who depend upon proper service and reasonable rates.[6] It creates a question of grave public concern, how the great volume of debt incurred under high price level will be borne by the companies which are under special obligation to the public, are vested with a public interest, are subject to regulation, and are entitled to consideration not found in ordinary industry.

Developments Since 1912

The standing of the debt is indicated in part by the relative utility developments over a period of years in relation to the changes in price level and earnings. Let us take a rapid survey, starting with pre-war conditions as reflected generally by the year 1912; next taking the immediate post-war conditions as indicated by 1922; then the pre-depression as represented by 1929, and finally present conditions as shown by 1931, or by the most recent available data. Charts 16 and 17 give the figures in graphic form.

The utility that has developed and forged ahead most rapidly is the electric. The principal data as to development and financial change are as follows:

TABLE 40

THE DEVELOPMENT OF THE ELECTRICAL INDUSTRY, 1912–1931

(Dollars in Millions)

	1912	1922	1929	1931
Funded debt............................	$1,084	$2,040	$5,075	$5,800
Total capitalization......................	1,926	3,968	10,150	11,600
Plant investment........................	2,099	4,290	10,400	12,300
Net earnings prior to interest charges.......	110	336	714	724
Interest requirements.....................	48	138	269	307
Net earnings times interest................	2.27	2.44	2.65	2.36

[6] It was not practicable to determine the distribution of debt among institutions and private holdings. No reports are made by the companies. There is no doubt, however, that utility bonds enter largely into institutional and funded investments, because they have been considered safe investments. Their present security has grave importance to colleges, universities, insurance companies, trust funds, and to hundreds of thousands of individuals who invested their savings in presumably well-protected securities. The extent of institutional holdings is indicated by a recent analysis of investments made by thirty colleges and universities. The total investments in all forms of securities and mortgages aggregated $537,000,000 of which $126,647,000 constituted public utility securities; and the latter were distributed $95,840,000 bonds, $19,483,000 preferred stock, and $10,324,000 common stock (Trusteeship of American Endowments, published by Wood, Strutters & Co.). Recent figures of insurance company investments show that fifty-two life insurance companies had $1,855,785,000 invested in public utility securities: $1,693,000,000 in bonds, $151,550,000 in preferred stock, and $11,235,000 in common stock.

Utility debt thus constitutes an extremely important part of the quasi-public investments. Its standing as to security has therefore exceptional significance, and its proper safe-guarding, in the depression and after, demands intelligent consideration.

CHART 16

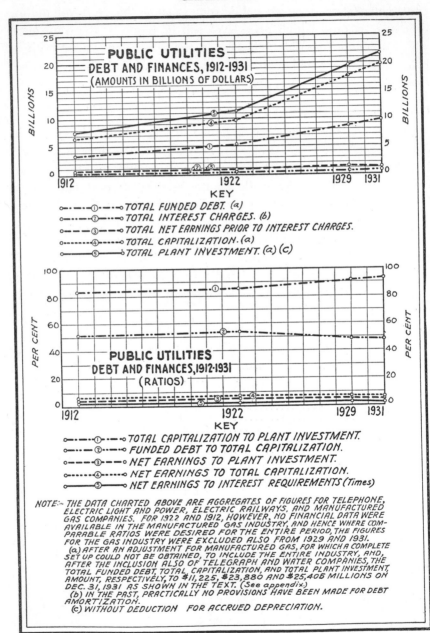

PUBLIC UTILITIES
DEBT AND FINANCES, 1912-1931
(AMOUNTS IN BILLIONS OF DOLLARS)

KEY
- ①---○ TOTAL FUNDED DEBT. (a)
- ②---○ TOTAL INTEREST CHARGES. (b)
- ③---○ TOTAL NET EARNINGS PRIOR TO INTEREST CHARGES.
- ④---○ TOTAL CAPITALIZATION. (a)
- ⑤----○ TOTAL PLANT INVESTMENT. (a) (c)

PUBLIC UTILITIES
DEBT AND FINANCES, 1912-1931
(RATIOS)

KEY
- ①---○ TOTAL CAPITALIZATION TO PLANT INVESTMENT.
- ②---○ FUNDED DEBT TO TOTAL CAPITALIZATION.
- ③---○ NET EARNINGS TO PLANT INVESTMENT.
- ④---○ NET EARNINGS TO TOTAL CAPITALIZATION.
- ⑤----○ NET EARNINGS TO INTEREST REQUIREMENTS (Times)

NOTE:- THE DATA CHARTED ABOVE ARE AGGREGATES OF FIGURES FOR TELEPHONE, ELECTRIC LIGHT AND POWER, ELECTRIC RAILWAYS, AND MANUFACTURED GAS COMPANIES. FOR 1922 AND 1912, HOWEVER, NO FINANCIAL DATA WERE AVAILABLE IN THE MANUFACTURED GAS INDUSTRY, AND HENCE WHERE COMPARABLE RATIOS WERE DESIRED FOR THE ENTIRE PERIOD, THE FIGURES FOR THE GAS INDUSTRY WERE EXCLUDED ALSO FROM 1929 AND 1931.
  (a) AFTER AN ADJUSTMENT FOR MANUFACTURED GAS, FOR WHICH A COMPLETE SET UP COULD NOT BE OBTAINED, TO INCLUDE THE ENTIRE INDUSTRY, AND, AFTER THE INCLUSION ALSO OF TELEGRAPH AND WATER COMPANIES, THE TOTAL FUNDED DEBT, TOTAL CAPITALIZATION, AND TOTAL PLANT INVESTMENT, AMOUNT, RESPECTIVELY, TO $11,225, $23,880 AND $25,406 MILLIONS ON DEC. 31, 1931 AS SHOWN IN THE TEXT. (See appendix)
  (b) IN THE PAST, PRACTICALLY NO PROVISIONS HAVE BEEN MADE FOR DEBT AMORTIZATION.
  (c) WITHOUT DEDUCTION FOR ACCRUED DEPRECIATION.

CHART 17

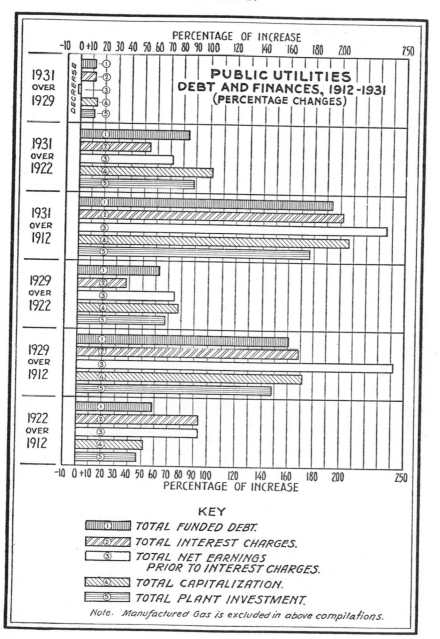

PERCENTAGE OF INCREASE

-10 0 +10 20 30 40 50 60 70 80 90 100   120   140   160   180   200   250

**PUBLIC UTILITIES
DEBT AND FINANCES, 1912-1931
(PERCENTAGE CHANGES)**

1931 OVER 1929

1931 OVER 1922

1931 OVER 1912

1929 OVER 1922

1929 OVER 1912

1922 OVER 1912

DECREASE

-10 0 +10 20 30 40 50 60 70 80 90 100   120   140   160   180   200   250
PERCENTAGE OF INCREASE

KEY

1 TOTAL FUNDED DEBT.
2 TOTAL INTEREST CHARGES.
3 TOTAL NET EARNINGS
    PRIOR TO INTEREST CHARGES.
4 TOTAL CAPITALIZATION.
5 TOTAL PLANT INVESTMENT.

Note. *Manufactured Gas is excluded in above compilations.*

This statement shows not only the enormous expansion of the electric utility, but also its stability in earnings. Since 1912, debt has increased more than five-fold, but the ratio to total capitalization has declined from 56 per cent to 50 per cent in 1931. For the same period, its net earnings advanced from $110 million to $724 million; its interest charges from $48 million to $307 million; and its ratio of earnings to interest requirements was slightly greater in 1931 than in 1912— 2.36 as against 2.27.[7] From the standpoint of earnings the present debt stands as well protected as the much smaller volume in 1912.

The electric railways, in contrast to the electric companies, have shown the most unfavorable developments since before the war.[8] The industry in 1912 had practically reached its maximum development and highest financial attainments. The results are shown as follows:

TABLE 41

THE DEVELOPMENT OF ELECTRIC RAILWAYS, 1912–1931

(Dollars in Millions)

	1912	1922	1929	1931
Funded debt...........................	$1,823	$2,500	$2,280	$2,480
Total capitalization......................	3,602	4,288	3,800	4,205
Plant investment........................	4,597	5,059	4,000	4,100
Net earnings prior to interest charges.......	173	213	133	129
Interest requirements.....................	105	156	123	134
Net earnings times interest................	1.65	1.37	1.08	0.96

Since 1912 the funded debt has increased somewhat, while the capital stock has declined slightly, and the ratio of debt to total capitalization advanced from 51 per cent to 59 per cent. Plant investment declined about $500 million, due to line abandonments. During the period there was little new construction; the improvements were limited largely to car equipment. In 1931, the total capitalization exceeded the plant investment, without taking into account the depreciation of the properties.

Retrogression of Street Railways

The net earnings of the street railways have decreased greatly, while interest requirements have increased materially. This change has taken place notwithstanding the fact that the fares have been raised from a

[7] Incomplete data for 1932 seem to indicate only a 10 per cent fall in the ratio.

[8] The details for the different utilities appear in the Appendix. For gas the corresponding data could not be obtained, but the industry, like the street railways, had largely reached its physical development before the war, and has advanced only with the growth of population.

level of five cents in 1912 to an average of about seven cents in 1931—when the interest requirements slightly exceeded the net earnings.

This retrogressive condition of the industry has been due to two major factors: (1) the difficulty in adjusting the fares to rising costs during and after the war, and (2) automotive developments. The tardiness of fare adjustment worked serious injury upon the street railways during and immediately after the war. By 1925, however, increases had been almost generally made, and since then the level has probably been as high as could be practically maintained, with due regard to volume of traffic. In many instances the increases have driven away riders, and the fares now appear as high as the traffic will bear. The present difficulties of the street railways, therefore, may be assigned principally to the automotive developments.

The influence of the automobile has been mostly two-fold. First, the buses have furnished a new, faster, more flexible, and more attractive transportation, and have, therefore, taken away traffic from street railways or have prevented the growth of traffic. Gradually, however, they have been brought extensively in co-ordination and control of the street railways so that their direct competition has been correspondingly eliminated. The second factor has been the enormous increases in automobile and truck traffic. This has not only taken away passengers from the street railways, but has produced street congestion, slowed down street railway operation, and reduced the attractiveness of the service.

Because of these conditions, including the interferences of the street railways with vehicular traffic, there are students of urban transportation who believe that the street railways will gradually disappear. There are others, however, who believe that they are essential for mass transportation, and that improvements and regulation will be effected so as to preserve the street railways as the principal medium of urban transportation. It is true that there have been many line abandonments in recent years. In many smaller cities, entire operation has been discontinued. Before a permanent balance between buses and street railways will be established, probably many lines and systems will go into discard. If street railways are to continue an important factor in urban transportation, a large part of their debt will have to be stripped off before they can function on a sound financial basis.

We shall not endeavor to forecast the future of street railways. We must, however, point to the decline in status during recent years, and to the serious problem with which the industry is confronted. In the face of present circumstances, the debt of the industry appears in a precarious position. It is inadequately secured by earning power. While the other utilities in 1931 had net earnings ranging from 2.36 to 3.99 times the interest requirements, the street railways did not earn the full interest charges.

At the close of 1931, approximately 20 per cent of the street railway debt was in default, and an even greater percentage in danger of default. For the other utilities, there have been few defaults. At the present time there are only few small companies in receivership. No important gas, electric, telephone, telegraph, or water company is in the hands of receivers, or appears in imminent danger of receivership.

Present Investment Status

Our survey of the different utilities indicates that, except for street railways, the long-term debt of the operating companies is well secured from the standpoint of earnings. On the basis of present and prospective conditions, most of the companies will be able to bear their interest burdens without serious financial handicap. The same conclusion follows our study of market quotations. These show clearly that with the exception of street railways, the utility bonds are generally regarded as well-secured, and are accepted as sound investments.

To indicate roughly the present investment standing of public utility debts, we present the following tabulation for January 1, 1933, which includes all the bonds listed on the New York Stock Exchange according to classification.[9]

TABLE 42
PRICE AND VALUE OF PUBLIC UTILITY BONDS

	Number of Issues	Average Price	Listed Bonds Par Value	Market Value
Gas and electric:				
Operating companies........	111	$95.08	$1,898,508,800	$1,805,074,090
Holding companies..........	15	69.78	233,554,600	162,966.822
Cable, teleph. and teleg., radio	28	98.17	1,044,853,536	1,025,759,288
Traction companies..........	37	51.06	568,042,600	290,056,256
Express company............	1	59.00	12,000,000	7,080,000
Water and central heating.....	4	102.05	32,563,000	33,230,250
Total...................	196	$87.72	$3,789,522,536	$3,324,166,709

[9] N. Y. Stock Exchange *Bulletin*, January, 1933, p. 9.

The significant figures are the average prices. While they ignore the variation in yield included in the averages, they show, nevertheless, that the operating company bonds stand well up to par, except traction, which are only about half of par. The holding companies class far below the operating companies.

Besides the bonds listed on the New York Stock Exchange, we have made a price and yield analysis of all bonds for which quotations for the latter part of 1932 were available. The total par value for the different groups is as follows:

Companies operating mainly gas and electric utilities......	$6,649,000,000
Telephone and telegraph companies....................	1,219,000,000
Water companies.....................................	238,000,000
Traction companies..................................	1,198,000,000
Total operating company bonds....................	$9,304,000,000
Holding company bonds.............................	2,230,000,000

The active bonds of operating utilities thus studied for price and yield represent therefore over 80 per cent of the total $11,225 million outstanding.

The classification follows as nearly as practicable the grouping by industry as previously presented. Here, however, there is considerable over-lapping between the different utilities; no sharp division of bonds by industry can be made. The price and yield study points to the same conclusion that, with the exception of street railways, the utility debt as a whole is well secured and is favorably considered as investment.[10]

Classification by Yields

From the standpoint of yield, we may make a five-fold grouping for our purposes. First, bonds bringing under 5 per cent on the market price, constitute first-class investment, with practically full security; second, those between 5 per cent and 7 per cent are reasonably well secured; third, between 7 per cent and 9 per cent inadequately secured; fourth, above 9 per cent manifestly in the dubious class; and, fifth, in default.

The bonds of operating utilities constituting the largest class were divided into three groups: (1) those exclusively electric, (2) exclusively gas, and (3) not exclusively gas or electric. For the exclusively electric

[10] Classification and explanation of debt, rate of yield, and default, are shown in Appendix II.

bonds, we found 54 per cent had a yield under 5 per cent, while for exclusively gas bonds 49 per cent came to less than 5 per cent. Of the exclusively electric bonds, 85 per cent bring 7 per cent or less; for exclusively gas bonds, 82 per cent. Of the electric, 5 per cent have a yield of 9 per cent or over; while the exclusively gas have 18 per cent, bringing 9 per cent or over. Bonds that are not exclusively gas or electric have 41 per cent under 5 per cent; 73 per cent yield 7 per cent or less; and 13 per cent yield 9 per cent or over, or in default. As a rough approximation, we may state that for the entire group, that is mainly gas and electric, 45 per cent are fully secured; about 32 per cent reasonably secured; 12 per cent inadequately; 10½ per cent poorly; and one-half per cent in default.

The same general analysis may be made for telephone and telegraph companies. In these utilities, however, a few large companies dominate, and largely set the level of security for the industry. On the basis of yield, 77 per cent are first-class, bringing 5 per cent or less. The second group has only 2 per cent; the third 1 per cent; but on the other extreme, about 20 per cent bring a yield of 9 per cent or over. This large percentage of dubious security is due to telegraph, and to smaller telephone companies that occupy poor territory or are operating against competition. The Bell securities come altogether in the first class.

The traction companies occupy by far the most unfavorable status among the utilities. There is practically no first class security. Less than 1 per cent of the bonds yield under 5 per cent. In the second class, there are 12 per cent; in the third 4 per cent; but in the fourth, 52 per cent have a yield of 9 per cent and over; and fifth, 31 per cent are in default. The market obviously is not optimistic over street railways.

Security of Operating and Holding Company Debt Compared

While for the most part, except for electric railways, the operating utility bonds are well or reasonably secured, the situation is quite different when we turn to the holding company bonds. In this group, we have included in our tabulation an aggregate of $2,230 million. Their distribution by yield approximates the street railways. Less than one-half of 1 per cent come within the first group of a 5 per cent yield and under. Next 14 per cent come between 5 per cent and 7 per cent; only 8 per cent in group 3. At the other extreme 67 per cent have a yield of over 9 per cent, while 11 per cent are in default. Holding company and traction bonds are mostly inadequately secured. They are not sufficiently supported by earnings, and occupy an unsatisfactory investment position. Both face serious difficulties for the future.

The far-flung holding company systems had a mushroom growth during the decade before the stock exchange collapse in 1929. Their development had been lavishly lauded because of the proclaimed economies in management, which were promised through consolidation and co-ordination, through system planning, and through centralized financing. The expected results might have been partly attained if the systems had been erected upon solid financial foundations. The basic weakness in the financial structures was the over-payment for the properties and the excessive fixed charges which resulted from the combinations. The purchases were largely made under competitive bidding between holding company groups. The prices paid were not only high enough to induce the local owners of the properties to sell, but to out-bid other competitive groups. Payments were made largely through bond issues and preferred stock.

Even under normal circumstances, the holding company systems would probably have found themselves in difficulty to support the extravagant financial structures which were erected. Only through gross overcharges to the operating companies for various fanciful services, could they expect to sustain their elaborate organizations. But with the financial collapse in 1929, the situation was rapidly changed. The public attitude toward the holding companies swiftly shifted from simple faith to cynicism.

With the advance of the depression, the holding company earnings have sharply declined. Furthermore, in various states the charges for management, financing, and other claimed services, were greatly reduced or completely eliminated. In the more extreme instances, insolvency was the prompt consequence. In other instances, the credit and financial structures have been hopelessly impaired. For the future the holding companies and their various management and financial affiliates appear of dubious value in any rational scheme of utility organization. In contrast to the extravagant expectations or promises of a few years ago, their position for the future was characterized as follows by a recent report of the New York Public Service Commission to the legislature of the state:

The underlying operating companies now must depend upon their own resources to raise capital, and they can do it on much more favorable terms than the holding companies. Companies that hold only securities and own no operating properties find it practically impossible to obtain funds and the market value of their securities has descended to depths of which no investor dreamed when he was enticed by rosy prospectuses and promises of great earnings to pass by the securities of operating utilities and invest in the securities of holding companies.

The holding company debt as a whole stands today as poorly supported. It rests mostly upon the underlying debt of the operating companies. It will probably result in a large proportion of loss to the holders. This condition stands in striking contrast to the operating companies, whose debt is reasonably well secured. In most instances, except street railways, unless there is a much greater decline in price level and shrinkage in business, the interest charges can be readily sustained. There are, however, companies which will find difficulty in meeting fixed charges on debt incurred on a much higher price level and under different economic prospects.

The intrinsic security of the public utility debt consists of the balance of earnings above interest requirements. The existing favorable balance is due to the fact that the volume of business has been largely maintained despite the depression, and that only slight reductions in rates have been granted to the consumers. As to volume of business, particularly the part that pertains to domestic consumption, it has kept its earlier level, and indeed has advanced somewhat during the depression. The losses in industrial business of the electric companies, for example, have been practically counter-balanced by the increase in domestic loads. The declines in gross revenues have been mostly balanced by reductions in expenses; and no drastic cutting of expenses has taken place. The operating companies, always excepting street railways, have fared extremely well in the depression. They are dealing extensively in public necessities and they are freed from the pressure of competitive business.

Prospective Rate Reductions

In studying the basic security of utility debt, consideration must be given to the fact that up to the present only slight reductions have been made in the rates to domestic users as well as to other classes who are normally served under non-competitive conditions. This includes commercial users and the service to municipalities and other governmental bodies. If we are to continue indefinitely on the present, or gradually falling, price level, it seems certain that increasing pressure will develop for rate reductions. Insistence upon revision has already gone far in the case of electricity, especially as to rates for domestic, commercial and municipal consumption. Unless prices and costs turn sharply upward, substantial rate reductions are certain to follow. This is true especially where class rates are distinctly out of line with the new level of costs and purchasing power.

But, while in many instances rate reductions are already overdue, adjustments are likely to be retarded. Just as during the upswing of prices and costs rate increases were delayed, so in the downward swing the decrease will be slow. The tardiness will be due in large measure to the opposition of the companies to the demands of the consuming public.

The utilities, especially the electric companies, occupy an exceptional position during the period of depression and business recovery under new price levels. To a large extent they serve under monopoly conditions and are, therefore, free from the direct competitive forces which in other industries have produced huge reductions in charges to the consumers. As against this monopoly position, the utilities are recognized as vested with special public interest and are subject to regulation by the state. The scope of regulation applies specially to the fixing of reasonable rates. Under the general system of regulation, as established not only by legislation but by a long line of court decisions, there is a clear legal basis of adjusting utility rates and earnings to changing costs and price levels.

Lag in Rate Regulation

In most states, the function of utility rate regulation is lodged with a special commission. This body has the responsibility of fixing reasonable rates. The general standard is that rates must be fixed high enough to cover the reasonable and necessary operating expenses including depreciation, plus taxes and a fair return on the "fair value" of the properties used in the public service. This formula provides the measure of the total revenues to which a company is entitled from its various classes of consumers. It is specifically designed to provide adjustments for change in costs and shift in price level.

Each of the three elements which must be provided for by the rates, operating expenses, taxes, and return,—involves changes in costs due to variations in prices. In each, however, there is greater lag in the utilities than in competitive business. Operating expenses continue longer on established levels than in other business where competition rules. Valuations on which fair returns are allowed are much slower of adjustment than where values are pulled down by ruthless competition through the slashing of charges to consumers.

The valuations on which utility rates are based are subject to final determination by the commissions. The determination of "fair value" requires special physical appraisals, with principal consideration to the cost of labor and materials at the time of the valuations, and with due regard to prospective price levels for a reasonable period in the future. While this formula is assumed to provide automatic adjustment of valuation to changing price levels, actually the application is extremely difficult and time consuming, because of the valuation procedure.

As a matter of basic law, physical valuations are necessary as a starting point for the final establishment of "fair value." The procedure is a judicial one. The commission holds hearings; the company has the right to present its evidence of value; and the principal element as recognized by law is reproduction cost less depreciation at the time of valuation. To establish the reproduction cost of the properties is a cumbersome and slow process. It facilitates the building up of high unit prices, large overheads, and intangibles to a point which off-sets the decline in price level. The burden of proving low reproduction cost usually rests upon municipal representatives or consumers. While the commission has a general responsibility to the public for reasonable rates, it seldom is in position to represent the consumers actively in preparing and presenting the necessary evidence of reproduction cost on the basis of which a proper valuation can be made. Usually the company side supporting a high valuation is well prepared and presented, and the consumers' side poorly. Consequently, the final determination of "fair value" and rates is likely to rest upon a one-sided record.

As a practical matter, the reproduction cost formula does not furnish the convenient and certain adjustment of valuations to changing price level as has been widely assumed in the economic and legal discussion. Retardation and maladjustment are the rule both during rising and falling prices. After three years of price declines, there are now few utility valuations in progress, notwithstanding the mounting criticism of rates. The very difficulty and expense of the undertaking holds back the effort to make the adjustment.

Investment versus Reproduction Cost

There is also a further practical difficulty with which the commissions are confronted. This applies at the present time especially to the electric properties. Since 1912, the total plant investment has increased approximately from $2,000 million to $12,000 million,—a six-fold increase. This means that the present properties were mostly constructed during the period of high prices, during the war and up to 1929. Hence, without regard to the usual tardiness of adjusting the valuations to reflect the fundamental changes in prices, the commissions are now confronted with reduction below the actual money cost of the properties. Taking the period as a whole from 1912 to 1931, the present reproduction cost would probably fall 30 per cent below the actual cost of the properties.[11] Since about 50 per cent of the investments were financed through the issuance of bonds, rigid application of reproduction cost would cut deeply into the security of the bonds. In the face of this situation, commissions will be extremely reluctant to fix valuations materially less than actual investment in properties, which would cut into the security of the bonds and reduce the financial stability of the companies.

The basic law of public utility valuation has never been rigidly fixed,

[11] This is the author's personal estimate, based on his experience and acquaintance with the far-reaching changes that have taken place, but not upon detailed cost determination and comparison. Copper, which bulks heavily in the electric properties, has declined on the average certainly over 50 per cent. Other construction materials and labor have been quoted more at nominal than actually attainable cost. Enormous improvements in methods of construction have taken place. The 30 per cent estimate is presented as reasonably conservative, but there is so far no clear indication how the basic changes which have occurred will be regarded by the commissions and courts. It would be possible through the building up of unit costs and through various allowances of overheads, to raise present replacement cost even beyond actual cost; but it is equally possible to reach a much greater cut than 30 per cent. It is this indefiniteness of valuation which creates conflict of interest and is fundamentally responsible for the ineffectiveness of regulation.

There is, moreover, the further factor of depreciation to be deducted from reproduction cost new. Few electric companies have made adequate provisions through reserve accumulations to take into account the various phases of plant depreciation, especially obsolescence which has accrued rapidly because of the swift technological development of the industry. A 30 per cent average depreciation would doubtless be sustainable on proper consideration of the facts. But a much lower or a negligible deduction may be established by the commissions and courts, depending upon their basic conception as to what constitutes depreciation in its relation to valuation and rate making.

and it furnishes such flexibility of application as may be justified or defended in the public interest. While the "fair value" rule has been interpreted as involving principally reproduction cost, less depreciation, the consideration of other elements, especially the actual cost of the properties, has always remained an integral part of the legal formula. Hence, with the great decline in price level, the utilities have already begun to back away from reproduction cost, and to sidle up to actual cost in the valuation for rate making. While during the rising and high price level they were probably responsible for the recognition of reproduction cost as the dominant element of "fair value," they now seek to limit the application of this rule so as not to reach below the actual cost of the properties used in the public service.

If the valuation rule of reproduction cost, less depreciation, were rigidly applied at the present time, it probably would result in forcing insolvency and receivership upon many operating companies. If rates were now to be fixed and maintained systematically according to economic conditions and strictly in accordance with the law of the land, the status of the utility debt would be materially different than it actually is and promises to be. Taking the electric industry as a whole, the gross plant investment figures of $12 billion might conceivably be reduced to a net of $6 billion at present reproduction cost, less depreciation.[12] If the net earnings were to be limited to 7 per cent on this amount, there would be a total of about $420 million as against the present interest requirement of $307 million. The margin of net earnings over interest would thus be reduced from 2.36 to about 1.30. Many companies would be hard pressed to meet their obligations, and a considerable number forced into receivership.

Debt and Rate Reductions

If the existing price level continues or declines further, the utilities will doubtless gradually be brought under increasing financial pressure as rates are reduced. The reduction, however, will be effected slowly and the retarded valuations will probably not reflect the greater part in the decline in prices. In the meantime, the companies will also be able to increase their net earnings through reductions in operating costs, including cuts in wage levels. They will also get the benefit of increasing

[12] Apply first 30 per cent reduction for price level, and next 30 per cent for depreciation to take into acount physical wear and obsolescence.

business. Under the actual conditions that are likely to prevail, there is sufficient reason for believing that the bulk of the debt, except street railways and holding companies, will be sustained by the earnings allowed under our system of regulation.

The companies which will be struggling with financial difficulties will probably be treated leniently by the commissions so as to avoid receivership and to preserve sufficient credit for financing. It is only in exceptional circumstances that financial pressure will be sufficient to force a company into solvency.

What has been said in the preceding paragraphs, applies especially to the electric companies, which today represent over half of the total utility debt and nearly half of the aggregate plant investment. The electric properties occupy the doubly fortunate situation of being monopolies and, therefore, not pressed by competitors, and of being still in the developmental stage as an industry. At the same time, however, they are subject to maximum reductions in valuations because of the large proportion of plant investment made at high cost levels.

With the recovery of normal business activity the electric companies, even on the lower price level, are certain to expand in all classes of business, especially residential. In the latter class the existing high rates have stood in the way of extensive utilization. While there has been a substantial drop in industrial sales during the depression, residential sales have steadily advanced. Notwithstanding the depression, there has been an increase both in number of consumers and the average consumption per customer.

The growth of residential use of electricity has large possibilities. The average consumption for the industry at large comes to about 40 kilowatt-hours per month, per customer. This is extremely low, and is due mostly to high rates and to lack of adequate effort on the part of the companies to develop the residential load. During recent years, however, much attention has been directed to this field of neglected business, partly because of its stability proved during the depression. Increasing consideration has been given not only to revision of rate structures so as to stimulate and make possible much greater domestic use, but also to energetic efforts on the part of the managements to facilitate the residential development. The meager 40 kilowatt-hour average can be readily expanded to 100 kilowatt-hours and probably to 150 kilowatt-hours within ten years.

That residential rates will be materially reduced within the next five or ten years, appears quite certain; and the same applies to commercial and municipal uses. At the same time the reductions, with the efforts to promote business, will probably result in much greater volume of sales and in greater economy, so that the companies are more likely to reap increases in net earnings rather than decreases.

Taking into account both the unstrict methods of regulation and the prospective expansion in business, also the possibilities of expense reductions, we may confidently believe that the bulk of the electric debt is adequately secured.[13] The same considerations apply also to gas and to other utilities. The manufactured gas industry is less likely to expand, but has also less to suffer from application of lower price levels to valuation, because a smaller proportion of the properties was erected during the high price period. The telephone industry, while resembling the electric industry in probable future growth of business and large expansion during the high price period, is, however, better situated in that a smaller portion of its construction was financed by bond issues. It probably also was less subjected to "write-ups" in connection with system consolidations. But the street railways are in an altogether different situation; they were losing business before the depression, and there is no clear prospect that their status will be materially improved with the passing of the depression.

The precarious position of street railways in many cases has had, however, a direct or indirect bearing upon the credit and even rates of electric and gas units affiliated within the same company or system. In such cases, the earnings of the other utility services are supporting the securities issued on behalf of the railways. Commissions hesitate to reduce electric and gas rates for fear that the entire structure would be impaired, although the financial pressure is due to lack of self-support, no matter what rates may be charged, on the part of the railways. But, sooner or later, an adjustment in electric and gas rates in line with rates in contiguous territory will become inevitable, and the company or system of which the railways form a part, may suffer

13 It is worth while, however, to point to the fact that there is insistent and growing demand for rate reduction throughout the country. This applies especially to domestic, commercial, and municipal consumption for which prevailing rates are generally high. If the pressure should result in sweeping reductions, and if there should not be the response of materially enlarged consumption, public utility debt would suffer loss in security. The huge mountain does quake with the crumbling plateau of high prices upon which it had been reared.

financially, and thus the weakness of the traction unit may be reflected in the other utility services.

2. RECOMMENDATIONS

We now turn to the large problem of general policies dealing with utility debts under the prospect of continued low or lower price level. The debts were mostly created under high levels, and will inevitably cause disarrangement by continuing through lower price levels. Their prompt adjustment would be desirable if practically attainable. But we can see no general formula which can be applied to all utility debt for adjustment to the new economic conditions.

For the most part, so far as security of the debt is concerned, no extensive adjustment will be necessary, except in the case of street railways and holding companies. The consumers, however, will be required to pay higher rates than fundamentally warranted, and stockholders will suffer losses in property equities and returns. While theoretically bondholders would be fully protected in basic values and returns if the debts were automatically scaled down in proportion to price level, as a practical matter no such policy of adjustment appears legally attainable. Furthermore, with earlier rise in prices, bondholders were compelled to suffer losses in purchasing power, while the stockholders gained at their expense. They lose through rising prices and profit from falling; so there is neither logical nor legal reason for their sacrificing their present advantages except as they may be compelled by the force of circumstances.

Each company will naturally strive to preserve its financial structure and to meet its obligations. The holders of debt will also strive to obtain all payments to which they feel themselves legally entitled under contract. The process of adjustment must practically be carried out through individual instances. It appears quite inconceivable that a sweeping formula of adjustment can be established and applied to all classes and varieties of utility debt. The fact that prices have fallen approximately 40 per cent in recent years, and that the purchasing power of the dollar has increased accordingly, does not change the terms of the debt contracts, and will not induce the holders to give up their rights if the earnings of the companies will permit their realization.

It is only in instances where the companies cannot meet their obligations that holders of debt will be willing to consider settlement for less than contract payment. But even in such cases, voluntary settlements are difficult without formal receivership and reorganization. To facilitate adjustments, receivership procedure may be simplified. The final disposition of claims, however, will depend largely upon individual circumstances.

There are, of course, exceptions; but mostly it seems quite inconceivable that the holders of utility debt would be willing to accept reductions from their legal rights except as found necessary under impending insolvency of the debtor companies. Even where receivership is threatening, the difficulty is usually insuperable to a creditor agreement which would avoid receivership. This is due to the variety in classes of creditors and to the wide spread of holdings. With a few holders of a single debt, voluntary adjustments are practicable. But in case of a large utility company with many kinds of debts and with thousands of holders, settlement without receivership is virtually impossible.

Receivership and Debt Adjustment

When a large company has reached the point where it cannot bear its load of debt, its only practical course is receivership and subsequent reorganization. This procedure furnishes the only realistic course for debt adjustment to changing economic conditions. It is, of course, true that under the new circumstance all utility debts created under high price level before the depression, will be more burdensome to the debtors than had been expected. They involve huge shifts in equity and returns between creditors and stockholders. Indirectly they will also affect rates paid by consumers. As the companies may be able to bear their burden, the relative loss of stockholders must be accepted as an unavoidable consequence of our system of regulation and financial policies. This situation, however, does not stand seriously in the way of economic recovery and the ability of the companies to meet their duties to the public service.

In current financial discussion there is the frequent assumption that the failure to make general debt adjustments to the new conditions, will bring losses to investors, and especially to funded investments held by quasi-public institutions. This view is quite unfounded. To the extent that the utility companies will be able to meet their contract obligations, all holders of the debt—institutional or otherwise—will receive greatly augmented purchasing power. They will gain by holding to their contract rights. Where, however, insolvency is incurred, then the holders of the debt are forced to accept the best settlement that can be finally reached. Whether they lose or still gain through the shift in price level, depends upon individual instances and can hardly be provided for by general formula of adjustment.

Public Rights Not Sacrificed

Existing utility debts, we surmise, will have to be accepted as they stand. In the meanwhile, however, the public rights to proper service and reasonable rates stand legally ahead of all creditor interests. This at least is nominally the law. When the commissions have fixed reasonable rates and have provided for proper service, and if then there is sufficient net revenue left above operating expenses and taxes to pay the interest on outstanding debts, the companies will meet their obligation according to contract. But if with reasonable rates and proper service the net earnings are not sufficient to pay the interest, insolvency follows; then comes the time for readjustment of debts to new conditions. In the process of such readjustment, however, even in the course of receivership, the underlying rights of the public to proper service and reasonable rates continue unaltered. The public interest is legally paramount, and the rights of creditors are secondary.

There is a common misapprehension as to the public effect of a utility receivership. While such a situation is never desirable, still it has no really serious public consequences. The receiver becomes the operating and financial manager of the company. The duties to the public are not diminished. The powers of the commission over service and rates are not abrogated or reduced. The ultimate financial settlement and reorganization do not alter the public rights to proper service and reasonable rates. Where the public loses through receiverships is usually through inadequate protection of basic rights. This, however, is unfortunately true generally of our system of regulation. The real difficulty is that regulation does not furnish the public protection that it is assumed to provide.

While the existing rights of the holders of utility debt can hardly be altered drastically in accordance with the change in price level, the fact nevertheless stands clear that the large volume of debt does involve difficulties both to protecting the public interest as to service and rates and in dealing with investors. Properly considered, the public interest to be protected through regulation includes investors as well as consumers. Revision of regulation in the future must have co-equal regard for both classes of the public. It should take into account the constant shift in price levels to which our economic organization is subjected. Until a general system of currency and price control has been established, we may expect virtually incessant fluctuations in price levels, which will affect the relationship between holders of debt, stockholders and consumers.[14]

Debt Limitations and Amortization

For the future, to meet shifting conditions, provisions should be made in part for the limitations of debt as a means of financing public utility extensions and improvements, and in part for the amortization and retirement of debt within fixed periods of time. Public utility financing in the past has had excessive dependence upon debt, and too many kinds of debt. Financing should be greatly simplified; there is no basic reason why debt should be extensively employed. A company is entitled to a fair return on its properties without regard to kinds of financing. Consequently the ordinary distinction between debt and stock has no real signification from the public standpoint. For the future there should be increasing recourse to capital stock financing, which will avoid the special difficulties created by debt with changing price levels.

In many instances, however, the fact that extensive bond issues exist, precludes the possibility of satisfactory financing through capital stock in the future. Moreover, while there is no basic reason for debt financing, there is no valid objection either to the issuance of bonds if the amount comes safely within the earnings permitted by a commission under the system of regulation regularly administered. But if bonds are issued, they should be subjected to systematic amortization as a part of regulation. In the past, practically no provisions have been made for

---

[14] The necessity of meeting high fixed charges tends also to exert pressure upon management against improvement in service and experimentation with lower rates, especially with promotional classification. The management inevitably feels the immediate necessity of preserving a safe margin of net earnings above interest and other fixed charges. It will hardly venture, therefore, to give up immediate revenues derived from high rates for the ultimate benefit of larger utilization stimulated by reduction in rates. It is with this particular respect that many of the municipal plants have the striking advantage in facing the new era. They have largely amortized their investment, and are practically free from the restraining burden of the fixed charges left over from costs of a bygone period.

debt amortization. Debts have seldom been paid when due; they have been mostly refunded, or defaulted. Normally, as extensions and improvements have been made, new debts have been piled upon the old. The total volume has grown larger and larger, and now stands as an obstacle to prompt adjustment to changing conditions.

The danger of unamortized debt appears not only in shifting price levels, but also with respect to changing economic status of companies and industries. Where a utility, like electric, is on the upgrade, mounting debt is no particular obstacle to development if there is no decline in price level. But when an industry has reached its normal growth, then the situation is different, quite apart from price level.

We have the striking illustration of the street railways. During the 1880's and 1890's, up to about 1910, they were on the developmental grade. During those years, huge and increasing bond issues were made without provision for amortization. Then almost suddenly development stopped, and new basic factors appeared. Before the change was understood and adjustments could be made to meet the new conditions of automobile competition, the possibility of debt amortization had passed. The time for amortization was during the three decades before 1910, when the need for amortization was not apparent.

At the present time the gas companies might well undertake a vigorous course of amortization before competition with electricity develops to a point of reducing materially the earning power of the gas properties. The electric companies, which still are surging forward rapidly, should regard the experience of other industries and provide for amortization during the developmental era, while the possibility of amortization still exists. They should not wait until the ability has vanished. No industry is safe against the competition of progress. None can rely upon its own permanence in our economic organization.

Future Policy for Financial Stability

As a matter of future policy, it would be desirable to require systematic amortization as a part of our regulatory system. No utility debt should be issued except as authorized by a commission in the interest of the public. The approval should provide adequate protection of the debt, limiting the amount to certain earning power and to amortization within a definite period of years.

Such requirements could be readily imposed upon future utility financing. While they can probably not be imposed retroactively upon outstanding debt, the commission could use indirect means of compelling the companies to institute reasonable amortization provisions. When an issue comes up for refunding, the commission can impose subsequent amortization; and it can give notice that it will not approve any future refunding unless in the meanwhile a proper policy of amortization has been adopted by the company.

To institute such a program of amortization will require special legislation by the states. This is necessary for the protection of investors as quite distinct from rights of consumers to proper service and reasonable rates. Public utility bonds should have the highest attainable investment standing; they should be protected by all reasonable safeguards. The principal protection that can be practically established is the amortization of debt. A comprehensive plan of safeguarding financial stability in utility investments will require also simultaneous reconstruction of policy as to rate base, rate procedure, and financial control of the companies. Without such comprehensive revision of policies, the problem of debt can hardly be satisfactorily solved for the future.

Consideration of policy with regard to debt created under past price levels raises also the question of instituting a program of inflation, or more palatably called "reflation," so as to reestablish approximately the pre-1929 level. This question involves not only public utilities but all debt which has continued from the higher price era. It is concerned, however, primarily not with adjustment of debt to lower price level, but with basic currency control for the reestablishment of prior prices and their subsequent stabilization. This leads to consideration of monetary and banking policies, a comprehensive program of public employment, and other far-reaching economic and political objectives, which, of course, call for national action but are beyond the scope of this particular study.[15]

15 Both in gathering and tabulating the data used, and in the analysis and preparation of this chapter, the author has relied heavily upon the able and devoted assistance of Mr. Nathaniel Gold, lecturer on public utility accounting and regulation in the College of the City of New York, and Mr. Winthrop A. Toan, Investment Statistician. The author assumes responsibility for all opinions and conclusions expressed.

Chapter Six

THE DEBTS OF INDUSTRIAL CORPORATIONS

SUMMARY

The Facts

THE *long-term* indebtedness of industrial corporations is about $10.5 billion (1932) compared with a plant investment estimated at $48.1 billion in 1930—or about one-fifth the tangible asset value (pp. 174–83).

The *short-term* (current) debts of industrial corporations are $10.8 billion (1932) compared with current assets of $51.3 billion (1930) (pp. 174–83).

Total industrial debts increased 75 per cent between 1913 and 1920, but only 21 per cent between 1920 and 1929. From 1929 to 1932 they declined over 18 per cent. In the first period the major part of the growth in debt was in short-term debt. Between 1920 and 1929 the growth was in long-term debt while short-term debt remained fairly constant. After 1929 short-term debt was greatly reduced while long-term debt remained relatively constant (pp. 174–83).

The credit position of industrial corporations taken as a whole (based on the relation between assets and liabilities) was so good in 1929—current assets alone being twice the total of both short- and long-term debts—that the impairment caused by the depression was at first of minor importance (pp. 180–83).

The growth in corporate income from 1920 to 1929 was roughly commensurate with that of corporate debts and there is no evidence of reckless borrowing during that period for corporations as a whole (pp. 177–82).

Since 1929, however, corporate long-term debts have slightly increased (2 per cent) while the total net income for all corporations reporting to the Federal Government had in 1931 vanished and turned into a deficit ($5.6 billion in 1929; deficit of $1.9 billion in 1931) (p. 177).

Broken down into major divisions manufacturing shows the largest long-term indebtedness ($6 billion in 1930, or 57 per cent of all industrial corporations); service comes next with only one-fourth of this amount ($1.8 billion or 17 per cent) and trade a close third ($1.4 billions or 14 per cent). Construction shows the smallest indebtedness

($357 millions or 3 per cent). The mining and quarrying industry has long-term debts of $960 millions or 9 per cent of the total (pp. 183–86).

In manufacturing somewhat over one-half the total debt is short-term accounts payable, bank borrowings, corporate notes; in trade and construction debts are largely short-term, five-sixths and two-thirds of their total debts respectively; mining shows an almost equal division between long- and short-term (pp. 183–86).

The bulk of the long-term debt ($13.3 billions or 60 per cent of the total) of manufacturing industries is in metals (especially steel and copper), food products (including tobacco) and chemicals (including oil). In textiles, lumber and leather debts are almost entirely short-term; in the others fairly evenly divided between short and long (pp. 183–86).

Of the five major groups two—manufacturing and service—showed credit improvement (comparing debts and assets) from 1926 to 1929, while construction maintained its position and both trade and mining showed a lowering of credit ratios (pp. 188–91).

In the first year of the depression the credit position of each group except mining remained steady (p. 191).

At the end of 1930 current assets of manufacturing corporations were 4.4 times current liabilities; while those of trade, mining, service and construction ranged from 2.6 to 2.1 in the order given (p. 191).

In 1929 the credit condition of large companies was vastly superior to small ones—the large showing assets 4.8 times the liabilities, and the small 3.1. The difference was particularly striking in construction: large, 5.7 as against 1.9 for the small (pp. 194–95).

Since 1929 the contrast has been even more marked. At the end of 1931 the current liabilities of large companies had been reduced more than 38 per cent while assets declined less than 20 per cent; but the assets of small concerns have declined faster than liabilities (pp. 194–95).

While the depression has taken a serious toll the volume of failures has been surprisingly small—the excess failures due to the depression have amounted to less than 4 per cent of the liabilities of all industrial corporations in 1929. In manufacturing the figure is lower still—2.4 per cent (p. 197).

Judged by the record of failures the pressure of debts has been alleviated in recent months. Failures reached their peak in the first months of 1932 and have steadily declined in each successive quarter since. In the last quarter of 1932 liabilities of failed concerns were only 40 per cent greater than the average for the boom years of 1928–9 (pp. 195–200).

The facts show that the debt situation in industry, though serious, is not cataclysmic nor is it a mass problem (p. 200).

The recovery in the price of better quality industrial bonds in the third quarter of 1932, bringing them to a level only 18 per cent below the peak of 1929, is a striking indication of the relatively sound position of these industries (pp. 200–202).

Recommendations

Mass remedies are not called for. The problem is one of individual enterprises to be dealt with separately (p. 202).

The problem of industrial debt does not come primarily from over-indebtedness or low prices but from low activity and bank instability. Profits would quickly appear in most corporate industries—even at present low price levels—with as little as a 30–40 per cent increase in production and sales (p. 203).

The bankruptcy laws should be recast to prevent a single creditor or a small group from resisting an equitable adjustment of a corporation's debt burden. This would allow corporations to be reorganized smoothly and continue to function without the disrupting results of receiverships (p. 202).

Further bank liquidation should be prevented (p. 202).

Pressure should be applied for a downward revision of short-term interest rates (p. 202).

The recommendations are merely of an interim character and are made on the assumption that a wide program to promote recovery will increase business activity (p. 203).

---

1. THE FACTS

AN adequate study of industrial debt must give answers to three major questions: first, what is the absolute amount of industrial debt; second, what have been the recent changes in industrial debt in relation to industrial assets and income—and particularly in relation to current assets; and third, to what extent is industrial debt bearing so heavily on industry as to impede economic recovery. The first two questions are concerned primarily with matters of fact and will be considered in sections covering (1) all industry, (2) five major divisions of industry, (3) large versus small corporations, and (4) separate industries. In each of these sections the discussion will be divided into two parts: the first covering the developments culminating in the collapse of security prices in 1929; and the second covering developments since that time.

Before presenting the factual material, certain questions of classification and of reliability must be taken up. The term "Industrial Corporation" is a catchall to include all corporations not elsewhere covered in this volume. This means that it includes all corporations except "Railroads," "Public Utilities," and "Financial Corporations." The major groups included are "Mining," "Manufacturing," "Trade," "Construction," and "Service" [1] Corporations.

In appraising the figures given certain warnings should be kept in mind. The basic estimates for the years 1926 to 1930 are reasonably exact. They are derived from the figures compiled from corporation tax returns by the Treasury Department and published in Statistics of Income. To the extent that corporations filed consolidated tax returns, a certain amount of intercorporate indebtedness is not covered in the figures. This amount is presumably not very great and is to an important extent a matter of bookkeeping rather than real debt.[2] The figures for 1913 and 1921 are necessarily less reliable than those for the later years, as comparable figures were not published by the Treasury Department before 1926. The figures for 1931 and 1932 are likewise less reliable than the immediately preceding figures as the Treasury compilations have not yet appeared. The estimates for the first two and last two years have been checked by estimates based on independent material and should be sufficiently accurate for practical purposes.

(a) TOTAL CORPORATE DEBTS

Parallel with the expansion of industry during the 20th century has come an increasing volume of industrial debt. The total debt of industrial corporations at the end of 1929 amounted to approximately $27 billion, an increase since 1913 of 125 per cent. Nearly three-fifths of the increase came during the war and immediate post war period. The $12 billion debt of 1913 had increased to roughly $21 billion [3] by 1920. In the depression of 1921, short-term debt declined heavily so that by the

---

[1] Service Corporations include restaurants, hotels, theatres, barbershops, laundries, professional services, etc.

[2] Consolidated returns are, with certain exceptions, allowed only where one corporation owns 95 per cent of the stock of its subsidiary. A debt of subsidiary to parent or vice versa should not be treated as an obligation of the enterprise but only of the *legally separate* part.

[3] This figure was obtained by taking the long-term debt as estimated for 1921 and adding short-term debt estimated by the method indicated in Table 43 for 1921, which resulted in a figure of $16,750 million for short-term debt in 1920.

end of the year the total debt amounted to only $18.5 billion. It then increased at a fairly steady rate to a peak in 1929. Thereafter, the total debt declined rapidly as short-term indebtedness was repaid, reaching a figure somewhat over $21 billion, a decline of approximately 20 per cent between 1929 and 1932. Table 43 gives the figures in detail.

TABLE 43

DEBTS OF INDUSTRIAL CORPORATIONS(a)

(In Million Dollars)

	Current Debt —Notes and Accounts Payable	Fixed Debt— Bonds and Mortgages(c)	Total Debt	Ratio of Fixed Debt to Total Debt
1913.................	$ 8,544	$ 3,738	$12,282	.302
1920(b)...............	16,750(b)	4,820(b)	21,570(b)	.224(b)
1921 (depression year)...	13,700	4,820	18,520	.260
1926..................	15,650	9,440	23,090	.322
1927..................	15,830	8,410	24,240	.347
1928..................	16,450	9,320	25,770	.362
1929..................	16,850	10,170	27,020	.376
1930..................	15,390	10,680	26,070	.408
1931..................	13,300	10,658	23,958	.445
1932..................	10,800	10,450	21,250	.492

(a) See next page for citations of source.
(b) Very rough estimate.
(c) Approximately one-fifth of this fixed debt is represented by real estate mortgages and only a small part of this is represented by urban properties. Hence there is only a negligible amount of duplication with the figures given in Chapter III.

Sources of data and method of estimate:

1913 Total figure derived from data on corporate debt.—Annual report of the Commissioner of Internal Revenue 1914, pp. 99–109. Figure includes figures for "Industrial and Manufacturing" companies (including mining), "Mercantile" and a portion of "Miscellaneous" allocated on a basis of 1923 and 1924 figures of corporate debt. Total 1913 debt is allocated between fixed and current on the basis of the ratio shown in the Capital Stock Tax Returns for 1923 and 1924 as reported in Statistics of Income 1924, pp. 50–54 and Statistics of Income 1925, pp. 38–43. The figure for fixed debt is consistent with a figure of $2,652 million reported by Moody's for the funded debt of all industrial corporations listed in Moody's at that time. Moody's Industrial Manual, 1928, p. xlii.

1921 Fixed debt estimated by averaging Moody's estimates for all industrial corporation *notes*, bonds and mortgages for 1920 and for 1922 (none given for 1921) (Moody's Industrial Manual 1925, p. 1) and adjusting for presence of notes on the assumption that Fixed Debt bore the same relation to notes plus fixed debt in 1921 as the average relation in 1926, 1927 and 1928. The figures of notes plus fixed debt for the latter three years were taken from Moody's Industrial Manual, 1928, p. xlii and the figures for fixed debt were those given below in the table.
Current debt in 1921 was estimated by assuming that it bore the same relation to "other loans" of reporting member banks in leading cities at the end of 1921 as current debt in the years 1926 to 1930 bore to "other loans" in these years. The correlation between changes in current debt of Industrial Corporations and "other loans" of reporting city banks was very close, the ratios from

1926 to 1930 being respectively .562, .549, .553, .564, and .552. The average (.556) was employed. Figures for "other loans" taken from Annual Report of the Federal Reserve Board, 1931, p. 110.

1926   Figures for Fixed and Current Debt from Statistics of Income 1926, pp. 18–20, 362–400, adjusted for balance sheets not tabulated by the Treasury Department. It was assumed that 96 per cent of all industrial corporation debt was covered by returns tabulated.

1927   Statistics of Income 1927, pp. 371–372. Assumed 97 per cent of debt covered by returns tabulated.

1928   Statistics of Income 1928, pp. 380–381. Assumed 98 per cent of debt covered by returns tabulated.

1929   Statistics of Income 1929, pp. 332–333. Assumed 97 per cent of debt covered by returns tabulated.

1930   Statistics of Income 1930, pp. 266–267. Assumed 98 per cent of debt covered by returns tabulated.

1931   Assumed same change in fixed debt between 1930 and 1931 as estimated by Moody's (i.e. minus 22 million dollars) Moody's Industrial Manual, 1932, p. xli. Current debt estimated as in 1921.

1932   Current debt estimated as in 1921. Figures for "other loans" of reporting member banks in leading cities taken from Federal Reserve Bulletin, January 1933, p. 41. Fixed debt estimated by deducting from 1931 estimate obligations maturing in 1932 (estimated on basis of partial listing in Moody's Industrial Manual 1931, pp. a24–a26, and more complete listing in Moody's Industrial Manual 1932, p. a22 et sec. for second half year), and adding the total industrial issues (new and refunding) reported in the Commercial and Financial Chronicle for each month.

Since 1913 the changes in long-term debt and in short-term debt did not run parallel, the short-term debt being extensively liquidated during depressions. Between 1913 and 1920, long-term debt increased only 30 per cent from $3.7 billion to $4.8 billion, while, under the stress of war conditions, short-term debt nearly doubled, increasing from $8.5 billion to $16.7 billion. Between 1920 and 1929 the rates of growth were reversed. Long-term debt increased steadily and much more rapidly, reaching $10 billion in 1929. Short-term debt, on the other hand, declined over 20 per cent in the depression year of 1921, recovered most of this drop in the following two years, and then very gradually increased to reach a figure in 1929 little greater than it held in 1920, on the eve of the earlier depression. In the three depression years of 1930, 1931 and 1932, the short-term debt declined drastically, dropping to less than two-thirds its high figure of 1929. In the same three years long-term debt remained almost constant, declining slightly.

The different rates of increase in long and short-term debt have resulted in changes in the proportion of long-term to total debt, the long-term debt coming to hold a very much more important position. In 1913, 30 per cent of the industrial debt was composed of bonds and mortgages. By 1920, as a result of the war expansion of short-term debt, the long-term debt amounted to less than 25 per cent of the total. Since that time bonds and mortgages have increased relatively, being 37 per cent of the total debt in 1929 before the effect of the present depression had been seriously felt and more than 48 per cent in 1932 as a result of the heavy decline in short-term debt.

Relation Between Income and Debt

The growth in total industrial debt between 1920 and 1929 was accompanied by a roughly corresponding increase in corporate income. (See Table 44 and Chart 18.) The figures of corporate income fluctuate so much from year to year that it is not possible to get a true measure of growth. But if we compare the income in the boom year 1920 with that in the boom year 1929 there is an increase in income corresponding to the growth in debt. Thus, while debt increased in the nine years by 25.7 per cent, the net income of corporations making an income increased by 22 per cent, while the net income of all corporations combined—net income of those reporting income less the deficits of those suffering a loss—increased 26.7 per cent.

If we avoid boom and depression years and compare the average income from 1922 to 1924 with the average income from 1926 to 1928 the growth in income is clearly apparent, being at a more rapid average annual rate than the rate from the peak of the 1920 boom to that of 1929. (Income for corporations reporting income showed an annual rate of 3.8 per cent for the shorter period, against 2.0 per cent for the longer period, while the net income for all corporations increased at the annual rate of 4.8 per cent in the shorter, and only 2.8 per cent in the longer, period.) Whether the underlying conditions of income kept pace with the increase in debt cannot be closely measured.

Since 1929 the decline in corporate income has paralleled the decline in corporate business and the decline in debt has not kept pace in anything like the same proportion. It is fair to say that corporate income at the present time bears little relation to corporate debt and that the debt burden on industrial corporations will become inordinate if the volume of business and of income is to remain at the present low levels.

Character of Changes in Debt

Two conclusions stand out on examination of these figures: first, the well established conclusion that short-term debt is subject to great defla-

CHART 18

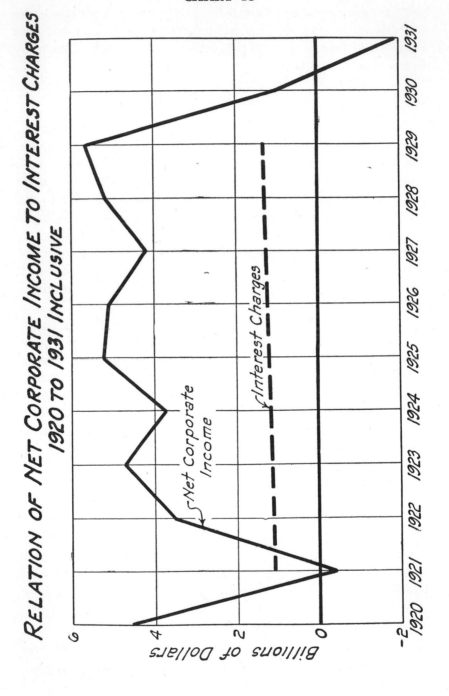

RELATION OF NET CORPORATE INCOME TO INTEREST CHARGES
1920 TO 1931 INCLUSIVE

tion during a depression; and second, the more important conclusion that corporate industry is financing its needs for increased capital through bonds and mortgages rather than through expansion of short-term debt. If we compare the boom year 1920 with the boom year 1929, short-term debt remained virtually constant while long-term debt more than doubled. The same conclusion is indicated if we compare the non-boom year 1926 either with the boom year 1929 or the non-boom-beginning-

TABLE 44

INCOME OF INDUSTRIAL CORPORATIONS(a)
(In Million Dollars)

	Income of Corporations Reporting Net Income	Deficit of Corporations Reporting No Net Income	Net Corporate Income
1920............	$6,040	$1,585	$4,455
1921............	2,775	3,192	417
1922............	5,097	1,600	3,497
1923............	6,196	1,477	4,719
1924............	5,359	1,626	3,733
1925............	6,591	1,372	5,219
1926............	6,613	1,520	5,093
1927............	5,870	1,708	4,162
1928............	6,833	1,652	5,181
1929............	7,364	1,715	5,649
1930............	4,030	2,977	1,053
1931............	2,140	4,040	1,900
Average, 1922–24.	5,551	1,568	3,983
Average, 1926–28.	6,439	1,627	4,812

(a) Source: Statistics of income

1920 pp. 9 and 10	1926 pp. 12 and 13
1921 " 10 " 11	1927 " 16 " 17
1922 " 16 " 17	1928 " 26 " 27
1923 " 11	1929 " 19 " 20
1924 " 14 " 15	1930 " 21 " 22
1925 " 11 " 12	1931, preliminary estimate made by assuming income

and deficit bore same relation to figures contained in Preliminary Report of Income 1931 (p. 12) that final reported figures in 1930 bore to preliminary figures, Preliminary Report of Income, 1930, p. 16.

depression year 1930. In the three years ending in 1929, long-term debt increased 36 per cent while short-term debt increased only 8 per cent. Even that increase in short-term debt which occurred can be more properly attributed to the difference between a non-boom and a boom year than to a secular growth in the amount of short-term industrial debt. In the four years beginning in the non-boom year 1926 and ending in 1930 before the depression had become far advanced, the growth in long-term debt was 43 per cent, while short-term debt declined slightly. This lack of an appreciable secular increase in short-term debt since the war combined with a very marked increase in long-term debt is a fact of considerable importance and one to be discussed below when we consider the changes in the debt-asset position of industry.

One other fact of importance should be noted,—the great decline in industrial debt which has taken place since the beginning of the current depression. While bond and mortgage debt has declined somewhat, short-term debt has been reduced over 35 per cent, or in absolute amount over 6 billion dollars. Because of this liquidation, the total debt of industrial corporations has been reduced over 20 per cent. Whether this decline in debt has placed industry in a better credit position, we will have to consider in the next sections.

The Relation of Debts to Assets

No adequate figures are available on which to base estimates of the assets of industrial corporations before the war and it is only in 1926 and thereafter that estimates of current assets can be made with a reasonable degree of exactness. For this reason we will confine the discussion of changes in the relation of debt to assets to the years 1926 to 1929 and from 1929 to the present. This will allow us to consider (1) whether or not the three years culminating in the peak year 1929 had seen a weakening in the credit position of industrial corporations and (2) whether or not the reduction in debt during the depression has improved their credit position.

Between 1926 and 1929, two developments took place which tended to have opposite effects on the credit position of industrial corporations. Current assets increased so much faster than current indebtedness that the current asset-current liability ratio improved, though slowly. (See Table 45 and Chart 19.) Current assets increased $4.7 billion, while current liabilities increased only $1.2 billion. As a result, current assets advanced from 3.28 times current liabilities to 3.33 times. Small though this gain was, it meant an improving current position for industry as a whole.

In the same three years bond and mortgage debt increased not only absolutely but faster than fixed capital (buildings, real estate and equipment). The gain in long-term debt amounted to $2.7 billion while fixed capital increased only $2.2 billion. This would indicate that some of the circulating capital of industry during this period was obtained by the

CHART 19

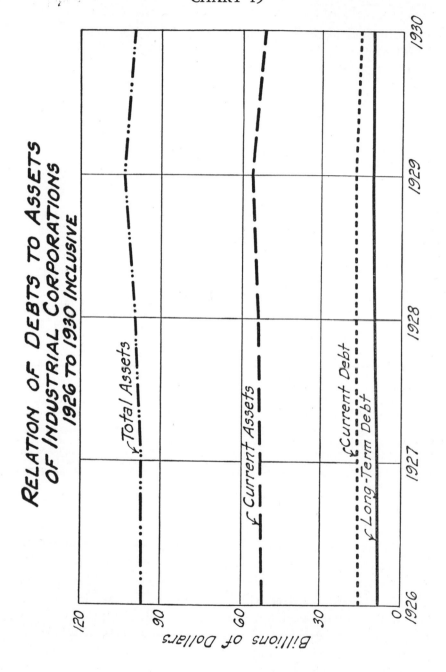

RELATION OF DEBTS TO ASSETS
OF INDUSTRIAL CORPORATIONS
1926 TO 1930 INCLUSIVE

Total Assets

Current Assets

Current Debt

Long-Term Debt

Billions of Dollars

120

90

60

30

0

1926   1927   1928   1929   1930

issue of bonds rather than by short-term borrowing, a tendency already suggested. Since much of the new long-term debt created will not mature for many years, industrial corporations will be for some years to come in a position superior to that in which they would have found themselves if they had obtained all circulating capital through short-term borrowing.

TABLE 45

RELATION OF DEBTS TO ASSETS OF INDUSTRIAL CORPORATIONS(a)

(Figures other than Ratios in Millions of Dollars)

	Debt			Tangible Assets			Credit Ratios		
	Current Debt	Bonds and Mort- gages	Total	Current Assets	Real Estate, Build- ings and Equip- ment	Total	Current Assets to Current Debt	Current Assets to Total Debt	Total Tangi- ble Assets to Total Debt
1926.......	$15,650	$7,440	$23,090	$51,400	$45,200	$96,600	3.28	2.23	4.18
1927.......	15,830	8,410	24,240	52,250	44,600	96,850	3.30	2.16	4.00
1928.......	16,450	9,320	25,770	53,650	45,500	99,150	3.26	2.08	3.85
1929.......	16,850	10,170	27,020	56,100	47,400	103,500	3.33	2.07	3.83
1930.......	15,390	10,680	26,070	51,250	48,100	99,350	3.00	1.97	3.80
Net Change									
1926-1929..	+1,200	+2,730	+3,930	+4,700	+2,200	+6,900			
1929-1930..	−1,460	+ 510	− 950	−4,850	+ 700	−4,150			
1926-1930..	− 260	+3,240	+2,980	− 150	+2,900	+2,750			

(a) Asset figures derived from Income Tax Statistics (for references see Table 43′ 1926-1930) were adjusted for incomplete tabulation in the same proportion as that applied to figures of debt (see Table 43). "Current assets" includes cash, notes and accounts receivable, inventory, tax exempt investments and one-half of other investments. Where other investments were included in miscellaneous in Statistics of Income it was assumed that investments bore the same relation to other miscellaneous as in 1930. "Fixed assets" includes only real estate, buildings and equipment. Debt figures from Table 43.

The combined effect of these two developments was to improve some- what the credit position of industry. Total debt increased $3.9 billion in the three years or 17 per cent, while the total tangible assets increased $6.9 billion or only 7 per cent, but most of the increase in assets had been of a liquid character while most of the increase in debt had been in the form of long-term obligations. It is apparent, therefore, that the period immediately preceding the depression was not one of reckless borrowing in so far as industry as a whole is concerned, a conclusion which is supported by the material available for particular industries.

Figures are not available to carry the analysis through the depression years but a slight indication of the probable development can be given by comparing the credit position of industry in 1930 with its position in 1929. In the first year of the depression current assets dropped $4.8 billion, while current debt dropped only $1.5 billion. The gain in current position made between 1926 and 1929 was practically cancelled. On the other hand, fixed assets and long-term debt increased slightly. Altogether, the credit position of industry was somewhat weakened by the liquidation of the first year of depression. However, the credit position taken as a whole had been so good in 1929—current assets alone being more than twice the total debt outstanding—that the impairment was of minor importance. The two additional years of depression have caused further liquidation of debt, mostly short-term, and a further reduction in current assets. How far this has undermined the position of industry will become apparent when we consider particular industries.

(b) DEBTS BY MAJOR INDUSTRIAL DIVISIONS

In breaking up the total industrial debt into the debt of the major divisions it is not possible to go back of the year 1926 with any reasonable degree of accuracy. Therefore, our statistical discussion will confine itself to the five years 1926 to 1930 and more general information will be given for the ensuing years. The figures can most easily be broken into six major groups: mining and quarrying, manufacturing, construction, trade including both wholesale and retail, service including amusements, theatres, hotels, restaurants and other service-rendering enterprises, and finally other industries including agricultural corporations and miscellaneous.

As is to be expected, the major portion of industrial debt is the debt of manufacturing corporations, while trade comes second. The division in the peak year of 1929 is indicated in Table 46.

The different distribution in short-term and long-term debt in the several industrial divisions should be noted. In the manufacturing industry somewhat more than half of the debt was short-term, consisting of both accounts payable to other enterprises, bank borrowings and a certain amount of corporate notes sold to the investing public. The fixed debt consisted mostly of corporate bonds, though including a small amount of unfunded mortgage debt. In wholesale and retail trade short-term debt

CHART 20

DIVISION OF LONG-TERM INDEBTEDNESS BETWEEN MAJOR INDUSTRIAL GROUPS 1930

$10,440,000,000

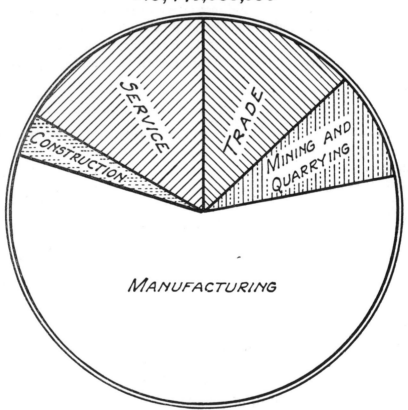

composed nearly five-sixths of the total indebtedness, the relatively small amount of fixed debt being to an important extent mortgages on the real estate employed in trade. In the mining and quarrying section debt was almost equally divided between long and short-term, the long-term being primarily bonded indebtedness. The construction debt, like that of trade, was primarily short-term, reflecting the normal process of financing new construction through short-term borrowing, while the larger part of the long-term debt was composed of mortgages on real estate. Debt of service industries was very largely dominated by the debt of hotels and

TABLE 46

DEBTS AND ASSETS OF MAJOR INDUSTRIAL GROUPS IN 1929(a)

(Figures Other than Ratios in Millions of Dollars)

	Liabilities			Tangible Assets			Credit Ratios	
	Notes and Accounts Payable	Bonds and Mortgages	Total Debt	Current Assets	Real Estate, Buildings and Equipment	Total	Current Assets to Current Liabilities	Total Tangible Assets to Total Debt
Manufacturing......	$ 7,650	$ 5,620	$13,270	$33,100	$29,200	$ 62,300	4.32	4.69
Trade.............	5,910	1,290	7,200	15,000	5,120	20,120	2.56	2.80
Mining and quarrying	1,000	1,070	2,070	3,080	7,490	10,570	3.08	5.10
Service............	985	1,610	2,595	2,110	3,920	6,030	4.67	2.32
Construction.......	872	361	1,233	1,757	885	2,642	2.02	2.14
Others...........	423	219	652	1,053	785	1,838	2.49	4.34
Total...........	$16,850	$10,170	$27,020	$56,100	$47,400	$103,500	3.33	3.83

(a) *Statistics of Income*, see Table 43.

moving picture companies, a debt consisting of both mortgage bonds and mortgages on the real estate employed in these enterprises.

The debt of manufacturing corporations in 1929 can be further broken up into the major divisions shown in Table 47 and Chart 20.

The bulk of the fixed debt is in the three categories, metals, food and chemicals. This covers the steel and copper industries which have large assets and heavy debts, the tobacco industry with its debt and the oil refining industry with its huge assets as well as a large debt. With the exception of the textile industry, the lumber industry and that of leather and shoes, the debt in each industry is roughly divided between long-

and short-term obligations. In the three exceptional industries the debt is primarily short-term. An explanation for this difference can be found in the fact that corporate concentration has progressed least far in these industries. They, more than any others in the country, represent the old style of individual or family entrepreneurship and it is to be expected

TABLE 47

DEBTS AND ASSETS OF MANUFACTURING INDUSTRIES IN 1929(a)

(Figures Other than Ratios in Millions of Dollars)

	Liabilities			Tangible Assets			Credit Ratios	
	Notes and Accounts Payable	Bonds and Mortgages	Total Debt	Current Assets	Real Estate, Buildings and Equipment	Total	Current Assets to Current Liabilities	Total Tangible Assets to Total Debts
Metal and metal products..	$1,910	$1,590	$3,500	$11,132	$9,620	$20,752	5.84	5.94
Food products, beverages and tobacco............	1,300	1,010	2,310	4,433	3,820	8,253	3.41	3.58
Chemicals and allied substitutes (including oil refining)	1,043	1,200	2,243	4,948	6,260	11,208	4.73	5.00
Textiles and textile products	1,190	269	1,459	3,676	2,510	6,186	3.09	4.24
Lumber and wood products.	613	245	858	1,633	1,780	3,413	2.67	3.98
Printing and publishing....	386	310	696	1,081	930	2,011	2.80	2.89
Paper pulp and products...	202	362	564	981	1,260	2,241	4.85	3.60
Stone, clay and glass products	275	218	493	830	1,360	2,190	3.02	4.45
Rubber and related products	189	258	447	690	506	1,196	3.65	2.68
Leather and leather products	207	37	244	811	273	1,084	3.92	4.45

(a) *Statistics of Income*, see Table 43.

that in these industries the resort to borrowing through bonds would be small while bank borrowing would play a larger role. As a larger proportion of an industry becomes concentrated in a few large units there appears to be a definite tendency for capital to be supplied to a greater extent through bonded indebtedness, as for instance in the oil and steel industries.

Debts in Relation to Assets—Manufacturing

Of more importance than the absolute amount of debt are the changes in debt in relation to assets. Table 48 and Chart 21 give the debt and assets for each of five major divisions of industry for the years 1926, 1929 and 1930.

CHART 21

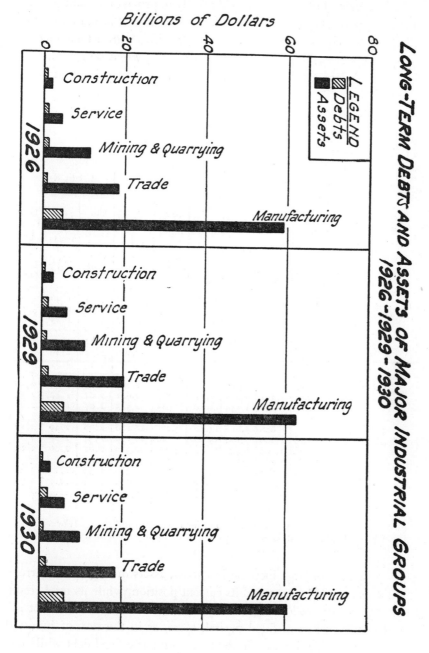

Billions of Dollars

LONG-TERM DEBTS AND ASSETS OF MAJOR INDUSTRIAL GROUPS
1926-1929-1930

LEGEND
Debts
Assets

1926
Construction
Service
Mining & Quarrying
Trade
Manufacturing

1929
Construction
Service
Mining & Quarrying
Trade
Manufacturing

1930
Construction
Service
Mining & Quarrying
Trade
Manufacturing

Manufacturing industry as a whole greatly improved its credit position in the three years culminating in 1929. Short-term debt increased slightly while long-term debt increased very considerably, with a total increase in debt of 1,230 million. At the same time both current assets and fixed assets increased to such an extent as to make a total gain in assets of

TABLE 48

INDUSTRIAL DEBT BY MAJOR DIVISIONS(a)

(Figures Other than Ratios in Millions of Dollars)

		Liabilities			Tangible Assets			Credit Ratios		
		Notes and Accounts Payable	Bonds and Mortgages	Total Debt	Current Assets	Real Estate, Buildings and Equipment	Total	Current Assets to Current Debt	Current Assets to Total Debt	Total Tangible Assets to Total Debt
Mining and Quarrying	1926...	$ 940	$1,050	$1,990	$2,910	$8,300	$11,210	3.24	1.46	5.65
	1929...	1,000	1,070	2,070	3,080	7,490	10,570	3.24	1.49	5.10
	1930...	1,050	960	2,010	2,515	7,400	9,915	2.39	1.25	4.94
Manufacturing	1926...	7,520	4,520	12,040	31,000	27,800	58,800	4.12	2.57	4.88
	1929...	7,650	5,620	13,270	33,100	29,200	62,300	4.33	2.49	4.70
	1930...	7,000	6,010	13,010	30,900	29,600	60,500	4.42	2.37	4.65
Construction	1926...	672	242	914	1,405	664	2,069	2.09	1.54	2.26
	1929...	872	361	1,233	1,757	885	2,642	2.02	1.42	2.14
	1930...	787	357	1,144	1,630	915	2,545	2.07	1.42	2.22
Trade.....	1926...	5,210	608	5,818	13,920	4,260	18,180	2.68	2.40	3.12
	1929...	5,910	1,290	7,200	15,000	5,120	20,120	2.54	2.08	2.80
	1930...	5,130	1,360	6,490	13,400	4,980	18,380	2.61	2.06	2.84
Service....	1926...	855	877	1,732	1,310	2,910	4,220	1.53	......	2.44
	1929...	985	1,610	2,595	2,110	3,920	6,030	2.14	......	2.33
	1930...	981	1,753	2,734	2,140	3,960	6,100	2.18	......	2.23

(a) Figures derived from *Statistics of Income* for 1926, 1929 and 1930. (For references see Table 43.) The same ratios of tabulated debt to total debt were assumed for each year as in Table 43.

3,500 million. The large increase in current assets in relation to current liabilities very greatly improved its current position, while its total credit position was improved though to a lesser extent since bonded debt increased nearly as fast as fixed capital. Here, as in the case of industry taken as a whole, the increase in debt was primarily fixed debt while the increase in assets was in large measure current assets. The credit position of manufacturing industry as a whole, strong in 1926, had thus become exceedingly strong by the end of 1929, with current assets more than four times current debt and two and one-half times total debt.

In the first year of the depression the credit position of manufacturing industry remained approximately constant, the ratio of current assets to current liabilities improving slightly, while the ratio of total assets to total liabilities declined slightly. Less comprehensive information covering manufacturing industry suggests that this development during the first year of the depression was carried into the second year, so that by the middle of 1931 the excellent credit position of manufacturing industry had not been seriously impaired, though undoubtedly the quality of many particular assets included in current assets had declined. After the summer of 1931, manufacturing industry as a whole became more seriously involved.

In wholesale and retail trade the credit position was somewhat lowered in the period from 1926 to 1929, though even at the height of the boom current assets were more than two and one-half times current liabilities and fixed liabilities were relatively small. In three years liabilities had increased $700 million and current assets only $1,120 million, while fixed liabilities increased $682 million and fixed assets increased only $860 million. In the first year of the depression the proportion of current debt to current liabilities improved slightly, though again it is necessary to keep in mind that the quality of current assets declined. Since 1930 the credit position declined somewhat, so that today current assets are probably not greatly in excess of double the current liabilities and fixed debt in the vicinity of a quarter of the current debt.

Mining and Quarrying

In the mining and quarrying division the credit position declined steadily after 1926. Between 1926 and 1929 current liabilities increased practically in proportion to current assets. Fixed liabilities remained relatively constant and fixed assets declined over $800 million. This left the industry as a whole in a poorer condition in its total debt-asset ratio, even though the current ratio remained constant. In the first year of the depression this position was further impaired. Current liabilities increased slightly while current assets declined more than $500 million. Fixed debt declined approximately as much as fixed assets. By the end of 1930 the current assets were less than two and one-half times current liabilities and appear to have declined to a lower ratio since.

Service and Construction

In the service industries the current credit position was steadily improving between 1926 and 1929 as short-term debt increased only $130 million, while current assets increased $800 million. On the other hand, fixed liabilities increased nearly $800 million, while fixed assets increased only $1 billion. This latter alteration reflects the increased mortgage and bonded indebtedness based on hotels, moving-picture houses, etc. In the first year of the depression certain of the larger units in the amusement industry were in financial difficulties, but as a whole the industry's credit position altered little. Its later difficulties have been largely connected with its real estate mortgage and will be discussed in that connection.

The credit position of the construction industry was not seriously changed between 1926 and 1929. Construction debt and assets both increased. Between 1929 and 1930 debt and assets declined somewhat, likewise with no important effect on the credit ratio. Here, however, the importance of the change in the quality of the current assets becomes greater as investment in construction projects tended to become less liquid.

It is not possible to break up changes in debt of manufacturing industries with any reasonable degree of accuracy. Information to throw light on the condition of separate manufacturing industries will have to come from statistics which cover only parts of each industry and will be considered below.

Inter-Industry Comparisons

For these five major industrial groups, two—manufacturing and service—showed credit improvement between 1926 and 1929, while construction maintained its position and both trade and mining showed a lowering of credit ratios, though only in the case of mining was the decline of serious proportions. On the whole, we may say that industry did not overburden itself with debt in the years immediately culminating with the year 1929. The weakening ratio in mining was due not primarily to added debt but to a decline in assets while the increase in debt in other industrial groups was fully counterbalanced by a more than proportionate increase in assets or in a favorable shift in their quality.

In the first year of the depression, the credit position of each group except mining remained steady. Mining itself continued to decline. At the end of the year 1930 the current ratio for the five industries was as follows:

Manufacturing	Current assets	4.42	times	current liabilities
Trade	"	"	2.61	"	"	"
Mining	"	"	2.39	"	"	"
Service	"	"	2.18	"	"	"
Construction	"	"	2.07	"	"	"

Since 1930, all five industries appear to have lost in credit position.

(C) DEBTS OF LARGE AND SMALL CORPORATIONS COMPARED

With the increasing growth in the size of corporate activity, a discrepancy has often appeared between the statistics covering large corporations and those covering small corporations, so that generalizations about an industry as a whole tend to disguise rather than clarify the actual condition of the industry. Fortunately for this report, Moody's Investors' Service has prepared elaborate compilations of the debt of 334 large industrial companies representing more than a quarter of the total fixed industrial debt in the country. The information covering these companies is assembled in Table 49, according to major industrial divisions. In Table 50 are given figures for smaller corporations obtained by deducting the figures for the large companies included in Moody's compilation from the total for each industrial group given in Table 48. Chart 22 gives a graphic picture of these data.

In comparing the two tables one fact stands out with great clarity. In each case and for each year the current condition of the large companies is vastly superior to that of small companies of the same industrial group. This is shown in the summary of current ratios for 1929 given below:

	Large companies	Smaller companies
Mining and quarrying	4.01	2.88
Manufacturing	5.05	4.12
Construction	5.67	1.87
Trade	3.89	2.48
Total	4.83	3.12

CHART 22

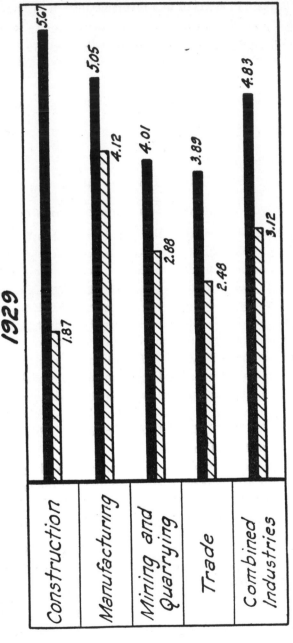

CREDIT CONDITION OF LARGE VS. SMALL CORPORATIONS
Ratios of Current Assets to Current Liabilities in Four Industrial Groups
1929

Construction — 5.67 / 1.87
Manufacturing — 5.05 / 4.12
Mining and Quarrying — 4.01 / 2.88
Trade — 3.89 / 2.48
Combined Industries — 4.83 / 3.12

LEGEND
Large Companies
Small Companies

Figures for the fixed assets of larger and smaller corporations are not available, though it is apparent that with the exception of the mining industry the large corporations raised a larger proportion of their capital through bonded indebtedness. In spite of this larger proportion of fixed

TABLE 49

DEBTS OF LARGE INDUSTRIAL CORPORATIONS(a)

(Figures Other than Ratios in Millions of Dollars)

		Liabilities			Assets	Credit Ratios	
		Notes and Accounts Payable	Bonds and Mortgages	Total Debt	Current	Current Assets to Current Debt	Current Assets to Total Debt
Mining and Quarrying. 38 companies.	1926	$107.1	$298.5	$405.6	$545.3	5.09	1.34
	1929	175.1	165.6	340.7	701.5	4.01	2.02
	1930	152.0	198.5	350.5	613.2	4.04	1.75
	1931	132.2	167.5	299.7	488.8	3.70	1.63
Manufacturing. 237 companies.	1926	1,581.4	2,072.8	3,654.2	7,352.1	4.65	2.02
	1929	1,696.4	2,119.2	3,815.6	8,543.7	5.05	2.24
	1930	1,330.6	2,126.5	3,457.1	7,825.0	5.88	2.26
	1931	1,002.2	2,093.7	3,095.9	6,808.5	6.80	2.20
Construction. 13 companies.	1926	26.9	26.2	53.1	143.7	5.35	2.71
	1929	33.9	41.0	74.9	192.1	5.67	2.56
	1930	26.3	39.5	65.8	165.7	6.30	2.52
	1931	19.6	43.6	63.2	140.7	7.18	2.23
Trade. 46 companies.	1926	193.7	81.6	275.3	749.7	3.87	2.72
	1929	258.4	257.0	515.4	1,003.9	3.89	1.95
	1930	212.1	154.4	366.5	943.6	4.47	2.57
	1931	188.9	153.7	342.6	892.7	4.72	2.60
Total. 334 companies.	1926	1,909.1	2,479.1	4,388.2	8,790.8	4.60	2.00
	1929	2,163.8	2,582.8	4,746.6	10,441.2	4.83	2.21
	1930	1,721.0	2,518.9	4,239.9	9,547.5	5.55	2.25
	1931	1,342.9	2,458.5	3,801.4	8,430.7	6.28	2.22

(a) Compiled from *Moody's Investment Survey*, Vol. 24, No. 44 (June 2, 1932), pp. 2215 to 2219.

debt there can be little doubt that for each of the industrial divisions the large companies were in a credit position very much superior to that of the smaller companies.

Relative Credit Standings

When we come to changes in credit position the differences between the large and small companies became even more clearly marked. The credit position of both the large and the small companies improved between 1926 and 1929, but since that time the current credit position of the 334 large companies has improved to a surprising degree while the credit position of the smaller companies appears to have declined somewhat. Thus in 1929 current assets of the large companies were 4.83 times current liabilities whereas at the end of 1931 current assets were

TABLE 50

DEBTS OF SMALLER INDUSTRIAL CORPORATIONS(a)

All Industrial Corporations Except the 334 Reported in Table 46

(Figures Other than Ratios in Millions of Dollars)

		Liabilities			Assets	Credit Ratios	
		Notes and Accounts Payable	Bonds and Mortgages	Total Debt	Current	Current Assets to Current Debt	Current Assets to Total Debt
Mining and Quarrying. All but 38 companies.	1926	$833	$751	$1,584	$2,365	2.84	1.49
	1929	825	904	1,729	2,379	2.88	1.38
	1930	898	761	1,659	1,902	2.12	1.15
Manufacturing. All but 237 companies.	1926	5,939	2,447	8,386	23,648	3.99	2.83
	1929	5,954	3,501	9,455	24,556	4.12	2.60
	1930	5,669	3,883	9,552	23,075	4.07	2.42
Construction. All but 13 companies.	1926	645	216	861	1,261	1.96	1.47
	1929	838	320	1,158	1,565	1.87	1.35
	1930	761	317	1,078	1,464	1.92	1.36
Trade. All but 46 companies.	1926	5,016	527	5,543	13,170	2.63	2.38
	1929	5,652	1,033	6,685	13,996	2.48	2.20
	1930	4,918	1,206	6,124	12,457	2.54	2.04
All industrial corporations, including service and miscellaneous. All but 334 companies.	1926	13,741	4,961	18,702	42,609	3.10	2.28
	1929	14,686	7,587	22,273	45,659	3.12	2.05
	1930	13,669	8,161	21,830	41,702	3.05	1.91

(a) Derived from Tables 43, 46 and 47.

6.28 times. Current liabilities had been reduced over 38 per cent, while current assets declined less than 20 per cent. In contrast, the current assets of the smaller companies declined at a slightly faster rate than current liabilities.

With respect to fixed debt the large corporations were also less seriously affected in their credit position than were the smaller companies.

In the first year of the depression the former reduced their bond and mortgage debt, whereas the smaller companies increased theirs by over 10 per cent. It is clear that while the credit position of industry as a whole remained constant or declined somewhat during the first two years of the depression, the large companies greatly improved their position while the smaller companies suffered the more seriously.

This same discrepancy appears in each of the four industrial divisions for which figures are available. For manufacturing, for trade, and for the construction industry the credit position of the large companies improved with the first two years of depression as they liquidated their current debt without any corresponding reduction in their current assets. The smaller companies suffered a loss in current assets without a fully corresponding decline in current liabilities. In mining, the position of both large and smaller companies declined but that of the smaller companies declined very much more rapidly.

(d) DEBTS BY SEPARATE INDUSTRIES

When we come to specific industries the available statistics of debt become less satisfactory except as we deal with separate and individual companies. It is probable that if time were allowed a figure for the debt of each industry and its credit condition could be obtained from trade associations and other sources. Under press of time it is necessary to limit the discussion to figures immediately available. Three sets of material will be considered: first, the record of business failures as published in Dun's Review; second, the more detailed information in Moody's survey of large companies already mentioned; third, the recent course of industrial bond prices.

Commercial Failures

The figures for commercial failures published in Dun's Review do not distinguish between corporate failures and the failures of unincorporated enterprises. In using them it will, therefore, be necessary to keep in mind that a small proportion, perhaps 10 or 15 per cent, of manufacturing enterprises are conducted by individuals or partnerships and that of trade enterprises roughly 50 per cent of the business is done by individuals and partnerships. Not even approximate figures are available for the proportion of service enterprises (hotels, restaurants, etc.) conducted by

TABLE 51

COMMERCIAL FAILURES, 1928-1932(a)

Manufacturers:	Number of Insolvencies					Liabilities (In Millions of Dollars)				
	1928	1929	1930	1931	1932	1928	1929	1930	1931	1932
Iron foundries and nails	119	148	103	181	286	$5.2	$6.2	$3.0	$19.8	$19.9
Machine and tools	325	295	330	409	506	11.6	15.6	18.8	52.0	32.8
Wools, carpets and knot goods	28	20	30	54	61	3.3	.5	2.0	5.5	3.0
Cottons, lace and hosiery	15	16	26	11	38	1.8	2.2	4.6	4.8	8.3
Lumber, carpenters and coopers	969	1,135	1,041	751	891	50.8	53.6	55.2	44.7	66.1
Clothing and millinery	557	500	579	707	840	10.3	8.0	16.4	14.6	23.3
Hats, gloves and furs	193	183	215	215	277	3.2	3.1	5.4	5.2	7.4
Chemicals and drugs	85	102	94	102	156	3.7	1.3	3.2	4.4	9.1
Paints and oils	13	21	20	26	44	.3	.3	1.2	2.6	1.6
Printing and engraving	172	174	212	260	384	3.6	2.6	7.2	9.5	13.0
Milling and bakers	494	462	449	493	554	7.0	5.6	6.3	7.8	8.6
Leather, shoes and harness	155	151	150	203	248	6.5	2.7	7.5	5.9	14.9
Tobacco, etc.	75	76	73	100	115	1.0	2.4	1.5	2.2	2.5
Glass, earthenware and brick	94	102	115	106	237	2.6	6.8	7.7	10.5	11.6
All other	2,630	2,622	2,841	2,794	2,642	71.6	79.8	98.6	93.9	128.1
Total	5,924	6,007	6,278	6,412	7,279	182.5	186.7	238.6	283.5	350.1
Service	1,105	1,172	1,132	1,159	1,258	24.4	20.5	20.9	44.0	51.5
Trading	15,372	14,245	17,261	19,011	21,366	200.9	204.2	252.0	291.4	379.7
Brokers, insurance agents, etc.	1,441	1,485	1,684	1,703	1,919	81.8	71.8	156.7	97.5	147.0
Total	23,842	22,909	26,355	28,285	31,822	$489.6	$483.3	$668.3	$736.3	$928.3

(a) Dun's *Review*, Vol. 41, No. 2025, p. 11 (Jan. 21, 1933).

corporations, while brokers, insurance agents, etc., are presumably for the most part unincorporated. Commercial failures by industrial groups are given in Table 51, both by number of failures and by millions of dollars of liabilities for the years 1928 to 1932.

In examining this table one important fact stands out. The liabilities in 1932, the worst of the five years covered, amounted to less than twice the liabilities of failed enterprises in the semi-boom and boom years of 1928 and 1929 and in total amounted to approximately three per cent of the liabilities of industrial corporations (this is a comparison of the liabilities of both incorporated and unincorporated enterprises which failed with the liabilities of corporations only). The total liabilities of concerns failing in the three depression years was approximately one billion dollars greater than the liabilities would have been if failures had continued at the 1928–29 rate. Thus the excess failures of both corporate and unincorporated enterprises due to the depression amounted to less than four per cent of the liabilities of all industrial corporations as they stood in 1929. If we take the figures for manufacturing corporations alone the excess liabilities presumably attributable to the depression amounted to only 2.4 per cent of the liabilities of all such corporations.

Thus, while the depression has taken its serious toll, the volume of failures has been surprisingly small considering the facts, (1) that industry has steadily declined until it is operating at little better than half its normal capacity, (2) that the banks in their drastic liquidation in the fall of 1931 and spring of 1932 forced the repayment of commercial loans to the extent of over $4 billion, or virtually 25 per cent of commercial loans outstanding, in less than a year, and (3) that bank suspensions locked up almost half a billion dollars of commercial deposits during the same period.

Strains Eased Before Bank Holiday

The recent quarterly figures for commercial failures given in Table 52 indicate that the pressure of debt had been somewhat alleviated during the latter part of 1932. (See also Chart 23.) Both the number of failures and the total amount of liabilities reached their peak in the first months of 1932 and have steadily declined in each successive quarter since. In the last quarter of 1932, the liabilities of failed concerns were only approximately 40 per cent larger than the average quarterly failures in 1928 and 1929. In the light of the declining rate of failures and the relatively

CHART 23

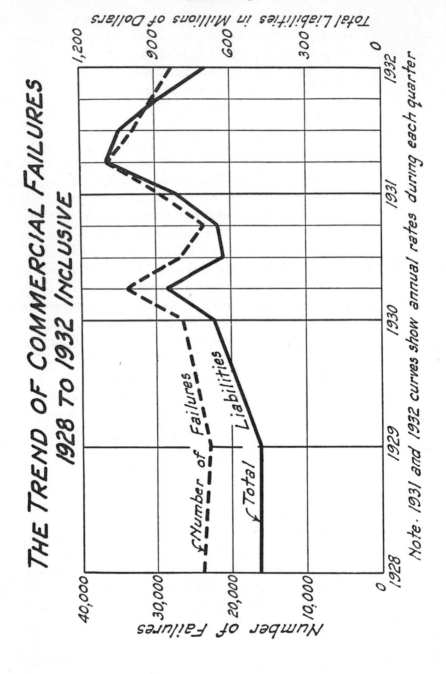

THE TREND OF COMMERCIAL FAILURES
1928 TO 1932 INCLUSIVE

Total Liabilities in Millions of Dollars

Number of Failures

£Number of Failures

£Total Liabilities

Note. 1931 and 1932 curves show annual rates during each quarter

small volume of failures under the tremendous pressure toward insolvency exerted on industrial concerns by the low rate of production and
by the bank liquidation and insolvency, it must be concluded that the
debt situation in industry, though serious, is not of cataclysmic proportions nor is it a mass problem.

TABLE 52

COMMERCIAL FAILURES

Quarterly Record, 1931–1932

	Number of Failures	Liabilities (In Millions of Dollars)
1931—1st quarter............	8,483	$214.6
2nd quarter............	6,624	155.9
3rd quarter............	5,863	161.3
4th quarter............	7,315	204.5
1932—1st quarter............	9,141	275.5
2nd quarter............	8,292	261.8
3rd quarter............	7,574	220.3
4th quarter............	6,943	169.9

With respect to the largest companies this same conclusion results
from an examination of the figures compiled by Moody's Investment
Service, though the figures only cover the period to the end of 1931.
They cover 334 corporations distributed among 39 industrial groups.
Treating the figures by industries and not by separate companies, 34 industries showed current assets more than three times current liabilities
while only 5 showed a lower current ratio. These were:

					Ratios
Coal and coke.............	Combined figures for	8	companies		2.94
Copper mining.............	"	"	"	10 "	2.71
Food canning.............	"	"	"	3 "	2.90
Drug chains.............	"	"	"	2 "	2.96
Restaurant chains.........	"	"	"	4 "	1.87

Four other industrial groups, however, showed such heavy funded
debt in relation to their current assets and liabilities as to make their
long time position not wholly satisfactory, even though their current
position was excellent. These were:—

Bread making	Combined figures for	4	companies	
Dairy	"	"	"	6 "
Meat packing	"	"	"	4 "
Retail Department Stores	"	"	"	18 "

The remaining industries, both with respect to current position and
funded debt, were in excellent shape, 25 of them having actually im-

proved their current position between 1929 and the end of 1931. Eleven of them showed current assets ten times current liabilities. Up to the beginning of 1932, then, the large companies were as a whole, in as sound a position as in the years 1926 to 1928, though certain industries and certain companies were in an unsatisfactory position or in actual financial difficulties. While this conclusion applies to the end of 1931, there is much to indicate that substantially the same condition prevailed at the end of 1932, that is, with the bulk of the larger companies solvent and in a reasonably good to excellent current position, and certain industries and companies in difficulties. Here again the debt problem appears to be not a mass problem but one easily localized and dealt with on an individual basis.

Bond Prices

One further source of information is available which will throw light on the subject of industrial debt, the record of industrial bond prices in recent months. Moody's Investment Service publishes a chart covering the changes in yield for 40 industrial bonds grouped into four classes or grades. This chart covering the years 1929 to 1932 is given below (see Chart 24). Its ups and downs directly reflect the changes in bond prices and roughly indicate their magnitude. The most prominent feature of the chart is the violent break in the prices of all four classes of bonds in the third quarter of 1931 at about the time that England left the gold standard. This was followed by the subsequent recovery in the third quarter of 1932. By the end of 1932 all classes, except Aa bonds, had returned to a level at or above that held in the middle of 1931. The marked recovery of the second and third grade bonds covered by the Baa index is a striking indication of the relatively sound position of these industries, in the presence of most unsatisfactory industrial conditions. At the end of 1932 their prices were only 18 per cent lower than their average price in 1929.

It must be kept in mind that these indexes reflect the course of prices for the better quality bonds and those of more important companies listed on the New York Stock Exchange. Only about half (by face value) of all industrial bonds are listed on the exchange, while only 60 per cent of the latter were rated by Moody's as Baa or better at the end of 1931. The indexes are nevertheless a fair indication of the drop and recovery

CHART 24

Prices of Industrial Bonds
1929–1932

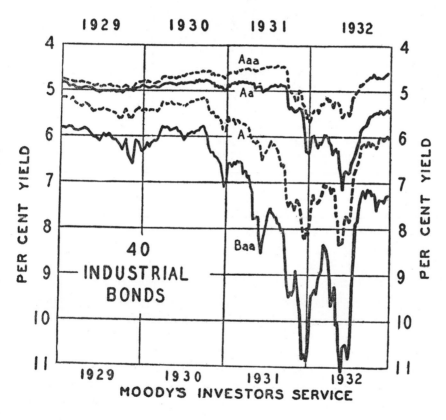

MOODY'S INVESTORS SERVICE

of industrial bond prices in general and are representative of a very large proportion since many unlisted securities would compare very favorably with those listed.

2. RECOMMENDATIONS

In closing this summary study of industrial debt, six conclusions stand out: *first,* industry as a whole did not over-borrow and thus weaken its credit position in the boom period culminating in 1929; *second,* industrial debt has declined markedly in the three years of the depression, current debt dropping more than 35 per cent; *third,* except for isolated cases, the credit position of larger companies has not become serious, since their ratios of current assets to current liabilities have been maintained at a high level; *fourth,* the effects of the depression on credit position have been very much more seriously felt by the smaller companies than the larger companies; *fifth,* industrial bond prices, though violently depressed during the fall of 1931 and the spring of 1932, had recovered their loss by the end of 1932 and show no indication of general industrial failure, being not out of line with their 1929 prices when consideration is given to the present unsatisfactory rate of industrial production; and *sixth,* the prospect of a whirlwind of industrial failures is not likely to develop from the conditions of industry itself, though such might develop from a general breakdown of the banking system.

In the light of these findings how should the problem of industrial corporation debt be met? This survey has suggested that the problem is not a mass problem but one for individual enterprises to be dealt with separately. Three steps could be taken to give relief.

First, reorganize the bankruptcy law so as to prevent a single creditor of a corporation or a small group of creditors from resisting an equable adjustment of the particular corporation's debt burden. This would allow corporations to be reorganized smoothly and to continue to function as economic enterprises, without the disrupting influence of receiverships. Such action would reduce the significance for industry as a whole of the larger financially weak companies and further isolate their influence.

Second, insure that no further bank liquidation of the drastic nature which occurred in the fall and winter of 1931–32 shall take place.

Third, apply pressure for a downward revision of the interest rates for short-term obligations which have shown little tendency to drop since the beginning of the depression.[4] Ease in money has found no important reflection in the lower interest charges for bank credit to customers. The combined effect of lower interest rates on short-term borrowing and a cessation of bank liquidation would greatly improve the debt position of smaller industrial companies and would enable the bulk of them to engage in any move toward business recovery.

Before closing this section on industrial debt one further statement should be made. It is clear that if business enterprise is to function at something like half its capacity for a long period of years, in other words if business is not to improve during the next three to four years, the treatment of industrial debt suggested here would be altogether inadequate. On the other hand, if economic recovery were to be immediate and rapid the problem of industrial debt would virtually disappear, excepting for that small fringe of companies which, under a competitive system, are expected to succumb. This conclusion would stand whether recovery were to take place at the existing level of prices or at a somewhat higher level. The present low rates of profit (or high loss) for the bulk of industrial companies appear to grow primarily out of the low functioning of the economic machine and to a minor extent only out of unsatisfactory price relationships. Increase production and sales 30 to 40 per cent at existing prices and it seems probable that in most corporate industries profits would quickly appear.

The suggestions for the treatment of debt made here are necessarily of an interim character and are offered on the assumption that moves in the direction of recovery will be made which will restore industry to a more nearly normal rate of activity. With such a development industry should be able to recover the highly favorable credit position which it held in the years from 1926 to 1929. To the present writer, the problem of industrial debt appears to be a problem growing out of bank instability and industrial inactivity, not out of overindebtedness or a drop in price level.

[4] For instance, at the beginning of 1932, interest rates charged to customers were higher than at the beginning of 1928 for three important groups of banks,—New York City banks, banks in eight other northern and eastern cities and banks of 27 southern and western cities. Between the beginning and the end of 1932 the rates charged by the New York City banks declined approximately 10 per cent, those charged by northern and eastern cities 4 per cent, and those by southern and western cities remained constant. *Federal Reserve Bulletin*, Jan. 1933, p. 21.

Chapter Seven

THE DEBTS OF FINANCIAL CORPORATIONS

SUMMARY

FINANCIAL corporations having long-term debts include life insurance companies, real estate companies, investment trusts, and finance companies (p. 205).

Long-term debts of financial institutions amounted to $24.7 billion in 1929 and $27 billion in 1930 (p. 205).

The long-term obligations of all life insurance companies (paid-up premiums on policies) grew from $4 billion in 1913 to $17 billion in 1931 (p. 206).

The bonded indebtedness of real estate companies increased from $150 million in 1913 to $5 billion in 1931 (p. 207).

The bonded indebtedness of investment trusts outstanding at the end of 1932 is estimated at about $230 million (p. 207).

The long-term debts of the three leading finance companies were $135 million in 1929 and $78 million in 1932 (p. 209).

The long-term debts of holding companies (railroad, public utility, etc.) are estimated at about $5 billion in 1929 and $6 billion in 1930 (p. 210).

Only the real estate companies and some of the holding companies are experiencing difficulty in meeting their obligations. Other financial corporations appear to be well able to handle current interest charges on their bonded debts.

Measures for dealing with real estate bonds are described in Chapter Three. See Chapters Four and Five for suggestions affecting holding companies in the public utility field.

Chapter Six describes the debt of industrial corporations in the United States. In order to obtain a complete picture of all corporate indebtedness of a long-term nature, account must also be taken of the bonded debt of financial corporations.

Financial institutions include banks and trust companies, whose debts are all short-term and are reported in Chapter Twelve; they also include stock and bond brokers, investment bankers and trusts, companies financing retail sales of automobiles, pianos, radios, etc., real estate and holding companies, insurance companies, building and loan associations, mortgage, note or pawn brokers, etc. Of these institutions, life insurance companies, real estate companies, investment trusts, and finance companies have incurred debts of a long-term nature.

Debt Statistics for 1929 and 1930

Data on the debts of financial corporations are available in the Statistics of Income for 1929 and 1930 compiled from income-tax returns of corporations submitting balance sheets to the Bureau of Internal Revenue in the United States Treasury Department. Table 19 in the Statistics of Income for both these years shows the assets and liabilities of all reporting corporations submitting balance sheets as of the last day of the calendar year or at the close of the fiscal year nearest thereto. Under the head of liabilities this table shows notes and accounts payable, bonded debt and mortgages, and miscellaneous liabilities not distributed. Notes and accounts payable are current debts; bonded debt and mortgages constitute long term debt; and miscellaneous liabilities are almost entirely accounted for by bank deposits, which are short-term debts, and by the value of outstanding life insurance policies and annuities, which are long-term obligations.

These three items, as shown in Table 53, constituting all the debts of all reporting financial corporations, excepting banks, whose deposits are excluded, aggregated $33,339 million in 1929 and $34,598 million in 1930. The long-term indebtedness of financial institutions in 1929 and 1930, however, represents the sum of items 2 and 3 in Table 53 (notes and accounts payable being current debt) which was $24,685 million in 1929 and $26,959 million in 1930.

The total debt of financial companies cannot be estimated for a pre-war year or a post-war depression year because the Statistics of Income for those years do not show the liabilities of reporting corporations. Nor can it be estimated for a later year than 1930 because the latest available Statistics of Income are for 1930.

It is possible to break down the long-term debts of financial corporations into the several financial groups so as to show the share of each in the total for 1929 and 1930. Although the liabilities of all financial companies are consolidated in the Statistics of Income, information has been obtained for some of the companies so that at least a partial picture of the distribution of the total long-term debt can be obtained.

Debt of Life Insurance Companies

The item on the balance sheet of life insurance companies which roughly corresponds to total deposits on a bank's balance sheet is that of "net reserves." This item is the accumulation of that portion of the cur-

TABLE 53

DEBTS OF FINANCIAL CORPORATIONS, 1929 AND 1930(a)

(Reporting to the U. S. Bureau of Internal Revenue)

	1929	1930
1. Notes and accounts payable................	$8,653,695,722	$7,639,569,158
2. Bonded debt and mortgages(b)..............	10,135,213,115	11,078,582,833
3. Net reserves, life insurance companies.......	14,550,000,000	15,880,000,000
	$33,338,908,837	$34,598,151,991

(a) Adapted from *Statistics of Income* for 1929, Table 19, p. 333; 1930, Table 19, p. 267.

(b) Real estate bonds account for approximately one-half of this item in both years. The remainder was presumably the debt of holding companies: railroad, public utility, etc.

rent premiums which are not used in the payment of current death claims and expenses. It represents the total amount of premiums paid in on outstanding life insurance policies and is classified as a long-term obligation of the companies to their policy holders. We have, therefore, used this figure of net reserves to indicate the trend of the total debt outstanding of life insurance companies.

The data shown in the following table have been estimated by increasing to 100 per cent the reserves of the 52 companies reporting to the Association of Life Insurance Companies, whose total assets comprise about 92 per cent of the total assets of all life insurance companies in the United States.

TABLE 54

GROWTH OF RESERVES OF LIFE INSURANCE COMPANIES(a)

(In Millions of Dollars)

1913........	$4,040	1930........	$15,880
1921........	6,740	1931........	17,000
1929........	14,550		

(a) Association of Life Insurance Presidents.

Real Estate Companies

In the chapter on "Urban Mortgage Debts," the volume of real estate securities outstanding at the end of certain years is estimated. According to these estimates the volume of real estate bonds outstanding at the end of selected years was as follows:

TABLE 55

TOTAL VOLUME OF REAL ESTATE BONDS OUTSTANDING
(In Millions of Dollars)

1913	$150	1930	$5,040
1921	502	1931	5,017
1929	4,918		

It will be seen that the volume of real estate securities outstanding more than tripled between 1913 and 1921, and that it multiplied almost ten times from 1921 to 1929, since which time it has remained relatively stable. Less than 2 per cent of these bonds outstanding in 1931 were short-term obligations. This type of indebtedness is also covered in Chapter Three, but it is not duplicated in the debt summary in Chapter One.

Investment Trusts

Beginning in 1925 investment trusts have done a considerable amount of long-term bond financing. From 1925 to 1930, inclusive, bond issues for investment trusts totaled $384 million. The amount of such financing in 1925 and 1926 was inconsiderable, but in 1927 they issued $90 million worth of bonds and comparably large amounts in each of the following three years. Since 1930, however, these companies have offered no new bonds for sale.

Table 56 shows the volume of investment trust financing, not including fixed trusts, during 1925–1930.

TABLE 56(*a*)

INVESTMENT TRUST FINANCING

1925	$425,000
1926	1,542,500
1927	89,704,750
1928	104,198,275
1929	84,446,800
1930	103,737,500
Total	$384,054,825

(*a*) Keane's *Manual of Investment Trusts* (1932), p. 1758.

In order to determine the bonded indebtedness of investment trusts outstanding in particular years, account must be taken of retirements of these issues. Data are available on the funded debt outstanding on December 31, 1929, 1930, 1931, and 1932 of a group of nine investment trusts having total net assets at the last year-end of over $126 million. Prior to 1929 the bonded indebtedness of these companies increased, but since 1929, as Table 57 shows, their funded debt has decreased almost 40 per cent. The companies included in this table cover a representative cross section of all investment trusts and it is reasonable to assume that the same ratio of decrease obtained among the investment trusts as a

TABLE 57(a)

FUNDED DEBTS OF INVESTMENT TRUSTS

(As of December 31)

	Total Net Assets, Dec. 31, 1932	1929	1930	1931	1932
American International.........	$17,768,772	$24,987,000	$23,750,000	$20,967,000	$14,182,000
Capital Administration.........	5,420,582	5,000,000	3,982,000	3,660,000	3,417,000
United Founders Group(b)......	44,089,284	52,447,200	51,679,000	43,944,100	23,747,400
General American Investors....	15,023,030	7,500,000	7,000,000	6,700,000	6,600,000
Adams Express Company.......	16,549,160	9,889,500	9,911,000	9,911,000	9,773,000
American European Sec........	7,708,519	4,000,000	4,000,000	4,000,000	3,057,000
General Public Service.........	8,993,037	14,971,000	13,943,000	9,200,000	6,500,000
Investment Co. of America.....	3,779,117	5,000,000	4,750,000	3,491,500	2,734,000
Standard Investing Corp.......	7,094,270	9,500,000	9,073,000	8,059,000	6,998,000
Total....................	$126,425,771	$133,294,700	$128,088,000	$109,932,600	$77,008,400

(a) Information furnished by Arthur A. Winston, Director of Statistical Department, Allied-Distributors, Inc., 63 Wall Street, New York.

(b) As of November 30.

group. On this assumption the total funded debt of all these companies outstanding on December 31, 1932, was about $230 million.

A review of the operations of eight leverage management investment trusts during 1930, 1931, and 1932 shows that in only one case was cash interest and dividend income, after paying expenses, insufficient to cover bond interest charges fully. The ratio of net income to interest charges on outstanding bonds ranged from 0.98 for the General Public Service Corporation in 1931 to 8.72 for the Tri-Continental Corporation in 1932.[1]

[1] *Management Trusts—Their Operations, Their Present Status, and Their Outlook,* by Arthur A. Winston, Director of Statistical Department, Allied General Corporation, New York City.

Retail Sales Finance Companies

Another type of financial institution that has incurred long-term indebtedness are the companies engaged in financing retail sales of automobiles, pianos, radios, etc. The bulk of this business is done by three companies: The Commercial Credit Company, The General Motors Acceptance Corporation, and The Commercial Investment Trust. These companies have issued bonds in small amounts in recent years. Table 58

TABLE 58(*a*)

LONG-TERM DEBTS OF FINANCE COMPANIES

(Amounts in Thousands)

	1929	1932
Long-Term Debt:		
Commercial Credit Company................................	$8,250	$9,422
General Motors Acceptance Corporation......................	80,500	48,160
Commercial Investment Trust.............................	46,081	20,357
Total long-term debt..................................	$134,831	$77,939
Net Income before Interest Charges:		
Commercial Credit Company................................	$13,421	$2,716
General Motors Acceptance Corporation......................	35,073	13,071
Commercial Investment Trust.............................	11,695	7,039
Total net income before interest charges....................	$60,189	$22,826
Interest Charges on Long-Term Debt:		
Commercial Credit Company................................	$475	$565
General Motors Acceptance Corporation......................	4,400	2,750
Commercial Investment Trust.............................	2,530	1,320
Total interest charges..................................	$7,405	$4,635

(*a*) Data supplied by Mr. Percy Hall, associate of Lahey, Fargo and Company, New York.

shows their bonded indebtedness, net income before interest charges, and the interest charges on their long-term debt for 1929 and 1932, the only years for which this information is available. It will be seen that these companies reduced their long-term debts by 42 per cent from 1929 to 1932, achieving this reduction both by bond retirements and by short-term bank loans. Net income before interest payments declined 62 per cent during the three-year period due to the decrease in the volume of business done. It was 8.13 times interest charges in 1929 and 4.92 times in 1932.

Total Long-Term Debts

The foregoing estimates of the long-term debts of financial institutions are consolidated in Table 59. This table accounts for all but $4,802 million of the entire long-term debt of all financial corporations

TABLE 59

LONG-TERM DEBTS OF FINANCIAL CORPORATIONS

(Amounts in Millions of Dollars)

	1913	1921	1929	1930	1931
1. Life insurance companies....	$4,040	$6,740	$14,550	$15,880	$17,000
2. Real estate companies......	150	502	4,918	5,040	5,017
3. Investment trusts..........	......	......	280	....	230
4. Finance companies.........	......	......	135	....	78
Total..................	$4,190	$7,242	$19,883	$20,920	$22,325

in 1929, and for all but $6,039 million in 1930 of the total reported in *Statistics of Income*. The difference is probably represented, as has been suggested, by the debts of holding companies.

Chapter Eight

THE DEBT OF THE UNITED STATES GOVERNMENT

SUMMARY

The Facts

ON March 15, 1933, the gross federal debt was $21.7 billion and the current deficit was $1.4 billion (p. 213).

The gross public debt on March 15, 1933, comprised a bonded long-term debt of $14.2 billion and short-term debts totaling $7.5 billion (pp. 213–17).

During the fiscal year 1933 it is estimated that interest charges on the federal debt will be $695 million and that retirements will be $427 million, or a total debt service of $1.1 billion. It is further estimated that total ordinary receipts of the federal government during 1933 will be $2.6 billion, or 2.34 times the current debt service (p. 214).

The gross federal debt per capita is now $173.69 compared with $139.40 in 1929, $208.97 in 1922, and $12.00 in 1914 (p. 228).

The gross federal debt is now 7.2 per cent of the estimated national wealth compared with 4.4 per cent in 1929, 7.2 per cent in 1922, and 0.6 per cent in 1914 (p. 227).

The debt service on the public debt is now 2.53 per cent of the estimated national income compared with 1.4 per cent in 1929, 2.1 per cent in 1922, and 0.06 per cent in 1914 (p. 228).

There were federal deficits in 1931 and 1932 and another deficit is indicated for 1933. From June 30, 1930, to March 15, 1933, the federal debt increased by $5.5 billion, or 34 per cent. This increase since 1930 compares with the decrease of $9.3 billion between 1919 and 1930 (p. 220).

The federal debt is retired by annual appropriations to the sinking fund, by receipts from foreign governments on their debt accounts, from surplus receipts in the general fund, and from miscellaneous receipts. During 1919–1932 funds from all these sources retired $9.3 billion of the public debt. Continued payments by several foreign governments are in doubt, and no net reductions in the federal debt have been made since 1930 (pp. 223–27).

Of all interest-bearing securities of the United States government outstanding in 1930, 57.2 per cent were held by corporations and 10.5 per cent by private individuals (pp. 229–30).

The treasury has met 43 per cent of its total deficit since July 1, 1930, by long-term bond issues and 57 per cent by intermediate issues of treasury notes and by short-term issues of certificates and bills. These issues have repeatedly been oversubscribed by the padding of bids, a practice that has serious drawbacks (pp. 234–36).

Recommendations

Two courses are open to the federal government for debt reduction: one is genuinely to balance the national budget for 1934 and thereby not only stop the further rise in the public debt caused by the financing of recurring deficits, but also resume the net reduction of the debt from sinking fund appropriations and from treasury surpluses. The other course is to refund existing obligations at lower rates of interest than they now bear (pp. 237–38).

Adoption of the so-called capital or extraordinary budget is suggested for capital outlays and emergency relief expenditures so as to prevent prospective federal borrowing of billions of dollars for emergency relief for farmers, home owners, and the unemployed from hopelessly unbalancing the current or operating budget and damaging the federal credit. Under this proposal only the carrying charges on bond issues for capital outlays and relief purposes would be covered in the current budget. If this plan had been in effect since 1930, it is estimated that there would have been deficits in 1931 and 1932 of $77 million and $1,545 million, instead of actual net deficits of $903 million and $2,885 million, respectively (pp. 241–44).

An estimated saving to the federal treasury of $92 million could be effected from a conversion of all outstanding Liberty bonds into 3 per cent bonds. Such a saving would help to balance the budget (pp. 247–48).

Elimination of the tax exemption feature of federal issues is recommended. Removal of this feature, it is estimated, would increase federal revenues from $100 to $300 million; increased revenues would probably be offset in part, however, by higher interest rates on treasury offerings (pp. 248–49).

1. THE FACTS [1]

THE purpose of this chapter is to describe the debt of the federal government: its size and composition, recent changes in it, sources of funds for its reduction, its relation to the national wealth and income and other categories of domestic indebtedness, the distribution of federal securities among individuals and institutions, changes in price, interest rates, and interest payments on government issues, and the way in which the treasury has met its recent deficits. Ways and means of reducing the federal debt burden will be considered, and the probable effect upon it of currency inflation will be examined.

The net change in the gross public debt at any time represents the net excess of expenditures over receipts, plus any decline in the general fund balance, plus borrowing necessitated by advances to the Reconstruction Finance Corporation. On June 30, 1932, the end of the last fiscal year, the total gross debt of the federal government amounted to $19,487 million. It stood at $21,711 million at the close of business March 15, 1933. The deficit of the current fiscal year, growing at the average rate of about five and one-half million dollars a day, had reached $1,413 million on March 15, 1933. It is hazardous to forecast the probable deficit for the fiscal year 1933 since tax collections when this was written had not yet fully reflected the effect of the revenue act of 1932 which increased the rates on individual and corporate incomes. President Hoover, in his budget message to Congress last December, estimated that the deficit for 1933 [2] would be $1,645 million.

The composition of the federal debt on January 31, 1933, is shown in Table 61. It will be seen that the total interest-bearing debt of the federal government outstanding at that time was $20,454 million, or 98 per cent of the total gross debt, and an increase of $1,293 million over the figure for June 30, 1932. The interest-bearing debt consists of long-term bonds and short-term treasury notes, certificates of indebtedness, and treasury bills. The non-interest-bearing debt consists of matured debt on which interest has ceased and miscellaneous items bearing no interest, including United States notes.

Bonds made up $14,230 million of the public debt at the end of January, or 69.5 per cent of the total interest-bearing debt and 68 per

---

[1] Table 60 and Chart 25 summarize the basic data used in this chapter.
[2] Reference to years in this chapter is to fiscal years.

TABLE 60

BASIC DATA ON FEDERAL GOVERNMENT DEBT

(Dollars, except per Capita Figures, in Millions)

	1933	1929	1922	1914	Percentage Changes		
					1933 over 1929	1929 over 1922	1922 over 1914
1. Total long-term debt	$14,237(a)	$12,155	$15,965	$968	17.1	−23.8	1,549
2. Total short-term debt	$7,474(a)	4,776	6,999	220	56.5	−31.7	3,081
3. Gross debt (1+2)	$21,711(a)	16,931	22,964	1,188	28.2	−26.3	1,841
4. Interest charge	$695(b)	678	991	23	2.5	−31.6	4,209
5. Public debt retirements	$427(b)	550	423	......	−22.3	30.0	......
6. Total debt service (4+5)	$1,122	1,228	1,414	23	−8.6	−13.2	6,048
7. Total ordinary receipts	$2,624(b)	4,033	4,109	735	−34.9	−1.8	459
8. Ratio, total receipts to debt service	2.34	3.28	2.91	31.96	−28.7	12.7	−91
9. Gross debt per capita	$173.69	139.40	208.97	12.00	24.6	−33.3	1,641
10. National wealth(c)	$300,000	385,000	321,000	192,000	−22.1	19.9	67
11. Percentage, gross debt of national wealth	7.2	4.4	7.2	0.6	63.6	34.7	1,100
12. National income(d)	$40,000	85,000	66,000	36,000	−56.5	39.4	88.5
13. Percentage, debt service of national income	2.53	1.4	2.1	0.06	78.6	−33.3	3,400
14. Wholesale commodity price index (BLS)	59.8(e)	95.3	96.7	68.1	−37.3	−1.5	42

(a) As of March 15, 1933.
(b) Estimated. Appropriation for 1933 was $640 million for interest on public debt.
(c) Estimates of National Industrial Conference Board for 1914 and 1929. U. S. census estimate for 1922. Estimate of Cleveland Trust Company for 1932.
(d) Estimates of W. I. King for 1914 and 1922. Estimates of National Industrial Conference Board for 1929 and 1932.
(e) For February, 1933.

CHART 25

The Federal Debt in Relation to National Wealth and Income

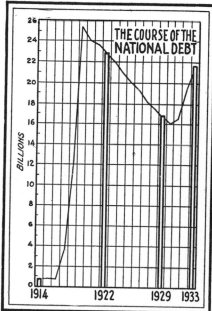

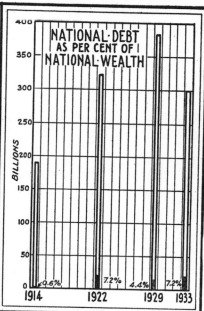

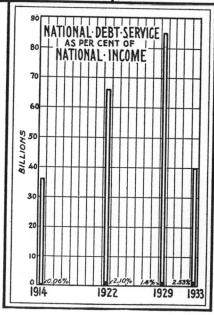

TABLE 61

PUBLIC DEBT, JANUARY 31, 1933, CLASSIFIED BY CHARACTER

I. *Interest Bearing*
  1. Bonds

a. Pre-war bonds......................	$806,017,570.00	
b. War-Liberty bonds..................	8,201,309,150.00	
c. Treasury bonds....................	5,222,842,600.00	
Total bonds.....................		$14,230,169,320.00
2. Treasury Notes		
a. Government Trust Funds		
(1) Civil Service Retirement Fund.....	$219,600,000.00	
(2) Foreign Service Retirement Fund...	2,110,000.00	
(3) Canal Zone Retirement Fund......	2,133,000.00	
Total Government Trust Funds....	$223,843,000.00	
b. Other...........................	3,074,531,600.00	
Total treasury notes..............		$3,298,374,600.00
3. Certificates of Indebtedness		
a. Adjusted Service Certificate Fund......	$127,300,000.00	
b. Other.............................	2,157,547,100.00	
Total Certificates of Indebtedness...		$2,284,847,100.00
4. Treasury Bills..........................		640,717,000.00
Total interest bearing.............		$20,454,108,020.00

II. *Matured debt on which interest has ceased*

1. Pre-war bonds..........................	$1,617,050.26	
2. War-Liberty bonds......................	8,248,050.00	
3. Treasury notes........................	12,762,200.00	
4. Certificates of indebtedness..............	21,493,400.00	
5. Treasury bills.........................	9,844,000.00	
6. Treasury savings certificates..............	658,150.00	
Total matured debt on which interest has ceased.....................		$54,622,850.26
III. *Total debt bearing no interest*...............		292,976,263.75
Total gross debt.................................		$20,801,707,134.01

cent of the gross debt. There has been a decrease during 1933 in the amount of bonds outstanding of $19 million. Except for a small issue of postal savings bonds, no bonds have been sold by the government during 1933.

Treasury notes accounted for $3,298 million of the federal debt at the close of January compared with $1,465 million on June 30, 1932. The increase of 125 per cent in the volume of these obligations was chiefly due to six note issues during the year, totaling $2,691 million and maturing in 1934, 1936, 1937, and 1938. One issue of treasury notes amounting to $600 million matured on December 15, 1932.

Certificates of indebtedness outstanding on January 31, 1933, amounted to $2,285 million, or 11 per cent of the gross debt. Outstanding obligations of this character decreased $712 million during the first seven months of the fiscal year.

Treasury bills, a type of federal short-time obligation authorized in 1929, accounted for $641 million of the public debt at the end of January. These bills are issued on a discount basis and are payable at maturity without interest. They are chiefly used to raise money during the periods between the regular quarterly borrowing operations.

Table 62 gives a preliminary statement of the public debt as of January 31, 1933. This statement shows the debt classified by character and issue. For each issue it shows the interest rate, the date redeemable or payable, and the amount outstanding. The table indicates that bonds constitute two-thirds of the public debt, that $1,933 million of First Liberty bonds are now eligible for redemption, and that $6,268 million of Fourth Liberty bonds become callable this year. The table shows also the maturities of $3,298 million of treasury notes during 1934–37, the maturities of $2,285 million of certificates of indebtedness on or before January 1, 1934, and the maturities of $641 million of treasury bills during February, March, and April, 1933. It will be seen that the federal debt is very flexible. Much of it will mature in small instalments over a long series of years. A large part of it may be retired or refunded whenever the condition of the treasury permits. About one-half of it—the war Liberty bonds, the certificates of indebtedness, and the treasury bills—matures or becomes eligible for redemption this year.

Tables 63 and 64 show the issues and maturities of interest-bearing securities of the United States, exclusive of trust funds and other special issues, from July 1, 1932, to February 8, 1933. These issues and maturities resulted during the period in a net increase of $1,429 million in the short-term debt of the United States. Meanwhile, the long-term bonded debt remained unchanged at about 14¼ billion dollars. The treasury was continuing to finance its deficits by short-term loans. the decline and rise of the public debt by obliging the government to

Changes in the Federal Debt Since 1916

Federal borrowing is influenced by various factors. The inflation and deflation of business and agriculture have had an inevitable effect upon undertake new activities in both fields with resulting changes in receipts and expenditures. Changes in the level of commodity prices affect the purchasing power of payments for interest and retirement of public indebtedness. The necessity of refunding operations undertaken to provide for maturing debt or to obtain more favorable rates of interest also influences governmental borrowing. National emergencies, however, such as wars and business depressions, have the most marked effect upon the trend in governmental indebtedness. Wars have had the greatest influence on the public debt which reached two peaks, in 1866 and in 1919, after the Civil and World Wars. During the past seventeen years the federal debt has been especially sensitive to the World War and the depression of 1929–33.

From 1890 until 1917 the federal debt remained relatively stable at slightly more than one billion dollars. At the close of 1916 it amounted to $1,225 million. With America's entry into the World War, however, it rose during 1917 to $2,976 million. By 1919, as a result of huge loans to our Allies and colossal expenditures at home and abroad, the federal debt reached $25,482 million, the high water mark of our fiscal history. At least three-quarters and probably a higher percentage of the present debt of the federal government, as well as debt service charges, may be attributed to the World War. The annual interest charge on the war debt in 1919 exceeded one billion dollars, a sum equal to about one-quarter of the total annual cost of running the federal government.

It has been the post-war policy of the treasury to reduce this great obligation almost as rapidly as the economic condition of the country and the requirements of the budget would permit.[3] Thanks to this policy of debt reduction and to a decade of prosperity, the federal debt fell to $16,185 million in 1930, or $9,297 million below the 1919 peak. This decline amounted to an average reduction during the interval of $845 million each year. Meanwhile, the remaining debt had been refunded at a lower rate of interest and future maturities so distributed as to dates and amounts that they could be readily handled out of current income or with a minimum of new financing. The record of the treasury in its public-debt transactions after the war deserves high praise, despite the fact that the debt could have been retired to even a greater extent than it was.

[3] During the period, 1921–1929, normal income tax rates were thrice reduced; otherwise the debt might have been reduced even more rapidly than it was.

TABLE 62

PRELIMINARY STATEMENT OF THE PUBLIC DEBT JANUARY 31, 1933

(On the Basis of Daily Treasury Statements)

Bonds:			
2% Consols of 1930		$599,724,050.00	
2% Panama Canal Loan of 1916–36		48,954,180.00	
2% Panama Canal Loan of 1918–38		25,947,400.00	
3% Panama Canal Loan of 1961		49,800,000.00	
3% Conversion bonds of 1946–47		28,894,500.00	
2½% Postal Savings bonds (5th to 44th Series)		52,697,440.00	$806,017,570.00
First Liberty loan of 1932–47:			
3½% bonds	$1,392,227,350.00		
4 % bonds (converted)	5,002,450.00		
4¼% bonds (converted)	535,982,800.00	$1,933,212,600.00	
4¼% Fourth Liberty loan of 1933–38		6,268,096,550.00	8,201,309,150.00
Treasury Bonds:			
4¼% bonds of 1947–52		$758,983,300.00	
4 % bonds of 1944–54		1,036,834,500.00	
3¾% bonds of 1946–56		489,087,100.00	
3⅜% bonds of 1943–47		454,135,200.00	
3⅜% bonds of 1940–43		352,994,450.00	
3⅜% bonds of 1941–43		544,916,050.00	
3⅛% bonds of 1946–49		821,400,500.00	
3 % bonds of 1951–55		764,491,500.00	5,222,842,600.00
Total bonds			$14,230,169,320.00
Treasury Notes:			
3 % Series A-1934, maturing May 2, 1934		$244,234,600.00	
2⅛% Series B-1934, maturing Aug. 1, 1934		345,292,600.00	
3 % Series A-1935, maturing June 15, 1935		416,602,800.00	
3¼% Series A-1936, maturing Aug. 1, 1936		365,138,000.00	
2¾% Series B-1936, maturing Dec. 15, 1936		360,533,200.00	
3¼% Series A-1937, maturing Sept. 15, 1937		834,401,500.00	
3 % Series B-1937, maturing Apr. 15, 1937		508,328,900.00	
		$3,074,531,600.00	
4% Civil Service retirement fund, Series 1933 to 1937		219,600,000.00	
4% Foreign Service retirement fund, Series 1933 to 1937		2,110,000.00	
4% Canal Zone retirement fund, Series 1936 and 1937		2,133,000.00	3,298,374,600.00
Certificates of Indebtedness:			
3¾% Series A-1933, maturing Feb. 1, 1933		$144,372,000.00	
3¾% Series TM-1933, maturing Mar. 15, 1933		660,715,500.00	
2 % 1st Series, maturing Mar. 15, 1933		33,594,600.00	
2 % Series B-1933, maturing May 2, 1933		239,197,000.00	
1½% Series TJ-1933, maturing June 15, 1933		373,856,500.00	
1¼% Series TS-1933, maturing Sept. 15, 1933		451,447,000.00	
¾ % Series TD-1933, maturing Dec. 15, 1933		254,364,500.00	
		$2,157,547,100.00	
4% Adjusted Service Certificate Fund Series, maturing Jan. 1, 1934		127,300,000.00	2,284,847,100.00

TABLE 62—*Continued*

PRELIMINARY STATEMENT OF THE PUBLIC DEBT JANUARY 31, 1933

(On the Basis of Daily Treasury Statements)

Treasury Bills (Maturity Value):

Series maturing Feb. 8, 1933	$75,056,000.00	
Series maturing Feb. 15, 1933	75,480,000.00	
Series maturing Feb. 23, 1933	60,000,000.00	
Series maturing Mar. 1, 1933	100,000,000.00	
Series maturing Mar. 29, 1933	100,039,000.00	
Series maturing Apr. 12, 1933	75,090,000.00	
Series maturing Apr. 19, 1933	75,032,000.00	
Series maturing Apr. 26, 1933	80,020,000.00	640,717,000.00
Total interest-bearing debt outstanding		$20,454,108,020.00
Matured Debt on Which Interest Has Ceased:		
Old debt matured-issued prior to Apr. 1, 1917	$1,617,050.26	
4% and 4¼% 2nd Liberty loan bonds of 1927–42	2,780,200.00	
4¼% 3rd Liberty loan bonds of 1928	4,427,550.00	
3¾% Victory notes of 1922–23	19,150.00	
4¾% Victory notes of 1922–23	1,021,150.00	
Treasury notes, at various interest rates	12,762,200.00	
Certificates of indebtedness, at various interest rates	21,493,400.00	
Treasury bills	9,844,000.00	
Treasury savings certificates	658,150.00	54,622,850.26
Debt Bearing No Interest:		
United States notes	$346,681,016.00	
Less gold reserve	156,039,088.03	
	$190,641,927.97	
Deposits for retirement of national bank and Federal reserve bank notes	96,945,449.50	
Old demand notes and fractional currency	2,040,299.35	
Thrift and Treasury savings stamps, unclassified sales, etc.	3,348,586.93	292,976,263.75
Total gross debt		$20,801,707,134.01

The coming of depression, however, put an end to the diminution of the total debt and introduced a new emergency in federal finances. In 1931 the treasury experienced its first peace-time deficit since 1915. Another deficit followed in 1932 and further deficits are indicated for 1933, and for 1934 unless President Roosevelt succeeds in balancing the budget for 1934. Under the stress of these conditions the total federal debt increased by $4,616 million from June 30, 1930, to January 31, 1933, or 28.5 per cent. This increase since 1930 of $4,616 million in the public debt compares with the decrease of $9,297 million between 1919 and 1930. Half the ground won since the war has been lost. Moreover, as a result of the depression and of federal deficits in 1931–1933, the government has failed to effect a reduction of $1,230

TABLE 63

ISSUES OF INTEREST-BEARING SECURITIES OF THE UNITED STATES EXCLUSIVE OF TRUST FUND AND OTHER SPECIAL ISSUES FROM JULY 1, 1932, TO FEBRUARY 8, 1933

Date	Issue	Rate of Interest(a)	Amount Issued
1932			
July 13	Treasury bills maturing Oct. 11, 1932............	.385	$75,278,000
20	Treasury bills maturing Oct. 19, 1932............	.400	75,923,000
27	Treasury bills maturing Oct. 26, 1932............	.466	83,317,000
Aug. 1	Treasury notes, series B-1934..................	$2\frac{1}{8}$	345,292,600
1	Treasury notes, series A-1936..................	$3\frac{1}{4}$	365,138,000
10	Treasury bills maturing Nov. 9, 1932............	.529	75,217,000
17	Treasury bills maturing Nov. 16, 1932...........	.485	75,016,000
24	Treasury bills maturing Nov. 23, 1932...........	.419	62,350,000
31	Treasury bills maturing Nov. 30, 1932...........	.325	100,500,000
Sept. 15	Treasury notes, series A-1937..................	$3\frac{1}{4}$	834,401,500
15	Certificates of indebtedness maturing Sept. 15, 1933.	$1\frac{1}{4}$	451,447,000
28	Treasury bills maturing Dec. 28, 1932............	.233	100,665,000
Oct. 11	Treasury bills maturing Jan. 11, 1933............	.192	75,954,000
15	Treasury notes, series B-1937..................	3	508,328,900
19	Treasury bills maturing Jan. 18, 1933............	.140	75,110,000
26	Treasury bills maturing Jan. 25, 1933............	.195	80,295,000
Nov. 9	Treasury bills maturing Feb. 8, 1933............	.217	75,056,000
16	Treasury bills maturing Feb. 15, 1933............	.206	75,480,000
23	Treasury bills maturing Feb. 23, 1933............	.168	60,000,000
30	Treasury bills maturing Mar. 1, 1933............	.134	100,000,000
Dec. 15	Treasury notes, series B-1936..................	$2\frac{3}{4}$	360,533,200
15	Certificates of indebtedness maturing Dec. 15, 1933.	$\frac{3}{4}$	254,364,500
28	Treasury bills maturing Mar. 29, 1933............	.085	100,039,000
1933			
Jan. 11	Treasury bills maturing Apr. 12, 1933............	.204	75,090,000
18	Treasury bills maturing Apr. 19, 1933............	.235	75,032,000
25	Treasury bills maturing Apr. 26, 1933............	.182	80,020,000
Feb. 1	Treasury notes, series A-1938..................	$2\frac{5}{8}$	277,516,600
8	Treasury bills maturing May 10, 1933............	.177	75,228,000
			$4,992,592,300

(a) For Treasury bills, average rates on a bank discount basis are shown.

million in the public debt as contemplated by the sinking fund provisions. In other words, the total cost of the depression to the federal treasury has been almost six billion dollars.[4]

Part of this increase, to be sure, is offset by the fact that, during the era of plenty, the public debt had been retired at a rate faster than originally anticipated. Thus a reserve had, in effect, been set up upon which the treasury was justified in drawing in order to avoid imposing new tax burdens in a time of stress. This reserve, however, has now been exhausted. Another probable offset, amounting to $1,107 million to March 15, 1933, represents net payments from credits established on account of the purchase by the Secretary of the Treasury of the

[4] Table 65 shows the surpluses and deficits of the Federal Government since 1920.

TABLE 64

MATURITIES OF INTEREST-BEARING SECURITIES OF THE UNITED STATES EXCLUSIVE OF
TRUST FUND AND OTHER SPECIAL ISSUES FROM JULY 1, 1932, TO FEBRUARY 8, 1933

Date	Issue	Rate of Interest(a)	Amount Matured
1932			
July 13	Treasury bills issued Apr. 13, 1932..............	1.049	$76,200,000
20	Treasury bills issued Apr. 20, 1932..............	.621	75,600,000
27	Treasury bills issued Apr. 27, 1932..............	.630	51,550,000
Aug. 1	Certificates of indebtedness issued Feb. 1, 1932....	3⅛	227,631,000
10	Treasury bills issued May 11, 1932..............	.676	76,744,000
17	Treasury bills issued May 18, 1932..............	.425	75,000,000
24	Treasury bills issued May 25, 1932..............	.289	60,050,000
31	Treasury bills issued June 1, 1932..............	.321	100,022,000
Sept. 15	Certificates of indebtedness issued Sept. 15, 1931..	1⅛	314,279,500
15	Certificates of indebtedness issued Dec. 15, 1931...	3	398,225,000
28	Treasury bills issued June 29, 1932..............	.408	100,466,000
Oct. 11	Treasury bills issued July 13, 1932..............	.385	50,278,000
15	Certificates of indebtedness issued Mar. 15, 1932..	3⅛	333,492,500
19	Treasury bills issued July 20, 1932..............	.400	75,923,000
26	Treasury bills issued July 27, 1932..............	.466	83,317,000
Nov. 9	Treasury bills issued Aug. 10, 1932..............	.529	75,217,000
16	Treasury bills issued Aug. 17, 1932..............	.485	75,016,000
23	Treasury bills issued Aug. 24, 1932..............	.419	62,350,000
30	Treasury bills issued Aug. 31, 1932..............	.325	100,500,000
Dec. 15	Treasury notes, series, 1932.....................	3¼	600,446,200
28	Treasury bills issued Sept. 28, 1932..............	.233	100,665,000
1933			
Jan. 11	Treasury bills issued Oct. 11, 1932..............	.192	75,954,000
18	Treasury bills issued Oct. 19, 1932..............	.140	75,110,000
25	Treasury bills issued Oct. 26, 1932..............	.195	80,295,000
Feb. 1	Certificates of indebtedness issued Feb. 1, 1932....	3¾	144,372,000
8	Treasury bills issued Nov. 9, 1932..............	.217	75,056,000

$3,563,779,200

(a) For Treasury bills, average rates on a bank discount basis are shown.

obligations of the Reconstruction Finance Corporation. These loans, it is expected, will sooner or later be repaid to the treasury and applied by law to the reduction of the public debt.

TABLE 65

ANNUAL SURPLUSES OR DEFICITS, 1920–1934(a)

1920...........	$212,475,198	1928......	$398,828,281
1921...........	86,723,772	1929......	184,787,035
1922...........	313,801,651	1930......	183,789,215
1923...........	309,657,461	1931......	−902,716,845
1924...........	505,366,987	1932......	−2,885,362,299
1925...........	250,505,239	1933......	−1,644,631,707(b)
1926...........	377,767,816	1934......	− 818,014,287(c)
1927...........	635,809,921		

(a) Including public debt retirements, and for 1933 and 1934 assuming no cut in expenditures, no new taxation, and full foreign government payments.
(b) Official budget estimate.
(c) Official budget estimate revised to take account of supplemental budget messages.

In order to carry out its policy of continuous debt reduction after the war, the federal government made certain provisions for retiring the debt at a progressive rate.

Sinking Fund

In the first place, it set up a sinking fund for the retirement of the Liberty bonds and Victory notes issued to finance the costs of the conflict. The sinking-fund act of March 3, 1919, provided for the annual appropriation to the fund of $253,404,865: a sum equal to $2\frac{1}{2}$ per cent of the total amount of the government's war debt outstanding on July 1, 1920, less the total amount of the par value of the obligations of foreign governments held by the treasury on that date. In addition, the act provided for the payment into the sinking fund of an amount equal to all the interest that would have had to be paid on all obligations retired through the sinking fund since its establishment. Under this second provision, annual appropriations to the fund increase and likewise annual debt retirements due to sinking-fund operations. When the sinking fund was set up, it was calculated that these two payments into it would result in the retirement in twenty-five years of that part of the war debt not covered by the repayment of loans to the Allies.

By means of the sinking-fund device, $3,992 million of the public debt had been retired by the end of 1932. Appropriations to the sinking fund for public debt retirement were $410.8 million in 1932. In 1933, it is estimated that they will be $426.5 million and in 1934 $439.7 million. Although the sinking-fund retirements have been continued as a charge against the budget, they have not resulted since 1930 in the intended reduction in the outstanding debt because of new borrowing.

Receipts from Foreign Governments

In the second place, it was provided that payments by foreign governments of principal and interest on their indebtedness to the United States should be applied with certain exceptions to reduction of our federal debt.

Under the provisions of section 3 of the first Liberty bond act and section 3 of the second Liberty bond act, as amended and supplemented, the Secretary of the Treasury is authorized to apply any payments made by foreign governments on account of the principal of their obligations given for cash advances under authority of those acts to the redemption or purchase of bonds issued under said acts at not more than par and accrued interest. If such bonds cannot be so redeemed or purchased, he shall apply such payments to the redemption or purchase of any other outstanding interest-bearing obligations of the United States which may at such time be subject to redemption or which can be purchased at not more than par and accrued interest.

All payments on account of the principal of loans made under authority of the Liberty loan acts must be applied to debt reduction. Payments on account of interest on such loans are not specifically required by law to be used for debt retirement, but may be used to meet expenditures chargeable against ordinary receipts.

In each of the foreign debt settlements as approved by specific acts of Congress, provision is made whereby the debtor government can, at its option, make payment of the principal and interest due thereunder in any obligations of the United States issued since April 6, 1917, in the form acceptable under general regulations of the Treasury Department governing transactions in United States obligations, which shall be accepted at par and accrued interest to the date of payment, irrespective of the maturity dates of such obligations. The act approved June 17, 1929, excepted unmatured treasury bills from the class of obligations of the United States available for this purpose. When foreign payments are made in obligations of the United States, the obligations are cancelled and the debt reduced accordingly. Generally speaking, obligations of the United States will not be used in making the payments unless they can be purchased below par and are still quoted in the market at or below par when the required 30 days' advance notice is given to the treasury with respect to the form of the payment next due.

Included in the debt settlements with Belgium, Czechoslovakia, France, Rumania, and Yugoslavia are amounts due not only on account of cash advances under the Liberty loan acts, but also on account of other indebtedness to the United States from sources such as the sale on credit of surplus war materials by the War and Navy Departments, of relief supplies by the American Relief Administration and by the United States Grain Corporation, and of services by the United States Shipping Board. When payments are received on account of the principal of the indebtedness under any of these five debt settlements, the amount required to be used for debt retirement is the percentage of the total principal payment that the indebtedness on account of cash advances included therein bears to the total indebtedness as funded. No indebtedness on account of cash advances is included in the debt settlements with Austria, Estonia, Finland, Hungary, Latvia, Lithuania, and Poland, and consequently payments received from these seven countries are not required by law to be used for debt retirement.[5]

From 1919 to 1931, $1,545 million, or 59 per cent of total foreign debt payments, was applied to debt retirement. Of this total, $906 million represented interest payments and the remainder payments on principal. In 1931 foreign cash repayments of principal amounting to $48.2 million were applied to public debt retirement, but no interest payments were so used. In 1932 no foreign repayments either of principal or interest were received. In 1933, $69 million and in 1934, $90.8 million foreign repayments of principal have been budgeted for debt redemption.

On November 15, 1932, fifteen foreign governments owed the United States $11,446 million on funded debt agreements pledging them to pay the principal and interest of their obligations in regular instalments continuing to 1987 and totaling over twenty-two billion dollars. Five other countries were indebted to the United States for varying amounts, but had not concluded any agreements as to repayment.

Recent developments raise a question regarding the continuity of this source of federal-debt reduction. World-wide economic disaster led several countries to default on their payments due in December, 1932, and negotiations now under way between the new administration and the debtor nations may result in further revision of the war debts. Continued payments by several of the countries were conditioned unofficially upon continuance of German reparation payments, which were terminated by the Lausanne agreement. Thus it is highly probable that some or all of the debtor countries will be unable or unwilling fully to perform their debt agreements. Whatever new arrangements are made will be bound to reduce the funds available for the retirement of our public debt. Under these circumstances, the treasury would have to meet a larger proportion of its outstanding obligations from domestic receipts.

It is also noteworthy that any or all of the existing provisions of law

[5] *Annual Report,* Secretary of the Treasury, 1930, pp. 59–60.

as to retirement of the public debt could be changed by Congress if it wished to adopt a different policy from that heretofore pursued. In years past proposals have been made in Congress for retarding the rate of public-debt retirement and utilizing foreign payments to meet current costs of government operation as a means of affording relief to taxpayers. Such proposals, however, have been vigorously opposed by the Treasury Department.

Surplus Receipts

A third source of funds for federal debt retirement is the surplus of ordinary receipts over ordinary expenditures. The Secretary of the Treasury may at any time use any surplus in the general fund, over and above that necessary for the maintenance of an adequate working balance, for debt reduction. During the fiscal years 1920–30, inclusive, debt retirement from surplus receipts totaled $3,459.5 million. No debt has been retired from this source since 1930 owing to deficits in 1931 and 1932. Increases in the total public debt as a result of the deficits of 1931 and 1932 had about offset the retirements from surplus receipts over the preceding eleven years.

Certain internal revenue and miscellaneous receipts are also available for debt retirement. These include estate taxes paid in bonds and notes, the proceeds of franchise taxes on net earnings of the federal reserve banks and the federal intermediate credit banks, gifts, forfeitures, etc. Receipts from these sources contributed $232 million toward the retirement of the public debt from 1918 to 1932. The sums realized from these sources are comparatively small and have diminished rapidly since 1922.

Table 66 shows the funds allocated to federal debt retirement for the period 1919–1932, classified according to source. The table indicates that the sinking fund, the treasury surplus, and foreign payments have been chiefly responsible for the great reduction in the public debt during the period. During the fiscal years 1919–1932, funds from all these sources retired $9,227 million of the public debt. As has been seen, no net reductions in federal debt took place in 1931 or 1932, on account of deficits in those years. Security issues and retirements during 1931 resulted in an increase of $616.2 million in the gross debt, and an increase of $2,685.7 million for 1932.

TABLE 66

PUBLIC DEBT RETIREMENTS BY SOURCE, FISCAL YEARS 1919 TO 1932

Sinking Fund..................................... $3,991,683,000

Foreign Payments:
    Cash repayments of principal..................... $433,072,000
    Bonds, etc. received as repayments of principal..... 205,447,000
    Bonds, etc. received as interest payments.......... 906,369,000

                                               $1,544,888,000

Surplus (1920–1930)............................. $3,459,512,000
Miscellaneous revenue receipts..................... 230,782,000

    Total public debt retirements..................... $9,226,865,000

National Debt Compared with Wealth and Income

The debts of nations, like those of individuals, should be considered in relation to their total wealth and public debt carrying charges in relation to their current incomes, for both have important bearings on their capacity to repay.

Estimates made by the National Industrial Conference Board based on the decennial censuses of wealth, debt, and taxation, show that between 1914 and 1922 the total wealth of the United States increased from 192 to 321 billion dollars. Dr. Leonard Ayres of the Cleveland Trust Company estimates that the national wealth in 1929 stood at $385 billion, and that it had fallen by 1932 to $301 billion. On the basis of these estimates of the nation's wealth, the federal debt was 0.6 per cent of our wealth in 1914, 7.2 per cent in 1922, 4.4 per cent in 1929, and 7.2 per cent in 1933, assuming that the wealth of the nation has fallen to about $300 billion. While budget deficits have been increasing the federal debt during the depression, our wealth and income have shrunk, which makes the burden still heavier. Since the beginning of the economic war which the world is now waging, the ratio of the federal debt to our national wealth has risen 2.8 per cent. It has increased over 6 per cent since 1914, and has again attained the post-war peak ratio of 7.2 per cent reached in 1922 during the post-war depression, but it is only about two-thirds as much as it was at the end of the Civil War.

Coming to a comparison of public debt service and national income, the estimates of Willford I. King show that from 1914 to 1922 the realized income of the American people rose from 36 to 66 billions of current dollars. The National Industrial Conference Board places the national income for 1929 at $85 billion and for 1932 at $40 billion.

Comparing the total carrying charges on the public debt (interest and principal) with these estimates of the national income, the debt charge was six-hundredths of one per cent of the national income in 1914, 2.1 per cent in 1922, 1.4 per cent in 1929, and 2.53 per cent in 1932. Thus this ratio almost doubled between 1929 and 1932.

This startling rise in the ratio of debt service to income is largely attributable to the abrupt decline in the national income since 1929. When it is recalled, however, that the federal debt amounted to nearly 10 per cent of our wealth at the close of the Civil War, it will be concluded that the public debt of the United States has not expanded beyond manageable bounds. Nevertheless, it is widely believed that federal expenditures must soon be brought within the federal income.

Debt Compared with Population and Commodity Prices

Another measure of the federal debt burden is the gross debt per capita. This figure stood at $11.83 in 1915, the lowest point it had reached since 1861. By 1919 it had risen to $240.09, a record high. The rapid retirement of the public debt after the war reduced the per capita burden to $131.38 in 1930, but the quick growth of the debt in the next three years brought the per capita figure up to $173.69 in 1933 or back to its 1925 level. The increase in the last three years of $42.31 in the gross federal debt per capita compares with a drop of $108.71 during the period from 1919 to 1930.

Another significant consideration is the effect of declining commodity prices on debts, since most of the security for debts is commodities in some form. Before the panic of 1920, relatively few debts had been incurred at a high price level. By 1929, as Professors G. F. Warren and F. A. Pearson have pointed out, the whole debt structure—public and private, national and international—was adjusted to a commodity price level of about 150, taking 1910–1914 as 100. At this level of prices the present debt burden would not be especially heavy. But their index of wholesale commodity prices, which stood at 226 in 1920 and at 139 in 1929, has subsequently fallen to its pre-war level. For February of this year it stood at 87.3. Investors in government securities profit from declining prices because they are paid back with dollars that have a higher purchasing power than the dollars which they invested. But the government suffers like other borrowers from declining prices because its payments of interest and principal on the public debt are in effect increased, at a price level of 90 or less, by 60 per cent or more.

Interest payments on the public debt during 1930–32 amounted to $1,870 million. Payments of principal on the public debt during this period amounted to $1,186 million. In other words, since prices began to fall sharply in 1929, the federal government has expended more than three billions on the public debt in dollars of higher buying power than those it originally borrowed. Fortunately for investors in federal issues, they can still collect in full from the treasury as their securities mature. But the capacity of the government to repay depends in turn upon the income of the taxpayers which, under the combined pressure of falling commodity prices and the low volume of economic activity, has suffered such a severe deflation that in many cases and areas the burden of taxes and private debts has become intolerable.

It remains, finally, to compare the federal bonded debt with other types of long-term indebtedness in the United States. Based on the estimates of the various classes of public and private debts outstanding in the latest available year, made by the other contributors to this volume, this comparison shows the following percentage relationships. The long-term federal debt is—

35 per cent of all public indebtedness in the United States
100 per cent of the funded obligations of steam railroads
102 per cent of the long-term debts of public utilities other than railroads
136 per cent of all fixed industrial corporate indebtedness
167 per cent of all farm mortgage debts
41 per cent of all urban real estate obligations
11 per cent of all long-term debts outstanding in the United States

Distribution of Holdings of United States Securities

In the event of the refunding of government bonds at lower rates of interest or the funding of part of the floating debt, the distribution of the holdings between individuals and institutions would become of great interest, for it would indicate the extent to which such operations would depend for success upon the cooperation of individual and institutional investors.

The latest information pertaining to the distribution of holdings of interest-bearing securities of the United States government pertains to the year 1930. The figures include securities issued under the Federal Farm Loan Act and by United States possessions. The data represent available information on the holdings of the securities indicated, and account for 83 per cent of all outstanding interest-bearing securities in 1930. The holdings of federal reserve banks, mutual savings banks, and federal land banks and the holdings of the Treasurer of the United States are not represented in the data taken from Statistics of Income and consequently have been included in addition. The statistics taken from Statistics of Income were obtained in the case of corporations from balance sheets submitted with income tax returns, and in the case of individuals from the returns reporting net income of $5,000 and over.

The Treasury Department points out that the statistics are subject to the following limitations: (a) the data are requested merely for informational purposes; (b) a large number of taxable corporations do not submit balance sheets; (c) the following persons submit no income tax returns: corporations specifically exempt from income tax under revenue acts; foreign corporations having no office or agent in this country; nonresident alien individuals with no taxable income from sources within the United States; (d) data are not available for individuals with net incomes under $5,000. Subject to these limitations, Table 67 shows the distribution of the holdings of all interest-bearing securities of the United States government outstanding in 1930.

It will be seen from the table that the securities were held as follows:

57.2 per cent were held by corporations, including banks
11.0 per cent were held by the Treasurer of the United States
10.5 per cent were held by individuals
3.3 per cent were held by federal reserve banks
0.8 per cent were held by mutual savings banks
0.09 per cent were held by federal land banks
17.11 per cent were unaccounted for

According to a recent estimate by former Under Secretary of the Treasury Ballantine, bank holdings now amount to about one-half of the obligations outstanding. About one-third of the national debt is now in the short-term and intermediate classification which the banks consider prime for their own portfolios, and the above table shows that they hold the bulk of such securities. Nor are the bank holdings of the long-term bonds small. Insurance company holdings of government securities make a sizable addition to the bank holdings, and it is thus apparent that individual investors possess a relatively small portion of the securities. The distribution of the obligations is an exceptionally important matter at this time, owing to the need for funding part of the floating debt and the contemplated plans for converting Liberty bonds into lower coupon long-term bonds. The small proportion of outstanding issues in individual hands will make the problem a fairly easy one.

Prices of Government Securities

The conditions affecting the market for federal securities include price changes and money rates as reflected in current yields, the demand for particular maturities, and the "thinness or otherwise" of the market in respect of its ability to take a given volume of new issues. During the fiscal year 1932 United States securities were, with the exception of treasury bills, issued at par. During the current fiscal year the market for United States long-term government bonds has continued to improve, except for a decline on the eve of the banking holiday when banks sold government securities in large quantities to meet withdrawals of bank deposits. On March 17, 1933, eleven out of thirteen active government bond issues were selling above par, having regained all the losses registered before the bank and stock exchange holiday.

Table 68 compares the prices and average yields of treasury bonds by quarters in 1929, 1930, 1931, 1932, and 1933 to date with the prices and yields of domestic bonds during that period. The government bond price is Moody's average for eight treasury bonds. The domestic bond price is Moody's AAA index covering thirty high-grade bonds, including ten railroad, ten public utility, and ten industrial bonds.

Interest Rates and Payments on Federal Issues

One of the major developments in the handling of the federal debt after the war was the refunding operations which effected a substantial reduction in the interest rate. The average rate of interest on the public debt was 4.225 per cent on June 30, 1920. Nine years later the average rate had fallen to 3.946 per cent, and on June 30, 1932, it was 3.505 per cent, a decline due, in part, to the larger proportion of short-term, low-interest issues in the total debt. The last long-term treasury bond issue, that of 1951–55, floated on September 15, 1931, for $800 million, carried an interest rate of only 3 per cent. Liberty and treasury bond issues were

TABLE 67

TOTAL OUTSTANDING INTEREST-BEARING SECURITIES OF UNITED STATES GOVERNMENT AND HOLDINGS THEREOF, 1930

(Including Securities Issued under Federal Farm Loan Act and by U. S. Possessions)

(In Millions of Dollars—Par Value)

	Amount	Date	Source
Total outstanding amounts:			
Gross debt of United States Government	$16,185.3	6/30	U. S. Public Debt Statement
Noninterest-bearing debt	231.7	6/30	" "
Total interest-bearing debt	$15,953.6		
Securities issued under Federal Farm Loan Act	1,802.1	6/30	Annual Report of Secretary of the Treasury, 1931, p. 555
Securities issued by U. S. possessions	119.7	6/30	Bureau of Insular Affairs, United States War Department
Total	$17,875.4		
Holdings:			
Individual		1,889.9	12/31 or any— Statistics of Income from Returns, 1930, p. 17
Corporation		10,228.2	date in 1930 " p. 27
Federal reserve banks		590.9	6/30 Federal Reserve Bulletin, August, 1930, p. 527
Mutual savings banks		152.5	6/30 Annual Report of Comptroller of Currency, 1930, p. 105
Federal land banks		16.9	6/30 Condition Report of Federal Land Banks, June 30, 1930
Treasurer of United States:			
To secure deposits of national banks	45.8		6/30 Finance Volume of Secretary of Treasury, 1930, p. 646
To secure circulation of national banks	666.2		" " p. 646
To secure postal savings fund	158.5		" " p. 647
In trust for:			
Adjusted service certificate fund	629.2		" " p. 113
Civil service retirement fund	156.9		" " p. 114
Foreign " "	1.0		" " p. 116
District of Columbia teachers' retirement fund	3.3		" " p. 115
Government life insurance fund	176.7		" " p. 120
Indian trust funds	29.5		" " p. 649
Securing funds of insolvent national banks	25.5		" " p. 649
Postal savings system	28.5		" " p. 648
Comptroller General	3.3		" " p. 649
Alien Property Custodian	25.5		" " p. 649
In lieu of surety bonds	27.7		" " p. 649
American Red Cross permanent building fund	.4		" " p. 649
Custody Account of Secretary of Interior	.5		" " p. 649
District of Columbia workmen's compensation act	.2		" " p. 649
Federal Farm Loan Board	.6		" " p. 649
U. S. Housing Corporation	.1		" " p. 649
Total		1,979.4	
Total holdings accounted for		$14,857.8	

selling on March 17, 1933, at prices to yield interest at rates ranging from 0.59 to 3.48. Interest rates on treasury notes issued during 1933 range from 2⅛ per cent to 3¼ per cent. Certificates of indebtedness issued during 1933 carry interest rates of ¾ per cent and 1¼ per cent, the lowest levels in federal fiscal history; but the last certificate issue, that of March 15, sold at 4 and 4¼ per cent. Discount rates on treasury bills have fluctuated widely. On a bank discount basis the rates on the treasury

TABLE 68

DOMESTIC AND GOVERNMENT BOND PRICES AND YIELDS, 1929–1933

	Thirty Domestic Bonds(a)		U. S. Government Bonds(b)	
	Price	Average Yield	Price(c)	Average Yield(d)
Jan. 1, 1929	$102.14	4.62	$103.40	3.59
April 1, 1929	100.81	4.70	100.94	3.67
July 1, 1929	99.20	4.80	101.04	3.68
Oct. 1, 1929	99.20	4.80	100.64	3.67
Jan. 1, 1930	101.47	4.66	104.29	3.51
April 1, 1930	102.64	4.59	105.08	3.46
July 1, 1930	103.32	4.55	106.09	3.37
Oct. 1, 1930	106.07	4.39	106.37	3.34
Jan. 1, 1931	104.68	4.47	106.17	3.33
April 1, 1931	105.89	4.40	105.65	3.38
July 1, 1931	106.25	4.38	106.91	3.32
Oct. 1, 1931	98.88	4.82	103.92	3.71
Jan. 1, 1932	91.11	5.34	95.48	4.27
April 1, 1932	94.58	5.10	97.78	3.74
July 1, 1932	90.13	5.41	100.61	3.65
Oct. 1, 1932	102.30	4.61	103.78	3.54
Jan. 1, 1933	103.99	4.51	105.15	3.41(e)
Feb. 1, 1933	105.89	4.40	105.89	3.36(e)

(a) Moody's AAA index, including 10 railroad bonds, 10 public utility bonds, and 10 industrial bonds.

(b) Average 1st of month prices of eight treasury bonds.

(c) Bonds included in average of 8 issues: 4¼s 1952, 4s 1954, 3¾s 1956, 3⅜s 1947, 3⅜s 1940–43, 3⅜s 1941–43, 3⅛s 1949, 3s 1955.

(d) Monthly averages of daily figures for 3 issues, compiled by the Treasury Department. Bonds included in average of 3 issues: 4s 1954, 3¾s 1956, 3⅜s 1947.

(e) Yield for first day of month—average daily figures not available.

bills issued during 1933 range from .085 per cent to .529 per cent. This general decline in interest rates on federal issues reflects the decline in the open market money rates, which have fallen to their lowest level since the World War, as well as the difficulty of finding other satisfactory investments.

Reductions in interest rates and in the federal debt during 1920–1930 resulted in a decline in annual interest payments up to 1932. On June 30, 1920, the computed interest charge on the federal debt was $1,016.6

million. By June 30, 1931, the computed annual interest charge had been reduced to $589 million. At the close of the fiscal year 1932 this charge had increased to $672 million. In 1933, $640 million has been budgeted for interest on the public debt, and the estimate of appropriation for 1934 is $725 million. The rising cost of the debt service since 1931 reflects increased governmental borrowing to cover recurring deficits. A balanced federal budget obviously would ease the annual interest charge on the public debt.

Apropos of this, former Secretary of the Treasury, Ogden L. Mills, in an address on January 31, 1933, said:

If we keep on pumping out government securities, a point must be reached at which the question arises not necessarily as to the ultimate credit standing of the government, but as to its ability to maintain the value of its securities in the face of a constantly increasing volume. When this point is reached, banks and investors hesitate to buy because of the fear of future depreciation. Interest rates will tend to rise with each new issue. Ultimately the point might be reached where central bank credit has to be invoked to support the credit of the government, and when that point is reached we have entered the field of destructive inflation. . . .

From the standpoint of the treasury a balanced budget should permit large saving in interest charges, not only through the prevention of a further increase in the public debt, but because it would enable the refunding on favorable terms of bonds bearing a high rate of interest, and which by October, 1933, will be callable in an amount not far from $7,000,000,000. A lower interest charge on such a large volume of government securities would affect long-time interest rates. . . .

How the Treasury Handles Its Deficit

As we have seen, the federal government experienced heavy deficits in 1931 and 1932. According to the daily treasury statement for March 15, 1933, the deficit of the current fiscal year stood at $1,413 million at the end of that day. The sum of these deficits down through March 15, 1933, including public debt retirements and the treasury subscription of $500 million to the capital stock of the Reconstruction Finance Corporation, was $5,206 million. In appraising the financial position of the government, allowance should be made for its subscription to the capital stock of the Reconstruction Finance Corporation, which was charged in the budget for 1932, and for its net advances to the corporation which are financed through public debt accounts as required by law. According to the 1932 report of the Secretary of the Treasury and the daily treasury statement for March 15, 1933, net payments to the corporation from its establishment to March 15, 1933, plus subscription to its capital stock, totaled $1,607 million. The treasury expects the corporation to return these funds "at a not too distant date." "Thus, of the amounts added to the public debt during this depression period," reads the last annual report of the Secretary of the Treasury, "over a billion dollars is represented by assets which will be realized on and will furnish funds which can be applied to debt retirement."

In planning the financing of these deficits, the treasury has been guided by conditions in the money market. These conditions were firm at the end of the calendar year 1931 and early in 1932, but became progressively easier after February, particularly as affecting short-term open market rates. Rates on new government issues with maturities up to one year followed this general trend. Since rates on treasury bills are determined by competitive bidding, and the bills are for shorter maturity than any other form of United States securities sold in the open market, the correspondence between short-term open market rates and rates on new treasury issues is most marked for these securities. Rates on new issues of treasury bills were below rates at which certificates (of longer maturity) were issued during the calendar years 1931 and 1932. In view of the already large amount of early maturities outstanding, however, the issuance of securities of longer maturity as conditions warranted, even at somewhat higher rates, was deemed by the Treasury Department to be in the interest of sound and orderly management of the public debt. Thus, in the financing of 1931–33, maturities have gradually been shifted from the shorter to the longer issues as market conditions have warranted.[6]

About 43 per cent of the total deficit of $5,206 million, incurred from July 1, 1930, to March 15, 1933, has been met by bond issues totaling $2,216 million. Three such issues were made during 1931 and 1932: one on March 16, 1931, of $594.2 million at $3\frac{3}{8}$ per cent maturing in 1941–43; one on June 15, 1931, of $821.4 million at $3\frac{1}{8}$ per cent maturing in 1946–49; and one on September 15, 1931, of $800.4 million at 3 per cent maturing in 1951–55. The issue of June 15, 1931, was over-subscribed almost 700 per cent; that of September 15 only $17\frac{1}{2}$ per cent. There have been no bond issues during the current fiscal year to date, except a small issue ($18 million) of postal savings bonds.

[6] *Annual Report*, Secretary of the Treasury, 1932, pp. 66–68.

Reliance on Short-Term Loans

The remainder and larger part of the deficit has been financed by intermediate issues of treasury notes (with maturities from 2 to 5 years) and by short-term issues of certificates of indebtedness (with maturities up to 12 months) and by treasury bills (with maturities up to 93 days). The most recent intermediate issue was that of 277 million in five-year 2⅝ per cent treasury notes dated February 1, 1933, which was over-subscribed 31.2 times. The last large treasury operation arose in connection with the maturity of $695 million of 3¾ per cent certificates of indebtedness on March 15, 1933, when $943 million of new certificates were sold at 4 and 4¼ per cent. An exceptionally keen demand has existed for all short-term government obligations, as they are considered especially suitable investments for commercial and savings banks and institutional investors generally.

Repeated oversubscription of treasury offerings brought a warning from Secretary Mills on January 26 against the padding of bids. The large oversubscription of recent treasury offerings should not be regarded, he said, as an indication that idle funds are available in an amount even remotely approaching the total subscribed for.

This great volume of subscriptions is due in large measure to the fact that many subscribers are deliberately applying for amounts far in excess of their requirements, anticipating that under the treasury's percentage allotment they will receive a reduced amount approximating their actual needs. This practice of padding has steadily increased until it has now reached such proportions that the department must consider measures to deal with it in the interests both of the subscribers and the treasury.

The practice of padding offers for federal loans has serious drawbacks. First, it gives an erroneous impression of the borrowing capacity of the government. Second, it makes it more difficult for the treasury to gauge the ability of the market to absorb future issues. And, third, it may embarrass subscribers themselves in case they receive allotments beyond their resources. This happened in England last November in connection with the conversion of the British debt. As yet, however, the treasury has not found a way of preventing the practice.

Recent federal deficits have thus been met by borrowing, by the "mopping up" process, to use Secretary Mill's pungent phrase. In mopping up deficits, other things get "mopped up" also, as the editor of the *New York Times* observed. One of them is the heavier interest charge on the public debt. Meanwhile, under the system of short-term financing by the treasury, new capital and idle funds have been virtually "warehoused" in these short-term issues. The return on them has been small, so that with little hope of appreciation in price, the money has been lodged in these issues mainly for liquidity and safety.

2. RECOMMENDATIONS

At a time when measures to ease the burden of various groups of borrowers are being proposed to Congress and the country, methods by which the federal government can reduce the burden of its indebtedness must also be considered. For the burden of public debt and taxation has far-reaching effects on business recovery.

Two ways of reducing the federal debt can promptly be dismissed as out of the question. One is the method of default; the other is the method of redeeming part of the public debt with new currency issued for that purpose. Neither of these needs to be employed because the treasury is still able to meet its debt service and its credit is still good. No one doubted the capacity of the federal government to repay its debts when in 1919 they reached the unprecedented total of more than $25 billion, and no one now can seriously challenge its capacity to meet the carrying charges on a debt of $22 billion. To be sure, business was booming during the period of war financing and the commodity price level was more than twice its present height. The national income today is only three-fifths of what it was in 1919. As a result, the debt burden of $22 billion is harder to carry than a $25 billion burden was fourteen years ago. Nevertheless, it seems safe to prophesy, especially in view of the energetic measures President Roosevelt has taken to safeguard the national credit, that the government will neither default nor resort to the printing of fiat money.

Short of default and inflation, there are two courses open to the federal government for debt reduction. One is to balance the national budget and thereby not only stop the further rise in the public debt caused by the financing of recurring deficits, but also commence debt reduction through operation of the sinking fund and from treasury surpluses. The restoration of the full effectiveness of the sinking fund requirements will involve net reduction in the debt; reduction of debt out of surpluses would represent *additional* reduction since the surplus is calculated on the basis of expenditures including statutory debt retirements. The other course is to refund existing obligations at lower rates of interest as time and opportunity permit.

Balancing the National Budget

The problem of balancing the national budget raises a number of important questions. In the first place, some economists argue that it is not necessary to balance the budget in lean years. On this point a sub-committee of the Committee on Unemployment and Industrial Stabilization of the Progressive Conference reported in November, 1931, as follows:[7]

In order that governmental employment may operate to counteract rather than to reinforce business depression, it is necessary that expenditures be expended at just those times when revenues fall off and budgets are straitened. A government in the strong financial situation of ours, backed by our generally strong national economy, need not and should not be afraid of using public credit freely or of incurring deficits at such times; relying on balancing the budget from surpluses secured in more prosperous years. The effect of government expenditures on economic stability is more important than accurate balancing of the budget in each single year. There need be no fear that borrowing will depress business by removing funds from the general capital market at a time when business expansion is not calling for such funds in anything like normal volume; provided measures are taken to mobilize the lending power which actually exists, e.g., by thawing out frozen credits. Even increased taxes, whose yield and burden are likely to be deferred a year or more, with short-term borrowing an anticipation of their yield, can not depress business as much as prompt expenditures can stimulate it. By the time the taxes come to be paid, business may be in a stronger position to pay them.

Of course, it is not always possible to tell exactly where we are on the curve of prosperity and depression, or where the next swing will take us. And hence the borrowing policy should be used with caution to avoid the temptation to general inflationism in normal times. Such borrowings should be for a short term of years, and stringent measures should be taken to see that they are retired on the return of prosperity. The point is that if taxes are sufficient to support the government in the general run of good times and bad, a deficit in an admittedly very bad year need not be thought to necessitate desperate efforts at retrenchment to balance the budget.

This argument has much merit. It is a question, however, how long the federal budget can go unbalanced without jeopardizing government

[7]Messrs. J. M. Clark, J. Russell Smith, Edwin S. Smith, and George Soule. Their report appears in the Hearings before a subcommittee of the Committee on Manufactures of the United States Senate on the bill (S.6215) to establish a National Economic Council, at pp. 737–752.

credit. There were deficits in the fiscal years 1931 and 1932; and there will be another deficit in 1933. Enactment of the economy and beer bills by the special session of the 73rd Congress reduced the prospective deficit for 1934 by $675 million to about $200 million, a margin which President Roosevelt may further reduce when he comes to reorganize the administrative branch of the national government. The progress made since March 4 toward a balanced budget has done much to renew confidence in the integrity of the federal credit.

Government credit has two distinct limitations: first, the amount that can be raised through taxation to meet interest and amortization charges on government loans, and, second, the capacity of the banks and investing public to subscribe to these issues. If the government continually spends more than it receives, fear of inflation develops, hoarding begins, trade and production slacken, unemployment increases, commodity and security prices fall, bank loans decline, and purchasing power dries up. The far-reaching effects of public confidence in the federal credit make a balanced budget for 1934 seem imperative. Heavy borrowing for public works would appear, therefore, to be an unwise policy at the present time, unless such loans are segregated in an extraordinary budget and special provision made for carrying and amortizing them. Short of actual experience with such measures as a huge federal public works program, financed by a federal bond issue, the efficacy of government borrowing as a means of stimulating economic recovery remains in the realm of opinion. If borrowed funds were spent, not on palliatives in the hope that prosperity would soon turn the corner, but in such a way as to stimulate real recovery from the depression, an increase in the federal debt would be justifiable.

A continuing flow of government issues, failing a balanced budget, may also affect the capital market. The repeated pumping out of federal securities in recent years has flooded the market and presumably absorbed a large volume of investment funds that might otherwise have gone into corporate issues (assuming that a considerable quantity of such issues is awaiting a better capital market) and thus stimulated the capital equipment industries upon whose revival business recovery largely depends. A balanced budget, therefore, in so far as it permitted the government to retire from the money market as a constant seeker of new funds, would have a stimulating effect upon the capital market to which some look for the initial impulse toward recovery.

The first point of attack, then, in the effort to readjust the federal debt, is to balance the national budget. The appropriation bills adopted in the recent—and last—short session disclosed no effective desire on the part of a majority in Congress to produce a really balanced budget. President Hoover's "balanced" budget for 1934 did not include provision for sinking fund obligations and it presupposed that no new obligations of any kind would be incurred. Meanwhile, the Reconstruction Finance Corporation continues to borrow funds from the treasury to loan to railroads, banks, insurance companies and others; and numerous bills have been introduced in Congress for the relief of farmers, veterans, debtors, and the unemployed, the adoption of any of which would place additional burdens upon the federal treasury and make inevitable a further increase in the public debt during the fiscal years 1933 and 1934. To suggest ways and means of balancing the federal budget would be outside the scope of this chapter. The new administration has gone a long way toward achieving this goal. The point to be emphasized here is the obvious one that there can be no reduction in the public debt until Congress achieves a genuinely balanced budget. The debt, indeed, will grow until receipts equal expenditures.

If Congress failed to balance the budget year after year, it is conceivable that the banking community might bring pressure to bear on the government to compel such action. Bankers might condition their subscription to future federal offerings upon the enactment of economies in Washington. They might at least require higher interest rates to induce them to extend financial aid. The bankers have employed such tactics in several American cities, notably New York City, where they demanded and obtained a reduced budget as a price for further loans. The wisdom of these tactics in New York was questioned by Professor McGoldrick of Columbia University, who said:

If the bankers are to assume to dictate to cities, there are certain responsibilities that must inevitably go with this dictation. The bankers cannot attempt to prescribe economy and avoid the responsibility if unwise and deceptive economies result. . . .

He continued:

The banks are the most important agency for control under present arrangements. This is not merely an opportunity; it is a responsibility. There is little room for pride in the way these responsibilities were exercised in the last decade. I think we can confidently predict that if the bankers do not show that they are prepared to act with a greater regard to general well-being in the next decade, they will be superseded by some other type of social control.

Proposal for an Extraordinary Budget

Another aspect of the budget problem, relevant to the federal debt, is the question of separating current expenses from capital outlays in the federal budget. The proposal has recently been made that the Treasury Department set up two budgets: an operating budget and an extraordinary budget. The operating budget would show on the expenditure side the expenses of running the government, including current obligations and debt redemption; on the income side, it would set up the revenues and the surplus which are anticipated to meet these expenditures. The extraordinary budget would present on the expenditure side the cost of the major properties which are acquired, the investments made in public enterprises and the sums required to finance emergency relief, loans, and public works, while on the income side it would enumerate the revenues, borrowings, receipts from the sales of capital assets, and surpluses in funds which are available to finance the expenditures. Those who urge this device maintain that it would only be necessary to balance the operating budget, covering current operating expenditures and debt service from current revenues. Capital outlays, such as those for the construction of public works and for emergency relief, would be provided for from bond issues correctly adjusted to the life of the improvements or loans and would be set up in a separate capital or improvement budget as part of a long-term financial program. It is argued that capital expenditures are rarely incorporated in state and local governmental budgets, and that business corporations are also in the habit of capitalizing improvements by amortizing the cost over a period of years. Adoption of this scheme, it is believed, would decrease the demand for total revenue, lower requirements for taxation, and postpone to prosperous years the burdens which cannot be borne by hard-pressed taxpayers at present. It would make for a balanced operating budget and adjust federal financing to the business cycle.

In a statement on January 16, 1933, entitled "Balancing the Budget, Federal Fiscal Policy during Depression," a group of economists at the University of Chicago urged this type of budgeting.

We recommend that elasticity in federal revenues should be sought in the future by the planned control of the federal debt—that federal debt should be permitted to increase in times of depression and be rapidly retired during prosperous times; that the borrowings for 1934 should not be less than the sums required to finance emergency relief, loans, investments, and public works.

Economists hold that the balancing of budgets should be regarded as a series of long-term operations; deficits should be incurred during periods of depression, and the public debt correspondingly reduced during periods of prosperity. The long-term budget would be balanced with reference to economic cycles. Ordinarily the budget can be balanced on an annual basis, but when practiced during a period of depression, the load of taxation is inappropriately heavy and tends to prolong the depression. Some economists believe that the definite tying-up of public works with the funds to be used, such as would be attainable through a segregation of this type of expenditure, would facilitate the long-term planning of public works programs.

Except in times of national emergency such as war, it has been the traditional policy of the federal government to budget its capital and operating expenditures together. The treasury books make no distinction between the current running expenses of government, on the one hand, and loans to private enterprise and investments in capital equipment, on the other. Until 1931 the United States Government was practically on a pay-as-you-go basis. Post offices, public buildings, port developments, federal highways, and warships are capital expenditures of annually recurring amounts which the federal government has taken in the stride of its current financing. It has been able to embody capital expenditures in its operating budget by adequate revenues in prosperous times, although they cannot be paid out of current receipts in periods of depression. To make the change now urged and capitalize improvements would be an innovation in federal financial practice.

There are those who doubt whether the proposed change would be a wise one. Generally speaking, it is noted that capital improvements made by the federal government differ from those of business corporations in that the former are not self-supporting in character, while they recur from year to year. Some students of public finance hold that it is desirable for governments to pay from current revenue for annually recurring amounts of capital expenditures, except those which are of self-supporting character.[8] Moreover, as Secretary of the Treasury Mills

[8] Cf. *Capital Expenditures*, a Report of the United States Chamber of Commerce, Revised Edition, February, 1930, p. 21.

pointed out, "no matter how the treasury set up its accounts, the fact of a huge increase in the public debt would remain. The failure to cover our sinking fund requirements would not disappear. The increased amount of government securities outstanding would not be retired. The uncertainty as to the government's position in the money market as a borrower would not disappear, but rather would be increased. The difficulties incident to the management of the public debt under existing conditions would become more complex rather than less. Fancy book-keeping might give a false sense of security to the unwary and a specious argument to the spenders, but it would not alter the fact that the United States government will have closed three fiscal years with large deficits and with a large increase in the public debt. . . ." [9]

If this plan had been in operation during the last three fiscal years, the major items which would have been classified in an extraordinary budget are those shown in Table 69. It will be seen from the table that, if the major loans and investments of the federal government had been segregated in an extraordinary budget, there would have been a net surplus in 1930 of $633 million, and net deficits in 1931 and 1932 of $77 million and $1,545 million, respectively. The cumulative deficit of the last two years would have been $1,622 million rather than $3,788 million.

Advocates of an extraordinary budget point out that the principle has been employed by the treasury, in part, in its treatment of advances to the Reconstruction Finance Corporation for the purpose of making its loans. Up to December 30, 1932, the corporation had loaned $1,502 million. Only $500 million of the funds from which these loans were made (representing the capital of the corporation) appears in the budget. The remaining billion dollars has been made available through the sale of debentures purchased exclusively by the treasury. It is contended that advances to the Shipping Board should likewise be withheld from the current budget. It is also argued that, by not including allowances for public debt retirements among expenditures to be covered by current revenues in the 1934 budget, the President has given partial recognition to the principle of an extraordinary budget. And, finally, it is asserted that subsidies to, and income from, government-owned corporations are

[9] In a speech before the Columbia Institute of Arts and Sciences, January 31, 1933. For a thorough analysis of this question see "Extraordinary Budgeting of Federal Finances," by Charles R. Weaver, *Editorial Research Reports*, February 10, 1933.

TABLE 69(a)

U. S. LOANS AND INVESTMENTS SUBJECT TO CAPITALIZED SEGREGATION

(In Millions of Dollars)

Class of Expenditure	1930	1931	1932
Agricultural Marketing (revolving fund)...................	$150	$191	$137
Construction Loan Fund (special) United States Shipping Board...	20	30	46
Seed-grain loans..	5	....	....
Farm Loan Bureau (annual special fund).................	1	....	....
Inland Waterways Corporation...........................	2	3	....
Public Works..	271	437	520
Supplemental public works appropriations, Dec. 20, 1930....	....	116	....
Loans to farmers in drought and storm-stricken areas......	....	43	....
Agricultural credits and rehabilitation (emergency relief)....	....	6	10
Capital stock, Reconstruction Finance Corporation.........	....	....	500
Capital stock, Federal Land Banks.......................	....	....	125
Capital stock, Federal Intermediate Credit Banks..........	....	....	2
Total loans and investments........................	$449	$826	$1,340
Total ordinary receipts.............................	4,178	3,317	2,121
Total ordinary expenses............................	3,994	4,220	5,007
Net surplus or deficit..........................	$184 surplus	$903 deficit	$2,885 deficit
Net surplus or deficit with loans and investments removed..................................	$633 surplus	$77 deficit	$1,545 deficit

(a) Source: *Editorial Research Reports*, February 10, 1933, p. 108.

not properly pictured in the budget. On June 30, 1932, the United States government owned securities totalling $13,442 million, the net income from which was applied to reducing the bookkeeping deficit.[10]

Those who urge the extraordinary budgeting of federal finances consider it desirable if only as a step toward the breakdown of expenditures by social and economic functions rather than by administrative units. The change would be sound, they say, from an accounting point of view, and most desirable in adjusting the tax load upon the basis of the country's capacity to pay. Its success in this latter respect would depend upon the extent to which expenditures were kept down during good times; if they were not, and if the public debt was not greatly reduced during boom periods, the extraordinary budget scheme would admittedly be an extravagance.

The ideal method of keeping the federal accounts, which would eliminate many faulty practices in government bookkeeping, would be to set up a classified income and expenditure statement and show all receipts and expenditures in one general budget with separate subdivisions or accounts for (1) current receipts and expenditures, (2) debt service,

[10] *Ibid.*, pp. 108–112.

(3) capital improvements, (4) self-liquidating expenditures, (5) government-owned corporations and utilities, and (6) the District of Columbia.

In the current account would be shown, on the income side, the current revenues of the federal government, including tax receipts and the net income accruing to government-owned corporations; and on the expenditure side, the current expenses of running the government. In the debt service account would be shown the funds appropriated and earmarked for debt retirement and the expenditures of principal and interest on the public debt. In the capital improvement account would be entered capital outlays for public works and the investments made in public enterprises. In the self-liquidating account would appear expenditures expected to be repaid, such as for the capital stock and debentures of the Reconstruction Finance Corporation, loans to the United States Shipping Board, loans to farmers, and the like. In the fifth account would be shown the expenditures and receipts of government-owned corporations, such as the Panama Railroad, the Inland Waterways Corporation, and the war emergency corporations. Under this head would also come the Post Office Department, virtually a public utility operating, for the most part, on a self-supporting basis. Net income accruing to government-owned corporations and utilities would apply to reduce deficits or swell surpluses in the current account; their deficits, if any, would be entered on the expenditure side of the current account. Finally, there would be a separate account in the general budget for the District of Columbia, a municipal corporation whose accounts should be kept separately from those of the federal government.

Thus there would be one general budget, but with separate accounts for the various and essentially different categories of expenditure and receipts. Expenditures for capital outlays, such as for public works, should be excluded from the current operating account and included in the capital improvement section of the general budget. The cost of such improvements should be met by borrowing and the carrying charges on debt so incurred should be provided out of current revenues and shown under debt service. All emergency non-recurring expenditures would be accounted for in the self-liquidating account, such as treasury advances to the Reconstruction Finance Corporation and loans to farmers and mortgage companies. The only valid charges against current revenues for such transactions are for reserves to cover possible losses.

As a result of this system of bookkeeping, the government would have a classified income and expenditure statement and the country would have a clearer picture of the federal finances. This system would avoid many abuses in governmental accounting. It would also avoid the danger inherent in an extraordinary budget—that it might become a catchall, like the French extraordinary budget, for miscellaneous expenditures whose inclusion in the current budget would unbalance it.

Refunding the Federal Debt

A second method of easing the debt burden open to the federal government is to refund existing obligations at lower rates of interest. It is doubtful whether the treasury could accomplish heavy refunding operations under most favorable conditions in the absence of adequate budget legislation. And a balanced budget depends in turn on budget legislation, the curve of business activity, and the trend in governmental receipts and expenditures.

In a message to Congress last January, President Hoover said: "It is essential that the government undertake at an early moment the refunding of outstanding high interest-bearing Liberty bonds into bonds bearing a lower rate of interest." It was also essential, he added that "a portion of our short-term borrowing should be converted into longer-term issues." Both operations present a problem to the Roosevelt administration calling for prompt action.

The floating and intermediate debt of the federal government now amounts to about $7.5 billion, or 34 per cent of the total debt. If a substantial part of the early maturities of this floating debt were converted into notes or long-term bonds, the way would be cleared for refunding the Liberty bond issues. Such conversions, to be sure, if they increased the supply of government bonds, might weaken the market for the refunding process.

Meanwhile, there is still outstanding $8,201 million in Liberty bonds, or about 38 per cent of the total debt. Of this total, $1,392 million consists of First Liberty loan bonds at $3\frac{1}{2}$ per cent, $5 million at 4 per cent, and $536 million bearing $4\frac{1}{4}$ per cent; and $6,268 million consists of Fourth Liberty loan bonds bearing interest at $4\frac{1}{4}$ per cent. (The Second and Third Liberty loans have been retired in part through refunding operations.)

The first Liberty loan bonds have been eligible for redemption since

June 15, 1932, and the Fourth Liberty loan will be callable on October 15, 1933. A three-month notice of payment issued on an interest date is required on the First Liberty loan, and a six-month notice on the Fourth Liberty loan.

Possible Saving by Conversion of Liberty Bonds

Annual interest on the First Liberty loan bonds totals $71,707,324. If these were converted into 3 per cent bonds, the government would save $13,710,946 a year in interest charges. Annual interest payments on the Fourth Liberty loan bonds amount to $266,394,103. If these were subsequently refunded at 3 per cent, a further saving of $78,-351,207 would result. The combined saving from a conversion of all outstanding Liberty bonds into 3 per cent bonds would be $92,062,153—a handsome contribution to a harassed budget. (Increased interest charges resulting from conversion of floating into funded debt might offset some of this saving.) A reduction of one per cent or more on such a large volume of government securities would lower long-time interest rates, increase bond prices, stimulate the capital market by inducing industry to offer and the market to absorb corporate issues, and thus create one of the conditions deemed essential to business recovery. Senator Carter Glass has urged that the treasury promptly convert some or all of these vast obligations into new bonds bearing lower interest rates, thereby "enabling a staggering Congress more surely to balance the budget." Extensive refunding of the Liberty bonds will probably depend, as has been seen, upon a balanced budget, budget legislation, conversion of some of the short-term debt into long-term bonds, and conditions in the money market.

There is ample precedent for such refunding, both at home and abroad. The governments of Great Britain and France recently converted their war debts with great success. During the summer of 1932 Great Britain refunded her 1917 war loan, which amounted to 2,087 million pounds bearing interest at 5 per cent, into a new loan bearing interest at $3\frac{1}{2}$ per cent. Further conversions accomplished in December, 1932, and February, 1933, brought the total to 2,352 million pounds, an operation of unprecedented magnitude. The consequent saving to the British treasury amounts to 38 million pounds annually or about $130 million at the current rate of exchange. Responding to pleas of patriotism and prosperity, all but $2\frac{1}{2}$ per cent of the 3 million British bondholders surrendered their 5 per cent bonds, which were not even callable, for issues bearing 3½ per cent. France followed suit by converting $3,400 million of bonds originally issued between 1915 and 1928 at 5, 6, and 7 per cent into a single 75-year loan at 4½ per cent—with a consequent saving to the French treasury of $40 million a year. And in the United States the Victory loan was retired in 1923 and the second and third Liberty loans were retired beginning in 1927. These operations reduced the average rate of interest on the interest-bearing debt of the United States from 4.18 per cent in 1919 to 3.81 per cent in 1930. Since that date the rate of interest on federal securities, as we have seen, has steadily declined.[11]

Factors Affecting Debt Management

The favorable reaction of the market to federal government securities in recent months may be reversed in the future by three possible developments: elimination of the tax-exemption feature of federal issues, extensive public borrowing for public works and emergency relief, and adoption by Congress of currency-inflation devices.

Elimination of Tax-Exemption

One factor affecting rates on government issues has been the tax-exemption feature. Since 1929 all issues of treasury bills, notes, and certificates have been exempt, both as to principal and interest, from both the normal and surtax rates of the federal income tax, as well as from state and local taxation. The First Liberty loan is exempt from surtaxes, and the Fourth Liberty loan is exempt only from the normal tax. Under existing law all of the income from new bonds issued in any future refunding operations will be subject to the present high surtax rates of the federal income tax. In the course of refunding operations, the bulk of the outstanding federal securities now wholly tax exempt could be made subject to the surtaxes in a relatively few

---

[11] On December 27, 1932, Representative La Guardia of New York introduced in the House of Representatives a joint resolution to reduce the interest rates on all outstanding bonded indebtedness of the United States by 29 per cent. The resolution would authorize the Secretary of the Treasury "to issue new certificates in exchange for all outstanding government bonds and other certificates of interest-bearing indebtedness bearing the new interest rates, which shall equal 71 per centum of the interest rates now paid on the respective issues of bonds or certificates or Liberty loans. . . . " This resolution has not been heard of since its introduction. If adopted, it would probably be challenged in the courts as violating the constitutional prohibition against impairing the obligations of contract. It is interesting to note that a refunding of Liberty 4¼s at 3 per cent would involve a reduction of 29.41 per cent in the rate of interest.

years, if Congress so ordered. In order to reach corporate income from federal securities, which income if exempt from normal tax is completely exempt, Congress would also have to remove the normal tax-exemption feature, since corporations constitute an important group of security holders. And, assuming the early adoption of a constitutional amendment to prohibit future issues of tax-exempt securities, the income from the new securities issued by the federal government would become taxable by the states. In any event, elimination of tax-exemption would impair the attractiveness of federal issues and probably require the treasury to pay a higher premium.

On the other hand, the loss in tax revenue to the federal and state governments from the exemption of securities probably exceeds the savings in interest due to the tax-exempt status of their securities. The volume of securities wholly exempt from the federal income tax has grown to approximately $26 billion. In addition, there are some $12 billion of federal securities which are exempt from the normal tax only. Estimates of the loss to the federal government in income tax receipts from the exemption of these securities vary from $100 million to $300 million, based on the income tax rates provided in the Revenue Act of 1921, the levels of which were restored by the Revenue Act of 1932. Efforts to abolish tax-free bonds by constitutional amendment failed in Congress in 1923 and 1924, but new efforts in this direction were made by Senators Ashurst and Hull in the last session of the 72nd Congress. Various other methods of reaching tax-free income without a constitutional amendment have been suggested by reputable authorities. These include a proposal for taxation at "penalty rates" of tax-free securities found in estates and inheritances, and a proposal to increase the rates in the upper brackets of the estate and gift taxes.

Whatever the merit of these proposals, the growing volume of tax-exempt securities constitutes a serious economic evil. As Secretary Mellon remarked in 1921, it "encourages the growth of public indebtedness and tends to divert capital from productive enterprise." At a time when new taxes are badly needed to balance the budget, this avenue of retreat should be closed and the flow of capital back into business channels facilitated. Congress should promptly submit to the states a constitutional amendment to permit taxation by the federal and state governments of income derived from future issues of their securities. And it should provide that all of the income from new bonds issued in the course of future refunding operations be subject at least to the surtax rates of the federal income tax.[12]

Borrowing for Emergency Relief

A second development that might endanger debt conversion would be the adoption by Congress of extensive schemes for public expenditures, financed by borrowings from the market. Under this head come federal loans to farmers, home owners, banks, and railroads, unemployment relief and public works, payment in full of the adjusted service compensation certificates, debt adjustment and mortgage moratorium bills, and other financial relief legislation. If such borrowings were not kept within reasonable limits or segregated in an extraordinary budget, they would result in deteriorating government credit, debt conversions would be impossible, and the lowering of long-term interest rates would be indefinitely delayed.[13]

Inflation of the Currency

It remains, finally, to consider the effect of currency inflation on refunding operations and on the federal debt in general. Presumably, the purpose of currency inflation would be to raise the general price level. The failure of managed currencies to raise prices appreciably abroad suggests the probable futility of similar efforts in this country. Floods of paper money would have to be issued to have any substantial effect on prices.[14] As prices rose, currency would depreciate in value. As the purchasing power of money declined, confidence in the currency might diminish. Bank depositors and holders of United States currency or securities would convert them into gold, if the law allowed, as they did in the early weeks of 1933. To the extent that currency was redeemed in gold, to that extent would gold reserves be depleted. If those reserves were reduced below their legal minimum, either Congress

---

[12] For a thorough and able discussion of this subject, see "Tax Burdens and Tax-Free Securities," by Richard M. Boeckel, *Editorial Research Reports,* January 25, 1933.

[13] Loans authorized by the Reconstruction Finance Corporation from its establishment on February 2, 1932, to December 31, 1932, totaled $1,937 million. The corporation receives its funds from the treasury and is expected to repay them ultimately. The Secretary of the Treasury in his last annual report recommended that legislation be enacted, providing that upon the retirement of the capital stock of the corporation, the amounts repaid to the treasury be applied to the reduction of the public debt. The repayments of the funds advanced by the treasury to the corporation on its notes under the terms of existing law will be automatically so applied.

[14] Unless inflation was brought about by reducing the gold content of the dollar.

would have to lower the legal reserve ratio, or the treasury would have to suspend gold payments as President Roosevelt did in his proclamation of March 5. In the latter event, the country would then be, at least temporarily, on an inconvertible paper currency basis, with its money decreasing in value as it increased in quantity. (Only $9,472,701 of the new emergency currency was in circulation or in the hands of issuing banks on March 16. The new banking legislation provides for swift retirement of the excess currency, the issue of which will terminate when the President declares the emergency at an end.) If inflation went far enough, however, it would have disastrous effects on the economic life of the nation.

The effect of a voluntary policy of currency inflation upon confidence is a major consideration. It is a principle of public finance that the volume of currency in circulation is dependent upon the effective demand for this particular form of exchange media. To force currency into circulation to such an extent as to produce inflation, that is, to such an extent as to influence the demand for currency, would probably set in motion forces the operation of which would be eventually anything but moderate.

How would inflation affect the national debt? If it succeeded in raising prices, it would raise the prices which the federal government has to pay for services and materials and thus increase current expenditures and reduce any possible treasury surplus otherwise available for debt retirement. Since the bulk of the present federal debt was incurred, prices have declined—sharply in 1920 and since 1929. As prices decline, the value of the dollar increases. As the value of the dollar increases, the burden of the national debt increases. Interest payments on the national debt increase in value to the holder of government bonds as prices fall, but the taxes required to meet the annual interest charges become steadily more burdensome to the taxpayer. This circumstance is well brought out by Professor Shultz, who writes: [15]

Today the funds which the federal government draws from its taxpayers and devotes to retirement of the federal debt are worth more in purchasing power than the funds which the federal government derived from its loans in 1918 and 1919. Because the federal government must redeem its war debt in years when money is worth more, in purchasing power, than in the years when its debt was incurred, it is compelled in effect to pay a bonus on such

[15] William J. Shultz, *American Public Finance and Taxation* (1931), p. 164.

part of its war costs as were financed by borrowing. This bonus goes to the subscribers to the war loans who have retained possession of their federal bonds. They are in the position of having loaned cheap money to the government and of being repaid in dear money.

All this would be reversed, however, if currency inflation succeeded in inflating prices. Price inflation would ease the burden of the federal debt to the treasury and the taxpayers at the expense of the bondholders; the government's loans would be repaid in cheaper dollars. The higher prices rose, the easier debt payment would become. If inflation went far enough, the United States could devalorize its public debt as France, Italy, Germany, and other European countries escaped their internal war debts. What effects a violent inflation would have on our general economic life can be surmised from the post-war experience of the countries that chose this course. But such speculation is beyond the scope of this chapter.

The Gold Clause

It may be argued that the United States could not escape its internal debt because of the so-called gold clause. When the treasury offers federal securities for sale, it states that the principal and interest thereof will be payable in United States gold coin of the "present standard of value," i.e., of the present weight and fineness. Were the gold content of the dollar reduced below its present standard and payments of principal and interest made in dollars so debased, it would involve a breach of contract on the part of the federal government and investors in federal securities would promptly appeal to the courts for payment in full. The Supreme Court would then be confronted with a choice between (1) requiring the government to pay in undebased gold coin, a decision which would increase the federal debt by as much as the dollar was debased and either drive the country off the gold standard or quickly exhaust our gold reserves, and (2) upholding payment in debased dollars, which would reduce the burden of the federal debt by so much. Faced with these alternatives, the Supreme Court might well find that the national welfare counselled choice of the lesser evil and sanction payment of the federal debt in gold coin of the new standard of value.

Devaluation of the currency by reducing the number of grains of gold in the dollar would involve the abrogation of all contracts, private as well as public, containing the gold clause. It is estimated that there are $75 billions of debts having such a gold provision. There are legal opinions holding that the courts would probably take the view that such gold contracts are impossible of performance and might, therefore, be abrogated in the public interest.

Professor John Hanna of the Columbia University Law School raises some knotty questions in this connection. Writing to the editor of *The New York Times,* he says in part:

The federal government has recently threatened to send citizens to prison for retaining gold in their possession. These same citizens owe at the present time billions of dollars in obligations containing a clause requiring payment in gold of "the present standard of weight and fineness." The government has outstanding about twenty billion dollars of gold promises. If a creditor has a contract for gold and a debtor has an obligation to pay gold and the government seizes all the gold and not only refuses to sell any of it but makes it illegal even to retain it, what can the creditor and the debtor do about it? . . . Does this excuse the individual from paying gold to the extent at least that if he tenders lawful money he can prevent the further accumulating of interest and costs? . . .

Admitting that most creditors will be willing to take payment in whatever form of lawful money is offered, Professor Hanna remarks that some creditors will be obdurate and changes in conditions may create a real spread between gold and paper values. The question then will almost certainly arise as to the power of the government to require creditors to allow debtors to pay off gold obligations with an equal nominal though less actual value of paper money.[16]

[16] *New York Times,* April 2, 1933.

Chapter Nine

THE DEBTS OF STATE AND LOCAL GOVERNMENTS

SUMMARY

The Facts

ON January 1, 1933, the total debt of state and local governments was $19.3 billion compared with $17 billion in 1929, $9.8 billion in 1922, and $4.8 billion in 1914 (p. 258).

The gross funded state and local debt on January 1, 1933, was $18.7 billion or 14.7 per cent of the nation's internal long-term debt burden. Only 2 billions of this were state debts. In 1926 the state and local funded debt amounted to $22.5 billion (p. 258).

In 1933 state and local long-term debts are 13 per cent above 1929, about double what they were in 1922, and almost four times their level in 1914 (p. 258).

The total annual service on these debts is now $1.5 billion compared with half a billion dollars in 1914. Interest charges comprised $887 million and retirements $607 million of the total debt service last year (p. 258).

Total tax collections in 1932 for all state and local governments combined were almost five times the entire carrying charges on their debts in that year (pp. 265–66).

State and local debts per capita were $154.50 in 1932, $140.92 in 1929, $88.92 in 1922 and $50.30 in 1914 (p. 258).

State and local debts were 6.43 per cent of the national wealth in 1932; and the carrying charges on them were 3.74 per cent of the national income (pp. 263–64).

Tax delinquency is becoming increasingly widespread, although some sections, notably New England, are relatively free from abnormal delinquency (pp. 267–68). High rates of delinquency tend to accompany high debts (p. 268).

Despite the favorable ratio of tax collections to debt service for state and local governments as a group, 1,120 public units are estimated to have defaulted on their bonded obligations up to February 1, 1933. No states, however, were in default at that time [1] (p. 270).

---

[1] Arkansas has subsequently defaulted on its entire state and district highway debt of $140 million.

Among the chief causes of local defaults are the mounting tide of tax delinquency, inability to fund floating debt, failure of banks containing public funds, unlimited issue of special assessment bonds, excessive borrowing, and general economic distress (pp. 271–72).

Recommendations

The redistribution of debt maturities so as to refund obligations whose payment is either impossible or imposes a strain and to postpone principal payments on specific issues for 3 to 5 years (pp. 273–74).

Lower interest charges on state and local debts through federal refinancing of their obligations and by the extension of state credit to municipalities (pp. 274–76).

Reallocation of state revenues from the gasoline tax and other newer tax sources to redeem local debts (pp. 276–77).

State receiverships of bankrupt municipalities, in extraordinary cases, to readjust abnormal debts to capacity to pay (pp. 277–80).

State control of funding and refunding by debt commissions to provide a mechanism for widespread debt readjustment for many localities in contrast to receiverships for unusual cases (pp. 280–82).

Resort to debt reduction through bondholders' agreements, if receiverships are not authorized (p. 282).

State review of prospective local and state bond issues (pp. 285–86).

Revision of state budget laws to assure orderly state and local financing, prevent excessive borrowing, and restrict the use of scrip (pp. 288–89).

Federal aid to state and local unemployment relief to relieve budgetary strains causing borrowing (p. 290).

Local and state effort through current and capital budgeting to economize and to plan the use of credit (p. 290).

------

1. THE FACTS [2]

STATE and local indebtedness forms a part of public and private debt which, while not large relative to the total, is one if not the most difficult to the deal with by reason of the excessive number and diversity of districts having incurred debts. Because of their rigid character, state

------

[2] Table 70 and Chart 26 summarize the basic data used in this chapter.

and local bonds usually remain a fixed charge upon budgets without possibility of alteration during the course of their terms.

As a charge fixed until the discharge of the obligations, debt service renders state and local economy difficult by reducing the margin of discretion in lowering public costs. The debt charges decrease the ability, especially of local governments, to pay for social services, particularly for unemployment relief. Property taxes, already high for a prosperous era, are rendered burdensome in some communities and exorbitant in other areas. The natural tendency to tax delinquency during a depression is intensified by high levies to redeem debts incurred during the flush "nineteen twenties." The burden of fixed charges is a stimulus to defaults by municipalities which virtually renders them bankrupt corporations.

No blanket characterizations of state and local borrowing, however, are applicable to all units and no causes of fiscal distress uniformly prevail throughout all areas. Consequently, an understanding of the debt structures and their burdens under the impact of the depression must identify the nature and extent of the debt and differentiate between the situations which call for remedy.

At the date of this writing, February, 1933, no comprehensive and dependable statistics exist to measure even the amount of outstanding debt of local governments. Their very number, estimated at 150,000 districts in the United States, is unknown. A reasonably accurate record exists, however, of state debts, the reporting of which is far better performed. Estimates of local debts must vary from the federal decennial census of public debt when it is released during the next year or two. That census was utilized in this study for the base year of 1922. To this was added all new obligations issued during the next decade, of which a dependable record exists, and from it were deducted the retirements of principal pro-rated between states according to the ratio for the annual and decennial retirements of all state and local debts in the United States. The estimates are serviceable in gauging debt burdens and the relative place of this class of obligations in the total debt structure.[3]

[3] Date of obligations issued and retired 1923–32 were derived from the published records and office files of *The Bond Buyer* through the courtesy of its editor. The gross debt, sinking fund accumulations, and net debt figures are the estimates of the United States Treasury through 1931 and of *The Bond Buyer* for 1932. The temporary debt figures, admittedly unreliable, are presented in order to afford a working estimate for a complete picture of indebtedness.

CHART 26

STATE AND LOCAL DEBTS IN RELATION TO TAX RECEIPTS AND NATIONAL WEALTH AND INCOME

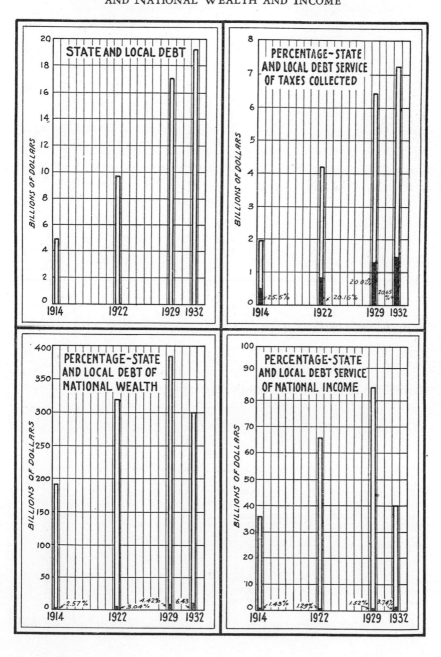

TABLE 70

Basic Data on State and Local Debts

(Dollars in Millions)

	1932 (Jan. 1, 1933)		1929		1922		1914
	Amount	Per Cent Change	Amount	Per Cent Change	Amount	Per Cent Change	Amount
1. Temporary debt..........	$600	33.33	$450	28.57	$350	100.00	$175
2. Gross funded debt........	$18,685	12.86	$16,556	75.75	$9,420	98.27	$4,751
3. Total debt...............	$19,285	13.40	$17,006	74.06	$9,770	98.34	$4,926
4. Interest charges.........	$887	13.43	$782	74.16	$449	97.80	$227
5. Debt retirements.........	$607	19.02	$510	26.87	$402	46.18	$275
6. Total debt service.......	$1,494	15.63	$1,292	51.82	$851	69.52	$502
7. Total taxes collected.....	$7,232	12.09	$6,452	52.85	$4,221	114.81	$1,965
8. Percentage debt service of taxes collected.........	.2065	3.15	.2002	−.69	.2016	−21.06	.255
9. Debts per capita........	$154.50	10.34	$140.92	57.47	$88.92	58.85	$50.30
10. National wealth.........	$300,000	−22.08	$385,000	$19.94	$321,000	67.19	$192,000
11. Percentage debt of national wealth................	6.43	45.48	4.42	45.39	3.04	18.29	2.57
12. National income.........	$40,000	−56.52	$85,000	39.39	$66,000	88.57	$35,000
13. Percentage debt service of national income........	3.74	167.14	1.52	8.53	1.29	−9.79	1.43
14. Wholesale commodity price index................	60.4	−36.6	95.3	−1.5	96.7	42	68.1

Debts in Amounts and by Population

On December 31, 1932, the estimated state and local net funded indebtedness was $16,570 million, the gross funded debt was $18,685 million, and the temporary debt was $600 million, making a total indebtedness of $19,285 million. The figure first given is utilized for comparisons and distribution of amounts between states. Of the total, $2,008 million were state debts, leaving $14,561 million of net funded local obligations. Table 71 traces the growth of state and local debt for a 92-year period from 1840, when it first assumed proportions large for that day, to the current figures demanding attention.

TABLE 71

State and Local Net Debt, 1840–1932(a)

			Increase Over Previous Year	
Year	Amount Net Debt (ooo omitted)	Per Capita Debt	In Amount Debt (ooo omitted)	In per Capita Debt
1840	$220,000	$12.89	....	....
1850	305,000	13.15	$85,000	$0.26
1860	375,000	11.93	70,000	−1.22
1870	868,600	22.53	493,600	10.60
1880	1,056,916	21.07	188,316	−1.46
1890	1,137,200	18.07	80,284	−3.00
1902	1,869,438	23.77	732,238	5.70
1912	3,821,896	39.88	1,952,458	16.11
1922	8,689,740	79.09	4,867,844	39.21
1932	16,570,353	132.75	7,880,613	53.66

(a) U. S. Treasury estimates, Federal Decennial Census of Debts, 1913 and 1922, H. C. Adams' *Public Debts*, and estimated for 1850.

The table reveals three periods in our debt history. Before the Civil War borrowing reached its peak in a per capita debt of $13.15 in 1850. The post-Civil War expansion and inflation raised debts to a new level with the per capita peak in the early "seventies." During the following deflationary period the amount of debt slowly rose, but per capita borrowing declined, so that the per capita debt at the end of the century was approximately the same as 30 years before. The moderate inflation after the turn of the century marked the beginning of a new debt era. The increase in debts from 1902 to 1912 of $1,952 million was greater than the outstanding debt of $1,869 million in 1902. The rising price level of the World War period and subsequent years was accompanied by the greatest increase of debt per capita in American history. The 127.4 per cent rise from 1912 to 1922 represented a net debt increase of $4,867 million. The 90.7 per cent rise during the decade ending 1932, or $7,880 million, is impressive in itself but acquires more meaning when stated in population terms. The per capita growth of $53.66 produced a net debt of $132.75 per person. In brief, the gross debts per person during the period of marked acceleration, 1914 to 1932, more than tripled from $50.30 to $154.50.

The 90.7 per cent increase of net debt from 1922 to 1932 is a total figure which obscures wide local variations. For example, in Idaho the increase was 8.27 per cent, while in Florida it was 447.73. The distribution of variations for all states is as follows:

TABLE 72

PERCENTAGE INCREASE IN STATE AND LOCAL DEBTS, 1922–1932

Up to 25 Per Cent	25.1 to 50 Per Cent	50.1 to 75 Per Cent	75.1 to 100 Per Cent	100.1 to 125 Per Cent	Over 125 Per Cent
Idaho	Georgia	Arizona	California	Arkansas	Alabama
Kansas	Oklahoma	Colorado	Kentucky	Louisiana	Florida
Minnesota	Virginia	Connecticut	New Hampshire	Maine	Illinois
Montana	Washington	Delaware	New York	Maryland	Michigan
Nebraska		Indiana	Texas	Rhode Island	Missouri
N. Dakota		Iowa	Wisconsin	S. Carolina	New Jersey
S. Dakota		Massachusetts		Tennessee	N. Carolina
Utah		Mississippi		Vermont	Pennsylvania
		Nevada			West Virginia
		New Mexico			
		Ohio			
		Oregon			
		Wyoming			

The median class of increase in state and local debts is 50 to 75 per cent, with 13 states in this class. Yet 23 states register a higher per cent rise, 17 showing from 100 to 150. Of the states with marked acceleration seven are southern (Alabama, Arkansas, Florida, Louisiana, North and South Carolina, and Tennessee); four middle Atlantic (Maryland, New Jersey, Pennsylvania, and West Virginia); three New England states (Maine, Rhode Island, and Vermont); and three middle western (Illinois, Missouri, and Michigan). In contrast are the two groups with an increase below 50 per cent. The eight states with a rise of less than 25 per cent (Idaho, Kansas, Minnesota, Montana, Nebraska, North and South Dakota, and Utah) form a single contiguous area of northwestern prairie and mountain states. The four states with a debt rise of 25 to 50 per cent (Georgia, Oklahoma, Virginia, and Washington) are scattered geographically but bear a relation to the agricultural breakdown which consistently acted as a break to further debt in the northwest. The slow rate of increase of the eight northwest states merely means that this group already had reached the peak of new loans before 1922 and has been endeavoring to redeem debts since with a moderate amount of new borrowing.

Debts in Relation to Population

During the decade 1922–32, the population increase for the United States was 13.6 per cent. Restated, the local and state debt rise is explainable by population to the extent of 13.6 per cent. The actual rise of 90.7 shows, therefore, that 77.1 per cent of the debt was due to causes other than the growth of the country.

Of special interest is the rate of debt growth in the fifteen states where the population growth was so retarded as to be less than half that of the United States as a whole. Six of the states with the lowest debt rate are in this class. In sharp contrast, however, five others in the same class (Maine, Missouri, Arkansas, South Carolina, and Vermont) increased their debts in excess of 100 per cent. In a group of equal size, fifteen states, the rate of population growth exceeded the average for the country. Yet in only six of them did the rate of debt increase exceed the country's average rate.

In other words, despite the repressive effect of meager population growth upon debt increase in a small minority of states, indebtedness in the others departed from the normal direct relationship to improvement costs for enlarging communities by following the opposite course. Excessive borrowing occurred in slow growing communities and slow or moderate borrowing in fast growing areas. This situation, of course, has intensified the per capita burden of state and local debts. In slow growing areas residents have suffered a growth in debt per person even where the rise in the total amounts of debt was moderate. The 1930 census has blasted the hopes of many cities whose borrowing has been related to an expected population growth that will probably not materialize. The diminution in the rate of growth of many cities inevitably means a heavier weight in the debt load per person than was expected when the debts were incurred.

Debt Burden as Affected by Price Changes

Since the principal and interest of debts are paid in dollars constantly changing in value, the actual burden (which is the annual retirement charges rather than the nominal amount of capitalized obligations) must fluctuate with the price level. A sharp conflict of opinion exists, however, as to the effect of falling prices upon debt burdens. Administrators confronted with the difficult mechanics of budget making view a price fall as inescapably adding to debt burdens. Economists, such as Pigou and Taussig, on the other hand, dissent with qualifications which escape the immediate view of officials. Nevertheless, when declining production and savings accompany the price fall, economic theory is more ready to admit a rise in the burden which administrators insist follows from the intensified difficulty of extracting dollars from the taxpayers.

Stated in terms of the wholesale price index of the U. S. Bureau of Labor Statistics (1926 = 100) the state and local debts are shown below for comparisons during two decades. The difference in the price level between 1926 and 1932 added to the actual weight of debts (but not to their nominal amount) approximately six billion dollars, resulting in a total state and local debt weight of twenty-two and a half billions in 1932. Of special import is the effect upon the rate of change. Instead of a per cent increase of 126.4 the actual weight of debts as adjusted to prices rose only 78.82 per cent from 1912 to 1922. The opposite result, however, marked the last decade. Instead of a per cent increase of 90.7 from 1922 to 1932, the readjusted rate of increase was 153.44 per cent. The figures are as follows:

	1912	1922	1932
Amount added to debt by lower prices....	$1,154,212,592	$2,208,553,760	$5,981,897,433
Readjusted debt outstanding...	4,976,108,592	8,898,293,760	22,552,250,433

Approximately two-fifths of the present debt service of states and localities is a result of the war and post-war inflation. Computing all state and local borrowings for construction projects between 1914 and 1930, Dr. Clarence Heer in the Report of the President's Committee on Social Trends finds that $6,775 million out of $14,181 million of bond issues were a result of inflation in construction prices above the 1913 level. Since interest and retirement charges on pre-war debts were not affected by post-war inflation, Dr. Heer concludes that "the aggregate debt service charges will probably keep on increasing during the next few years even though the trend of construction costs be downward. Debt service will continue to increase as long as the amount of new bond issues exceeds the amount of bond retirements. An excess of bond issues may be expected as long as a considerable proportion of the bonds retired consist of pre-war issues and as long as current costs remain above the 1913 level." [4]

Despite the marked antipathy towards new issues in 1932, this prediction was fulfilled for at least that year, with a net debt increase of $300 million. The recent rise in the annual retirements to $600 million, combined with the decrease in new issues, points to a very moderate net increase in debt service in the near future; and if the depression continues or deepens the margin of the excess of new issues over retirements may be so narrowed, if not eliminated, as to render the debt service stationary. The outstanding fact is that the debt service has and is mounting through the depression period and that a future increase, although less in amount than in previous years, is a likelihood but not a certainty in 1933. Accordingly, budget makers are faced with an enlarging debt service which represents the scissors movement of two-fifths of the debt attributable to inflation combined with necessity of repayment in deflated prices.

Relation of Debts to Wealth and Income

The effect of a changing price level upon debt burdens, as well as the measure of the burdens themselves, is best shown by the relation

[4] *Recent Social Trends,* vol. II, pp. 1351–52.

of debts to wealth and income. The table below traces the relationship for an 82-year period, 1850–1932, between net debt and taxable wealth.

TABLE 73

TAXABLE WEALTH IN RELATION TO POPULATION AND DEBTS, 1850–1932

(Dollars in Millions)

Year	Total Taxable Wealth	Per Capita Wealth	Per Cent Net Debt to Taxable Wealth	Wholesale Price Index (1926=100)
1850	$7,136	$308	4.27	
1860	16,160	514	2.32	61
1870	24,055	624	3.61	87
1880	41,642	830	2.54	65
1890	61,204	975	1.86	56.2
1902	91,289	1,150	2.05	58.9
1912	173,986	1,820	2.20	69.1
1922	300,298	2,731	2.89	96.7
1932	239,731	1,921	6.91	62.6

Except for not unimportant variations, the per cent of net debt to taxable wealth discloses no extreme variations except for the first and last years, 1850 and 1932. The year 1850 approximately marked the climax of the pre-Civil War borrowing and 1932 represents the combined effect of a lower price level, shrinkage in wealth, and an inherited debt whose amount had been accelerated by the previous inflationary period. Similarly the ratio of 3.61 per cent of net debt to taxable wealth in 1870 is a product of post-Civil War expansion and inflation, while the opposite condition prevailing in 1890 is expressed by the lowest percentage of 1.86 of debt to wealth.

Of significance also is a comparison of the two columns, "per capita wealth" and "per cent of net debt to taxable wealth." By and large, per capita wealth grew faster than the debt burden during the latter part of the last century; and subsequently, despite the huge rise in per capita debts, taxable wealth tended to rise in a corresponding amount until 1922 or shortly afterwards. Thereafter, the ratio of debt to wealth steadily rose notwithstanding the phenomenal expansion of wealth until 1929. In that year the ratio was higher than in any prior year in American history. So when the depression whittled away the wealth base the already high ratio jumped in 1932 to the abnormal ratio of 6.91 per cent of net debt to wealth.

The net decline in taxable wealth and private income from 1922 to 1931 is a fact paramount to the entire analysis. During the nine-year period, the taxable wealth decreased 20.17 per cent and income per capita shrunk slightly further to 22.43 per cent.[5] So uniform was the decline in taxable wealth that but six states report an increase and of these, Florida may be dismissed by reason of abnormalities. Three disclosed very moderate rises, leaving only the two states of New Jersey and California with substantial wealth increases. Reducing private income to a per capita basis, the picture is even darker with but two states revealing an increase. The bulk of the states show an income decline well above the average. Indeed 31 states report a decline in excess of 25 per cent. In 12 of these states, the state and local debt had mounted from 50 to 100 per cent during the past decade and in 10 the debt increase was in excess of 100 per cent.

Recapitulating the relation of state and local debts to wealth and income, the following table reveals the burdens for the two years, 1922 and 1931–32 and indicates their relative changes:

TABLE 74

RELATIVE DEBT BURDENS 1922 AND 1932

Year	State and Local Debt	Taxable Wealth	Ratio of Debts to Wealth	Private Income	Ratio of Debts to Income
1922	$8,689,740,000	$300,298,043,000	2.89	$60,195,000,000	14.43
1931–32	16,570,353,000	239,731,912,000	6.91	52,703,000,000	31.44

The increased ratio of debt to taxable wealth from 2.89 per cent in 1922 to 6.91 per cent in 1931–32 was a rise of 139 per cent. The

TABLE 75

AMOUNT OF INCREASE IN RATIOS OF STATE AND LOCAL DEBTS TO INCOME, 1922–1932

Up to 5 Per Cent	5.1 to 10 Per Cent	10.1 to 15 Per Cent	15.1 to 25 Per Cent	25.1 to 35 Per Cent	Over 35 Per Cent
Delaware	Connecticut	Arizona	California	Alabama	Arkansas
Idaho	Georgia	Colorado	Maine	Louisiana	Florida
Kansas	Indiana	Illinois	Missouri	Michigan	Mississippi
Nebraska	Iowa	Kentucky	New Mexico	New Jersey	N. Carolina
S. Dakota	Minnesota	Maryland	New York	S. Carolina	Tennessee
	Montana	Massachusetts	Oregon		
	Nevada	N. Dakota	Pennsylvania		
	New Hampshire	Ohio	Rhode Island		
	Utah	Oklahoma	Texas		
	Vermont	Virginia	W. Virginia		
	Wisconsin	Washington			
		Wyoming			

[5] Computed from 1922 Federal Census of *Wealth, Debt and Taxation*, the 1932 Federal Committee Report on *Double Taxation*, and the income reports of the Brookmire Economic Service.

increase in the ratio of debt to private income during the decade of from 14.43 to 31.44 per cent, was a growth of 187 per cent. In 1932, the state and local debt formed so large a proportion of taxable wealth of all kinds as to be above the seven per cent ratio usually accepted as a conservative limit in 21 states and above 10 per cent in eight states.

Table 75 shows the variations in increased debt burdens in the various states. The figures give the percentage of increase in the ratios of debts to income between 1922 and 1932.

The Relation of Taxes to Debts

In the face of a decline in production, savings, private income, and taxable wealth, what has been the trend of taxes imposed by state and local governments to meet debt payments and other expenses? The expansion in the tax burden of all states and their subdivisions is traced for the nine-year period, 1922–31, in Table 76.[6]

TABLE 76

THE TREND OF TAXES, 1922–1931

	Taxes Collected		Increase of Taxes		Increase per Capita	
	1922	1931	Amount	Per Cent	Amount	Per Cent
States.........	$868,000,000	$1,967,000,000	$1,099,000,000	126	8.03	100
Counties......	745,000,000	958,000,000	213,000,000	29	0.94	14
Cities.........	1,627,000,000	2,978,000,000	1,351,000,000	83	0.29	62
Other divisions.	981,000,000	1,188,000,000	207,000,000	21	0.65	7
Total.......	$4,221,000,000	$7,091,000,000	$2,870,000,000	67	18.91	48.7

Notwithstanding the moderate tax expansion of counties and minor divisions, the rise of state and local taxes as a whole was 67 per cent during the same period during which debts rose 90.7 per cent. The per capita tax rise was 48.7 per cent as against a per capita debt growth for the decade of 66.15 per cent. Stating the tax burden in amounts per capita, rather than in rates of increase, the total burden was $38.84 in 1922 and $57.76 nine years later, a rise of nearly $18.92 per person.

Of this total, general property taxes grew from $31.71 to $42.87 per capita, a rise of $11.16 per person, while the burden of all other state and local taxes mounted from $7.13 to $14.89 per capita, or an

[6] Report of Federal Committee on *Double Taxation*, pp. 203–204.

expansion of $7.76 to every inhabitant. Since state and local bonds rest so largely upon the general property tax, it is pertinent to point out that, viewing the federal, state, and local tax system as a whole, the burden of all taxes other than property levies decreased $1.90 per capita. The property tax expansion alone accounted for a net growth of $9.66 per capita of all taxation in the United States. Consequently, the repayment of state and local bonds is rendered hazardous to the extent that the redemption process is continued mainly from property tax receipts.

A comparison between the tax growth and debt rise by states shows that, in the main, the two increases are outgrowths of the same conditions and tend, despite exceptions, to accompany each other. Of the 20 states with the highest tax growth, 12 are states with excessive rates of debt expansion. Conversely, all the 12 states with the lowest tax rise, were, with two exceptions, relatively moderate borrowers. The inflexible character of municipal functions has rendered difficult the reduction of local expenditures during the depression to correspond to a shrinking tax base and at the same time to afford funds to pay for debt service. Of 106 cities reporting in 1930 to the Municipal Administration Service, 71 increased expenses over the previous year, but in 1931 decreases were effected by 47 out of 80 municipalities.[7]

Mr. C. E. Rightor's analysis of city tax rates compares the levies of 256 cities in 1931 and 1932. The average in the former year was $34.99 and in the latter year was $35.03 per $1,000 valuation, an average rise of four cents in all cities.[8] Of the 256 cities, a majority either decreased or held their tax rates relatively stationary, showing an effort to protect public credit and taxpayers, while the increases mainly were attributable to welfare and unemployment expenses. More hopeful as an earnest of tax reduction is the collation of reports from 279 cities in 39 states, as of January 1, 1933, by Mr. Carl H. Chatters. The amount of city taxes levied decreased in 31 states and, of the eight states with rises, only Connecticut, Massachusetts, and New York cities increased their levies above five per cent over the previous year. Twelve states report net decreases in the reporting cities of more than 10 per cent in local levies.[9]

[7] F. L. Bird, "Present Financial Status of 135 Cities in the United States and Canada," p. 6.

[8] National Municipal Review, December, 1932.

[9] Computed from Report of Hearings before Subcommittee of Senate Committee on Manufacturing, p. 177.

Tax Delinquencies and Credit

To the extent that high property taxes prove uncollectable the base of public credit, as well as the financing of services, is weakened and often put in serious jeopardy. To measure the degree of tax delinquency is difficult, if not impossible, because no reporting machinery exists for all public units. Likewise for the districts for which data can be collected the information becomes obsolete rapidly with new years and new economic conditions.

As recently as 1931 tax collections were proceeding normally in many states, contrary to the popular notion. A survey of all the federal census reports for 1931, available on February 1, 1933, discloses that in 205 cities located in 37 states the ratio of property tax receipts to tax levies increased from 1929 to 1931 in 18 states and decreased in 19 states. The 1931 record of the state governments was even superior to that of the cities. A total of 19 disclosed an increase in the per cent of collection, 12 a decline, while 7 imposed no property tax or did not report.[10]

Conditions are radically different, however, in 1933. Tax delinquency is now occurring unevenly over the country. A section like New England is relatively free from abnormal delinquency, while areas like the northern lake sections and southern and western farm districts are struggling with mounting failures to collect. Areas with marked delinquency were spotted by the Bureau of Agricultural Statistics in a 1932 survey which estimated that 1931 taxes were delinquent on nearly 40 million acres in five states (Michigan, Minnesota, Wisconsin, South Dakota, and Oregon), representing 16 per cent of their total area.[11] That the extent of delinquency is becoming cumulatively greater is observed from the report of the same bureau showing the increase in the number of farm foreclosures for delinquent taxes to be from 4.2 to 7.4 per 1,000 farms between 1926 and 1931.[12]

More recent statistics indicate a more widespread delinquency and higher ratios of uncollected taxes. Individual industrial cities throughout the country, such as Milwaukee and Detroit, are currently reporting abnormal increases in uncollected taxes which are obscured by general reports. An effort to procure the latest figures in 1933 resulted in returns from nine sample states whose trends are recapitulated.[13]

[10] Computed from the office records of the U. S. Bureau of the Census.
[11] Release, Mr. Donald Jackson, June 14, 1932.
[12] "The Farm Real Estate Situation, 1930–31," Table 9.
[13] Correspondence with tax officials of the respective states.

Massachusetts is free from unusual difficulty. Mississippi disclosed only a 6½ per cent delinquency in state taxes with an estimated higher ratio for local levies. A 3.77 per cent delinquency in 31 Kansas counties in 1928 had grown to 13.5 per cent in 1932. Arizona's delinquent taxes were 37.5 per cent larger in 1932 than in 1931. Oregon's delinquency grew from 13.54 in 1928 to 15.47 in 1930 and jumped to 26.28 in 1931. Virginia's local tax collections were 14 per cent delinquent in 1932 in contrast to 11.6 per cent in 1931. Of Washington's 1932 tax levies 29.7 per cent were uncollected at the end of the year and of all outstanding taxes 44.4 per cent were uncollected. North Carolina school tax delinquencies mounted from 3.9 per cent in 1929 and 5.1 per cent in 1930 to 12.8 per cent in 1931; and Pennsylvania's 12.2 per cent delinquency in 1930 was estimated appreciably higher the next two years.

These figures gain weight since they refer to all subdivisions within the states. By the same token they require analysis since they obscure more threatening situations where the percentages are alarmingly higher for individual units. Thus one-third of the North Carolina counties collected less than 80 per cent of taxes in 1931, while two-thirds were estimated to be in the same class in 1932.

Relation of Delinquency to Debts

The relationship between the amount of delinquency and the weight of debt is confirmed by several studies, of which the most important is the 1932 report of the tax delinquency committee of the National Tax Association. Analyzing the figures for 72 cities, the committee found that "in nine cities with a debt in excess of $200 per capita, collections for 1930 averaged 90.5 per cent, whereas in 12 cities with a per capita debt of less than $50, collections for that year averaged 96.7 per cent. Likewise, 21 cities with a debt exceeding 10 per cent of the assessed valuation collected 91.2 per cent of the 1930 levy, whereas 21 cities with a debt of less than five per cent of assessed value collected 96.1 per cent."

An analysis of the debt, the extent of defaults, and the percentage of taxes collected in 1932 of 30 Florida cities discloses a connection between all three factors. The relative size of the defaults to debts and the number of suits for collecting due debts varied with the degree of tax delinquency.[14] While high debts and high rates of delinquency are both reflections of the same economic condition, and especially of real

[14] Figures derived from *The Bond Buyer*, September 24, 1932.

estate speculation, the high debts once incurred tend to intensify the difficulty of tax collection by keeping tax rates at so high a level as to make delinquency likely.

The Cost of Debt Service

Figures on the burden of interest charges for states and large cities are available but those for all subdivisions can only be estimated. The burden of debt retirements can only be guessed at. The failure of the Census Bureau to report debt retirements compels an estimate even for the units for which interest payments are reported.

The one complete statement that can be made from reported data relates to interest charges for states. In 1922 they expended $41 million for this purpose out of a total expenditure of $1,280 million, while in 1930 they paid $101 million out of a total of $2,290 million. The proportion of total expenditures devoted to interest rose but slightly over one per cent in eight years. The per cent in the earlier year was 3.2 and in the latter year 4.4. Nevertheless, the percentage increase in interest charges was 146 per cent and the amount of the increase, $60 million, was far in excess of the total interest charges of 1922. Municipal interest charges for 261 cities in 1922 totaled $214 million out of $2,223 million expenditure, absorbing 9.62 per cent of the total; and for 310 cities in 1932 interest cost $405 million out of $3,810 million, absorbing 10.63 per cent of the total.[15]

The total estimated debt service of states and localities affords two significant measures of the weight of the debt burden: the per cent of debt service to taxes collected and to national income. The growth of the debt service in itself is arresting with a total of $502 million in 1914, mounting in progressive stages to $851 million in 1922 and $1,292 million in 1929 and reaching $1,494 million in 1932. The per cent of taxes collected which were absorbed by debt service, however, shows a rather remarkable uniformity. The percentages are approximately the same for 1922, 1929 and 1932—between 20 and 21 per cent. The figure for 1914—25.5—is appreciably higher than for later years when the indebtedness was so much greater in amount. Debt service takes only a slightly larger proportion of total budgets at the end of the past decade than it did at the beginning. Debt charges have enlarged proportionately with total costs. They arouse more anxiety now merely because their fixed nature renders their payment unavoidable under a lower price level when other charges are being reduced.

[15] *Double Taxation,* pp. 215–20.

The ratio of debt service to the national income grew from 1.43 per cent in 1914 to 1.29 in 1922, to 1.40 per cent in 1929 and to 3.74 per cent in 1932. The constant expansion of wealth and income made possible the carrying of the debt service with no greater absorption of private income in 1929 than in 1914. The depression, however, caused an abnormal jump in the burden of debt to income. The figures cited above show the burden to be 167 per cent heavier in 1932 than in 1929. How burdensome is the result is disclosed by the trend of all expenditures, state and local, in North Carolina. In 1928–29, the debt service of $31 million absorbed 26 per cent of all expenditures. Marked reductions were made in all other expenses, but the 1931–32 debt charges of $36 million absorbed 37 per cent of total costs. These fixed charges tended to offset strenuous efforts for economy.[16]

Defaulting Municipalities

That the burden of meeting these debt charges, combined with the lessening of tax capacity, causes an over-strain to local finance is evidenced by the inability of over 150 local units of North Carolina, according to the 1932 report of its tax commission, to meet maturing bond payments. A large number, however, were in technical default for a period until their obligations were refunded.

What constitutes a default is a question given varying answers. The widest interpretation includes so-called floating debt for which no legal authorization exists. Only under this interpretation are any states in default. Restricting the term to its legitimate use to describe an extended inability of a public unit to meet bonded obligations, no states had defaulted up to February 1, 1933. (Arkansas has subsequently defaulted in a total of $140 million state and district highway bonds.) A total of 1,120 local governments are estimated to have been in default at that time. The distribution of the defaults, occurring in all except six states, is shown as follows:

Number of Defaults	Number of States
None	6
1– 5	11
6– 25	20
26– 50	6
51–100	2
Over 100	3

[16] *Report of the North Carolina Tax Commission*, 1932, p. 51.

To relate the defaults to debt increases and tax burdens is difficult when the reporting unit is the state, for varying conditions within states belie quick generalizations. Yet of the 17 states where defaults were excessive (on a relative scale) nine were in the class of rapidly increasing debts. In 11 of them the income per capita had shrunk at rates in excess of the average for the country; and in six the increase of the tax burden had been above the average rate. In 10 of these states, however, the rise of the tax burden was well under the average increase and was slight in several of them. The taxes levied had already been so high in many states with moderate tax increases that the shrinkage in wealth and income has now imperiled credit even without local extravagance. The situation has in many cases become so acute as seriously to cripple conservatively conducted governments.

Causes of Defaults

The two classes of obligations most likely to disintegrate local finance and cause defaults are the types for which reports are most fragmentary. The first class comprises tax anticipatory notes and short-term loans which are issued incidental to budget administration. They incur no unusual hazards in prosperous periods. The mounting tide of tax delinquency, however, has made it difficult for local governments to meet payments at maturity on short-term obligations regardless as to how conservatively they may have managed their finances. Since state bond laws often do not contemplate funding of accumulated short-term paper many local units are embarrassed by maturing notes which they neither can pay nor fund into bond issues. The Fall River receivership, for instance, with its background of losses in the cotton industry was precipitated by the accumulation of unpaid short-term loans. In more conservative communities, tax delinquency produces a similar embarrassment by wiping out expected assets. Both types of localities were penalized by failures of banks in which deposits of public funds were insecurely protected and where suspension forced defaults otherwise avoidable. The result has been that the causes of bankruptcies are not largely confined to special types of short-term obligations. Of those recorded 13.91 per cent have been of school districts, 17.19 per cent of counties, and 30.40 per cent of municipalities.

The second type of debts most likely to cause defaults have been special assessment bonds supported either by a pledge of municipal taxes or solely by liens against individual properties. Their amount runs into the hundreds of millions, and their defaults into the hundreds if not thousands of instances, but failure to report makes impossible an accurate estimate. The speculative fever of the "nineteen twenties" had its inevitable outgrowth in speculative public financing—in improvements which were virtually part of real estate promotion schemes. Even legitimate improvements were financed by methods which were well adapted to boom periods but which, lacking safeguards, proved disastrous in a depression. This has been especially true of special assessment bonds, which customarily are free of legal limitation of amount, and to a less extent of general corporate obligations. The limitation of the latter according to a statutory ratio to assessments has been found thoroughly unsatisfactory. The proportion of recorded defaults traceable to special assessment bonds is 21.36 per cent; and, if to this figure is added obligations of special districts, the proportion rises to 38.46 per cent. The direct and inevitable effect of special assessment bonds is to retard tax collections and to stimulate defaults because property owners in arrears on assessments do not pay taxes on property which they may lose to the holders of the assessment liens.

While a deflation period and general economic distress inexorably tend to bankruptcies, the number and degree of defaults are contingent upon immediately precipitating causes which are often controllable. For example, the issuance of loans out of proportion to economic resources has occurred in conservative communities by reason of meaningless debt limits and the overlapping of jurisdictions whose pyramided limit would permit a total indebtedness in some New York districts of $53\frac{1}{2}$ per cent, and in Oregon of 78 per cent of assessments. Faulty debt limitation cannot in itself produce defaults, but limitation is a control device whose presence or absence means the control or lack of control of the conditions which precipitate defaults—particularly when the economic structure is weakened. In Massachusetts, for instance, the debt supervision of local credit has forestalled the development of situations in many cities analogous to Fall River in their lessened economic capacity.

2. RECOMMENDATIONS

American states have not worked out machinery for administering the finances or of adjusting the obligations of defaulting municipalities. Nor has any state constituted a satisfactory method of forestalling bankruptcies by local units and of assuring a sane exercise of borrowing power regardless of defaults. The value of an analysis of defaults consists not merely in understanding the relatively few cases of bankruptcy, but in appreciating that these abnormal cases are representative of a much larger group of incipient defaults and indicative of the need of sane financing throughout the United States.

Three major remedies for the present maladjustment of debts—which is a maladjustment both to economic conditions and to governmental mechanism—are called for: an immediate reduction in debt service by a readjustment of the manner of paying for principal and of controlling interest charges; second, administrative machinery to execute readjustment measures; and third, a permanent mechanism for future use in supervising credit and finance.

Adjusting Principal of Debts

American governments have not accepted, nor has the distress of the depression prompted, any suggestion for repudiation, either open or concealed, by a wholesale scaling down of debt principal. So quickly do conditions change, however, that a reduction of principal is not impossible in some instances—especially for individual communities. It is relatively simple in a number of Florida municipalities, for example, which divide their debt into Class A obligations, a debt proper whose amortization is definite, and Class B bonds, a debt whose payment is contingent upon the realization of uncertain assets.

While the possibility exists of an unavoidable reduction in principal in isolated cases—through bankruptcy proceedings later described—the immediate need is for a planned rearrangement of debt maturities which defers payment of the principal for a definite period or until the economic capacity of the districts permits resumption of repayments. Here the problem is relatively simple and can be adequately met if forethought is taken. Briefly, the funding and refunding authorizations to localities (and if need be to states) can, first, permit the issuance of new loans for obligations whose immediate payment either is impossible or a fiscal strain; and second, they can allow the grading or arrangement of the maturing serial installments so that the first installment becomes due the fourth to the sixth year after the date of issuance.

Virtually a moratorium on principal would be declared for three to five years—not on the whole debt, but upon the particular bond issues of the particular districts for which the loans would be approved. The authorization, preferably stated in broad terms, should permit loans for three classes of obligations: (1) bonds and notes whose payment is due without assets to meet the obligations; (2) floating debt represented by operating deficits and liabilities caused by a proved inability to collect delinquent taxes and special assessments; and (3) the principal and interest of debts due in the immediate future (represented by all or part of the debt service of serial and sinking fund bonds or notes) whose immediate payment is uncertain or which constitute an excessive drain upon the individual communities for which loans would be approved. To the foregoing groups a fourth class for refinancing might be added— the "callable bonds" permitting refunding at lower interest before the dates of maturity. This last type of authorization, it may be noted, affords a controlled relief in paying interest through new loans instead of the loans for the same purpose which are being floated promiscuously without safeguards.

Reducing Interest Burdens

No ready means exists for lowering interest charges of states and municipalities. New loans carry the same, if not higher, interest as the retired loans. Refinancing because of weak credit, if not controlled, brings its own penalty in high interest. The most inviting prospect for reducing interest lies in the utilization of federal credit through the Reconstruction Finance Corporation. Obviously the present design of the Reconstruction Finance Corporation is foreign to this purpose on either one or both of two counts, namely the high interest rates charged by the Reconstruction Finance Corporation and its avowed aim to limit loans to the stabilization of business and promotion of new enterprise.

It requires a strained interpretation, however, to differentiate between several types of borrowing approved by the Reconstruction Finance Corporation and loans to refinance municipal bonds whose debt charges absorb private income and probably private capital. By February 3, 1933, loans of $101,948,000 had been approved for agricultural credit corporations, a not unimportant part of the proceeds being utilized by farmers to pay taxes and debt service. By January 23, 1933, loans had been extended to railroads to pay $19,624,815 in state and local taxes, $25,994,000 to pay federal taxes, and $118,886,996 to meet the indebtedness of railroads.[17] Of course, unless the Reconstruction Finance Corporation voluntarily or by congressional act reduces interest rates no value whatsoever would accrue to municipalities in financing through federal credit. Senator Wagner has proposed to limit the interest rate on federal loans to one-half of one per cent more than the rate paid by the Reconstruction Finance Corporation on the federal bonds from whose proceeds loans are made.

A group of executives of metropolitan cities in February, 1933, proposed to Congress that Reconstruction Finance Corporation credit be extended to the purchase of municipal securities, including tax anticipation warrants, at an interest rate of six per cent. Devoid of any advantage of low interest, the proposal was a striking revelation of the stringency of credit which forced cities, unable to get credit at banks, to appeal to Congress. Although the plan was rejected at the time, federal refinancing of local obligations is one practical measure which may be forced upon the country by catastrophic events. An obstacle is the extensive refunding program of the federal government in 1933, combined with the prospective bond issues for unemployment plans, which threatens to absorb the federal credit immediately available.

If refinancing through federal credit is impossible, neither is refinancing through state credit a likelihood. In brief, the preponderant number of state constitutions, as a result of frenzied financing in the pre-Civil War and post-Civil War periods, prohibit the extension of state credit to municipalities. In a small number of jurisdictions the state can underwrite local obligations—a plan proposed by Governor Ely of Massachusetts for bankrupt municipalities. Aside from these instances, however, the states would be compelled to avoid legal difficulties to sustain indirect grants of credit. The creation of a municipal credit corporation, with a statewide jurisdiction, would be feasible if not imperiled by a legal cloud as to its validity. One method that would quiet all legal doubts, and at the same time raise difficulties in adoption, is a state constitutional amendment authorizing the floating of state bonds for this purpose. The 1933 California legislature is seriously considering an amendment authorizing a $55,000,000 state bond issue to buy up, at four per cent, irrigation and reclamation district bonds bearing five and six per cent interest.

[17] Memoranda furnished by the Washington office, Reconstruction Finance Corporation.

An analogous plan, already adopted, is the Arkansas 1932 refunding act under which the state agreed to assume $47 million of road district bonds, exchanging state bonds bearing 4½ per cent interest for local securities carrying 4½ to 6 per cent interest. The plan, now in process of consummation, has aroused protests from bondholders, however, and has awakened fears concerning the solvency of the state. Similar was the 1932 Texas act providing for the state assumption of county and district liabilities for their contributions in aid of the state highway construction. An estimated $110 million of local bonds will be assumed by Texas which has diverted the proceeds of one cent of the gas tax, yielding $10,762,333 in 1932, to the extinguishment of the debts. Governor Connor of Mississippi proposes the refinancing of the $147,701,344 local debt of his state through state credit, the prerequisite of restored state finances being an impediment in Mississippi as well as other states. Like other measures of debt relief, state assumption of local debt is not a general solution but is applicable only to special cases where the state credit will not be imperiled by assumption and where no other alternative is open for local relief.

Reallocation of Revenues to Redeem Debts

The Arkansas and Texas measures involve the use of state credit or revenues for state assumption of local obligations, the first alternative in a reallocation of revenues by states to lighten local debt costs. Instead of state assumption of debts the state may, however, divert the proceeds of designated state revenues to localities with stipulations that the money be utilized for debt service. Such a course is being followed by Arkansas, Delaware, Florida, Illinois, Michigan, Tennessee, and Wisconsin in diverting gasoline tax receipts for the payment of county road bonds. During 1931, state gas taxes to the amount of $27,451,735 were allocated for the payment of county road bonds. The Florida plan for redeeming bonds of crippled localities is based on allocation of the proceeds of a three cent gas tax for that purpose.

Reallocation of resources may also be made by allotments of so-called state aid to local units either for definite functional purposes or without stipulation concerning the object of the local use of the funds. By the former method, local taxes now consumed by service demands are freed for debt service and under the latter method the localities are free to utilize the state aid for services or debt payments in their own discretion. Approximately $125 million was disbursed by states in 1932 for county road and city street construction and repair and a much larger sum was expended for state school aid. The effect of the customary state aid in relieving local debt pressure is greatly lessened since local functions have been built up and are administered under the expectancy of state aid as a regular revenue source and not as a gratuitous subsidy.

For the purpose of debt administration, waiving aside other considerations, the dedication of state aid revenues to the extinguishment of local debt claims is superior to blanket aid, at least for the years immediately ahead. Validity is attached to this device since, viewing the entire tax structure, equity demands the reallocation of burdens by relieving over-taxed property and shifting a share of the load to taxes which the state is best fitted to administer—state gasoline, income, and luxury taxes. Similarly, the reallocation of the burden of paying for poor and unemployment relief, at least in part, from local to state and federal budgets will immediately relieve the financial strain in many communities which find almost impossible the complete discharge of obligations to bondholders and to the unemployed.

Receiverships of Bankrupt Municipalities

The lack of state administrative machinery to supervise the finances of defaulting municipalities, and indeed an almost equally widespread lack of supervision of local indebtedness in general, threatens to jeopardize any plans for safeguarding credit. Since the most aggravated cases of heavy debt loads and weakened credit are in defaulting communities the administrative plan first considered must be state receiverships of bankrupt districts. Franklin D. Roosevelt, as Governor, proposed this to the New York 1932 legislature. Initially the receivership is designed to fill a conspicuous gap in American law. Through the very lack of receivership provisions creditors are forced to sue a municipality to obtain a court judgment for amounts due and, failing payment, to apply for a writ of mandamus directing local officials to levy taxes sufficient to pay the obligations. Neither judgment nor mandamus are productive of repayment of debts when a municipality's credit is weakened and revenues are diminishing. Until 1931, American states had never provided for receiverships, except for instances like the substitution of the Shelby Taxing District for Memphis in 1879.

Slight help was derived from these precedents by Massachusetts when

$5,725,000 of Fall River's obligations were in default, actual or prospective. According to Mr. James Jackson, chairman of the state appointed receivership commission, Fall River's default was due to: (1) failure to keep expenditures within collectible income, (2) failure to reduce assessments in time to correspond with the shrinkage in true valuations, and (3) failure to provide sufficiently for uncollectible taxes with the ensuing creation of a temporary and floating debt lacking assets. The state-appointed commission, which will administer the city's finances until the defaulted debt is repaid, is vested with powers which are the best defined of any act in the specification of authority. The commission can: (1) liquidate the accumulated floating indebtedness; (2) control the incurrence of obligations and expenditures through the state board's power to approve all appropriations, expenses, and debts; (3) assume responsibility for tax and revenue collection; (4) assess valuations; and (5) make recommendations regarding administrative performance. The commission's conduct of affairs has been marked by the successful funding of floating debts, a severe reduction in salaries, the abolition and merger of a number of functions and positions, the increase in tax collections, and a decrease in assessments.[18]

The local mismanagement back of the Fall River receivership similarly underlay the threatened default of North Bergen, New Jersey, in 1931 when the state named a receivership commission whose authority was to fund $8 million of unpaid notes, reappraise all property, control borrowing, and advise in budget making.[19] These ends have been accomplished in coöperation with the local officers, a new set of officials having displaced the officers responsible for mismanagement both in North Bergen and Fall River.

In 1931 North Carolina authorized the appointment of an administrator of finance by the state director of local finance in event a locality fails to pay the interest and principal of a debt when it is due. During the two years since the passage of the act, at exactly the time when municipalities were defaulting, no receiverships have been named. Instead the state recognized realistically that economic conditions, not local dereliction, has caused the fiscal embarrassment of the localities. Indeed

---

[18] Data as to Massachusetts, New Jersey, and North Carolina receiverships derived in conferences with officials in these states.

[19] Three other New Jersey municipalities recently petitioned for a state receivership. Significantly, in all the four New Jersey cases, the municipal officials themselves requested the receivership.

the broad supervisory powers vested in the state rendered possible a control of the debt redemption process without resort to a receiver who would have been superfluous except in event of a recalcitrant municipality. An opposite attitude was displayed by the North Carolina municipalities which solicited advice from the state director of local finance. By permitting the funding or refunding of many local obligations, the state commission of local finance has eased the financial strain in many localities and so has warded off crises which would induce receiverships.

Conditions which Call for Receiverships

Three possible contingencies warrant the creation of state receiverships: (1) local gross maladministration to which the locality is indifferent; (2) state assistance in reorganizing debt and fiscal administration when local processes break down, and (3) state administration of finances when local debts are to be readjusted in decreasing the principal or interest of obligations. Only the first two situations were contemplated under the few plans adopted before 1933 in the United States; and Oregon was the first state by 1933 legislative action to authorize officially the compromise of local obligations. After a local district has been in default for six months, a receivership may be initiated by the local district officials or by the owners of 25 per cent of the bonds in default, either of whom may petition the court for the appointment of an "administrator." Under his guidance, the debts may be adjusted, compromised, liquidated, or refunded according to a plan which, upon receiving judicial approval, ensues in the discharge of the administrator and ending of the receivership. The Oregon law was drafted with the needs in mind of a number of municipalities, notably Astoria, which are expected to take immediate advantage of its terms.

The provincial boards of Ontario and Quebec are clothed with the power to readjust interest and compromise principal payments. During the year following its inception, the Quebec Commission has considered but one case of refinancing, approved January 28, 1933, in which the amount in principal is unchanged and the same interest rate is retained. "I do not believe," declares the commission's secretary, "that it will be necessary, except in one or two very special cases, to order a reduction in the amount of the principal as well as a decrease in the rate of interest." [20] Lacking authority to scale down debts American receivers could be vested with the duty of controlling the funding and refunding process and of making the agreements with bondholders which now are painfully worked out by bondholders' committees which legitimately endeavor to "get what they can" for the investors they represent.

The designation of the precise authority of the receivership body, within the enumerated limits of powers set forth in the state enabling act, should be made at the time the receivership is petitioned for and sanctioned. Here any one of several alternatives could initiate a receivership: (1) the petition of the local governing body; (2) the petition of a majority of the electorate; (3) the request of the state agency supervising local finance, or (4) the petition of the bondholders filed with a court of competent jurisdiction setting forth the facts and praying for the approval of a receivership. When a state supervisory agency exists, the head of the agency would act as chairman of the receivership commission, personally or through a representative, and the other members would be named by the court. Continuous supervision of local finances, when it requires local residence, would be exercised by one or more appointees of the commission. Termination of the receivership—probably as important as its institution—may be specified as the date when arrangement for payment of debts has been consummated and the fiscal status of the locality has received approval by the appointing court as satisfactory upon the recommendation of the state fiscal supervisory agency.

State Commissions Supervising Refunding

The receivership, as a device, is inherently adapted to individual cases of aggravated ills and not to the solution of state-wide problems. For this reason Florida authorized the refunding of local obligations into 60-year bonds. From the same motive North Carolina has refrained from appointing receivers and has chosen to control all local borrowing through a single state commission of local finance which reviews, approving or rejecting, all local bonds and notes before their issuance. Virtually the commission reviews funding and refunding issues since the local units, with a few exceptions, refrain from initiating improvement bonds.

Michigan in 1932 resorted to state administrative control of local

[20] Personal letter, February 1, 1933.

refunding of bonds in order to safeguard local credit. The plan created a state public debt commission, consisting of the state treasurer, attorney-general, and the auditor general. The commission's jurisdiction comes into play whenever a municipality defaults on payment of its obligations, or when a default is impending within 60 days, or when the "condition of the municipality, in the opinion of the commission, warrants refunding as a matter of sound financing." The commission has power (1) to permit the refunding, in whole or in part, (2) to prescribe reasonable conditions upon which refunding bonds may be issued, or (3) to deny permission to refund when it is not in the public interest.

Both in the stage of authorizing refunding bonds, just described, as well as in the stage of debt redemption, the commission possesses discretionary authority to insure orderly administration. In the local redemption of refunding bonds, the state commission may require the levying of additional taxes or collection of other revenues to be applied to the debt service. Likewise, the permission to refund is conditioned upon the local compliance with the state requirements that all receipts of taxes or special assessments, against which the obligations originally were issued, should be applied on the repayment of the refunded bonds.

While the Michigan plan involves no control over local expenditures and singles out alone for control the redemption of the obligations, which are threatening the credit of the municipality, the authority of the state commission is ample to safeguard the repayment of all debts whose default would militate against the credit of the state and its sub-divisions. From May 4 to November 18, 1932, the commission passed upon 19 applications by cities and authorized the refunding of city bonds for $20,264,440. Twenty-five applications from other districts added two millions more to the approved refunding issues.

A commission of this nature is better suited for supervision of debts throughout the state when all the local units are commonly confronted with debt problems than through receiverships, advisable as they are for exceptional cases. A review commission is desirable, if not imperative, because the authority to fund and to refund should broadly enable any refinancing necessary to ease debt loads under safeguards insured by the commission. Commissions of this type should be vested with authority: (1) to review the refunding of bonds and the grading of their maturities, (2) to pass on funding of deficits from uncollectible taxes and other causes, (3) to review the adjustment of interest through agreements reached between bondholders and local officials, (4) to supervise the disbursement of state funds dedicated to the retirement of local debts, and (5) to be represented on any receivership commission named by a court and supervision of its work.

"Scaling Down" Through Bondholders' Agreements

If neither new credit nor tax resources are allocated for local debt service, an impetus will be given to the virtual reduction of part of the principal and interest load in districts diverting an excessive proportion of diminishing resources to their debt service. Agreements between bondholders' committees and Florida municipalities, notably Coral Gables, are the result of realistic acceptance of the rule of redemption of debts "according to ability to pay." The $9 million debt of Coral Gables was refunded in 1931 by the issuance of $4 million of Class A obligations payable within 20 years and $5 million of contingent Class B bonds, having a maturity date neither for principal nor interest. To the payment of Class B bonds are pledged the collections of delinquencies, special improvement liens, income from non-governmental properties owned by the city, and surplus revenues.

West Palm Beach, with an annual debt service of $2 million, agreed with its bondholders that the maximum tax levy for all purposes should not exceed more than half that sum, reserving $425,000 for current operations and the remainder for debt service. For the first 10 years under the agreement, the city's bonds will carry but half of the interest formerly paid and a portion of the budget will be devoted to buying up the depreciated bonds for retirement.

Receiverships for Local Governments

The previous and present congresses have seriously considered so-called bankruptcy measures, the McLeod bill, the Fletcher bill, and the Wilcox bill. The first named proposal would have permitted defaulting districts to come under a court receivership whose relief was to consist of the postponement of all debt service for two years rather than a compromise of the amount or interest of debts. The relief accorded would have been limited to defaulting localities by suspending all payments, except for current operations, without changing in any way the terms of indebtedness. The merit of the bill consisted in giving a "breathing spell" to extreme cases of distress, whose future number is uncertain; and its demerit consisted in evading the problem of liquidation and in failing to accord relief to the larger number of localities not in default but likely to default.

The earlier Fletcher and the later Wilcox proposals differed in details but both authorized a uniform procedure for bankruptcy proceedings for local units in the federal courts. If the Fletcher bill may be dismissed as symptomatic of the desire for official receivership machinery, attention must be directed towards the more carefully prepared Wilcox bill. Initiation of the proceedings would be by the local unit, not the bondholders, which would file a petition in a federal court, attaching a copy of a plan of adjustment of claims carrying the consent of creditors owning more than one-half of the debts of the district. The adjustment plan would comprise the adjustment of the claims of creditors, the possible pledging of public property not used for governmental purposes, and provide means for the plan's execution. The procedure of judicial review would involve hearings, the presentation of detailed tax, debt, and wealth schedules, and the consideration of alternative plans. Judicial approval would be contingent upon the consent of creditors holding three-fourths of the claims and authorization by state law for the districts to take necessary action.

No clear-cut provisions are contained for administering the measure which merely contains a gesture in that direction by authorizing the court to appoint a controller of revenues without definite powers. By reason of the fact that the proceedings would be through the federal government, not the state governments, the measure inevitably debars the court from interfering with the governmental or financial powers of the district other than to carry out the adjustment plan. Like all other proposals for federal receiverships, this plan possesses the immediate advantage of relief to defaulting localities, but its advantages are narrowly limited to districts in default and its administration is severely hampered because of lack of federal control over local taxes and finances. A bona-fide receivership, in the true sense of the word, calls for management of the finances of a corporation for the period, however brief, of the receivership so as to insure a restoration of healthy financing.

Consequently, practical administrative needs combine with constitutional questions to render difficult the creation of an adequate receivership mechanism. Constitutional limitations, on the one hand, forbid the federal encroachment upon state and local tax and finance powers, a limitation recognized in the Wilcox bill; and, on the other hand, states are debarred by the constitutional prohibition from enacting any law "impairing the obligations of contracts" which would discharge insolvent municipal debtors from liabilities. The clue for resolving the dilemma is contained in the clause of the Wilcox bill which requires the consent of a state for the filing of municipal petitions of bankruptcy in the federal courts. Clearly, concurrent action between the federal and state governments is essential to the administration of the bankruptcy proceedings.

The measure should expand the "consent" of a state to participation by the state in the proceedings through the exercise of its tax and finance powers necessary to administer the receivership. That is to say, the very readjustment of the debts entails a restriction of local taxes, expenditures and borrowing which the state alone can accomplish through a receivership agency, either a state appointed commission or a special receiver. The administration of the fiscal affairs of the local unit for the period necessary for rehabilitation (and no longer) is an inevitable part of a receivership to be performed by the state alone, while the composition of debts would require the sanction of the federal court. Ample legal precedents affirm the validity of a federal measure whose actual operation is permissive and dependent upon collaborating state action in accepting the provisions of the federal law and in instituting administrative machinery of its own consonant with the federal statute. Of course, any state receivership which compromised or settled debts without impairing the obligation of contracts could be undertaken separately by the state without federal sanction.

Inflation and Local Debts

The Florida agreements antedate the prospective compromises elsewhere because economic adversity first affected Florida. The question whether repudiation of debts, under whatever name, is invoked or not is related to the national currency policy of inflation or deflation. An inflationary policy will result in the lightening of the debt load; and, insofar as the debt problem is merely one of the relative size and heaviness of loads, inflation will effect a cure. Insofar as the problem is one of adjustment of debts to resources, needs, and economic practices, however, inflation will do nothing to effect a cure. Rather it will demand control machinery, elsewhere outlined in this chapter, to prevent excesses in borrowing which have characterized past inflationary periods. If deflation continues, the question hitherto evaded must be squarely faced in determining whether public obligations will be placed in the same status of private obligations by liquidation through bankruptcy.

An inflationary policy in 1933 may avoid a decision concerning the social ethics of liquidation of public debts analogous to private receiverships; but a decision, either ultimately or immediately, must be reached. Unless governments are to discriminate permanently in favor of private bondholders, the claims upon governments must be equitably adjusted without favoritism between classes of creditors. The social services, notably welfare relief and education, cannot be reduced below a minimum without irreparable wastage. If all the justly recognized claims upon government are viewed as, in a sense, obligations to creditors, the receivership equitably must apportion the diminished assets among all creditors, bondholders and otherwise. By creating machinery for a judicial review and approval of the apportionment plan, a liquidation as nearly impartial as is possible may be obtained. Preferably the receivership should be authorized and administered by states since it should be a permanent feature of state laws governing local finance and consistent with other features of supervision. If state action is too dilatory, federal authorization may be forced to avoid catastrophic consequences.

Review of Indebtedness

The question remains of according relief to the larger number of nondefaulting municipalities. This can be done through the previously described state refinancing commissions or by state debt review commissions. State refunding commissions are essentially temporary devices in that they are designed especially for depression periods. They possess a permanent value, however, in establishing machinery for the review of the funding of deficits, arising from faulty budgeting, and of refunding, caused from failure to provide for the redemption of debts. Normally, no excuse exists for either funding of deficits or refunding of unredeemed bonds; and, when a district is forced to do either, a set of circumstances is created in which state approval should be a prerequisite to a type of borrowing which otherwise should be illegal. At this point the value of the plan stops abruptly. It is devoid of curative power to prevent abuses or of forestalling the practices which have resulted in present debt loads. Indeed no state has created a mechanism to substitute for reliance upon the customary debt limits which miss the crucial question as to whether and how localities shall borrow under the limits that often afford wide loopholes.

Instead of contenting itself with negative, statutory restrictions the state should be of positive assistance to localities at the time a bond issue is proposed. For that time is the pivotal moment when the feasibility of issuance, the amounts and purpose, terms, maturities, and interest of the bond issue are considered. At that stage in the process the state agency supervising local finance should receive from every subdivision contemplating the floating of an issue a comprehensive debt report setting forth in full the facts relative to the proposed issue and all related data bearing upon local finance.

Debt reports of one kind or another are now required in a number of jurisdictions. The reports are all post-mortem in nature—filed long after the debts are incurred. The reporting process should be reversed to require a report prior to the incurrence of the obligation, setting forth the following types of information concerning which the state agency should review the proposed issue:

(1) *Relative to the Legality of the Bonds*

As to the local authorization of the bonds, the legal purpose of the issue, the amounts in relation to existing debt limits, and any other legal aspect.

(2) *Relative to the Economic Capacity of the District*

As to the assets supporting the bonds in respect to the record of assessed valuations and tax rates, a complete record of income and expenditures, a record of tax collection and possible delinquency, a record of special assessments and their collection, a record of public utility debt, a statement of the total debt resting upon property of the district by reason of overlapping or coterminous units.

(3) *Relative to the Proposed Business Plan of Paying the Indebtedness*

As to the local improvement budget, the term, interest, redemption and grading of maturities, and methods of sale.

Standardization of reporting in these matters will be feasible. The mere preparation of the report and consultation with state officials and their advice respecting desirable revisions would, in nine cases out of ten and possibly more often, be an adequate remedy against unbusiness-like or excessive borrowing. If the state desired to make its decision mandatory upon localities, in order to control the "tenth district," the state would only be doing by administrative action what it ineffectively attempts to do now by debt limits and minute statutory regulations. Neither the limits nor the regulations would be abolished, under this plan, but a review would be instituted to consider the desirability of new debts for an individual community at a given time instead of solely relying upon an arbitrary percentage to assessments for a uniform debt limit applicable to all districts at all times; and the present statutory regulations would gain flexibility with a number of them rendered unnecessary. A serious mistake would be made to transfer to a state agency the entire responsibility for local debt administration, either in respect to decisions for issuance or for redemption. What the state can do is to select those aspects of borrowing which affect the entire credit and tax burdens of the state and perform a review of affirmative value to localities.

Supplementary Action

A review of this sort would obviate the need of the previously discussed refunding commissions. Their task would be merged with the broader review, which, it must be emphasized, furnishes the key to a number of perplexing debt problems. Not only would a corrective be given to reliance upon the discredited debt limits and a method furnished for refinancing distressed communities, but a workable restriction of special assessment debt would be afforded where none is now available. Several proposals have been advanced to limit special assessments, and a few states have enacted restrictive statutes. Through all these measures runs the vitiating defect of applying a ratio to assessments which is peculiarly unsuited to special levies against selected parcels or areas within a jurisdiction.

The review plan obviates the need for an unsuitable special assessment limit by considering each bond issue, whether paid from general or special levies, in relation to all resources and liabilities of the district and its capacity to pay. Pyramiding of debts through multiple districts becomes controllable by a review aimed to consider all burdens on the area regardless of the district floating the issue. An impetus would be given to budgeting capital improvements by a review which required the local formulation of an improvement program and state recommendation for its betterment. No reason exists why the same procedure should not be applied to future issues of state governments which would be aided by a hearing, study, and reexamination of the merits of a proposed issue by a commission technically qualified to survey the subject.

Even without a debt review, the states will be remiss if they do not revise existing budget laws which now foster illicit borrowing. Temporary borrowing in anticipation of taxes should be reduced to a minimum by restricting its authorization and by rendering it unnecessary as far as feasible. Restricting its authorization can be accomplished by permitting temporary borrowing only up to one-half of the actual receipts of the previous year, repayment being obligatory before the end of the year. To reduce the need of this borrowing, payment of taxes on an installment basis, at least quarterly, will furnish most units with a continuous flow of receipts. Tax delinquency notes require redemption within two or three years after issuance. Any amount, representing notes based on uncollectible taxes, should be met by a budget appropriation except when an application to the state review commission obtains permission to fund the deficit in short-term bonds.

While 32 states possess budget laws applying to either or both counties and municipalities, the statutes in many cases are fragmentary and require revision to forestall operating deficits and to provide for budgeting of improvements. A planned local economy, conducive to sane borrowing, can be a consequence only of intelligent budgeting of capital outlays and the use of current tax receipts instead of bond proceeds for recurring outlays or for an appreciable proportion of capital outlays during a prosperous business period. The tendency towards the accumulation of debts of one type or another during a depression, such as for poor relief, adds a further reason for the unfailing use of current receipts for a large proportion of improvement outlays during a prosperous period.

One or both of two courses are being forced upon localities in order to balance budgets. The first is drastic economy in expenditure to prevent the tax load from being insufferably heavy while full payment of the debt service is continued. Defaults have been, and in the future must be, prevented by tax reduction through voluntary action of the municipalities in the bulk of cases, through state receiverships of recalcitrant municipalities in extreme cases, and by a permanent mechanism for the administrative review of public expenditures.[21] Second, with or without economy, the issuance of scrip is likely to expand under a credit stringency. Scrip justly bears the opprobrium of wild-cat financing

[21] The subject is discussed by the writer in the *Bulletin of the National Tax Association*, February, 1933.

which can be controlled if regulatory laws restrict its use to temporary and current financing. That is, scrip should be nothing more than temporary notes, issued against realizable assets, which are accepted by a public unit in payment of taxes and other obligations. The use of the scrip by the unit to pay expenses constitutes a forced means of selling notes, the interest going to the acceptors of scrip instead of to investors. Of course, the amount of scrip must be limited to realizable resources of the unit in order to prevent the accumulation of floating debt.

Conclusions

The burden of state and local debt is not known precisely. It can, however, be understood, and a policy for its administration evolved, by an estimate and an appreciation of its position—its changing position —in the structure of public finance and the economic world.[22] Public debt dynamically has changed as a fiscal and economic burden in a structure whose rate of change has so accelerated as to approach a dizzy whirl. State and local debt during the climax of the whirl has become relatively a much heavier burden, a greater drain upon resources. It is an impediment to the efforts of budget makers for economy and to relief alike to taxpayers and to the unemployed, a deterrent to social services and a stimulus to tax delinquency and the forfeiture of the private ownership of homes. At its fringes it has instigated municipal bankruptcies. While the relative position of these debts bulks larger, the rigid mold of state and local obligations has rendered the debt an almost inert ball ever whirling larger and out of control. Essentially, the problem is to transcend the inherited rigid mold and subject the debts to a control which will ease its burden, safeguard its processes, and constitute a sane and flexible instrument for administration in the future.

The control problem is complicated because there is not one problem, permitting a single solution uniformly applied, but a number of problems varying in degree and kind over the United States. The mere statement of the problems, as well as the formulation of remedies, requires a distinction between the use of state and federal power during emergencies and during normal periods. For instance, the state supervises local debt normally to keep localities "from going too deeply into debt; and in emergencies, it steps in after the city is already too deeply

[22] The reader is referred to the admirable exposition by William Withers in *The Retirement of National Debts*.

in debt." The control problem quickly changes form, notably from inflation. If consistently utilized, inflation will mitigate the debt burden but demand a control mechanism to guard against excesses. Without inflation machinery is needed even more urgently to liquidate debts. Consequently, control is to be exercised by:

(1) Local governments through current and capital budgeting and other techniques locally applied to achieve economy, assure social services, and protect and plan for the use of public credit.

(2) Receiverships of mismanaged and defaulting districts in extraordinary cases. Preferably the receivers should be appointed by the states. They can more readily get at the roots of mismanagement than the federal government which, if the states continue to be tardy, may be forced to authorize receiverships restricted to adjusting debt claims.

(3) Frank recognition that public credit, analogous to private credit, may be liquidated through bankruptcy proceedings which adjust principal and interest according to ability to pay.

(4) Realistic acknowledgment that the present distress is too widespread to be relieved through receiverships alone. The states must liberalize funding and refunding authorizations to cover all contingencies and safeguard liberal refinancing by approval of new issues by a state commission. By permitting the deferment of initial instalments of debt maturities, a moratorium on principal for the specific issues would be insured for three to five years.

(5) The realization of lower interest rates on refinanced issues; a consideration of the use for localities of state credit, if not constitutionally barred, and of federal Reconstruction Finance Corporation credit, if federal finances permit.

(6) Reallocation of state funds from newer tax sources, as the gas tax, for dedication to designated local obligations where the local general property tax threatens an utter breakdown.

(7) Reallocation of federal funds for unemployment relief which will relieve the excessive strain upon many local budgets.

(8) Redrafting of state laws governing local budgets to ensure orderly financing, compel adherence to budgetary terms, prevent excessive temporary borrowing, and restrict scrip to its legitimate use.

(9) Permanent planning for the sane use of state and local credit through a review of all bonds before their issuance by a state commission which, without assuming control over local discretion in borrowing, will establish an administrative limit of the economic capacity of public units to borrow in lieu of the present ineffectual reliance upon statutory debt limits.

Chapter Ten

SHORT-TERM BUSINESS DEBTS [1]

SUMMARY

IN this study all debts maturing within a year or less are treated as short-term, except those which originated as long-term items (p. 292).

Every credit advance, even of the same money, is included in the short-term debt total, but actual duplication of loans is avoided (p. 293).

Debts are also credits; cancellation of all domestic debts would neither increase nor decrease the national wealth (pp. 293–94).

There are two kinds of short-term debts: those incurred for business purposes, and those incurred for personal and household uses (p. 294).

Total short-term business debts are estimated at $98.5 billion on December 31, 1931, and $89.2 billion at the end of 1932, a decline of about 8 per cent (p. 294).

The major forms of short-term business indebtedness include bank deposits, bank loans for business purposes, brokers' loans, current liabilities of incorporated and unincorporated business concerns excluding bank loans, loans by life insurance companies on their policies for business purposes, and overdue rents, taxes, and insurance premiums (p. 296).

[1] Credit should be given for the generous help the author has received in the preparation of this chapter and the following chapter on personal and household debts, from many experts in the various fields of research, including Messrs. Leon Henderson and Rolf Nugent of the Russell Sage Foundation, Dr. Wilbur C. Plummer, Economist of the U. S. Department of Commerce, Dr. Grosvenor M. Jones, Chief of the Finance Division of the U. S. Department of Commerce, Dr. W. A. Berridge, Economist of the Metropolitan Life Insurance Company, Mr. David Gay of Standard Statistics Company, Mr. Charles A. Glover, statistician of the American Telephone and Telegraph Company, Major Milan V. Ayres, Analyst of the National Association of Finance Companies, Dr. Paul Atkins, Special Liquidation of Securities Office, Federal Reserve Bank Building, New York City, Mr. Guy H. Hulse, Secretary of the National Retail Credit Association, Mr. Adam Gostomski of Moody's Investors' Service, Mr. G. M. Jones of Dun & Bradstreet, Mr. M. Collins of the U. S. Veterans' Administration, Washington, D. C., Mr. Thomas J. V. Cullen, Editor of *The Spectator,* Mr. Glenn G. Munn of Paine, Webber & Company, Mr. A. J. Hutterly, Fiscal Agent of the U. S. Intermediate Credit Banks, Mr. H. F. Cellarius, Secretary of the United States Building and Loan League, Mr. Edgar F. Fowler, Secretary of the American Association of Personal Finance Companies, Mr. Dwight Mitchener of the Chase National Bank, Mr. Alexander Wall, Secretary of Robert Morris Associates, and from the authors of other sections of this study.

Bank debt to depositors is the largest and most important form of short-term obligations. Bank deposits dropped from $45.8 billion at the end of 1931 to $41.5 billion at the end of 1932. Total short-term bank loans declined from $22.2 billion to $18 billion during the same year. Meanwhile, brokers' loans fell from $932 million to $594 million, about one-fifth of which was loaned to business firms and current business liabilities dropped about $3 billion (pp. 297–99).

Short-term business debts in 1931 were 88 per cent of the entire short-term indebtedness in the United States and 86 per cent in 1932 (p. 301).

The total short-term debt of the nation is estimated at $51 billion in 1913, $102 billion in 1921, $150 billion in 1929, and $104 billion in 1932. Thus this type of indebtedness has declined during the depression to about its 1921 level, a drop of almost one-third (p. 301).

THE total short-term debt in the United States is made up of aggregates of estimated sub-totals, some of which are money loans and others are advances of credit of various kinds; but all of these obligations must be paid off in money within a relatively short time as contrasted with the long-term debt items which may run for several years.

For purposes of this study, we have not formulated any hard-and-fast definitions of short-term and long-term debts. All debts maturing within a year or less, however, are clearly short-term, except those which originated as long-term items. For example, a long-term bond issue issued thirty years ago which is now about to mature in three months, is not a short-term item for purposes of this study, although for purposes of bank credit analysis, such an item would be so regarded. On the other hand, all items of so-called "intermediate credit" are regarded as short-term, even if they run three or four years. Roughly speaking, we have regarded all "current debts" as short-term and have excluded from the short-term tabulation all items which may be called "fixed debts."

Relaying of Debts and Credits

One of the most striking features of any total estimate of current or short-term debts is the fact that there must be a great amount of double, triple, and even quadruple counting of relayed credit advances. For example, suppose a school teacher, the head of a family, deposits $1000 in a bank. The bank lends the $1000 to a wholesaler. The wholesaler advances $1000 of credit to a retail furniture store, while the retail store, in turn, advances $1000 of credit to the school teacher, enabling him to buy $1000 worth of furniture for his home. The same $1000 has been used as a credit advance four times and must be counted four times in the total aggregate short-term debt. The cancelling or offsetting credits and debts to avoid this kind of relayed double counting is fallacious. But, of course, actual duplication where the same specific loans are counted twice, must be avoided.

On the other hand, the multiple counting of relayed credit has a reverse aspect which is very striking. Suppose the retailer wants the payment for the furniture from the school teacher immediately. The school teacher draws his $1000 from the bank in the form of a check payable to the furniture store. The furniture store then pays the wholesaler and the wholesaler pays the bank the $1000 due it. Thus, again a $1000 transaction relayed three successive times wipes out $4000 in the total of short-term debt.

From the illustration of the relaying of credit advances it can be seen that the grand total of all short-term debt is of a very peculiar nature. The causes which operate to increase or decrease the total are multiplied several times in their effectiveness, so that the grand aggregate is more a mathematical phenomenon than real. Nevertheless, to get the entire total, very credit advance should be included.

On the other hand, if, as in the case of a consolidated balance sheet, we should attempt to eliminate all inter-business and inter-individual items, we should have to do the same thing with the long-term debt items and in the final table there would be no debt at all, as all the debts here shown are debts between Americans. A consolidated balance sheet of America would show only our national wealth and the debts owed to us by foreign nations as assets, since we are a creditor nation.

Debts Are Also Credits

Another noteworthy point in regard to a debt study is that it is also a credit study. We are studying just one side of all the double-entries in all the books of account of the United States. The total of all debt is also a total of all credit. If we are concerned with the strains on the debtor or borrower, we might also be concerned with the strains on the lender and creditor. Every debtor was trusted by his creditor and the creditor hoped to be paid. In answer to the so-called technocrats, what they call the "pathology of debt" is also the pathology of credit. The piled-up billions and billions of accumulated debt in the United States are also piled-up billions of accumulated credit.

If all the debts were cancelled by the creditors and forgiven, the real national wealth would not be increased or decreased by one item. The return of prosperity would not be hastened because the wiping out of all debt would greatly enhance the value of the monetary unit, resulting in lower prices, which would offset any gains expected from wiping out of debts. From both a moral and an economic point of view, the best way out of debt is to pay it. But regardless of any moral issue involved, there has been in the last few years an over-extension of credit which is now in the process of being reduced by charge-offs because of uncollectible debts. When a debtor cannot pay and the creditor can see no hope of getting him to pay, the items on the asset side of the creditor's balance sheet must be marked down. Large amounts of bills payable, notes payable and accounts payable will never be paid at all.

Personal and Business Short-Term Debts

In this study, the nation's short-term debts have been divided into two main classes: (1) those incurred for business purposes and (2) those incurred for personal and household uses. The present chapter is concerned with short-term debts which are strictly business obligations. Chapter Eleven will cover personal and household obligations.

No authoritative studies of all short-term business debts have ever been made. Their total aggregate amount can only be roughly guessed at. The attempt in this chapter to arrive at approximate totals for the years 1931 and 1932 is made, not with any pretense at exactness, but primarily to stake out a field for subsequent exploration and to sketch its outlines, as a matter of immediate public interest. Table 77 summarizes the best aggregate guess which the author can make of all the various items of short-term business debts in the United States at the ends of 1931 and 1932. The sums of all these items indicate a total indebtedness of this kind amounting to $98,522,000,000 on Dec. 31, 1931 and $89,240,723,904 on Dec. 31, 1932.

The totals of all the items in Table 77 are subject to a large percentage of error because there are probably some items of short-term debt which have been omitted, but even so, whatever totals we might calculate are unreal and are merely mathematical aggregations and can never be as significant as the basic fact that a consolidated balance sheet of America with all internal debts between Americans removed, as the accountants would remove them in such a balance sheet, would show us the only large nation in the world, not in debt. The total amount of short-term business credit outstanding at any one time has a questionable absolute significance on account of these multiplicative effects of successive relayed credit advances, but from one particular period of time to another, the relative changes in important sub-totals are significant, if two successive sets of totals are aggregated on a comparable basis.

Money as Debt

In order that our tabulation of all American short-term debts should be fully complete, it should, strictly from an accounting point of view, include the following forms of short-term debt:

1. Promises to pay which pass currently as money, including national bank notes, United States notes, Federal Reserve notes and in fact all forms of money except gold, which is the ultimate money.
2. Balances of Federal Reserve banks at the U. S. Treasury.
3. Reserves of member banks held in Federal Reserve banks.
4. Other deposits of member banks in Federal Reserve banks.
5. All other debts owed by banks to other banks.
6. Debts owed by banks to individuals and businesses. (Deposits)

But since all forms of bank notes pass currently as money, certainly a current debt owed by a Federal Reserve bank to another bank, or by any bank to any other bank should be regarded in the same category. Therefore, in Table 77 we have arbitrarily excluded all the debt items which pass as money and have also excluded all inter-bank debts. But these excluded items would make an interesting table by themselves.

Needless to say, this is an arbitrary demarcation. It is done to conform to general custom in thinking about money in relation to credit and it must not be forgotten that in studying debt we are studying credit. The two things are both aspects of one single economic phenomenon.

TABLE 77

SHORT-TERM BUSINESS DEBTS IN THE UNITED STATES FOR YEARS 1931 AND 1932

(Excluding Debt Items Considered as Money and Excluding Inter-Bank Items—Figures in Millions)

Forms of Short-Term Business Indebtedness	Outstanding Dec. 31, 1931	Outstanding Dec. 31, 1932
Short-term loans to banks by individuals and business enterprizes (deposits)...............................	$45,821	$41,500(a)
Loans by Federal Reserve Member Banks...............	19,261	15,000(b)
Loans by non-member banks...........................	12,045	11,000
Total Loans by Going Banks.......................	$31,305	$26,000
Estimated loans by suspended banks, which may still be regarded as collectible	865	1,000
Total Bank Loans................................	$32,170	$27,017
Less: Estimated total of long-term bank loans secured by real estate..	10,000	9,000
Total Short-Term Bank Loans.....................	$22,170	$18,017
Less: Estimated total of short-term personal bank loans for individual and household purposes. (Items 7 and 8 from Tables 82 and 83 of Chapter XI).....................	1,120	760
Total of Strictly Business Short-Term Loans..........	$21,050	$17,257
Loans to brokers for the account of "others" made by reporting member banks in New York City...................	13	4
Loans to brokers, reported by New York Stock Exchange, from private banks, brokers, foreign banking agencies, etc..	132	68
Loans by brokers to individuals (estimated)..............	746	475
Loans by brokers to business firms (estimated)...........	186	119
Loans by Reconstruction Finance Corporation............. (Of this total for 1932, loans to banks and trust companies were $594,597,707.)	....	1,356
Estimated Current Liabilities of incorporated business concerns, excluding debts due to banks...................	14,000	12,000
Estimated Current Liabilities of non-incorporated business concerns, excluding debts due to banks...............	3,000	2,200
Miscellaneous financing by factors, selling agents and other strictly business non-banking financing, not included above	1,000	1,000
Loans by life insurance companies on life insurance policies, for business purposes...............................	1,100	1,300
Loans by the United States Government on Government insurance policies and on Adjusted Service Certificates, for business purposes....................................	134	158
Short-term cash loans by small loan agencies for strictly business purposes. (From column 6 of Tables 82 and 83 of Chapter XI).......................................	340	304
Miscellaneous overdue rents, overdue taxes and overdue insurance premiums owed by business firms..............	1,000	1,500
Total Short-Term Business Debt...................	$98,522	$89,241

(a) Estimated total figures as of the end of 1932. At the time this study went to press, the final official figures for these items were not available.

In order to be consistent, all the short-term items listed above should be stated as numerical quantities so that an aggregate of the money items and inter-bank debts can be shown, but again, if such items are totaled and added to the total of the short-term debt in the United States in Table 77, the unreality and illusiveness of the final total is emphasized more than ever.

One of the peculiar fallacies which has developed out of debt studies is the notion that bank deposits are not debts—that having money in the bank is like having it in a safe. It is *your* money and you can get it any time you want it. Business firms show their money on hand as "cash in bank." But deposits are debts—short-term debts to individuals and businessses, owed to them by banks, and these debts of banks to their depositors constitute one of the most critical problems in the entire short-term debt situation. Depositors supposedly have a right to get their money back on demand, but many of the banks find themselves more or less unprepared to meet this demand.

Short-Term Bank Debts

Turning now to Table 77, we note that the total of bank deposits fell off from $45,800 million at the end of 1931 to $41,500 million at the end of 1932 partly because of withdrawals of cash and partly because of bank suspensions.

Deposits in suspended banks are not included in the published totals partly because such items are no longer current items. They tend to become more like long-term debts.

Federal Reserve Member Bank loans declined from $19,261 million at the end of 1931 to an estimated figure of $15,000 million at the end of 1932, while non-member bank loans declined from $12,045 million to about $11,000 million during the same time.

The estimated total of loans by suspended banks which may still be regarded as collectible, increased from $865 million to $1,000 million during the year. The total of all bank loans declined from $32,170 million at the end of 1931 to $27,000 million.

The estimated total of loans by suspended banks which may still be regarded as collectible, was worked out for each year as follows: Taking three years as the average time required for winding up the affairs of a bank, estimated totals of bank loans of suspended banks for three successive years ending with the year to be estimated, were added together and then divided by two on the assumption that about half of the loans can be collected. The total of the outstanding loans was estimated by first calculating the ratio of loans to deposits from the United States Comptroller's report of all banks, and then multiplying the official published figures for the deposits of failed banks by the calculated ratio which was taken as 62 per cent for the two years.

After the final totals of bank loans at the ends of the two years were finally arrived at, they were further reduced by deducting estimates of the totals of long-term bank loans for the two years. The figures for long-term bank loans secured by real estate were worked out from a study of the Comptroller's report for all banks as of June 30, 1931 and 1932 and stepped down to the ends of those years. A part of the long-term mortgage debt discussed in other chapters of this book is included in these figures, which were estimated to be $10 billion for 1931 and $9 billion for 1932.

Brokers' Loans

Loans for the account of "others" for both years was only a drop in the bucket as compared with what this item was in 1928 and 1929. The figure declined from $13 million at the end of 1931 to $4 million at the end of 1932, but the change was utterly meaningless. Brokers' loans reported by New York Stock Exchange from private banks, brokers, foreign banking agencies, etc. declined from $132 million to $68 million. Regular brokers' loans are included in the bank loans figures already discussed.

In order to estimate the total of all loans by brokers to their customers, inquiries were made in order to discover the proportion of loans to brokers by banks which are re-lent to customers. It was estimated by one authority that brokers not only re-lent all of the loans they borrow from banks, that in addition to this, they had $200 million of their own capital loaned out to customers at the end of 1931 and about $175 million at the end of 1932. The figures for "Brokers' Loans" by banks reported by the New York Stock Exchange was $587 million at the end of 1931 and $347 million at the end of 1932, so that the final estimate for loans by brokers to their customers was $932 million at the end of 1931 and $594 million at the end of 1932. (See Table 78.)

Another executive of a stock exchange firm, well versed in statistics

of brokerage houses, estimated that of the total of all loans to customers, about one-fifth is loans to business firms to carry securities and
about four-fifths is loans to individuals. On this basis, it was estimated
that loans by brokers to business firms to carry securities declined from
about $186 million at the end of 1931 to about $119 million at the
end of 1932. Similarly, it was estimated on the same basis, that loans
to individuals to carry securities, declined from $746 million at the
end of 1931 to $475 million at the end of 1932.

Loans by Federal Intermediate Credit banks declined from $117,-
935,171 at the end of 1931 to $92,383,370 at the end of 1932. These
loans are more liquid than loans by the Federal Land Banks. They show
a gradual decline partly by reason of paying off of loans and partly by
reason of the general features of the business situation.

There were no loans by the Reconstruction Finance Corporation at
the end of 1931, but at the end of 1932 there were $1,355,725,904
of these loans outstanding, $594,597,707 of which was loans to banks
and trust companies.

TABLE 78

ESTIMATED TOTAL OF LOANS BY BROKERS TO THEIR CUSTOMERS
(In Millions)

Items of Available Capital to Lend	Total Amounts Outstanding	
	At End of 1931	At End of 1932
Brokers' own capital (estimated)....................	$200	$175
Borrowed from "others".........................	13	4
Borrowed from private banks, brokers, foreign banking agencies, etc....................................	132	68
Borrowed from banks............................	587	347
Estimated total of loans by brokers to their customers	$932	$594
Amount estimated as loaned to individuals for speculation	746	475
Estimated amount of the above loaned to business firms	186	119

Another problem arises in connection with this total which has to do
with duplication. In cases where authorized but unissued long-term
bonds, held in the treasury of a railroad or other corporation, are
pledged as security for a loan by the Reconstruction Finance Corporation, and the pledged bonds are set up on the books of the borrower
as long-term debts, then it seems that such loan should be regarded as
long-term. Furthermore, many of the loans of the Reconstruction
Finance Corporation were made in such a way that they may become
long-term items before they are paid off.

Current Business Liabilities

Current liabilities of incorporated business concerns were calculated for 1931 and 1932 by a rather violent assumption, but it was the only method available for use in the short period of time allotted for this study. The figure of $29,400 million of notes and accounts payable of corporations, given on page 25 of *Statistics of Income for 1929,* published by the Bureau of Internal Revenue, were taken as a basis for estimated amounts of $26 billion for 1931 and $22 billion for 1932. It was assumed that about 60% of these totals were current liabilities exclusive of bank loans. These estimates should be further refined by careful studies of corporation statements and tabulations for the years to be estimated. The current liabilities, excluding bank loans, of non-incorporated business concerns were similarly calculated, but are merely a guess. Miscellaneous financing by factors, selling agents, etc. was estimated from very fragmentary information, but should be included in the table.

Both the long-term and the short-term debts of incorporated business concerns are discussed in another chapter. But one of the most baffling problems of the entire study is the problem of the long-term and short-term debts of non-incorporated business concerns.

The current liabilities of incorporated business concerns not including bank loans, declined from about $14 billion at the end of 1931 to about $12 billion at the end of 1932. Similarly and by the same method of estimating, which is very crude but the only method available in so short a time, it is estimated that the bank loans of incorporated business concerns declined from about $12 billion to about $10 billion during the same time.

For purposes of Table 77, it was estimated that current liabilities of non-incorporated business concerns, excluding bank loans, declined from about $3,000 million at the end of 1931 to about $2,200 million at the end of 1932. Likewise, it is believed that bank loans of non-incorporated business concerns declined from a similar amount of $2,500 million at the end of 1931 to about $1,800 million at the end of 1932. But these are very rough estimates.

Total Short-Term Debt 1931–1932

Having now discussed all the items of strictly business debt which are listed in Table 77, and noted that they total up to $98,522 million for the end of 1931 and $89,241 million at the end of 1932, we should also note that if we add to these totals the other totals of personal and household debt from Table 82 in Chapter Eleven, we get final totals of all the short-term debt in the United States, amounting to $112,421 million as of the end of 1931, as contrasted with the aggregate of $103,636 million as of the end of 1932, showing a decline of about eight per cent.

Taking these totals and working them backward for previous years, the author presents in Table 79 the following very rough guesses for the years 1913, 1921, 1929 in contrast to the above totals.

TABLE 79

SHORT-TERM DEBTS IN THE UNITED STATES

(In Billions of Dollars)

Kind of Debt	End of 1913	End of 1921	End of 1929	End of 1931	End of 1932
Short-Term Business Debt................	$47	$ 93	$128	$ 98.5	$ 89.2
Short-Term Personal and Household Debt...	4	9	22	13.9	14.4
Total Short-Term Debt.................	$51	$102	$150	$112.4	$103.6

In gathering the data for this chapter, the author found that almost nothing had been done along these lines by the large statistical and credit services. A dozen different credit and banking authorities were asked for estimates of the total current liabilities of all business concerns, but none of them had the data.

Chapter Eleven

SHORT-TERM PERSONAL AND HOUSEHOLD DEBTS [1]

SUMMARY

THE household is the largest and most important business in the nation in point of size: size of investment ($121 billion in housings and household equipment); number of people employed (23,000,000 housewives and many millions of domestic servants) and social importance (pp. 304–5).

At the beginning of 1933 there were approximately $14.4 billion of personal and household short-term debts outstanding as against $13.9 the year before—an increase of almost 4 per cent. But the most important elements of these totals are mercantile debts and short-term cash loans and the aggregates of these items declined from a total of $7.4 billion at the end of 1931 to $5.9 billion at the end of 1932, a real decline of about 20 per cent (Table 81 on p. 307). In this latter calculation, life insurance policy loans are left out because in a sense, they are in reality a cashing in of surrender values of life insurance and as loans they never have to be paid (p. 305).

Of $15 billion retail sales on credit in 1932, $11.5 billion, or 77 per cent, were sales on open charge accounts and $3.5, or 23 per cent, were on the instalment plan, with outstandings at the year's end of $2.5 billion on open account and $1.75 billion on instalment contracts. These figures are in contrast to $3.2 billion of open account debts and $2 billion of instalment debts outstanding at the end of 1931 (pp. 305–8).

Losses from uncollectible retail debts in 1932 were about $600 million and were about three times the normal losses for years like 1929 or 1930. The $600 million of losses from bad retail debts is divided about equally between open account debts and instalment debts (pp. 307–8).

Life insurance policy loans by insurance companies and premium notes outstanding at the end of 1932 were $3.8 billion of which less

---

[1] The estimates and figures given in this chapter are the outgrowth of two previous studies by the author (Franklin W. Ryan) one of which was entitled *Family Finance in the United States,* published in *The Journal of Business of the University of Chicago* for October, 1930. Another study, *Family Finance in 1930 and 1931,* was issued by the author on January 10th, 1932, in *The Franklin Plan Review.*

than 3 per cent were premium notes. This total constituted an increase of 171 per cent since 1929 (pp. 308–9).

The United States Government became the largest single small loan agency in the country in 1931 by advancing $1.3 billion to war veterans which was increased to $1.6 at the end of 1932, of which 90 per cent were probably for personal and household uses (pp. 309–10).

Short-term cash loans outstanding for personal and household purposes, by various small loan agencies, aggregated $1.7 billion at the beginning of 1933 as against $2.2 billion at the beginning of 1932 (p. 310).

Of this total small loan companies licensed under the "uniform law" account for $207 million at the start of this year as against $216 million last. During 1932 there was an unusually heavy charge of uncollectible loans—probably fully 6 per cent of outstandings (pp. 310–11).

Pawnbrokers' loans outstanding amounted to $240 millions as against $270 the year before (pp. 311–13).

Share loans of building and loan associations outstanding were $200 million compared with $220 million (p. 313).

Morris Plan and other "industrial banks" and endorsed note agencies accounted for $197 and $134 million (Tables 82 and 83).

Personal loans by commercial banks are estimated (very roughly) at $1.1 billion and $760 million—a decrease over 30 per cent in the year's span (p. 313).

Credit union personal loans outstanding increased from about $28 to $34 million (p. 316).

Loans by axias are estimated to have declined from $7 to $6 million because of their lack of legal status and relatively low business standards (pp. 316–17).

Personal loans outstanding by unlawful lenders ("loan sharks") are thought to have dropped from $120 to $95 million partly because of an increasingly aroused sentiment against them (p. 317).

"Remedial" and Hebrew Free Loan Societies and employee plans account for $45 and $44 million of outstanding personal loans at the beginning of 1933 and 1932, respectively (pp. 317–18).

It is, of course, impossible to make more than a shrewd guess at the amount of personal loans by individuals to each other, but the total of these outstanding at the beginning of 1933 is put at $1.5 billion compared with $1.0 billion the year before (pp. 318–19).

Overdue rents, taxes and insurance premiums probably increased from $2 to $3 billion in the same period (p. 442).

The sharp decline of about 20 per cent in short-term cash loans and instalment credit during the past year was more than overbalanced by the increase in life insurance loans—but, it should be noted, these do not have to be paid and are an offset against subsequent death benefits (pp. 320–21).

In the past 30 years, with brief reactions in 1907 and 1921, the American family plunged headlong into a load of debts which culminated in 1929 with probably 98 per cent of all families involved. The reverse process is now under way and possibly 10 to 15 per cent of American families are now out of debt (p. 321).

There is nothing fundamentally wrong with either charge accounts or instalment credit. The evils come from lack of judgment and control (p. 322).

It is much sounder, however, to save before one spends (p. 323).

Savings deposits usually increase and debts are paid off during a depression until savings seek active use and recovery begins (p. 324).

Savings deposits are now in fact on the increase—over 5 per cent for banks and 250 per cent for postal accounts in the past two years (p. 323).

The immediate problem today is to balance the budgets of each American family. If each American household could be so managed that it should be spending less currently than its income and be gradually saving a surplus, a very important part of our debt problem would be solved (p. 325).

———————

The household is the largest and most important business in the world. All other businesses exist for it and because of it. It is the primary industry while the others are secondary. It is largest in number of people employed, largest in amount of investment and of first rank in value and importance of its usefulness to society.

All commercial business enterprises are owned by families and individuals. Household activities are distinctly separate from commercial business activities and can be separately allocated even where families live on farms. In such cases, the household constitutes a separate entity from the farm as an enterprise.

Table 80, compiled by the author in 1930, gives figures for some of America's leading industries. The figures for each of these seven leading industries are impressive, but they decline in importance when compared with the business of the home. The total investment in housings alone in the United States on January 1, 1930, was $71 billion, according to the Copper and Brass Research Association. The total investment in household equipment at that time was also estimated by the author to be about $50 billion.

TABLE 80(a)

STATISTICS OF LEADING AMERICAN INDUSTRIES

Industry	Number of People Employed (In Thousands)	Annual Value of Products or Services (In Millions)	Estimated Capital Employed (In Millions)
Agriculture.............	8,400	$17,000	$57,000
Transportation.........	2,600	9,000	30,000
Construction...........	2,500	8,496	9,000
Textiles and their products	1,600	8,000	6,000
Iron and Steel..........	830	6,000	9,000
Machinery.............	886	5,300	3,000
Automobiles...........	370	4,000	3,000

(a) These estimates are based partly upon the U. S. census of manufactures for 1927, the U. S. census of agriculture for 1925, and federal income tax returns for 1928. The estimates for the construction industry are based partly upon figures supplied by Thomas H. Holden, of the F. W. Dodge Corporation.

The households of the United States are managed by more than 23,000,000 housewives and housekeepers, which is a greater number than the total of all the people employed in 1930 by seven of our largest industries, to say nothing of millions of domestic servants employed in American homes.

The product of the home is the growing family—new citizens in the process of development to take the place of the present generation when it passes on—and the value of this product cannot be estimated in money; but we are safe in saying that the importance and value of American children is enormously greater than the value of all the material products of American industry put together.

Table 81 shows the total estimated outstanding personal and family short-term debts at the end of 1931 as $13,898,850,082 and at the end of 1932 as $14,395,339,019. On subsequent pages the items making up these totals are discussed in detail.

National Retail Sales to Individuals and Families

The United States census figures for 1929 show sales by retail stores that year of $50,033,850,792 and $3,172,934,842 of other direct sales to individuals and families by manufacturers and others. But during this period there were fully $2 billion or more of direct sales to individuals and families by jobbers and wholesalers which would bring the total up to around $55 billion as opposed to the estimate by the National Bureau of Economic Research. Three years ago, Major Milan V. Ayres estimated that the total sales for 1929 were $55 billion. On the basis of these figures and more recent data, the following figures are taken for national retail sales for the last five years:

Year	Annual Sales to Individuals and Families (In Billions)
1928	$52.0
1929	55.0
1930	48.0
1931	41.0
1932	31.5

The estimate for 1932 is that of Dr. Julius Klein, of the United States Department of Commerce, given out in a radio talk January 1, 1933, and published by the *New York Times,* January 2, 1933, and is the same estimate as given out by R. G. Dun & Company for 1932 sales in *The New York Journal of Commerce* for January 5, 1933.

In Bradstreet's weekly for January 28, 1933, Professor Paul H. Nystrom of Columbia University estimated that retail sales totaled $28 billion in 1932. Mr. Guy H. Hulse, Secretary of the National Retail Credit Association, in a letter to the author, dated February 17, 1933, estimates the total for 1932 as $35.0 billion. The $31.5 billion estimate of Dr. Klein is exactly half way between these two estimates.

Open Account Debts and Instalment Debts for 1932

It has been found by statistical studies, carried on by different retail credit authorities, among whom are Mr. Guy H. Hulse, Secretary of the National Retail Credit Association and Mr. R. Preston Shealey of the Washington, D. C. Bar, that sales on credit are normally somewhat less than half of the total volume of sales during a given period of time. Dr. Wilbur C. Plummer, Economist of the U. S. Department of Commerce, as a result of studies carried out under his direction for one year, found that credit sales were 47 per cent of total retail sales. Taking Dr. Julius Klein's figure of $31.5 billion as the total of all retail sales in the United States for 1932, we can estimate on the basis of work

TABLE 81

SHORT-TERM INDEBTEDNESS FOR HOUSEHOLD PURPOSES IN THE UNITED STATES
IN 1931 AND 1932(a)

Class of Financing	Total Amounts Outstanding	
	At end of 1931	At end of 1932
1. Retail Open Account Debts..................	$3,200,000,000	$2,500,000,000
2. Retail Instalment Debts......................	2,000,000,000	1,750,000,000
3. Short-term Cash Loans (from Tables 82 and 83). (For personal and household purposes)........	2,223,083,000	1,720,000,000
Total of Retail Mercantile Debts and Short-term Cash Loans......................	$7,423,083,000	$5,970,000,000
4. Estimated total of Life Insurance Policy Loans by Life Insurance Companies. (For personal and household purposes.)........................	$2,269,146,545	$2,500,000,000
5. Estimated total of U. S. Government Loans to Veterans on Life Insurance and on adjusted service certificates. (For personal and household purposes.)..........................	1,206,620,537	1,425,339,019
6. Estimated total of Miscellaneous overdue rents, taxes, and overdue life insurance premiums....	2,000,000,000	3,000,000,000
7. Personal loans between individuals(b)...........	1,000,000,000	1,500,000,000
Total short-term Individual and Family Debt the United States.....................	$13,898,850,082	$14,395,339,019

(a) Life insurance policy loans as given in this table were estimated as follows: Of the totals of life insurance policy loans by life insurance companies, about two-thirds were for personal and household purposes and about one-third for business purposes. Of the totals of loans to war veterans by the U. S. Government on government life insurance and on adjusted service certificates, about 90 per cent of the total was for personal and household purposes and about 10 per cent for business purposes. The estimates of life insurance policy loans for business purposes have already been included in Table 77 of Chapter Ten.

In a letter to the author dated February 28, 1933, Mr. M. Collins, Director of Finance, U. S. Veterans Administration, Washington, D. C., estimated that the totals of outstanding loans by banks on U. S. Government adjusted service certificates, not yet redeemep by the government, were $75,000,000 at the end of 1931 and $60,000,000 at the end of 1932. But these totals are already counted in bank loans in Tables 82 and 83 and in Table 77 in Chapter Ten. About 10 per cent of these totals are for business loans and about 90 per cent for loans for personal and household purposes.

(b) Personal loans between individuals and families are inter-family and inter-individual items and if an accountant were to prepare a consolidated balance sheet of all American household debts, these debts between individuals and families would be taken out of such a consolidated balance sheet as is the regular practice in preparing consolidated statements.

already done that credit sales during 1932 were about $15 billion. This estimate has been checked and given tentative approval by Dr. Plummer and by other experts.

Of the total of $15.0 billion of total sales on credit during 1932, it is now estimated that about $11.5 billion were sales on open account and that about $3.5 billion were sales on the instalment plan. The ratio between the two forms of credit was worked out on the basis of figures for previous years.

Mr. Hulse writes that, in his opinion, credit sales are about 60 per cent of retail sales. He also says that losses from uncollectible retail debts are about three times as large in 1932 as in normal years. In other words, whereas, in normal years, retailers lose about $100 million on uncollectible open accounts and another $100 million on uncollect-ible instalment debts, the two figures were tripled for 1932 with a total of losses of about $600 million.

Dr. Plummer found in his credit studies, that three years ago, open accounts ran on the average about 72 days or ⅕ of a year and that two years ago they ran about 76 days. During the first half of 1932 he found that they ran 80 days. In view of the lengthening duration of open accounts, it seems probable that the total open accounts outstanding at the end of 1932 should be about $2.5 billion, a decline of about $700 million from the end of 1931.

In a letter to the writer dated February 10, 1933, Dr. Plummer states that his last credit survey for 1932, showed that the average length of time accounts receivable on instalment sales had increased materially over the corresponding period in 1931. It is his opinion that of the total of $3.5 billion of instalment sales during 1932, about 50 per cent, or $1,750 billion were outstanding and due at the end of the year. In 1931 the percentage was taken at 40 per cent. Of the $5 billion instal-ment sales during 1931, the total outstanding and due at the end of the year was taken as $2 billion. In other words, the decline in the instalment debt for the year 1932 was about $250 million.

Life Insurance Policy Loans and Premium Notes

According to the compendium of Official Life Insurance Reports for 1932, published by the Spectator Company, the total amounts of Life Insurance Policy Loans and Premium Notes outstanding of reporting companies at the end of each year from 1921 to 1931 inclusive were as follows:

1921	$1,058,073,020
1922	1,140,728,019
1923	1,198,108,368
1924	1,323,304,728
1925	1,445,507,242
1926	1,599,389,607
1927	1,784,973,470
1928	2,000,138,202
1929	2,379,360,387
1930	2,807,012,195
1931	3,369,146,545

These totals are made up about 95 per cent or more, of policy loans while premium notes are relatively small in amount. During the last three years shown in the above list policy loans without premium notes were: $2,290,079,713 at the end of 1929; $2,706,213,747 at the end of 1930; and $3,252,290,710 at the end of 1931. Premium notes outstanding totaled $116,855,835 at the end of 1931.

From the end of 1926 to the end of 1931 the total increase in policy loans and premium notes was $1,769,756,938 or at the average rate of increase of $353,951,387 per year. The increase from the end of 1929 to the end of 1930 was $427,651,808 and the increase from the end of 1930 to the end of 1931 was $562,134,350. Mr. Thomas J. V. Cullen, Editor of *The Spectator,* estimates that at the end of 1932 the total of policy loans and premium notes was about $3,800 million of which about $100 million were premium notes.[2]

Government Loans

The United States government, by entering the personal loan business in 1931 with a total of $1,340,620,537 loaned to war veterans at the end of the year, became the largest single small loan agency in the field. This amount increased to $1,583,339,019 at the end of 1932, but these amounts must be scaled down by about ten per cent to estimate the amount that can be classified as strictly personal loans. In Table 81 the 1931 total is scaled down to $1,206,620,537 and the 1932 total to $1,425,339,019.[3] These estimated amounts that have been deducted, which are approximately ten per cent of each of the totals, or $134,-000,000 for the end of 1931 and $158,000,000 for the end of 1932, are already shown in Table 77 in Chapter Ten.

During the last two years, it was estimated on the basis of questionnaire studies by the author, that life insurance policy loans, by life

[2] According to Mr. Cullen, the total amount of outstanding policy loans and premium notes increased sharply from January to June in 1932 at about the same rapid rate as of 1931. But after June there was a very noticeable slowing up in the increase so that his figure of $3,800 million for the total at the end of the year seems about in line with the increases of previous years and with the actual borrowings of last year.
According to estimates by Mr. Cullen, fully one-third of the life insurance policy loans by life insurance companies are business loans for strictly business purposes, while the remaining two-thirds are loans for household or individual purposes. But as regards life insurance policy loans by the United States government, advances on government insurance and on adjusted service certificates, a much larger percentage is for personal and household loans, and only about 10 per cent being used for business purposes.
[3] The amounts by which the totals of life insurance policy loans are scaled down, are very rough estimates and are based upon the opinions of the author and also upon the opinions of Mr. Thomas J. V. Cullen, Editor of *The Spectator.*

insurance companies, and U. S. Government advances to veterans were used to the extent of about 60 per cent, to pay off the different kinds of already existing debts and to pay off already existing open account debts and instalment debts, and that about 40 per cent of these advances were used for payments on new purchases.

But in this connection it must be noted that life insurance policy loans constitute a sale of insurance cash surrender values and never have to be paid off, so that they lose much of their significance as debts.

Note in Table 81, that the enormous increase in life insurance policy loans caused an increase in the total aggregate, but if we exclude all the items but the mercantile debts and the cash loans, we find that there was a very encouraging decrease in personal and household debts.

Short-Term Cash Loans During 1932

As a result of studies of the available data for 1932, it is estimated that the total of the short-term debt on account of personal cash loans at the end of 1932, excluding life insurance policy loans, brokers loans to individuals for speculation and loans between friends and relatives, was $1,720,000,000 as contrasted with the revised total of about $2,223,083,000 for the year 1931. The details of these estimates are given in Tables 82 and 83 together with the annual volume of loans and changes thereon.

Personal Finance Companies

Mr. Rolf Nugent of the Russell Sage Foundation gives us the preliminary estimates of the Foundation for 1930, 1931 and 1932 for loans by small loan companies licensed under the Uniform Small Loan Law or its approximate equivalent, which are predominantly chattel loan companies, but also include companies making wage assignment loans, co-maker loans and plain note loans. The figures for 1931 and 1930 are the result of several months of very thorough and painstaking compilations and calculations of all available public data, and a considerable amount from private sources. The figures for 1932 are more of a tentative estimate and not so accurate as those for 1930 and 1931, and are subject to later revision. The estimates are as follows:

	Total Volume of Loans Made	Debts Outstanding	Estimated Annual Loan Charges
1930	$361,800,000	$268,000,000	$86,000,000
1931	357,000,000	275,083,000	87,900,000
1932	300,000,000	260,000,000	83,000,000

In order to make the items in the subsequent classification of per-sonal loans in Tables 82 and 83 mutually exclusive, deductions from each of the items listed above have been made because of the fact that in some states other forms of personal loan agencies operate under the same statutes as the personal loan companies whose figures are estimated above.

During 1932 there were heavy charge-offs for uncollectible loans in the small loan business so that the average national loss for charge-offs was fully six per cent of the invested capital. The actual losses may be considerably greater than six per cent if the amount of loans found to be uncollectible exceed the estimates covered by the charge-offs. A small amount of new capital came into the business in 1931, but very little came in during 1932 and this was more than offset by charge-offs, withdrawals of capital, increases in cash balances in banks and by heavy liquidation of borrowings from banks by the loan companies.

It is estimated that of the total of $260 million invested in out-standing loans in this business, about ten per cent is for business loans and the remaining 90 per cent for personal and household loans.[4]

Pawnbroking

The pawnbroking business suffered severely during 1932, much worse than in 1931, on account of losses in the value of pledges and in the general difficulties which faced the business. The real losses resulted from sales of unredeemed pledges. In most cases, pawnbroking offices did not earn enough to cover their overhead costs. In general, pawn-brokers either made no profits or barely covered their costs in 1931, but as a rule, 1932 was a year of real loss to them. About one-fourth of all pawnbroking loans are for business loans and about 75% are for personal and household purposes.

The total volume of commercial pawnbroking loans was about $410 million in 1932 as against about $500 million in 1931, showing a decline of about $90 million. The total investment in the business declined from about $360 million at the end of 1931 to about $320 million at the end of 1932. A considerable amount of money was taken

[4] In *The Small Loan Situation in New Jersey in 1929*, by Dr. W. I. King, pp. 60–61, Dr. King found that of the total of loans which he studied, which was 16,079, all were loans for personal and household purposes except 1,612 loans or 10.03 per cent of the total *number* of loans. In *Ten Thousand Small Loans* by Dr. Louis N. Robinson, we also find some confirmation for the ten per cent estimate above, in Table 69.

TABLE 82

ESTIMATED VOLUME AND AMOUNTS OUTSTANDING OF LOANS BY SMALL LOAN AGENCIES IN THE UNITED STATES, 1932(a)

(Not Including Insurance Policy Loans)

(1) Small Loan Agencies	(2) Annual Volume of Loans Made	(3) Total Investment in All Loans Outstanding as of Dec. 31, 1932	(4) Annual Loan Charges	(5) Estimated Percentage of Business Loans	(6) Estimated Amount of Business Loans by Small Loan Agencies	(7) Final Estimates of Strictly Personal and Household Loans by Small Loan Agencies Outstanding Dec. 31, 1931
1. Small Loan Companies Licensed under the Uniform Small Loan Law or its Approximate equivalent which are predominantly chattel loan companies, but also include companies making wage assignment loans, co-maker loans and plain note loans....	$300,000,000	$260,000,000	$83,300,000		$23,000,000	$207,000,000
Less: Estimated total of items counted elsewhere in this table..........	40,000,000	30,000,000	8,000,000			
Adjusted total to avoid duplication....	$260,000,000	$230,000,000	$75,000,000	10.0	$23,000,000	$207,000,000
2. Pawnbrokers......	410,000,000	320,000,000	115,000,000	25.0	80,000,000	240,000,000
3. Indorsed note lenders:						
a. Morris Plan and other industrial banking companies..........	240,000,000	180,000,000	18,000,000	33.33	60,000,000	120,000,000
b. Other indorsed note lenders......	32,000,000	20,000,000	4,800,000	30.0	6,000,000	14,000,000
4. Share Loans by Building and Loan Associations....	200,000,000	240,000,000	15,000,000	16.67	40,000,000	200,000,000
5. Credit Unions....	60,000,000	45,000,000	3,000,000	25.0	11,000,000	34,000,000
6. Axias....	30,000,000	25,000,000	3,000,000	70.0	19,000,000	6,000,000
7. Personal Loan Departments of Banks....	270,000,000	160,000,000	22,500,000	30.0	50,000,000	110,000,000(b)
8. Non-departmentized personal loans by commercial banks....	1,300,000,000	650,000,000	60,000,000			650,000,000(b)
9. Unlawful lenders of all kinds.... (All others in this list operate lawfully)	800,000,000	100,000,000	280,000,000	5.0	5,000,000	95,000,000
10. Remedial Loan Societies:						
a. Remedial Loan Societies (Pawnbroker Loans)....	37,000,000	32,000,000	4,800,000	25.0	8,000,000	24,000,000
b. Other Remedial Loan Societies....	10,000,000	8,000,000	2,000,000	12.5	1,000,000	7,000,000
11. Hebrew Free Loan Societies....	2,500,000	2,000,000		50.0	1,000,000	1,000,000
12. Employees Loan Associations....	25,000,000	12,000,000	600,000			12,000,000
Total............	$3,616,500,000	$2,024,000,000	$603,700,000		$304,000,000	$1,720,000,000

(a) See Footnote on Table 83, page 314.   (b) Subtracted from Total Bank Loans in Table 77, Chapter Ten.

out of the business by withdrawals of capital and by reducing bank loans, in addition to the losses that were suffered.

Share Loans by Building and Loan Associations

According to H. F. Cellarius, Secretary of the United State Building and Loan League, the estimated total volume of share loans by building and loan associations [5] was about $250 million during 1930 and about $225 million for 1931, while the loans outstanding were estimated to be $300 million on December 31, 1930 and about $270 million on December 31, 1931. Mr. Cellarius writes that he is unable to make estimates for 1932, but from other building and loan data available in New York and New Jersey, and from previous figures, it can be estimated that the total volume of share loans by building and loan associations was about $200 million during 1932 and that the total amount of this debt outstanding at the end of 1932 was about $240 million with annual loan charges of about $15 million.

Personal Loan Departments of Commercial Banks

During the year 1932 the total volume of loans made by personal loan departments of commercial banks declined from about $320 million during 1931 to about $270 million during 1932, while the loans outstanding also declined from around $180 million at the end of 1931 to about $160 million at the end of 1932. During the year a few more banks opened personal loan departments but any increase of loans in this way was more than balanced by many banks that stopped making loans in these departments or reduced them materially, and by the closing of some banks which had personal loan departments. About one-third of the total volume of loans of personal loan departments of commercial banks are for business purposes.

Non-Departmentized Loans by Commercial Banks

During 1931 the total volume of non-departmentized personal loans [6] by commercial banks was about $1 billion while the amount outstand-

[5] It has often been said that share loans by building and loan associations are not real additions to debt because, in a sense, the borrower is using his own savings, as represented by his pledged shares; but this objection seems inconsistent. The borrower from a pawnbroker also uses his own savings represented by his pledged jewelry in the same way. The total share loans by building and loan associations should be included in any summing-up of the volume of personal loans.

[6] There is a basic difference between two types of personal loans by banks. In recent years many banks have established "personal loan departments" in which all their per-

TABLE 83

ESTIMATED VOLUME AND AMOUNTS OUTSTANDING OF LOANS BY SMALL LOAN AGENCIES IN THE UNITED STATES, 1931(a)

(Not Including Insurance Policy Loans)

(1) Small Loan Agencies	(2) Annual Volume of Loans Made	(3) Total Investment in all Loans Outstanding as of Dec. 31, 1931	(4) Annual Loan Charges	(5) Estimated Percentage of Business Loans	(6) Estimated Amount of Business Loans by Small Loan Agencies	(7) Final Estimates of Strictly Personal and Household Loans by Small Loan Agencies Outstanding Dec. 31, 1931
1. Small Loan Companies Licensed under the Uniform Small Loan Law or its Approximate equivalent which are predominantly chattel loan companies, but also include companies making wage assignment loans, co-maker loans, and plain note loans	$357,000,000	$275,083,000	$87,900,000			
Less: Estimated total of items counted elsewhere in this table.........	50,000,000	35,000,000	10,000,000			
Adjusted total to avoid duplication....	$307,000,000	$240,083,000	$77,900,000	10.0	$24,000,000	$216,083,000
2. Pawnbrokers........................	500,000,000	360,000,000	130,000,000	25.0	90,000,000	270,000,000
3. Indorsed note lenders:						
a. Industrial Banks (Morris Plan and Others).............	320,000,000	230,000,000	24,000,000	35.0	50,000,000	180,000,000
b. Other co-maker and indorsed note lenders...................	40,000,000	25,000,000	6,000,000	33.33	8,000,000	17,000,000
4. Share Loans by Building and Loan Associations.....................	225,000,000	270,000,000	18,000,000	18.0	50,000,000	220,000,000
5. Credit Unions.................	60,000,000	42,000,000	3,000,000	33.33	14,000,000	28,000,000

6. Axias..................	60,000,000	35,000,000	3,800,000	80.0	28,000,000	7,000,000
7. Personal Loan Departments of Banks....	320,000,000	180,000,000	25,000,000	33.33	60,000,000	120,000,000(b)
8. Non-departmentized personal loans by commercial banks........	2,000,000,000	1,000,000,000	90,000,000	....	....	1,000,000,000(b)
9. Unlawful lenders of all kinds........ (All others in this list operate lawfully)	1,000,000,000	125,000,000	350,000,000	5.0	5,000,000	120,000,000
10. Remedial Loan Societies:						
a. Remedial Loan Societies (Pawnbroker Loans).............	44,000,000	34,000,000	5,100,000	27.0	9,000,000	25,000,000
b. Other Remedial Loan Societies.........	11,000,000	8,000,000	2,000,000	12.5	1,000,000	7,000,000
11. Hebrew Free Loan Societies..........	3,000,000	2,000,000	....	50.0	1,000,000	1,000,000
12. Employees Loan Associations.........	25,000,000	12,000,000	600,000	....	....	12,000,000
Total.........	$4,970,000,000	$2,563,583,000	$735,400,000		$340,000,000	$2,223,083,000

(a) These estimates and figures in Tables 82 and 83 bring up to date the figures of previous tables of former years 1930 and 1931 prepared by the author, in his article *Family Finance in the United States* published in the October 1930 number of *The Journal of Business of the University of Chicago*, and in an economic bulletin issued in *The Franklin Plan Review* on January 10, 1932, entitled *Family Finance During 1930 and 1931*. In preparing these two earlier publications and in making the present table, the author received the generous assistance of Mr. Leon Henderson and Mr. Rolf Nugent of the Russell Sage Foundation. The estimates of the annual volume and total outstanding of share loans by building and loan associations were furnished by H.F. Cellarius of the United States Building and Loan League. The first table of estimates of personal loans ever published was originally prepared by Mr. Leon Henderson and was issued in an interview with him entitled *Business Rescues the Small Borrower* which appeared in the *Business Week* January 22, 1930. The first table of estimated loan charges ever published was prepared by Mr. Rolf Nugent of the Russell Sage Foundation and was published in the *Magazine of Wall Street*, December 3, 1927.

(b) Subtracted from Total Bank Loans in Table 77, Chapter Ten.

ing at the end of the year was also about $1 billion. During 1932, there was a considerable curtailment of these loans many of which were merely personal notes without indorsers or co-makers. Many of the smaller banks that were closed or suspended had a large amount of personal loans. The annual volume for 1932 was reduced to about $900 million while the amount outstanding at the end of the year was about $650 million. Total interest paid was about $60 million. These estimates of non-departmentized loans by banks are rough approximations and are subject to a high percentage of error. They are not comparable in accuracy to the compiled figures for some of the other items such as those of the small loan companies.

Credit Unions

It was found that the annual volume of loans by credit unions was about the same in 1932 as in 1931, namely, about $60 million but that the capital in the business increased from about $42 million in 1931 to about $45 million at the end of 1932, as a result of the addition of new states in which credit unions may be formed. About one-fourth to one-third of the total volume of loans by credit unions are for business purposes.

Axias

During 1932, the form of credit society known as the axia suffered severely. These associations are found among the foreign population of our large industrial cities. They raise their capital by the sale of shares but sometimes they are not incorporated and thus have no legal status. In cases where they are incorporated they usually do not have the legal right to engage in money-lending. Borrowers are required to hold a minimum number of shares. The rates vary from 15 to 30 per cent a year. During the last year, many of them were ordered to liquidate by state officials because of their lack of legal status. Those that still remain in business were usually unprofitable during 1932 and it is expected that eventually a large part of the now existing business of axias will be liquidated. Whereas axias made about $60 million in loans during 1931, they made only about $30 million in loans during 1932. It is estimated

sonal loans are made. But the great majority of American banks have not established personal loan departments and yet they grant personal loans in amounts varying from bank to bank. By non-departmentized personal loans we mean those personal loans by banks which have not organized personal loan departments.

that the total capital investment in the business was reduced from about $35 million at the end of 1931 to about $25 million at the end of 1932. On account of its lack of legal status and the fact that the axia is not licensed or regulated by state officials, these estimates are merely rough approximations. About three-fourths of that total volume of loans by axias are for business purposes.

Unlawful Lenders

The total of loans by unlawful lenders, of all kinds, declined from a total volume of about $1 billion during 1931 to about $800 million during 1932. The capital employed in the business was reduced from about $125 million at the end of 1931 to about $100 million at the end of 1932. Loan charges during 1932 were about $280 million. It is strange to see this business declining, but during 1932 the causes which operated to cause declines in other forms of personal loans operated in this business also. Public sentiment also operated to reduce the volume. These unlawful lenders are of four main varieties, namely, illegal chattel loan companies charging 70 to 100 per cent a year, illegal plain note companies, charging as high as 150 per cent a year, salary buyers or wage assignment companies operating illegally and charging 20 to 40 per cent a month, and finally the unregulated high-rate pawnbrokers.

Remedial Loan Societies

There are a number of loan groups known as "remedial loan associations" originally established along philanthropic lines. For the most part they carry on a limited-dividend loan business. That is, they do not allow their net profits to exceed certain limits. Most of them have been fairly profitable in years past. Some of the associations do a pawnbroking business. Others lend on chattel mortgages while still others have both types of loan business. It is estimated that the total volume of loans made by pawnbroking remedial loan associations (not counting estimates already counted) declined from about $44 million during 1931 to about $37 million during 1932. Invested capital in this group declined from around $34 million at the end of 1931 to about $32 million at the end of 1932. A total volume of loans by remedial loan associations other than those doing a strictly pawnbroking business, declined from about $11 million during 1931 to about $10 million during 1932, but the investment in the business of about $8 million remained the same for the two years. Interest charges were about $2 million a year. It is estimated from one-eighth to one-fourth of all the loans of remedial loan societies are for business purposes. The reduction in total investment in the business of the remedial loan societies was largely due to lack of good risks.

Hebrew Free Loan Societies

In our large industrial cities, there exist a small number of Jewish remedial loan societies which for both the year 1931 and 1932 had about $1 million outstanding in loans. The great majority of the loans are made without any interest charge at all and in the extremely few cases where a charge is collected, it is a purely nominal fee intended to cover the costs. These Hebrew free loan societies stand out unique in our loan organization as probably the only loans made free of charge by organized loan agencies. It is estimated that about one-half of the total loans outstanding are for business purposes.

Employees Loan Plans

It is estimated that the annual volume of loans by employers to employees on various plans remained about the same for 1932 as for 1931, namely, about $25 million while the invested capital of about $12 million remained the same for the two years. These estimates are exclusive of figures already given for credit unions many of which are sponsored by large employers. In all of these plans the employee usually pays interest at the rate of six per cent.

Other Personal and Family Indebtedness

Having now discussed all the items in Tables 82 and 83 for the two years 1931 and 1932, let us now return to Table 81 which is a summary of all personal and family indebtedness for the two years. We see there three other items not yet discussed, namely, personal debts between individuals and families, overdue items such as rents, taxes and insurance premiums, etc., and finally loans to individuals and families for speculation.

As a result of fragmentary studies by the author over a period of two years, it appears that inter-family and inter-individual debts were at least $1 billion at the end of 1931 and that because of the unemployment situation this item increased to fully $1.5 billion at the end of 1932.

It is also roughly estimated as a result of discussions with several authorities who, like the author, have made merely broad estimates, that overdue items such as rents, taxes, insurance premiums increased from about $2 billion at the end of 1931 to about $3 billion at the end of 1932.

There is a question as to whether the item of speculative debts is strictly a household activity. It should not be included in Table 2 at all. Speculation is a sort of side line and partakes of the nature of a business activity. These loans are already discussed in the previous chapter.

Long-Term Household Debts about $10 Billion

There are no official figures available for the total of real estate mortgages on dwellings in the United States. But on the basis of available statistics from different sources, it can be calculated that the total is roughly $22.5 billion. This total is made up of $8 billion of mortgages by building and loan associations, $3.5 billion of first mortgages by insurance companies, $5 billion of first mortgages by private mortgage companies, $2 billion of second mortgages and other junior liens, and a final $1 billion calculated to be the proper allocation to farm homes out of the total of $9.4 billion of all mortgages on farms in the United States.

It would be improper to add the total of $22.5 billion of real estate debts to the total of current family debts to get the total of all family debts, both current and fixed, because in the United States about 60 per cent of all dwellings are rented and a large proportion of the $22.5 billion is thus owned by landlords. Nevertheless, the total of home-mortgage debts by families living in their own homes is probably at least $10 billion so that the total of all American family debts, both short and long-term, may be estimated at $25 billion by aggregating these estimates and others previously discussed. Long-term household debts are not tabulated in this chapter because they have already been covered in the chapter on mortgage debts in the United States.

On the other hand, families who are buying homes on the instalment plan may be considered as owning only an equity investment in their homes, which they are slowly increasing by savings.

It is probable that fully $1 billion or more of the real estate mortgages on homes in the United States has been incurred on account of current household needs, since we know that thousands of people use home-mortgage money for automobiles, furniture, and many other current expenditures. This, again is a very rough estimate.

Changes in Personal and Family Indebtedness

From a comparison of the items in Table 81 and those in Tables 82 and 83, for the two years 1931 and 1932, many striking changes may be noted.

Short-term cash loans declined fully 20 per cent, from around $2.5 billion at the end of 1931 to about $2 billion at the end of 1932, whereas the total for 1931 was only slightly less than for 1930 which was estimated by the author to have been nearly $2.6 billion. The year 1930 seems to have been the peak year for this type of short-term debts.

There was also a noteworthy decline in the volume of open account debts from $3.2 billion at the end of 1931 to about $2.5 billion at the end of 1932 and this decline was very similar to the 20 per cent decline in cash loans.

Both of these declines reflect the increase in the value of the dollar and the fall in prices as well as a falling off in buying power. But the most potent influences here was the real desire on the part of families and individuals to get more and more out of debt and on a cash basis.

The volume of instalment debts outstanding at the end of 1932, as contrasted with the amount at the end of 1931, shows the same tendencies as noted above. Falling prices helped to reduce the total sales and lack of buying power added another influence to cause the decline. On the other hand the length of instalment contracts increased making collections slower.

These three important declines in current or short-term items of household indebtedness were apparently more than overbalanced by the enormous increase in life insurance policy loans, reflecting the fact that unemployment conditions have forced millions of families to cash in on the surrender values of their insurance in force. The volume of such loans increased with heavy momentum all during 1931 and during the first half of 1932, but toward the end of 1932 there was a falling off in the volume, which has been interpreted as showing that American families are becoming better adjusted to the conditions of the depression.

Again, it must be noted that life insurance policy loans do not ever have to be paid. From this point of view, they present no serious problem. Many of them run on for years. In reality they are merely an offset against the value of American life insurance in force.

Disregarding life insurance policy loans of all kinds, the total of mercantile debts plus personal cash loans declined from a total of $7,423 million in 1931 to a total of $5,970 million at the end of 1932 and this was certainly a most striking contrast to the many years of increases in these items from 1900 to 1930.

The Expansion of Family Debts

During this 30-year period, with brief reactions in 1907 and 1921, the American family was plunging headlong into debt so that it is normal to have a period of decline in debts like the one we are now witnessing.

The American household's plunge into debt for commodities and for loans as well as for long-term financing, during the last thirty years, constitutes a most remarkable phenomenon. Fifty years ago, no one would have dreamed that our once predominantly thrifty (in the sense of being on a cash basis) population would in 1929 and 1930 become apparently not thrifty at all. No one would have predicted in those days, when most people "never got into debt and always lived within their means," that in 1929 and 1930 nearly every American family would be in debt. Extensive investigation by the author in 1928, 1929 and 1930, indicate that during that period, 98 per cent of American families were indebted in some way or other. The period 1930 to 1932 has seen a slight decline in this percentage to perhaps 85 to 90 per cent, but the getting-out-of-debt process is going on today with accelerated momentum. Today the "It Pays to be Thrifty" slogan of one of our leading New York department stores is meeting with increasing public approval as seen in the slight increase in ratio of cash retail sales to credit sales which has already occurred.

In the year 1910, the total volume of retail sales in the United States was about $20 billion and of this amount only about $2 billion was sold on credit. But in 1915, although retail sales had increased to about $21 billion the total of sales on credit had increased to about $3 billion. During the next five years while the World War was in progress and during the post-war boom, retail sales doubled in volume to $45 billion while total sales on credit tripled in volume to about $9 billion.[7]

This, in itself, was a remarkable change in American buying habits, but it was only the beginning. In 1925, with retail sales of $53 billion sales on credit had increased to $18 billion and from then on to 1930 the

[7] See *Journal of Business of the University of Chicago,* Vol. III (Oct. 1930) p. 417.

increase went on with heavier volumes but with signs of difficulties ahead. In 1930, with a national income of about $90 billion retail sales were $60 billion and sales on credit $30 billion.

During 1932 with total retail sales of $31.5 billion and sales on credit of around $15 billion we found our economic situation had gone back to about what it was in 1923 and 1924.

There is nothing fundamentally wrong with either the open charge-account system or with instalment buying. The $4,250 million of current debts for family purchases in these two categories at the end of 1932, can be called neither unsound nor unnecessary. Each debt is normally self-liquidating and is paid out of income. In general, the modern time-payment system has been beneficial to the American family, although in individual cases many families have gone more deeply into debt than they should. The evils of the modern credit system are not to be found in the debts themselves, but rather in the frequent lack of business and financial judgment on the part of both retailers and purchasers who get themselves into difficulties through lack of foresight.

This American system of getting into debt, like all economic situations, contains its own remedies and correctives. If a retailer overextends credit too freely, he will pay a penalty for it. But if his creditors are gained wisely, his net profits will increase. On the other hand, if a family goes too deeply or extravagantly into debt, it will suffer for it. But it also finds from experience that going into debt on sound principles has numerous advantages. Modern credit research is surveying and charting these problems, and the evils—if they are evils—are gradually being reduced or eliminated.

Personal Debts and Prosperity

According to the theories of Dr. Wesley C. Mitchell and Dr. Warren M. Persons, the business cycle generates itself. Each succeeding stage in the cycles of "depression, improvement, prosperity, decline, depression," grows out of the preceding stage. Should we adopt a *laissez-faire* policy toward the depression or should something be done? Some advocate "controlled inflation" but as yet no one seems to have a definite formula for what this remedy is.

Today there is a group of economists who say that the depression was partly caused by the fact that during the years 1926 to 1929, millions of families lived beyond their means, saved no money, and involved them-

selves thoughtlessly in debt. On the other hand, we hear it frequently
said that the way to end the depression is to get American families into
an orgy of extravagant living again, but this appears to be an admission
that the orgy of extravagant living from 1927 to 1929 was an economic
mistake.

There is no justification for any perverting of economic principles or
for false economic reasoning which neglects to base true prosperity on
the economic independence of each American family. It was Charles
Dickens who said many years ago:

Annual income twenty pounds, annual expenditure nineteen six, result
happiness. Annual income twenty pounds, annual expenditure twenty pounds
and six, result misery.

At the 1932 convention of the National Association of Mutual Savings Banks in New York City, the President of the association, Mr. Wil-
son C. Wing, said:

The kind of prosperity that we knew from 1921 to 1929 was largely based
upon a false assumption of future income. We were spending first and saving
later, and most of us tried to enjoy the expected benefits before the means
were at hand. Everyone was imbued with a sense of unwarranted optimism,
based upon false promises.
A sounder prosperity lies ahead through realization that we must save
before we spend.

After all, what is prosperity? Is it reckless spending and going into
debt or is it getting ahead in life? If we can define general prosperity as
that state of national economic welfare in which our individual American families are saving their money and piling up household surpluses,
then possibly, we are already laying the foundation for coming prosperity of greater stability than in the past.

Savings are Accumulating

The deposits in mutual savings banks increased from $9,465 million
on January 1, 1931 to $10,030 million on January 1, 1932, a gain of
$565 million. Again on January 1, 1933, the total was $9,970,947,424
showing an excess of $505 million over two years ago. During the same
period from December 31, 1930 to December 31, 1931, postal savings
increased from $243,795,000 to a total of $595,660,000. The total on
December 31, 1932 was $900,239,000.

In the September 15, 1932 issue of the economic bulletin of the Cleveland Trust Company is the following dictum from Colonel Leonard P. Ayres:

When the end of a prosperity comes, hundreds of thousands of people are heavily burdened with debts that have been lightly assumed. During the hard times that follow, these debts are steadily paid off, and savings accumulate. Eventually the savings predominate and seek active use, and recovery starts.

In a recent book entitled *"Business Adrift"* by Dean Wallace B. Donham of the Harvard Graduate School of Business Administration, the author says, in effect, that in a prolonged period of prosperity such as the one from 1924 to 1929, the great mass of people get to thinking that the prosperity will last indefinitely and forget their need for security in the future. In commenting on the period from 1921 to 1929, and on certain economic forces and factors which helped to bring about the depression of 1930 to 1933, he writes:

It should again be stated that this condition arose during a period when the great mass of our people engaged in industry and commerce had a very pronounced feeling of security, so that the competition of the want for security with the desire to possess automobiles and radios was abnormally low. The rapid extension of installment buying is evidence of this. I hazard the statement that unless the basis for security is greatly improved, a like condition will not recur during this middle period.

By "middle period" he means the next five to ten years. Of course the converse of this theory is that when depression and unemployment come, as they did during 1931 to 1933, the want for security will be uppermost in the minds of all those who still have employment so that they greatly reduce their standards of living in order to save money to build up reserves to give themselves a greater feeling of security.

In view of all these considerations, it is certainly justifiable to attempt to isolate the aggregate debts, both short-term and long-term of the American household, because if what Colonel Ayres, Mr. Wing and Dean Donham says is true, we must look to the condition of the basic indebtedness of American households to find some of the important signs which indicate that the business cycle is about to swing out of depression into the hoped-for period of gradual improvement.

This enormous business of the household, the largest business in the nation, with more than $100 billion invested in housings and household equipment, and managed by more than 23 million housewives, has more money invested and more people employed in it than all the rail-roads, oil wells and refineries, farms, steel industries, steamship lines, textile mills, chemical works and automobile factories in the United States.

The individual household is the basic unit in the economic structure,— more fundamental than retail stores, banks, railroads or factories. Every-thing begins and ends with the home. The household, by its activities, tends to augment the economic forces which bring about periods of im-provement, thus tending to lift us into prosperity and to accentuate and prolong prosperity; while, on the other hand, the household tends to make more precipitate a period of decline and to intensify and prolong a period of depression. The problem today is to balance the budgets of each individual American family unit so that each household will live on the average, within its income, and save a surplus, and make its own proportionate advancement in line with the general long-term improve-ment in our national economic condition and the gradual increase in our total national wealth.

Chapter Twelve

BANK DEBTS

Summary

The Facts

BANK debt, which is almost entirely short-term, is the most important type of internal debt because to an important extent it performs the function of money in the community. It amounted to $47 billion on June 30, 1932, of which $42 billion was debt to depositors including both time and demand deposits (pp. 328–30).

Time deposits accounted in June, 1932, for $25 billion or 60 per cent of bank debt to depositors. Demand deposits amounted to $17 billion or 40 per cent. The deposits in savings banks amounted to $10 billion or nearly 25 per cent of the total deposits while the remainder or $32 billion of deposits was in commercial banks. For these last, 79 per cent of the deposits were debt of banks which were members of the Federal Reserve System (p. 333).

Between 1913 and 1922, deposits of savings banks increased 46 per cent while those of commercial banks increased nearly 140 per cent. The latter increase was largely due to war-time financing and contributed to the extensive rise in prices during the period (pp. 335–36).

From 1922 to 1929 bank debt increased at a more normal rate, averaging about 4 per cent a year. In the seven years the deposits of savings banks increased from $6.3 billion to $9.6 billion while those of commercial banks increased from $31.6 billion to $44.7 billion. For the latter group of banks the increase was divided roughly between demand and time deposits, but as time deposits were very much smaller at the beginning of the period, they showed a larger per cent increase. The growth in time deposits of national banks was most marked (pp. 336–42).

Between 1929 and the summer of 1931, savings bank deposits continued to increase while those of commercial banks remained fairly constant during 1930, but declined in the first part of 1931 (p. 343).

In the eight months after June, 1931, over $10 billion, or 25 per cent of the commercial deposits of the country, disappeared or were destroyed, involving a major destruction of purchasing power. This "terrific bank liquidation" was a "general mass movement of unprecedented proportions" affecting all banks (pp. 343–44).

Bank debt remained fairly constant during the summer of 1932 and January, 1933, but fell violently in February and March before the moratorium, reductions in deposits amounting to at least 2.5 billion dollars in five weeks. Moratoria in states and nation postponed the further payment of bank debts to depositors (pp. 343–44).

The character of bank assets changed during the World War and after 1929, but remained relatively constant during the intervening years. In 1932, 61 per cent of bank assets was in loans as against 72.5 per cent in 1929 (pp. 345–46).

Between 1921 and 1929, 5,642 banks failed, or 20 per cent of all banks. They had deposits of $1.7 billion, or 3.7 per cent of total deposits. During 1930–32, 5,096 banks failed, or 24 per cent of the total number. Their deposits amounted to $3.3 billion, or 6.6 per cent of all bank deposits. Of all bank failures during 1921–32, 2,028 were member banks and 8,710 were non-member banks; of the suspended member banks, 1,609 were national banks and 419 were state banks. The bulk of the failures have been small banks in small towns (pp. 346–49).

Recommendations

To prevent further liquidation, it is recommended that the reserve banks create non-borrowed reserves by open market operations in sufficient quantity to make the outstanding volume at least equal to that in January, 1933 (p. 380).

To increase the willingness of banks to make loans or investments, it is recommended that the non-borrowed reserves in the banking system be increased considerably beyond the point at which further liquidation is halted (p. 381).

To increase the number of responsible borrowers, it is recommended that any new construction which is to be undertaken with the aid of the Reconstruction Finance Corporation be financed in the initial period by local borrowing from the banks to be underwritten by the Reconstruction Finance Corporation rather than by direct advances by that organization (pp. 382–83).

To obtain uniformity in banking rules, regulations, and inspection without fear of loss of banks to the system, it is recommended that all commercial banks be compelled to become members of the Federal Reserve System (pp. 383–84).

1. The Facts

B ANK debt is by far the most important single type of debt in the United States. In the form of obligations of banks to their depositors, bank debt makes up a large proportion of the money of the community. We have recently seen how vitally the community relies on this debt in the conduct of its daily business. The recent "bank holiday" placed in temporary abeyance the legal obligation of banks to pay their debts. The result was to bring many lines of business to a standstill and, if the holiday had been continued, it would have disrupted the whole of our business activity. Thus bank debt lies at the very heart of our economy and is perhaps its most sensitive element.

Bank debt is almost entirely short-term, and, though its magnitude would place it in the forefront of any general study of indebtedness, its importance in a study of long-term obligation lies less in its magnitude than in the influence which it has had in greatly increasing the burden of other forms of debt. As we trace through the changes in bank debt in the three years of the depression, it will become apparent how these changes have intensified the burden of debt in the community.

Total Bank Debt

The total indebtedness of banks on June 30, 1932, amounted to $47 billion. As Table 84 indicates, $42 billion of this represented debt to depositors. The following discussion will be almost entirely confined to this major item.

In considering this debt to depositors, it is necessary to break it up according to type of deposit, and according to type of bank. Deposits are usually classified either as demand deposits or time deposits. The first customarily represent debt which the banks are legally obligated to pay on demand or extremely short notice and consist almost entirely of checking accounts. Time deposits represent debt which the banks are legally obligated to pay only after notice of thirty days or more and usually consist of savings accounts.

It is also necessary to distinguish between time deposits in savings banks and time deposits in commercial banks. The former are of minor importance to this study since they do not perform the function of money. Time deposits in commercial banks, however, are so easily

TABLE 84

BANK DEBT IN THE UNITED STATES

Exclusive of the Debt of the Federal Reserve Banks
June 30, 1932

Total debt to depositors (bank deposits)(*a*)	$42,124,962,000
Debt due to banks(*b*).	3,755,070,000
Debt to Federal Reserve banks(*c*).	440,000,000
National bank notes(*d*).	652,168,000
Commercial debt(*e*).	319,017,000
Total bank debt.	$47,291,217,000

(*a*) Total deposits less "due to banks" (demand deposits) and time deposits of other banks. *Annual Report* of the Comptroller of the Currency, 1932, pp. 75, 76 and 77.

(*b*) "Due to banks" (demand deposits) plus time deposits and loans to banks. *Ibid.*, 1932, pp. 75, 76 and 77.

(*c*) Bills discounted by Federal Reserve banks. Federal Reserve *Bulletin*, December 1932, p. 749.

(*d*) *Annual Report* of the Comptroller of the Currency, 1932, p. 76.

(*e*) Bills payable and rediscounts less debt to Federal Reserve banks and loans to banks. *Ibid.*, 1932, pp. 75, 76 and 77. Also (*c*) above.

interchangeable with demand deposits that for some purposes they should be classified with the latter.

Differing Types of Banks

In distinguishing between types of banks, there are two important methods of classification which we can employ. First we can classify deposits according to the type of institution whose debt they represent, and second we can classify them according to the relation of the banks concerned to the Federal Reserve system. Table 85 shows the bank debt to depositors in 1932, distributed by the first method, and Table 86 shows the debt of banks doing a commercial banking business, distributed by the relation to the reserve system. Banks doing almost solely a savings bank business—having practically no demand deposits—are excluded from the second of these tables, as the Reserve system is primarily a commercial banking system.

Geographical Distribution of Banks

The geographical distribution of banks is given in Table 87. Figures are not available for the distribution of banks according to size but a fair indication can be obtained from the size distribution of national banks given in Table 88, and representing half the deposits of all commercial banks.

TABLE 85

DEBT OF ALL BANKS IN THE UNITED STATES, DISTRIBUTED BY TYPE OF BANK(a)

(As of June 30, 1932)

Type of Bank Charter	Number of Banks	Deposits (In Million Dollars)			Ratio of Deposits to Total Deposits of All Banks (Percentages)			Ratio of Deposits to Total Deposits of All Banks Except Savings Banks (Percentages)		
		Demand	Time	Total	Demand	Time	Total	Demand	Time	Total
Banks doing Commercial Business										
National Banks...........	6,150	$8,394	$7,266	$15,660	48.2	29.4	37.2	48.6	50.2	49.3
State Banks (commercial).......	10,455	3,206	4,210	7,416	18.4	17.0	17.5	18.5	29.2	23.2
Loan and Trust Companies........	1,235	5,697	2,988	8,685	32.8	12.1	20.6	32.8	20.5	27.3
Private Banks...........	227	20	21	41	.1	.1	.1	.1	.1	.1
Total Commercial Banks.........	18,067	17,317	14,485	31,802	....	....	....	100.0	100.0	100.0
Savings Banks										
Stock Savings Banks........	502	84	254	338	.5	1.0	.8			
Mutual Savings Banks........	594	4	10,035	10,039	.0	40.4	23.8			
Total Savings Banks..........	1,096	88	10,289	10,377						
Total...........	19,163	$17,405	$24,774	$42,179	100.0	100.0	100.0			

(a) Derived from *Annual Report* of the Comptroller of the Currency, 1932, pp. 76 and 77. Includes banks in Alaska and insular possessions. Time deposits include a small amount of time deposits due to banks which have been classified with debt due to banks in Table 84. California stock savings bank deposits are classed as time deposits of state commercial banks. See footnote, Table 90.

TABLE 86

DEBT OF ALL BANKS IN THE UNITED STATES EXCEPT SAVINGS BANKS, DISTRIBUTED BY RELATION TO FEDERAL RESERVE SYSTEM

(As of June, 1932)

	Member of Banks	Deposits (In Million Dollars)			Ratio of Deposits to Total Deposits of All Commercial Banks (Percentages)			Ratio of Deposits to Total Deposits of All Member Banks (Percentages)		
		Demand	Time	Total	Demand	Time	Total	Demand	Time	Total
Member Banks (a)										
New York City Banks(b)	36	$5,154	$803	$5,957	29.8	5.5	18.8	35.8	7.5	23.8
Other Reserve City Banks (62 cities)	340	5,433	4,599	10,032	31.4	31.7	31.5	37.7	43.2	40.0
Country Banks	6,604	3,826	5,261	9,087	22.1	36.4	28.5	26.5	49.3	36.2
Total Member Banks	6,980	14,413	10,663	25,076	83.3	73.6	78.8	100.0	100.0	100.0
Non-Member Banks (c)										
State Commercial Banks, Loan and Trust Companies and Private Banks(d)	11,087	2,904	3,822	6,726	16.7	26.4	21.2			
Total of all Commercial Banks	18,667	$17,317	$14,485	$31,802	100.0	100.0	100.0			

(a) Federal Reserve *Bulletin*, February 1933, p. 72. Figures are averages of daily figures during the month of June 1932.
(b) Central reserve city banks only.
(c) Derived by deducting deposits of all member banks (average of daily figures for June 1932) from deposits of all banks except savings banks (from Table 85) for June 30, 1932. The difference in character of two sets of figures introduces the probability of a small error in the figures for non-member banks. The discrepancy is unlikely to be important for the present discussion.
(d) California stock savings bank deposits classified as time deposits of commercial banks. See footnote, Table 90.

TABLE 87

GEOGRAPHICAL DISTRIBUTION OF BANKS AND BANK DEBT IN THE UNITED STATES, INCLUDING ALASKA AND INSULAR POSSESSIONS(a)

National Banks, Sept. 30, 1932. Other Banks, June 30, 1932

Geographical Division(b)	Commercial Banks				Savings Banks			Per Cent of Total
	National	State	Loan and Trust	Private	Stock	Mutual	Total	
New England	350	......	260	5	....	379	994	5.2
Middle Atlantic	1,517	392	578	42	1	179	2,709	14.2
East North Central	999	2,792	124	145	3	14	4,077	21.3
West North Central	1,033	2,986	122	22	456	2	4,621	24.2
South Atlantic	491	1,158	86	6	23	16	1,780	9.4
East South Central	293	1,019	......	2	4	....	1,318	6.9
West South Central	810	1,217	......	5	....	....	2,032	10.7
Mountain	265	442	16	......	3	....	726	3.7
Pacific	322	405	38	......	12	4	781	4.1
Alaska and Insular Possessions	5	44	......	......	....	....	60	.3
United States	6,085	10,455	1,235	227	502	594	19,098	100.0

DEPOSITS OF BANKS(d)
(In Millions of Dollars)

Geographical Division	Commercial Banks		Savings Banks		Total	Per Cent of Total Bank Deposits	Per Capita Deposits(c) (Number of Dollars)
	National	State, Loan and Trust, Private	Stock	Mutual			
New England	$1,476.5	$993.1	$....	$3,329.4	$5,799.0	13.7	$710.10
Middle Atlantic	5,610.5	7,249.1	26.3	6,103.1	18,989.0	45.0	723.09
East North Central	2,449.1	3,623.7	12.9	138.7	6,224.4	14.8	240.5
West North Central	1,231.2	1,266.2	108.1	62.7	2,668.2	6.3	200.66
South Atlantic	994.7	1,032.4	22.8	244.0	2,293.9	5.4	145.24
East South Central	443.2	379.5	3.4	......	826.1	2.0	83.55
West South Central	878.3	483.5	....	......	1,361.8	3.2	111.84
Mountain	337.3	229.0	19.4	......	585.7	2.0	232.59
Pacific	2,009.3	1,070.4	0	143.9	3,223.6	7.6	393.38
Alaska and Insular Possessions	30.8	176.0	......	......	206.8	.5	
United States	14,460.9	16,502.9	192.7	10,021.9	42,178.4	100.0	344.00

Table references, page 333.

Bank Debt in 1932

We can summarize the picture of bank debt in the summer of 1932 as follows. Debt to depositors, the largest and most significant part of bank debt, amounted to $42 billion. Twenty-five billion, or 60 per cent, of this debt consisted of time deposits, and was roughly divided between debt of savings banks, particularly mutual savings banks, and debt of banks doing both a saving and commercial business. Seventeen billion, or 40 per cent, of the bank debt to depositors consisted of demand deposits and was therefore subject to call at any time without notice.

Approximately half of this debt subject to demand was owed to depositors by national banks, while more than a quarter was debt of state chartered loan and trust companies, and the remainder was debt of state commercial banks and, to a negligible extent, the debt of private banks. Approximately 80 per cent of the debt, and 83 per cent of the demand debt, of these commercial banks was owed by banks which were members of the Federal Reserve System, though a host of small state commercial banks and trust companies were outside the system. With this picture of the major constituent in bank debt, we can proceed to examine the changes in bank debt which have taken place—first between 1913 and 1929, and then in the three depression years.

Changes Since 1913

The changes in the volume and character of bank debt during the last twenty years have been closely tied up with our business and political history. As Table 89 indicates, the total bank deposits more than doubled between 1913 and 1920. This very great increase can be directly attributed to war activity;—heavy increases in 1915 and 1916

(*a*) Bank figures—*Annual Report* of Comptroller of Currency, 1932, pp. 41, 42, 80, 92, 94, and 96.

(*b*) According to Census divisions.

(*c*) Population figures—15th Census of the U. S. 1930, Vol. I, p. 10.

(*d*) Totals for the various type banks in this table differ slightly from those given in Tables 85 and 86. This is due to the discrepancy in the call dates employed and to the type of figures reported by the comptroller of the currency. The data for State, Loan and Trust, and Private Banks were derived from the total of all banks as of June 30, less the figures for National Banks as of Sept. 30 and of savings banks as of June 30. The discrepancy resulting from the different dates is of minor importance so far as a general picture of distribution of bank deposits is concerned. California stock savings bank deposits are classified as time deposits of commercial banks. See footnote, Table 90.

TABLE 88

DEBT OF NATIONAL BANKS CLASSIFIED ACCORDING TO SIZE OF CAPITAL STOCK(a)

(As of December 31, 1931)

Size of Capital	Number of Banks	Total Deposits (In Million Dollars)	Proportion of Total Banks (In Per Cent)	Proportion of Total Deposits (In Per Cent)
Under $50,000..............	1,690	$452	26.5	2.3
50,000– 200,000.......	3,432	3,128	53.9	16.3
200,000– 500,000.......	814	2,446	12.8	12.8
500,000– 1,000,000.......	233	1,488	3.6	7.7
1,000,000– 5,000,000.......	168	3,411	2.6	17.6
5,000,000–25,000,000.......	29	3,139	.4	16.4
25,000,000–50,000,000.......	4	1,857	.1	9.6
Over 50,000,000............	3	3,325	.1	17.3
Total..................	6,373	19,245	100.0	100.0
Under $200,000............	5,122	3,580	80.3	18.7
200,000–5,000,000...........	1,215	7,345	19.1	38.1
Over 5,000,000.............	36	8,320	.6	43.2
Total..................	6,373	$ 19,245	100.0	100.0

(a) Derived from the *Annual Report* of the Comptroller of the Currency, 1932, p. 72.

as the banks helped to finance, first, the munitions manufacturers supplying weapons to foreign armies, and subsequently the war boom prosperity within the country resulting from the munition activity; similar rapid expansion in 1917, 1918 and 1919 as the American participation in the war called for extensive financing both for Allied and American purchases; and finally, a burst of expansion in 1920 as the post-war boom of that year called forth a further extension of bank credit. During the whole period over twenty billion dollars additional debt to depositors was incurred by the banks as they extended a roughly corresponding amount of credit to industry, governments and others. This rapid expansion—equivalent to nearly 12 per cent a year [1]—undoubtedly contributed in an important degree to the extensive rise in prices which is associated with the war period.

The depression of 1921 brought to an end the rising prices of the war period and introduced a long period of relative price stability lasting from 1922 to 1929 and ending with the present depression. During the years of relative stability the total bank debt continued to increase but at a rate more nearly in line with the country's underlying rate of economic growth. The reduction in bank debt in 1921 had been wholly

[1] Cumulative average.

reversed by the summer of 1922 and expansion of bank debt and credit continued until 1928 at rates ranging between 3.5 per cent and 8.8 per cent a year. Between June 1928 and June 1929 there was a slight drop in total bank debt. For the whole period from the boom year 1920 to that of 1929, the average rate of increase in bank debt was approximately 4 per cent. In the three years of depression, the volume of bank debt first increased slightly to an all-time high in 1930, then declined sharply in 1931 and precipitately in 1932.

TABLE 89

CHANGES IN DEBT OF ALL BANKS(a)

1913–1932

	All Banks		Savings Banks		Commercial Banks	
On or About June 30	Total Deposits (In Billion Dollars)	Change Over Previous Year (In Per Cent)	Total Deposits (In Billion Dollars)	Change Over Previous Year (In Per Cent)	Total Deposits (In Billion Dollars)	Change Over Previous Year (In Per Cent)
1913....	17.5	....	4.3	....	13.1	....
1914....	18.5	6.1	4.5	4.1	14.0	6.9
1915....	19.1	3.0	4.6	1.1	14.5	3.8
1916....	22.7	18.8	4.6	0.5	18.1	24.8
1917....	26.3	15.8	4.9	6.0	21.5	18.2
1918....	28.8	9.1	4.9	1.0	23.9	11.0
1919....	33.6	17.0	5.2	5.9	28.4	19.0
1920....	38.0	13.1	5.7	9.1	32.3	13.7
1921....	36.7	− 3.5	6.0	6.0	30.7	− 5.0
1922....	37.9	3.1	6.3	4.5	31.6	2.8
1923....	40.6	7.1	6.8	8.8	33.8	7.0
1924....	43.8	7.8	7.2	6.6	36.5	8.0
1925....	47.6	8.8	7.8	7.0	39.9	9.2
1926....	49.7	4.5	8.2	5.8	41.5	3.9
1927....	52.4	5.4	8.7	5.8	43.8	5.8
1928....	54.3	3.8	9.3	7.0	45.0	3.2
1929....	54.2	− 0.1	9.6	3.1	44.7	− 1.1
1930....	55.5	2.2	9.8	2.0	45.7	2.3
1931....	52.0	− 6.2	10.5	7.8	41.5	− 9.0
1932....	42.1	−19.1	10.4	− 1.5	31.8	−23.5

(a) 1913–1915 *Annual Report* of Comptroller of Currency, 1917, pp. 885–6. 1916–1920 *Annual Report* of Comptroller of Currency, 1920, p. 841. Other years in the corresponding Comptroller's Report. California stock savings bank deposits classed as time deposits of commercial banks. See footnote, Table 90.

In examining the changes in bank debt, we will consider separately five different periods, divided as follows: the war and immediate post-war period 1913 to 1922; the stable period 1922 to 1929; the early depression period 1929 to 1931; the period of great bank liquidation June, 1931 to June, 1932; and finally, the period beginning in June, 1932 and culminating in the national moratorium of March 4, 1933.

Each of these periods has different characteristics and a different significance for an understanding of the current problem of bank debt.

The Period 1913–1922

During the war period, 1913–1922, the major part of the great increase in bank debt was incurred in the growth of the commercial banks (see Table 89). The debt of savings banks increased between 1913 and 1922 only 50 per cent, while that of commercial banks increased 141 per cent. The absolute amount of the increase in commercial bank deposits was almost equally divided between demand and time debt (see Table 90), but as the time deposits were a small proportion of the whole in 1913, they showed a very much greater percentage increase, increasing over 300 per cent, while demand deposits increased only 86 per cent. In the same period, the national banks as a group showed the largest absolute growth in deposits, but the state commercial banks showed the largest percentage increase, their deposits almost tripling, while those of national banks doubled and those of loan and trust companies less than doubled. In 1913 national banks held 46 per cent of all commercial bank deposits and by 1922 they held only 43 per cent.

This decline in the relative position of the national banks was largely a result of the very growth in the time deposits of state commercial banks (including loan and trust companies), the growth amounting to something like six times (accurate figures are not available). However, if one considers only the demand deposits of commercial banks, the national banks somewhat more than held their own, increasing their proportion of the total from 50 per cent in 1913 to 51 per cent in 1922. The nine-year period also saw the development of the Federal Reserve System. Without any members in 1913, the system had developed by 1922 to such an extent (see Table 91) that 71 per cent of the deposits of all commercial banks and 80 per cent of their demand deposits were included in the system.

The Period 1922–1929

For the stable period from 1922 to 1929, we will first sketch the major changes in bank debt and then examine the more important of them in detail.

TABLE 90

GROWTH IN DEBT OF ALL BANKS IN THE UNITED STATES
DEMAND AND TIME DEPOSITS BY TYPE OF BANK(a)

1913–1932

(In Billion Dollars)

On or About June 30	Commercial Banks					Savings Banks		Total(a) All Banks
	National	State	Loan and Trust(a)	Time Deposits California Commercial Banks Not Subdivided	Total(a)	Stock	Mutual	
Demand Deposits								
1913.....	$ 5.1	$2.4	$2.6	$...	$10.2	$.3	$....	$10.5
1921.....	9.3	?	3.8	...	18.5	..	.2	18.7
1922.....	9.7	?	4.2	...	19.0	..	.1	19.1
1923.....	9.7	?	4.5	...	19.8	.1	....	19.9
1924.....	10.3	?	5.1	...	21.2	.1	....	21.3
1925.....	11.1	?	5.6	...	23.1	..	....	23.1
1926.....	11.4	?	5.8	...	23.9	.1	....	24.0
1927.....	11.6	6.4	6.8	...	24.9	.2	....	25.1
1928.....	11.6	6.3	7.3	...	25.2	.3	....	25.5
1929.....	11.1	6.3	7.4	...	24.9	.3	....	25.2
1930.....	11.8	5.8	8.1	...	25.7	.1	.1	25.9
1931.....	10.9	4.9	7.3	...	23.2	.1	....	23.3
1932.....	8.4	3.2	5.6	...	17.3	.1	....	17.4
Time Deposits								
1913.....	.8	.6	1.0	.4	2.9	.3	3.8	7.0
1921.....	3.7	?	2.0	.9	12.2	.4	5.4	18.0
1922.....	4.1	?	2.3	.9	12.6	.5	5.7	18.8
1923.....	4.8	?	2.4	1.1	14.0	.4	6.3	20.7
1924.....	5.3	?	2.7	1.2	15.3	.5	6.7	22.5
1925.....	5.9	?	3.0	1.3	16.9	.6	7.1	24.6
1926.....	6.3	?	3.1	1.4	17.7	.5	7.6	25.8
1927.....	7.3	6.7	3.7	1.1	18.8	.4	8.1	27.3
1928.....	8.3	6.6	3.9	1.0	19.8	.3	8.7	28.8
1929.....	8.3	6.6	4.0	.9	19.9	.3	8.9	29.1
1930.....	8.8	5.9	4.4	.8	19.9	.5	9.2	29.6
1931.....	8.6	5.1	3.9	.7	18.4	.4	10.0	28.8
1932.....	7.3	3.6	3.0	.6	14.5	.3	10.0	24.8
Total Deposits								
1913.....	6.0	3.1	3.6	.4	13.1	.6	3.8	17.5
1921.....	13.0	10.9	5.9	.9	30.7	.4	5.6	36.7
1922.....	13.8	10.2	6.5	.9	31.6	.5	5.8	37.9
1923.....	14.5	11.2	6.9	1.1	33.8	.5	6.3	40.6
1924.....	15.5	11.8	7.8	1.2	36.5	.6	6.7	43.8
1925.....	17.0	12.9	8.6	1.3	39.9	.6	7.1	47.6
1926.....	17.8	13.3	9.0	1.4	41.5	.6	7.6	49.7
1927.....	18.9	13.2	10.5	1.1	43.7	.6	8.1	52.4
1928.....	19.9	12.8	11.2	1.0	44.9	.6	8.7	54.2
1929.....	19.4	12.9	11.4	.9	44.7	.6	9.0	54.3
1930.....	20.6	11.7	12.5	.8	45.7	.6	9.2	55.5
1931.....	19.5	10.0	11.3	.7	41.5	.5	10.0	52.0
1932.....	15.7	6.8	8.7	.6	31.8	.4	10.0	42.2

(a) Derived from the reports of the Comptroller of the Currency for the respective years. The total deposits for the various types of banks have been reported regularly

Savings bank debt can be disposed of summarily. It increased rapidly (see Table 90) in 1922 and 1923 and steadily thereafter. The increase was at a rate of a little over 5 per cent a year. It is notable that the increase continued, though at a somewhat slower rate, through the speculative years from the summer of 1927 to the summer of 1929, suggesting that the speculative mania did not seriously affect savings bank depositors in so far as their savings were concerned.

The changes in commercial banks must be examined in more detail. The total commercial bank deposits increased in the seven years (June, 1922 to June, 1929) from 31 billion dollars to nearly 45 billion dollars, or 45 per cent. This growth was at the rate of a little over 5 per cent a year, a rate slightly faster than that usually employed as indicating the basic secular growth in the American economy.

That this rate of growth in commercial bank deposits is not out of line with growth in the years immediately preceding the war is indicated by the lines in Chart 27. The solid line shows the actual growth in the loans and investments of banks other than savings banks, a figure which we can treat as directly reflecting the deposits of such banks.

---

and can be regarded as reasonably accurate, with one major exception. In the California state reports on which the Comptroller relies in compiling his figures for state chartered banks, the time deposits of all state banks appear to be classed as deposits of stock savings banks. As the number of stock savings banks in California is very small compared to state commercial banks and loan and trust companies (11 against 183 in 1932) and as the stock savings banks are mostly small, the whole of the time deposits of California state banks (other than mutual savings banks) has been grouped with the deposits of commercial banks and in the totals is classed with time deposits of commercial banks. This introduces a very small error as a small part of these deposits is in stock savings banks.

In subdividing the total deposits between time and demand deposits reasonably accurate figures are available only in the last four years. In earlier years the reports for state banks contain an important item of "unclassified deposits." For national banks and for savings banks the unclassified item was negligible and has been included in time deposits. For loan and trust companies, the item was often considerable, representing as high as 46 per cent of the total deposits in 1925 but being negligible in 1913, 1921 and 1928. As the ratios between demand and time deposits were essentially the same in 1921, 1929 and for the average of 1929 to 1932 (respectively 33 : 67, 35 : 65, and 35 : 65) the total deposits were distributed between demand and time deposits according to the 1929–1932 ratio. This introduces an element of error for the 1921–1927 figures as there was a small increase in the proportion of time to demand deposits. The error does not exceed 2 per cent of the total deposits of loan and trust companies. For state commercial banks reasonably accurate figures were available for 1913 but not even approximate estimates could be made for the years 1921 to 1926. In 1927 and 1928 the unclassified deposits of state commercial banks were small and were arbitrarily allocated between time and demand deposits, thereby introducing an error, at the maximum of less than 3 per cent. In computing a total of the demand and of the time deposits of commercial banks, the total deposits of state commercial banks were arbitrarily divided between time and demand deposits according to the average ratio in the years 1929–1932. Such arbitrary action would be unjustified if we were to report such figures separately, but in the final total the error involved is minimized, being at the most an error of less than 5 per cent, with a high probability that the error is less than 2 per cent.

CHART 27

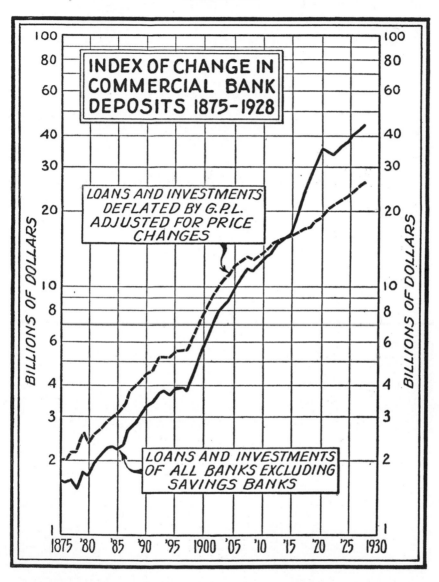

INDEX OF CHANGE IN
COMMERCIAL BANK
DEPOSITS 1875-1928

LOANS AND INVESTMENTS
DEFLATED BY G.P.L.
ADJUSTED FOR PRICE
CHANGES

LOANS AND INVESTMENTS
OF ALL BANKS EXCLUDING
SAVINGS BANKS

BILLIONS OF DOLLARS

TABLE 91

GROWTH IN DEBT OF COMMERCIAL BANKS

DISTRIBUTED IN RELATION TO FEDERAL RESERVE SYSTEM(a)

(In Billion Dollars)

June 30	Total Member Banks			Central Reserve City Banks			Reserve City Banks			Country Banks			Non-member Commercial Total(b)
	Demand	Time	Total	Demand	Time	Total	Demand	Time	Total	Demand	Time	Total	
1922	$15.2	$7.1	$22.4	$5.4	$.8	$6.2	$4.8	$2.3	$7.2	$5.0	$4.0	$9.0	$9.2
1923	15.4	8.3	23.8	4.8	.9	5.6	5.3	2.8	8.1	5.4	4.6	10.1	9.9
1924	16.5	9.2	25.7	5.7	.9	6.7	5.3	3.2	8.5	5.4	5.1	10.4	10.8
1925	18.0	10.4	28.4	6.3	1.1	7.4	5.9	3.7	9.6	5.8	5.5	11.3	11.4
1926	18.6	11.2	29.7	6.4	1.2	7.6	6.2	4.1	10.3	5.9	5.9	11.9	11.8
1927	19.0	12.2	31.2	6.8	1.4	8.2	6.2	4.5	10.7	6.0	6.3	12.3	13.5
1928	18.6	13.4	32.1	6.5	1.8	8.3	6.2	4.9	11.1	6.0	6.7	12.7	13.0
1929	18.9	13.3	32.3	6.9	1.6	8.5	6.2	4.8	11.0	5.9	6.8	12.7	12.4
1930	19.9	13.8	33.7	8.1	2.1	10.2	6.0	5.0	11.0	5.7	6.7	12.4	12.0
1931	18.0	13.5	31.6	7.2	1.8	8.9	5.7	5.3	11.0	5.1	6.5	11.6	10.0
1932	14.1	10.6	24.7	5.6	1.1	6.8	4.6	4.2	8.8	3.9	5.3	9.1	7.0

(a) Source: *Annual Reports* of Federal Reserve Board and Federal Reserve *Bulletin.*

(b) These figures were obtained by deducting total deposits of member banks from total deposits of all commercial banks (Table 89). Since the figures for member banks are presumably complete, any error in the figure for all commercial banks takes on a magnified importance in the figure for total deposits of non-member banks. Because of the differences in classification between time and demand deposits as reported by member banks and by state banks, it is not possible to segregate the time from the demand deposits of non-member banks.

The rate of growth in the years 1922 to 1927 is almost exactly the same as the rate of growth between 1908 and 1915. When the changes in price level are adjusted for, the lack of any abnormally rapid growth in commercial bank loans and investments is clearly indicated. In terms of commodities, the rate of increase in commercial bank portfolios was surprisingly steady, showing almost a straight line on the logarithmic chart for the twenty years from 1908 to 1927. The rate of growth was also very much slower than that during the periods 1875–1897 and 1897–1907. Thus it is clear that the growth in commercial bank debt in the eight years ending in 1929 was not at an abnormally rapid rate.

As in the war period, the time deposits of commercial banks increased in the stable period somewhat more rapidly than demand deposits. In the seven-year period the time deposits increased from 12.6 billion dollars to 19.9 billion, or at a rate of 7 per cent a year, while demand deposits increased only from 19 billion to less than 25 billion, or at a rate of 4 per cent a year. Presumably the more rapid rate of growth of time deposits was in part due to the ease with which commercial banks could reclassify deposits of customers and thereby gain the advantage of the lower reserve required by law. To the extent that such a reclassification took place, the more rapid increase in time deposits was not the result of a change in the fundamental character of the deposits but simply a product of a change in accounting practice and legal classification. If the deposits in 1929 were distributed on exactly the same basis that the 1922 deposits were distributed it is quite probable that the rate of growth of time and demand deposits in the period would be more nearly the same.

Growth of Time Deposits

When the total change in deposits of commercial banks is divided among the three major types of banks it is at once apparent that the abnormal increase in time deposits occurred almost entirely in the deposits of national banks. For both state commercial banks and loan and trust companies, the increase of demand and time deposits was practically the same during the seven years. Yet the time deposits of national banks more than doubled, while their demand deposits increased less than 15 per cent for the whole period. The per cent increase for each type of bank is given below:

TABLE 92

INCREASE IN DEPOSITS, 1922–1929

	Demand Deposits	Time Deposits(a)	Total Deposits
National banks............................	14%	102%	40%
State commercial banks......................	....	....	27%
Loan and trust companies...................	76%	74%	75%
All commercial banks....................	31%	58%	41%

(a) Exclusive of time deposits of California banks.

The above table also indicates that the deposits of state-chartered loan and trust companies showed the most rapid growth during the stable years, while the deposits of national banks grew less rapidly and those of state banks most slowly. The different rates of growth are reflected in the changed proportion of the types of banks at the beginning and end of the period. National banks held approximately the same proportion of all commercial deposits in 1929 as in 1922, but loan and trust companies had increased their share of all deposits from 21.4 per cent in 1922 to 26.1 per cent in 1929, a gain obtained almost entirely at the expense of state commercial banks.

As has already been indicated, the bulk of the deposits of commercial banks are held by member banks of the Reserve system. The changes in member and non-member bank debt to depositors are given in Table 92. The total debt of member banks increased 45 per cent in the seven years; demand deposits increased 25 per cent, while time deposits increased 85 per cent, so that the proportion of member bank deposits which were subject to payment on demand dropped from 68 per cent of total member bank deposits to 59 per cent. The relative position of the groups of large, medium and small sized banks did not change appreciably during the seven years. All groups increased their total debt to depositors. The smallest growth was shown by the non-member banks, which increased their deposits only 35 per cent. The large central Reserve city banks added 38 per cent to their deposits. Country banks added 42 per cent and Reserve city banks added 55 per cent, —the largest growth for any one group. The different size-groups all show the same more rapid growth of time than demand deposits, the central Reserve city banks showing the greatest discrepancy and the country banks the least.

The Period 1929–1931

In the first two years of the present depression, the savings banks continued to increase their debt to depositors (see Table 90). For commercial banks, however, an appreciable amount of bank liquidation took place.

The liquidation in this period was very unevenly distributed, being almost entirely a reduction in the deposits of state commercial banks. The deposits of national banks increased slightly (see Table 90) and those of loan and trust companies dropped slightly. The deposits of state commercial banks, on the other hand, were reduced by nearly 23 per cent.

When we examine the changes in the debt of commercial banks classified according to their relation to the Reserve system, it is apparent that the major liquidation was in small banks both member and non-member. In the first two years of the depression, the deposits of the big central Reserve banks increased slightly while those of the medium-sized Reserve city banks remained constant. On the other hand, the deposits of country banks and those of non-member banks (primarily small banks) declined very markedly, the former decreasing by over $1 billion or 9 per cent while the latter declined over $2 billion or 19 per cent.

The Period 1931–1932

The summer of 1931 ushered in a period of bank liquidation probably more rapid and more extensive than has ever before occurred in this country. In a period of eight months over $10 billion,[2] or practically 25 per cent, of the commercial bank deposits of the country disappeared from use or were destroyed. As the counterbalancing increase in currency in circulation was little more than $600 million, this meant that a major destruction of purchasing power took place. If we include the deposits of commercial banks as well as of currency in circulation as constituting the money of the community, then this liquidation destroyed over 20 per cent of the money which had been outstanding in 1931.

This terrific bank liquidation was not confined to any one particular

[2] Including $700 million deposits due by commercial banks to savings banks or to foreign banks, i.e., to banks outside the commercial banking system.

group of banks but was rather a general mass movement of unprecedented proportions. As Table 90 indicates, it affected national banks,
trust companies, and state commercial banks in a major degree, though
the last group suffered the heaviest liquidation, just as in the earlier
period it had been the only group to show important net liquidation.
The net reduction in deposits in each of these groups during the single
year June 1931 to June 1932 was as follows: [3]

National banks......................	19.5	per cent
Loan and trust companies..............	23.0	" "
State commercial banks..............	32.0	" "
Total commercial banks...........	23.4	per cent

The large and medium sized banks did not escape the liquidation as
they had in the earlier period, as their deposits were actually reduced
to a greater extent than those of country banks, though to a less extent
than those of non-member banks (see Table 91). The decline in the
deposits of these groups was as follows:

Central Reserve city banks............	23.6	per cent
Reserve city banks..................	20.0	" "
Country banks	21.5	" "
Non-member banks	30.0	" "
Total member banks............	21.9	per cent

The Period 1932–1933

Between the summer of 1932 and January 1933, the volume of bank
debt appears to have remained fairly constant, though complete figures
are not yet available. The deposits of the big New York banks increased
very greatly while those of Chicago central Reserve banks and those
of Reserve city banks remained constant and those of the country banks
declined considerably.

The first two months of 1933 saw a sudden burst of bank difficulties
culminating in the nation-wide bank holiday beginning March 6th.
January saw relatively little change, but in the four weeks from February 1st to March 1st, the deposits of New York City banks were reduced by over $1 billion while those of other reporting banks—mostly
large—were reduced by $800 million. Between March 1st and the bank
holiday there were further reductions in deposits amounting in the case

[3] Derived from Table 90.

of the New York banks to something like another half billion [4] and presumably a somewhat smaller reduction outside of New York— smaller because so many banks had already been closed by state bank holidays.

It is needless to say that such violent swings in the volume of bank debt—a debt which performs the function of money in the community —are of a thoroughly disorganizing nature. That the New York banks should lose or destroy nearly 25 per cent of their deposits in a five-week period is enough to indicate how sensitive to change bank debt may be. With such a reduction in debt already accomplished, and with the number of states in which bank holidays had been declared increasing daily, a holiday was declared in New York and in Illinois on March 4th and for the whole nation to take effect March 6th. The problem of bank debt to depositors had then become so acute that state and federal governments were prevailed upon to postpone the banks' legal obligations to their depositors by the declaration of these holidays, thereby postponing or preventing the insolvency which the necessity of meeting further debt to depositors would have brought in so many cases.

The Changing Assets of Banks

When the assets out of which this changing volume of bank debt must be paid are examined, it is apparent that their distribution between the two major categories, loans and investments, changed during the war and after 1929, but remained relatively constant during the intervening years. In 1914, 77.5 per cent of the portfolios of commercial banks consisted of loans and 22.5 per cent of investments. During the war, a large volume of government securities was added to the portfolio of commercial banks and became a permanent part of the earning assets of the system so that both in 1922 and 1929 28 per cent of the assets were investments. During the depression loans of all sorts have been greatly reduced, while large purchases of federal government securities have caused a net increase in investments even though investments other than governments have fallen. By the summer of 1932, 39 per cent of the earning assets of commercial banks consisted of investments, nearly 17 per cent being United States Government issues.

[4] The bank figures published since March 1st are incomplete and are difficult to interpret because of the new problems of classification brought by the new situation.

More detailed figures on bank assets show that loans on real estate and on securities increased relative to commercial loans of commercial bank portfolios. Though the relative increase in loans on real estate was great, these remained a small part of the total portfolio and hardly kept pace with the relative increase in time as against demand deposits of commercial banks. The depression brought a shift, both proportional and absolute, in portfolio distribution, as both commercial loans and loans on securities were liquidated while government securities were being purchased. Figures for the portfolios of national banks are given in Table 93.

Bank Suspensions

The difficulty in meeting bank debt, though greatly aggravated during the present depression, is no new phenomenon, as is shown by the long record of bank failures. In Table 94, the number of bank failures in recent years is indicated. Between 1921 and 1929 practically 20 per cent of the banks in the country were suspended, thereby locking up temporarily or permanently 1.7 billion dollars of deposits, or nearly 4 per cent of the average deposits of all banks during the nine-year period.

When the figures are broken up (Table 95) it is at once apparent that the bulk of the failures by number are those of very small banks. Seventy per cent of the failures were in towns with a population of under 1500 people, while two-fifths were in villages with less than 500 inhabitants. Clearly the very large number of failures reflects, to an important extent, these extremely small banks. More than 60 per cent of the banks failing had capital of less than $25,000.

Unfortunately, figures are not available to show what proportion of the deposits of failed banks was in these very small banks and what proportion in the larger ones, though it is apparent that large banks contributed an important part of the deposits of all closed banks since, in spite of the large number of very small banks suspended, the average deposits of suspended banks amounted to $300,000. A smaller proportion of national banks failed than state banks, while the state member banks showed fewer failures in proportion to their number than non-member banks. In the latter category nearly 25 per cent of the banks (open on the average during the period) were closed, thereby locking up 6.6 per cent of the deposits of non-member banks.

TABLE 93

NATIONAL BANKS(a)

DISTRIBUTION OF EARNING ASSETS

(In Billion Dollars)

On or About June 30	Loans	Investments	Total Loans and Investments	Investments U.S. Government Securities	Other Securities	Loans Loans on Real Estate	Loans on Stocks and Bonds	Other Loans Mostly Commercial
1914	$ 6.4	$ 1.9	$ 8.3	$ .8	$ 1.1	$ ..	$ 2.4	$ 4.0
1915	6.7	2.1	8.7	.7	1.3	.1	1.7	4.8
1916	7.8	2.3	10.1	.7	1.6	.2	2.2	5.4
1917	9.0	3.0	12.0	1.1	1.9	.2	2.3	6.5
1918	10.2	3.9	14.1	2.1	1.8	.2	2.6	7.4
1919	11.0	5.0	16.1	3.1	1.9	.2	3.4	7.4
1920	13.6	4.2	17.8	2.3	1.9	.2	3.1	10.3
1921	12.0	4.0	16.0	2.0	2.0	.3	2.7	9.0
1922	11.2	4.6	15.8	2.3	2.3	.4	2.9	8.0
1923	11.8	5.0	16.9	2.7	2.4	.5	3.0	8.4
1924	12.0	5.1	17.1	2.5	2.7	.5	3.1	8.3
1925	12.7	5.7	18.4	2.5	3.2	.6	3.7	8.4
1926	13.4	5.8	19.3	2.5	3.4	.7	4.0	8.7
1927	14.0	6.4	20.3	2.6	3.8	1.0	4.4	8.5
1928	15.1	7.1	22.3	2.9	4.2	1.3	5.1	8.7
1929	14.8	6.6	21.5	2.8	3.8	1.4	5.1	8.3
1930	14.9	6.9	21.8	2.7	4.1	1.5	5.5	7.9
1931	13.2	7.7	20.8	3.2	4.4	1.6	4.5	7.0
1932	10.3	7.2	17.5	3.3	3.8	1.6	3.2	5.5

Percentage of Total Portfolio

On or About June 30	Loans	Investments	Total	U.S. Govt	Other Sec	Real Estate	Stocks and Bonds	Other
1914	77.0	23.0	100.0	9.5	13.5	...	28.8	48.2
1915	76.5	23.5	100.0	8.8	14.7	1.7	20.1	54.7
1916	76.8	23.2	100.0	7.2	16.0	1.6	21.6	53.6
1917	75.0	25.0	100.0	8.9	16.1	1.5	19.4	54.1
1918	72.0	28.0	100.0	15.0	13.0	1.3	18.2	52.5
1919	68.6	31.4	100.0	19.7	11.7	1.1	21.4	46.1
1920	76.6	23.4	100.0	12.7	10.7	1.3	17.5	57.8
1921	75.0	25.0	100.0	12.0	12.5	1.7	16.8	56.5
1922	71.2	28.8	100.0	14.5	14.3	2.3	18.3	50.6
1923	70.0	30.0	100.0	15.9	14.1	2.7	17.7	49.6
1924	70.0	30.0	100.0	14.5	15.5	3.1	18.1	48.8
1925	69.0	31.0	100.0	13.7	17.3	3.5	19.9	45.6
1926	69.7	30.3	100.0	12.8	17.5	3.8	20.9	45.0
1927	68.6	31.4	100.0	12.7	18.7	5.2	21.8	41.6
1928	68.0	32.0	100.0	12.9	19.1	5.8	23.0	39.2
1929	69.0	31.0	100.0	13.1	17.9	6.6	23.8	38.6
1930	68.4	31.6	100.0	12.7	18.9	6.8	25.2	36.4
1931	63.2	36.8	100.0	15.6	21.2	7.6	21.7	33.9
1932	58.8	41.2	100.0	19.2	22.0	9.2	18.2	31.4

(a) Includes U. S. possessions.

Such a record of failures in a period free from serious depression suggests a basic fault in the banking system.

TABLE 94

BANK SUSPENSIONS(a)

	Number	Deposits (In Million Dollars)	Proportion of Total Banks at Middle of Year(b)	Proportion of Total Deposits at Middle of Year(b)
All banks:				
1921–1929	5,642	$1,722	19.8	3.7
1930	1,345	865	5.6	1.6
1931	2,298	1,692	10.4	3.3
1932	1,453	730	7.6	1.7
Member Banks:				
1921–1929	994	494	10.6	1.8
1930	187	380	2.2	1.1
1931	517	734	6.7	2.3
1932	330	270	4.7	1.1
	2,028			
National Banks:				
1921–1929	763	356	9.5	3.3
1930	161	173	2.2	.8
1931	409	439	6.0	2.3
1932	276	215	4.5	1.4
	1,609			
State Member Banks:				
1921–1929	231	138	16.5	1.3
1930	26	207	2.4	1.6
1931	108	294	11.0	2.4
1932	54	55	6.5	.6
	419			
Non-member Banks:				
1921–1929	4,648	1,228	24.3	6.6
1930	1,158	484	7.3	2.2
1931	1,781	958	12.4	4.7
1932	1,123	460	9.3	2.7
	8,710			

(a) Federal Reserve *Bulletin*, January, 1933, pp. 16 and 19. Also other tables in chapter for amount of deposits.

(b) For 1921–1929 base of percentage is average for the nine years.

During the three depression years, the volume of failures was greatly increased, particularly in the fall of 1931 and the first two months of 1932, i.e., in the six months prior to the creation of the Reconstruction Finance Corporation. In those six months, nearly 15 per cent of all the banks in the country were suspended while the volume of deposits of closed banks exceeded the volume in the nine years ending in 1929. In the three depression years, 20 per cent of the total banks in the country were closed, thereby involving over three billion dollars of

TABLE 95

BANK SUSPENSIONS BY SIZE OF TOWN OR CITY(a)

Population	Number of Suspensions			Per Cent of Total Suspensions		
	1921 29	1930	1931	1921 29	1930	1931
Less than 500...........	2,278	442	666	40.3	32.9	29.0
500– 1,000...........	1,133	278	402	20.1	20.7	17.5
1,000– 1,500...........	567	128	202	10.2	9.5	8.8
1,500– 2,500...........	537	137	225	9.5	10.2	9.8
2,500– 5,000...........	413	119	214	7.3	8.8	9.3
5,000–10,000...........	239	60	140	4.2	4.5	6.1
10,000–25,000...........	180	57	134	3.2	4.2	5.8
25,000 and over.........	295	124	315	5.2	9.2	13.7
Total..............	5,642	1,345	2,298	100.0	100.0	100.0
Under 1,500............	3,978	848	1,270	70.6	63.1	55.3
1,500–5,000............	950	256	439	16.8	19.0	19.1
Over 5,000.............	714	241	589	12.6	17.9	25.6
Total..............	5,642	1,345	2,298	100.0	100.0	100.0

(a) *Annual Report* of the Federal Reserve Board, 1931, p. 127.

deposits, or 6.5 per cent of the country's total deposits and a very much larger proportion of the deposits of commercial banks since few savings banks were closed. The increase in average deposits of failed banks from $300,000 in 1921–1929 to over $700,000 in 1931 indicates a greater increase in suspension of larger banks than of smaller ones. That the suspensions of large banks in 1932 were not greater is clearly to be attributed, to an important extent, to the activity of the Reconstruction Finance Corporation.

The actual loss to depositors does not amount to as large sums as the figures for bank suspensions would seem to indicate since many banks are subsequently reopened or, if they are not reopened, dividends are paid to depositors out of the proceeds of their liquidation. In the pre-depression period, approximately 60 per cent of the debt to depositors of closed national banks was finally paid, though in many cases only after long delay. Presumably, for the less well regulated state banks the proportion of loss is greater while during the depression the proportion of loss is greater for all banks. It is probable that the loss to depositors in the first three years of the depression was in the vicinity of two billion dollars,[5] at least half of which was incurred in the fall of 1931.

[5] Between $1.5 and $2.5 billion. No accurate estimate can be made.

The Problem of Depositors' Demands

That bank debt is a serious problem must be evident from these figures and from the national bank holiday and subsequent reopening of only part of the banks. The exact character of the problem which it presents is not so clear. Only as we have fully in mind the character of the banking system and changes in bank debt in recent years is it possible to perceive the true nature of the problem of bank debt.

On first thought it may appear that the problem of bank debt is one of arranging that the banks should be able to meet their debts whenever depositors make the demand. Yet a little consideration will make it clear that the banking system has not been organized to allow depositors *as a body* to demand payment of the debts owed to them by banks. Leaving out of account the banks only doing a savings business, the total deposits in the country amounted in 1929 to 45 billion dollars. Yet in that year the total gold stocks in the banking system amounted to less than 5 billion dollars. If the banks had been called on to pay their debt to depositors in gold they could have paid less than 12 cents on the dollar. If the depositors were willing to have the debt paid in currency then the banks could pay their debt with Federal Reserve notes which could be issued by the Reserve banks to the extent of $2.50 for every dollar of gold held as reserves against the note issue (plus certain other collateral) and with other forms of currency. By this means the banks could meet their debt at the very maximum only to the extent of 28 cents on the dollar. The desire of depositors to convert deposits into currency could not be satisfied to an extent greater than the total currency issuing power of the banking system. The banking system is thus fundamentally based on the assumption that all depositors will *not* attempt to convert their deposits into currency. In fact, the debacle in February and March, 1933, was precipitated by the demand for payment of less than five per cent of the total deposits in commercial banks.[6]

Currency and Deposits as Money

Even more important than the inability of the banks of the banking system to pay their debt to depositors in toto or even in major part by

[6] Between January 31 and March 8, 1933, $572 million of gold was withdrawn from the reserve banks and $1,490 million of federal reserve notes. Presumably an amount of gold and notes roughly corresponding were paid out to depositors by banks.

paying out currency, is the fact that, if they were periodically called upon to meet their debt en masse, the banking system as it is now constituted could not perform its function of supplying the bulk of the country's money. In order to understand this, it is first necessary to recognize the major role which bank deposits play as a form of money. Whenever a payment is made by check and that check is deposited without the withdrawal of currency, bank deposits have acted as a medium of exchange. The bookkeeping transfer of title to the debt of a bank by means of a check is comparable to the passing from hand to hand of a banknote. Both involve a form of bank debt, the note being a token of title to the obligation of a bank payable to bearer while the deposit is a bank obligation only to the registered owner of the deposit. Together bank notes and deposits constitute the larger part of the country's money and allow the community to carry on transactions with a minimum use of gold, silver or other forms of money. Of these two types of bank debt bank deposits are by far the more important part of our money supply. The total money in circulation in the United States during 1928 and 1929 averaged approximately $50 billion, and of this $45 billion, or nine-tenths were deposits or debt to depositors of commercial banks, as compared with less than $2.5 billion of bank notes and less than $2.5 billion of other forms of money in circulation. Commercial banks thus supplied approximately 95 per cent of the money for the country, most of it bank debt in the form of deposits.

As the banking system is at present organized, the total volume of money is particularly sensitive to the interchange of bank debt in the form of deposits and bank debt in the form of bank notes. An extensive withdrawal of deposits, i.e. the conversion of bank deposits into currency, tends to induce a contraction in the total money stock of the country by inducing extensive bank liquidation with the corresponding destruction of deposits. In ordinary times the two forms of money, currency and deposits, are freely interchangeable. The banks will cash checks, paying out currency and thereby reducing their debt to depositors, or banks will accept currency from depositors thereby increasing debt to depositors. Since currency is just as much money as are bank deposits, this interchange of deposits for currency or currency for deposits has no direct effect on the volume of money in the country and outside the vaults of the banks. The interchange may, however, have very important secondary effects. An extensive effort to convert deposits into currency may *induce* a destruction of deposits through wholesale liquidation. We have seen that there are definite limits to the extent to which deposits can be converted into currency. Within narrow limits the conversion of currency into deposits simply involves a shift from one type of money to another without any effect on the total volume of money. Beyond these limits, the conversion of deposits into currency—especially their conversion into gold—tends to reduce the reserves of the banking system and it is this which induces bank liquidation, with a corresponding destruction of deposits and reduction in the money stock of the country.

The Orgy of Bank Liquidation of 1931 and 1932

In the orgy of bank liquidation between the summer of 1931 and that of 1932, this effect is clearly suggested. During this period, net withdrawals amounted to only $1,180 million—$621 million [7] of currency withdrawn into circulation, and $559 million [8] of gold withdrawn for foreign account—yet the total decline in deposits was nearly $10 billion. A decline of over $8.5 billion of deposits resulted from factors other than withdrawals. Of this amount $1,421 [9] million could be accounted for by bank suspensions, but over $7 billion of bank liquidation would remain to be accounted for. An important proportion of this appears to be traceable to the repercussions growing out of the withdrawals of gold and currency.

In order to understand the indirect effect of the conversion of deposits into currency, it is necessary to examine first, the ways in which deposits are created and destroyed and, second, the role of reserves in the banking system.

How Deposits Are Created

Deposits are created (and destroyed) in three principal ways, involving respectively action by individuals or institutions other than the banks themselves, action by the banks, and the combined action of banks and individuals. The first of these ways is the one most commonly

[7] July 31, 1931, to March 31, 1932. Between July 31, 1931, and Dec. 31, 1931, $810 million of currency was drawn into circulation. Between Dec. 31, 1931, and March 31, 1932, $189 million of this was returned from circulation. Federal Reserve *Bulletins,* Oct. 1931, p. 595, and Jan. 1932, p. 11, and Aug. 1932, p. 484.

[8] Federal Reserve *Bulletin,* Aug. 1932, p. 486.

[9] Federal Reserve *Bulletin,* Feb. 1933, p. 77. Includes deposits of all banks suspended less deposits of banks reopened.

thought of—namely the incurring of a debt to depositors when people deposit currency [10] and the bank agrees to pay out on demand (or short notice) a corresponding amount of currency. The creation of deposits in mutual savings and stock savings banks in this country approximates this method.[11]

Our commercial banking system introduces two other methods whereby bank deposits are created or destroyed. A bank can create deposits, as it were, out of thin air—by making bookkeeping entries. This it can do by either of two methods. It can purchase securities—let us say government bonds—and pay for them with a check drawn on itself.[12] By this method the bank acquires securities and the seller of the bonds, on placing the check with the bank, acquires a deposit. Here there is no currency involved. The bank acquires the securities by simply making a book entry in favor of the seller. So long as the seller or his assignees rest content to possess a deposit with the bank, i.e., to have the bank indebted to them, no currency enters into the series of transactions. From the point of view of banking policy, it is only because the seller or someone to whom the title to the deposit is transferred (through the checking process) may force the debt to be paid in currency, that a bank has to have any currency at all in connection with such a creation of bank debt.[13]

In normal times the chance that a demand for payment in currency will be made is small and as a matter of banking practice only a relatively small reserve in currency or its equivalent needs to be kept. So long as the deposit is not destroyed by a withdrawal of currency it can exist alongside of deposits created by the first method and be indistinguishable from them. Both can perform the function of money in the community.

A bank can also create deposits by making loans. This process is in

[10] Currency is here used in the broad sense to include all forms of hand-to-hand circulating media. It does not include checks as these are only the "certificates of notification" whereby a change in legal title to bank deposits is facilitated.

[11] The most important difference is that in addition to receiving deposits of currency they also receive checks on commercial banks. The deposits in other banks to which they receive title by "collecting" the check serve the same purpose for a savings bank that currency serves.

[12] This transaction may be accomplished in several ways. For instance, the bank may make a loan to itself (or to a particular department in the bank) thereby creating a deposit, i.e., a debt to itself. By drawing checks on this account, the obligation is transferred from a debt to itself to a debt to an outsider. So far as the world outside the banks is concerned, the deposit is created, i. e., added to the debt of the bank, when the purchase of the securities occurs.

[13] Of course, the state may, and usually does, step in and require a legal reserve against such deposits.

essentials similar to that involved in the creation of deposits by security purchase. The bank, in making a loan to a customer, simply credits the customer with an amount in his deposit account. The borrower gives his note to the bank and in exchange the bank becomes indebted to the borrower or to his assignees. The newly created deposit in the name of the customer is as good in the purchase of commodities as is the deposit created by the direct placing of currency with a bank. By drawing checks against it he can normally pay for purchases quite as well as if he held currency. Here also the deposits created without any deposit of currency are indistinguishable from those created by means of a placing of currency with a bank and can equally perform the function of money.[14]

How Deposits Are Destroyed

Just as deposits can be created by the three methods considered above, so they can be destroyed by three methods involving action the reverse of the above. An individual can demand that a bank pay its debt to him in currency and the process of this deposit withdrawal destroys the deposit. The bank can sell securities in its portfolio to persons to whom it is indebted, that is, who have deposits with it, and thereby reduce its debt, with the corresponding reduction in deposits. Finally, a borrower at a bank can destroy deposits in it by repaying his loan with a check drawn against his own deposit account with the bank. In each case, just as a bank incurs a debt when a deposit is created, so a bank reduces its debt when a deposit is destroyed.

Since debts created by these three means become indistinguishable in the accounts of the bank, their importance lies in the difference in initiation and control. A bank has slight control over the action of individuals in creating or destroying deposits by means of currency deposit or withdrawal. Over the creation of deposits or their destruction by purchase or sale of securities, the bank has almost complete control, so long as there is a continuous market. The expansion or contraction of deposits through bank loans is the resultant of the interaction of bankers and borrowers and is not under the primary control of either.

It is in these last two methods of deposit destruction that we must find an explanation of the disappearance of the $7 billion of deposits not

---

[14] It should be noted that the so-called "deposit" of checks with a commercial bank does not create deposits except as the particular bank extends credit to its depositor as a matter of convenience. The checks only transfer title to deposits already created from one person to another.

accounted for by currency and gold withdrawals or by bank failures in
1931–1932.

Presumably this amount was destroyed, (1) by the action of the banks
in selling securities, (2) by the action of the banks in forcing the repayment of loans without making any corresponding new loans, or
(3) by the willing repayment of loans by borrowers who no longer
needed the funds, combined with the inability or unwillingness of banks
to make new loans.

We can at once attribute the destruction of something like $2 billion
of deposits to the direct action of commercial banks. In the eight-month
period from June 30, 1931, to March 31, 1932, these banks appear to
have reduced their portfolios through the sale of securities to the
extent of at least this amount.[15] The remaining drop must be attributed to the reduction of loans either as the banks forced repayment or
were unable to find safe borrowers to whom to lend when other borrowers repaid their loans. It seems probable that part of this loan liquidation was due to each cause. The selling of investments in a period
when security prices, particularly bond prices, were at sacrifice levels certainly suggests that the banks were under heavy pressure to liquidate and
that part of this pressure would take the form, on the one hand, of forcing repayments of loans and, on the other hand, of raising the standard
by which a prospective borrower was measured.

The Struggle for Reserves as Liquidation Pressure

What, then, was the pressure which forced banks to sell securities at a
heavy loss, which made them refuse to extend loans, which doubled and
tripled short-term interest rates and which could justify the application
of the term panic? Any answer to this question must necessarily be tentative. Only extensive study of the period will allow any conclusive
answer to the problem of causal relationships involved in this liquidation. Yet the major changes during the period can be made to fall into
such a clearly intelligible pattern by the introduction of a single causal
factor, that there is a high probability that this factor is itself at the

---

[15] The investments of all commercial banks dropped between June, 1931, and June,
1932, by $1,536 million. As the investments of reporting member banks (report-
ing little more than half of all commercial bank portfolios) increased by $622
million between March and June (Federal Reserve *Bulletin*, April, 1932, p. 235 and
July 1932, p. 427), it is probable that in March the investments of all commercial
banks were at least $2 billion below the June, 1931, figures. More accurate figures are
not available.

root of the liquidation. This factor was the depletion and fear of further depletion of bank reserve by the withdrawals of gold and currency which precipitated *a struggle between individual banks for the reserves remaining within the system.* To understand this struggle—a struggle the character of which was by no means evident to the participants—we must examine the rôle of bank reserves.

Since bank deposits are, or are treated as, obligations to pay currency on demand, a bank must maintain a reservoir out of which to draw such currency. Reserves are not earning assets and consequently it is to the interest of bank owners, for whom banks are private, profit-making enterprises, to keep the volume of reserves as low as possible. Depositors, on the other hand, require large reserves for the safety of their deposits. In the absence of law, the reserves would be determined by banking policy, with conservative bankers maintaining an adequate, and speculative bankers an inadequate volume. Prior to the Federal Reserve Act, the law had stepped in to raise the volume of reserves of all banks to levels more nearly comparable to those maintained by conservative bankers, though in many states the levels were far from adequate.

With the introduction and development of the Federal Reserve System, a curious change in reserve requirements was made, the implications of which do not appear to be fully realized. First the reserves of member banks were centralized in the twelve Federal Reserve banks, each bank depositing with the Reserve bank its currency reserves, except for a small amount of till money, and the legal requirements were altered to allow deposits with the reserve bank to count as legal reserves. In fact, they came to be the only form of legal reserve. For many reasons not germain to the present discussion, this centralizing of bank reserves greatly increased the flexibility of the banking system. At the same time, the deposits with the reserve bank were a very adequate reserve for a member bank. They could be converted into currency almost at a moment's notice and, so far as the member bank was concerned, were practically as good as currency in its vaults. They served the practical banking need which had formerly been served by currency reserves in the bank's own vaults, though the bank had to provide itself with till money in addition, an amount of currency which also performs the practical function of reserves at the present time, though no longer a part of the legal reserve.

"Borrowed Reserves"

If this centralization of reserves had been the only step taken with respect to reserves when the Reserve system was developed, the situation would have been little altered.[16] Actually, however, a second change was made which largely nullified the protection to depositors contained in the legal reserve requirement. A member bank was allowed to borrow from its Reserve bank on suitable collateral and to keep the proceeds of the borrowing with the Reserve bank *as part of its legal reserve*. This means that part of the legal reserve of a member bank may be borrowed reserve, or entirely fictitious in so far as practical banking is concerned. Under the new arrangement the effect, from the point of view of the protection of depositors, was the same as if the law had said to the banks, *you do not need to keep any specified amount of reserves either in currency or with your reserve bank, but, to the extent that your reserve falls below a certain ratio to your deposits you will pay a very small fine—the discount rate—on the difference and you must place with the authorities certain types of high-grade assets to the extent of the deficiency.* To the extent, then, that banks have "borrowed reserves," to that extent they have a smaller volume of reserves of the type which constitute a highly liquid bank asset and correspondingly contribute to bank saftey than conservative banking practice and the higher standard bank laws had allowed.[17]

This ability to borrow fictitious reserves to meet the legal reserve re-

---

[16] For the present purpose the lowering of the reserve ratio legally required is not of importance. It corresponded to the increased flexibility of reserves and was to some extent counterbalanced by the fact that till money, formerly included in the legal reserve, was no longer so included.

[17] It may be claimed that the borrowed reserves are reserves equivalent to currency, like any other reserve, since they can be converted into currency which can be paid out to depositors. This would seem to place the emphasis in the wrong place. If a bank has 5 cents in non-borrowed reserve with the reserve bank back of every dollar of deposits and is also in a position to borrow 5 cents in currency from it, its position is as good as if it has 10 cents in reserves, half of it borrowed. Likewise a bank with 10 cents in clear reserves with the reserve bank and also the power to borrow from the reserve bank is in a better position in so far as the depositors are concerned than one with 5 cents in reserve and also the power to borrow. In all cases, it is the *power* to borrow currency from the reserve bank, i.e., to quickly convert certain assets into currency, which is important in each case. This power (to rediscount) undoubtedly made the system of banks more flexible when the Federal Reserve System was developed and possibly therefore justified a lowering of reserve ratios. The borrowing of reserves adds nothing to the position of the borrower except, one, the meeting of the legal requirement and, two, the imposition of the small interest charge acting as it were as a fine. The depositors' position is not improved.

quirement, made it possible for the less conservative banks to get along in good times with as little reserves, other than borrowed reserves, as they liked and opened the way for the creation of bank debt with as little non-borrowed reserve back of it as that which, in earlier days, received the popular name of wild-cat banking. In considering the changing condition of bank debt, we must therefore examine the changes in reserves, not in terms of total reserves but in terms of borrowed reserves, on the one hand, and non-borrowed or what we will call clear reserves—those clear of a corresponding debt to the Reserve Banks—on the other. And our attention must be riveted primarily on the clear reserves.

Meaning of Clear Reserves

Because the term "clear reserves" will be used frequently in the following pages, it is necessary to give it precise definition. The term "clear reserves" is used here to indicate the deposits held by member banks in a Federal Reserve bank which are not counterbalanced by an equivalent indebtedness to the Reserve bank. Thus, for a single bank, its clear reserves would be its total reserves with the Reserve bank less its borrowings from the Reserve bank. For a group of banks the clear reserves should be the sum of the clear reserves of the separate banks. Unfortunately, the figures published by the Reserve banks do not make it possible to derive such totals. Therefore, when a group of banks is being considered here, the clear reserves of the group will be taken as the total reserves of the group less the borrowings from the Reserve banks by the group. In most cases this would give essentially the same figure as the sum of the clear reserves of the separate banks in the group. The importance of clear reserves as a separate category will become apparent as we proceed.

The Flow of Clear Reserves

The total volume of clear reserves on deposit with the Federal Reserve banks is subject to change as a result of three major independent influences:[18]—(1) a change in the currency in circulation within the country as a result of hoarding or increased business need for currency including that resulting from the closing of banking facilities; (2) a

[18] Among minor influences are changes in the volume of government deposits with the reserve banks—an increase decreasing the reserves available to member banks; changes in the deposits of foreign banks; changes in the currency holdings of member banks.

flow of gold into or out of the monetary system as a result of gold import and export,[19] new gold production, or the flow of gold into or out of the arts; and (3) the creation or destruction of reserves by the open market operations of the Reserve banks themselves. As currency or gold flow into the banks, they are redeposited with the reserve banks, thus creating clear reserves for the depositing banks.[20] The deposits created by open market operations of reserve banks arise from the payment for purchases of bills or securities by the Reserve banks.

In addition to being subjected to the influences which affect the reserves of the banking system as a whole, the reserves of individual banks may be shifted among members of the system with no net effect on the total clear reserves of the whole system. This can be brought about in many ways, of which the four most important are (1) the normal flow of funds between banks as a result of the shifting currents of business, (2) the action of individuals in transferring their deposits from one bank to another in the system, presumably for reasons of safety, (3) the building up of deposits by one bank in another bank in the system, and (4) the expansion or contraction of loans and investments by particular banks. The first of these we may disregard since in the course of the normal banking business there is a rough tendency for the flow of funds to cancel out ever periods of time. The transfer of deposits from one bank to another involves a transfer of title to clear reserves from one bank to the other. So far as the first bank is concerned, this process is just as effective in reducing its clear reserves as would be the withdrawal of deposits in the form of currency.

Deposits of one bank in another bank are frequently built up, especially in the central Reserve city banks, as a form of secondary reserves. These deposits are usually acquired when one bank has a favorable balance of clearings against another bank [21] and, since they are subject to

[19] Changes in earmarked gold are here included as part of the import and export of gold.

[20] For purposes of simplicity we are excluding the influences of changes in national bank notes in circulation. To the extent that their volume changes, the volume of currency outstanding can change without any corresponding change in clear reserves. The actual changes in volume outstanding in recent years have been relatively small, except as they have involved a corresponding reduction in other forms of currency outstanding.

[21] That is, one bank has a larger amount of checks drawn against some other bank and placed with it for collection than the amount of checks drawn by its depositors against it and placed with the other bank for collection. On balance the second bank is in debt to the first. If the other does not require the payment of this debt by the transfer of clear reserves, it has a deposit or, as it appears in the published figures, a "due from banks" to its credit.

withdrawal at a moment's notice, they are in ordinary times almost as good as clear reserves. Under normal banking conditions, they can be converted into clear reserves without delay. For the profit-seeking bank they have the advantage that interest is usually paid on them, whereas clear reserves are not an earning asset. As we shall see, these secondary reserves are by no means equivalent to clear reserves in so far as meeting withdrawals by depositors is concerned.

The fourth process by which a shift in clear reserves between banks is brought about is through the expansion or contraction of loans and investments by a particular bank. It is primarily through this control of the volume of earning assets that a particular bank attempts to maintain its reserve position. An increase in a bank's loans and investments tends to cause its clear reserves to be drawn off into other banks as a result of adverse clearings, while a reduction of its portfolio tends to bring in clear reserves from other banks.[22]

Simultaneous Liquidation

It is important to note, however, that if all banks expand or reduce their portfolios equally and simultaneously, there will tend to be no loss or gain of reserves for any particular bank. For instance, if one bank reduces its portfolio in order to replace its depleted reserves or meet a debt to the Reserve bank and other banks are doing the same thing, the first bank may gain reserves only to lose them immediately to other banks as their liquidation brings reserves to them at the expense of the first bank. Only as a bank liquidates faster than other banks in the system would it be able to add to its clear reserves. If there were a wholesale bank liquidation in process, even the banks liquidating more rapidly

[22] The process in simplified form is as follows:—Suppose that Bank A finds its clear reserves below what it regards as a satisfactory level. It thereupon sells a security to Mr. B. who has a deposit account with Bank B. Mr. B. pays for the security with a check drawn on Bank B. Bank A sends the check through the clearing house and obtains a favorable balance due from Bank B, which it proceeds to collect. Bank B transfers to Bank A part of its clear reserves, and removes from its books the deposit in the name of Mr. B. The net effect of the sale of the security on Bank A would be to reduce its clear reserves. The net effect of the sale on Bank B would be to destroy part of its deposits and to remove part of its clear reserves. On the banking system taken as a whole, the effect of the sale is to decrease the total deposits in the system and to decrease total loans and investments. If Bank A sold the security to one of its own depositors it would not, of course, add to its clear reserves, but would simply destroy part of its deposits as it accepted a check on itself in payment for the security. A reduction of bank loans has an effect corresponding to that of the sale of a security, though the process is somewhat more complicated. Needless to say, the purchase of securities and the expansion of loans have the opposite effect.

would be likely to lose this advantage shortly as the laggard banks speeded up the calling of loans and sale of securities in an effort to counterbalance the adverse clearings which were daily being chalked up against them at the clearing house and tending to reduce their clear reserves and force them into debt to the Reserve bank.

Clear reserves appear to act as one of the major factors of control in the banking system. The action of any individual bank with respect to expanding or reducing its earning assets and correspondingly its deposits is a product of a wide variety of factors,—the various rates of interest, the discount rate, the temper of the business community, the quality of the bank's own assets, the demands for credit from its regular customers, the fluctuations in its clearing-house balances—favorable or adverse— and a host of other factors. Among the more important of these factors is the state of the bank's reserves and its borrowings from its Reserve bank. If adverse clearings have forced the bank heavily into debt to the Reserve bank,—i.e. very greatly reduced the bank's clear reserves,— it will tend to contract its loans and investment. Per contra, if in normal times it is receiving favorable clearings and is therewith reducing its debt to the Reserve bank or building up excess reserves,—i.e. clear reserves in excess of the legal reserve requirement—then it will tend to expand its portfolio. It should be noted, however, that in ordinary banking practice, instead of considering the usual banking situation as one involving clear reserves it is customary to center the attention on the legal reserve requirement and to discuss a particular situation in terms of debt to the reserve bank or excess reserves. Therefore, it is customary to say that expansion or liquidation is controlled in part by the borrowing at the Reserve bank and that it is in part regulated by the discount rate. While this last is undoubtedly true, the banker's *desire to hold clear reserves,* that is, his desire not to be indebted to the Reserve bank to the full amount of his legal reserve requirements, or his desire to hold excess reserves, appears to be the more basic fact through which the discount rate operates. Clear reserves perform the fundamental banking function of control that gold would have performed in the country before the development of the Reserve system *if there had been no legal reserve requirements.* As a banker would have had to hold a reserve of gold for the purely banking purpose of being in a position to meet demands and to have a measure of leeway, so today he holds clear reserves for this purpose,—an amount lessened by the fact that he can borrow from the Reserve bank to meet withdrawals or adverse clearings but an amount subject to the same desire on the part of bankers to hold that would exist with respect to gold in a banking system lacking both a central banking arrangement and legal requirements as to reserves.

The desire on the part of the bankers to hold clear reserves as part of the assets of their banks appears to meet a deep-seated desire to maintain a portion of the bank's assets in a highly liquid condition. The persistence with which important banks have maintained extensive excess reserves "in order to be in a liquid condition" is evidence of this. It appears to be a desire which increases with an increase in business uncertainty and in a time of bank runs and suspensions. Furthermore, it appears to be a desire which may result in extensive bank liquidation, if it is not met.

Consider what would happen if a widespread desire for greater liquidity were to arise and express itself in part in the desire for increased holdings of clear reserves while the clear reserves in the system remained constant. Since a bank normally adds to its clear reserves by reducing its portfolio the desire for clear reserves would translate itself into extensive liquidation as one bank tried to draw clear reserves away from other banks and in a parallel process of liquidation the latter took steps to prevent a loss in clear reserves. In such a situation, and so long as the desire to increase clear reserves persisted while the amount of clear reserves in the system remained constant, one would expect wave after wave of liquidation to succeed each other, a break in high-grade security prices as millions of dollars of government and other "blue ribbon" bonds were forced on the market, a drastic curtailment of business as loans were called and even the best grade of prospective borrower put off from day to day. In such an hypothetical situation one can see bankers throughout the country trying to decide what to sell next, daring to refuse extension of credit to some of their best customers, and wondering what is to stop the deluge of liquidation. Here is a type of bank liquidation which could arise entirely within the banking system and solely from the effort of banks to increase their holdings of clear reserves.

A similar type of liquidation would result from any insufficiency of reserves in the system, whether due to an increased desire of some banks to hold additional reserves or from a depletion of total clear reserves in the system, or from a combination of both.

Efforts of banks to increase or maintain a given level of reserves are dependent upon what, in different circumstances, they regard as adequate protection against the demands which are likely to be made upon them. We have already suggested that the proportion of clear reserves to deposits is no longer controlled by law in the case of member banks in the Reserve system. In times of normal business and high interest rates the banks of the country taken as a whole appear to regard the legal reserve requirement as unnecessarily high. In 1928 and the first part of 1929, the clear reserves of member banks as a body varied between 55 and 66 per cent of the "reserves" required by law, while the remainder was made up of the fictitious (but quite legal) borrowed reserves. The figures during the depression, however, very clearly suggest that in times of uncertain business conditions, and particularly in times of extensive bank runs, the measure of what constitutes a conservative holding of clear reserves is revised upward. As banks attempt to increase the liquidity of their position, or to maintain it as some banks become less liquid, it is reasonable to expect them to add to their clear reserves, their most liquid asset, —at the expense of their earning assets—a shift made less hurtful to their earning capacity because of the low rates of interest usually prevailing in such times on the most liquid types of loans and securities. The available figures also suggest that in uncertain times the legal limit has a certain psychological advantage as a standard. Banks appear to be particularly loath to show debt to the reserve banks on their balance sheets.

The Record of Clear Reserves

In examining the figures of clear reserves we will take up:—first, the changes in total clear reserves in the Reserve system and the causes of change during the last three years; second, the distribution and shifting of clear reserves between banks in the system; and finally we will consider the extent to which the changes in clear reserves and the bank liquidation of the three years of the depression might be interpreted as representing liquidation of the type just described and atributable primarily to the action of the banks themselves as they destroyed deposits in a vain effort on the part of some to increase their own liquidity and on the part of others to maintain their own solvency.

The changes in total clear reserves in the banking system are shown in Chart 28, along with an indication of the major elements causing change. From the summer of 1929 to that of 1930, the clear reserves in the system increased steadily from a low of $1,243 million in July, 1929, to

CHART 28 ᵃ

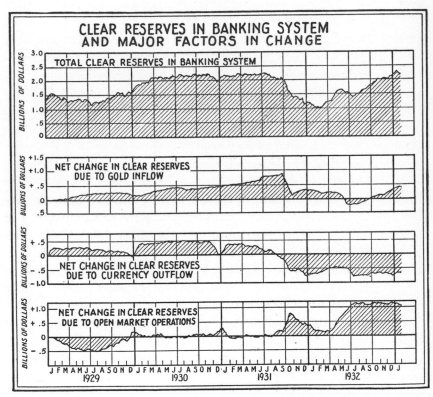

CLEAR RESERVES IN BANKING SYSTEM
AND MAJOR FACTORS IN CHANGE

ᵃ Figures derived from Federal Reserve *Bulletin*. Gold inflow indicates changes in "monetary gold" and is therefore only an approximate index of the changes in clear reserves due to gold flow.

$2,183 million in July, 1930. Of this increase of clear reserves, approximately $200 million came as a result of gold flowing into the country, $200 million came from a reduction of currency in circulation, and $500 million was the net result of the open market operations of the Federal Reserve banks.

As Chart 29 indicates, the first of the clear reserves which thus came into the system were held by the big New York and Chicago banks, which proceeded to build their clear reserves up to the legal line, thereby freeing themselves from debt to the reserve banks. By February, 1930, both groups were practically out of debt to the latter. In the same period, both reserve city banks and country banks were building up their clear reserves, i.e., getting out of debt to the reserve banks, but it wis not until August, 1930, that the Reserve city banks were virtually clear. The country banks as a group were never clear. In the summer and fall of 1930, between 20 and 25 per cent of their reserves were borrowed.

From the summer of 1930 to that of 1931, and except for the seasonal shift in December, the volume of clear reserves in the system remained fairly constant, as did their distribution throughout the system. (See Chart 30.) During the year there was a net inflow of gold of approximately $400 million but the currency in circulation increased by $300 million, so that the net addition to clear reserves from these two influences was only $100 million. The volume of clear reserves growing out of the open market operations of the reserve banks showed no appreciable net change.

The Effects of Europe's Difficulties

In June of 1931 a new element entered into the picture. Serious financial difficulties in Europe developed both in connection with war debt payments and with respect to important central European banking houses. These resulted in heavy draining of gold from Germany, the one year moratorium on war debts, the standstill agreement with respect to German short-term borrowings, and finally the severing of the relation between sterling and gold in September, 1931.

The unsettling effect of these events on the banking system of this country was reflected in an unseasonal increase in currency in circulation of $120 million, an inflow of gold of slightly larger proportions and a marked increase in the clear reserve of the big New York and Chicago banks. By August the clear reserves of these banks were increased over

CHART 29

Ratio of Clear Reserves to Legal Reserve Requirement

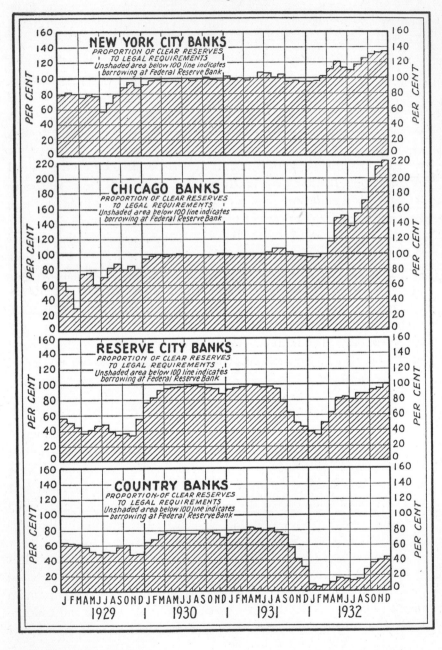

CHART 30

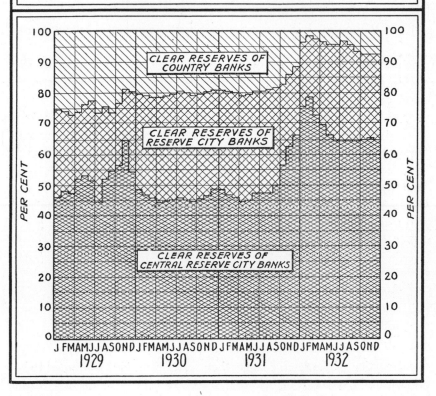

PERCENTAGE DISTRIBUTION OF CLEAR RESERVES
IN BANKING SYSTEM 1929-1932

CLEAR RESERVES OF
COUNTRY BANKS

CLEAR RESERVES OF
RESERVE CITY BANKS

CLEAR RESERVES OF
CENTRAL RESERVE CITY BANKS

PER CENT

PER CENT

J FMAMJJASOND J FMAMJJASOND J FMAMJJASOND J FMAMJJASOND
1929   1930   1931   1932

the legal limit by 5 and 10 per cent respectively, presumably reflecting the judgment of bankers that because of the unsettled conditions, increased reserves were now necessary for safety. In that same month the usual seasonal increase of currency in circulation occurred and its effect on the total volume of clear reserves in the system was counteracted by the open market operations of the reserve banks. Then, in the latter part of September the storm broke. England went off the gold standard on September 21st. In the six weeks which followed, the banking system of this country lost $724 million of clear reserves through gold outflow and $452 million through an increase of money in circulation. This $1,176 million in clear reserves was in part made good through the reserve banks which created $440 million of clear reserves, primarily by the purchase of bills in the open market.[23] But this left a net reduction in clear reserves of over $700 million, or a drop of 33 per cent in the total clear reserves within the system.

This loss was further accentuated by the action of the reserve banks in the following months. In November, there was a net return flow of gold amounting to $122 million, and no appreciable net change in money in circulation, but the reserve banks reversed their open market operations, and, by reducing their open market holdings to the extent of $243 million, caused a net reduction in clear reserves during the month of over $100 million. In December the usual seasonal increase of currency in circulation took place, but though the reserve banks did not take the customary action to counteract its effect, it was neutralized by an inflow of gold and a release of reserve deposits by holders other than member banks. In January and February there was a net export of gold, an influence counterbalanced in part by a small though less than seasonal return of currency from circulation. Added to the net loss in clear reserves due to these two outside influences was a heavy destruction of clear reserves by the action of the reserve banks themselves through a continued reduction in their holdings of bills and securities. This resulted in a further net drop in clear reserves of $382 million.

Clear Reserves Cut in Half

In the five and a half months from the middle of September to the end of February, the total clear reserves in our banking system were re-

[23] An addition of $20 million of clear reserves also came from the release of reserve deposits by other holders.

duced by these developments from $2,155 million to $1,021 million, or a drop of approximately 53 per cent. When it is recalled that in our banking system as now organized the clear reserves play virtually the same role for member banks that gold used to play before the Reserve system was adopted, it is clear that such a drastic decline in clear reserves must be expected to have drastic results. In the earlier days it would have resulted in a gold panic of major proportions. In the present instance it resulted in a reserve panic no less acute, as the head of the largest bank in the country no doubt recognized when he said, "The year 1931 ended in panic. . . " [24]

TABLE 96

LOSS OF CLEAR RESERVES TO MEMBER BANKS OF FEDERAL RESERVE SYSTEM(a)

September 16, 1931–February 29, 1932

(In Million Dollars)

1931–32	Outflow of Gold—Reduction in Monetary Gold Stock(b) (Negative means inflow)	Outflow of Currency into Circulation (Negative means return)	Net Loss in Clear Reserves from Influences Outside Banking System	Reduction of Clear Reserves through Open Market Operations of Federal Reserve	Reserve Deposits Absorbed by Other Holders than Member Banks and Other Adjustments	Net Loss of Clear Reserves to Member Banks
Sept. 16 to Oct. 31.	$724	$452	$1,176	$−440	$−20	$716
November........	−122	−4	−126	243	−11	106
December........	−46	111	65	−2	−53	10
January..........	45	−5	40	258	57	355
February........	62	−39	23	76	−72	27
Total........	$663	$515	$1,178	$135	$−99	$1,214

(a) *Annual Report* of the Federal Reserve Board, 1931, p. 36, and Federal Reserve *Bulletin*, April 1932, p. 229.

(b) Changes in monetary gold stock do not exactly correspond to the changes in gold holdings of reserve banks, but in the period under consideration there was a rough parallel. The discrepancies are covered in the "other adjustments" in the fifth column of figures above.

Effect of Reducing Clear Reserves

In Chart 29 it is possible to follow the effect of this great reduction of clear reserves on the different types of banks. For the big New York City banks, the excess reserves of the group, i.e., the clear reserves in ex-

[24] A. H. Wiggin, Address to stockholders of Chase National Bank, as reported in the *New York Times*, January 9, 1933.

cess of the legal reserve requirement, were quickly wiped out and the banks were forced into debt to the New York Reserve bank to a small extent. The big Chicago banks show a similar picture. It should be noted, however, that neither of these groups of banks suffered a really serious loss of clear reserves.

When we turn to the reserve city banks and the country banks, the picture is truly appalling. The clear reserves of the medium-sized reserve city banks fell from 94 per cent of the legal level to 34 per cent in the six months from August, 1931 to February, 1932, while those of the country banks dropped from 77 per cent to negligible proportions in the same period.

The extent to which the strong New York and Chicago banks were able to accumulate the major part of the clear reserves in the banking system is clearly indicated in Chart 30. These big banks increased their proportionate share of the total clear reserves from less than 48 per cent in August to over 78 per cent in February. If we regard the possession of clear reserves as a necessary safeguard to the depositors of any bank, we must consider the drawing away of reserves by the stronger bank from the weaker as a force tending to further weaken the latter.

That the reserve city and country banks were under a very considerable pressure to maintain their reserve position is clearly indicated by the steady melting away of their secondary reserves. Presumably they were either meeting adverse clearings by reducing their secondary reserves or else converting them into clear reserves to replace currency drawn into circulation. The loss of secondary reserves began as early as July, if not before, and continued precipitately until November, after which it continued at a slower pace until February. It should be noted that this change in rate of decline in secondary reserves corresponds to the change in the rate of decline in the clear reserves held by reserve city and country banks.

The Record of the Great Liquidation

When we come to the actual problem of examining the liquidation of banks over this period the published statistical series are by no means complete or satisfactory. Figures for the total earning assets of all member banks are not published except on call dates. The best that we can do is to examine the monthly figures for the deposits of central Reserve city, Reserve city and country banks, keeping in mind

that the deposits and earning assets tend to run parallel.[25] Chart 31
shows the total deposits of New York City banks. The decline in deposits between May and August is marked, but the decline does not
become precipitate until the last three months of the year. Accompanying the figures for deposits are figures showing the extent of the borrowed reserves (shaded area below the base line) and clear reserves
in excess of the legal requirements (back area above base line). Chart
31 shows the corresponding figures for the big Chicago banks, while
those for reserve cities and for country banks are shown in Chart 32.
In each case the story is the same,—a slow decline in deposits from
April or May to September and an almost cataclysmic decline from September to February.

It takes little imagination to see this liquidation, and most especially
that after the September loss of clear reserves, as a struggle among the
banks in the system for the existing clear reserves. The loss of gold
reduced the clear reserves of the New York banks, which proceeded
to sell securities and call loans in order to maintain their reserve position, thereby drawing clear reserves away from the reserve city and
country banks. The latter lost clear reserves both to the New York
banks and to the community as currency was drawn into circulation and
were forced to sell securities and call loans in order to prevent the
adverse clearings and to recoup their depleted reserves. This further
liquidation forced the New York and Chicago banks to liquidate further in order to retain the clear reserves which their more vigorous
liquidation had already brought to them. So long as there was a deficiency of clear reserves in the system in relation to the demand for
them there is no reason why this heart-breaking liquidation should
not have continued until half the banks in the system were closed by
the more rapid liquidation of the stronger banks and the stronger banks
were closed by the runs upon them induced by the wholesale bank
suspensions.

Aid from the Federal Reserve

This terrific liquidation appears to have been brought to a stop, in
so far as the big banks are concerned, and to have been slowed up
in so far as the smaller banks are concerned by the action of the Federal

[25] The fluctuations in earning assets and in total deposits ran roughly parallel during
the period for "reporting New York City banks" and for "other reporting banks."

CHART 31

CHANGES IN TOTAL DEPOSITS AND IN BORROWED RESERVES OR
EXCESS OF CLEAR RESERVES OVER LEGAL RESERVE REQUIREMENT
NEW YORK AND CHICAGO BANKS

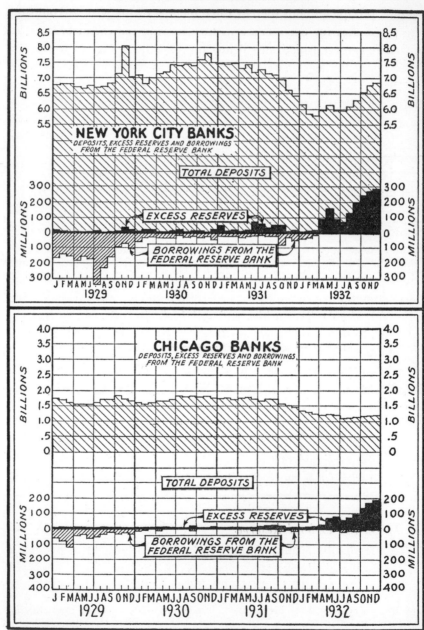

CHART 32

Changes in Total Deposits and in Borrowed Reserves or Excess of Clear Reserves Over Legal Reserve Requirement City and Country Reserve Banks

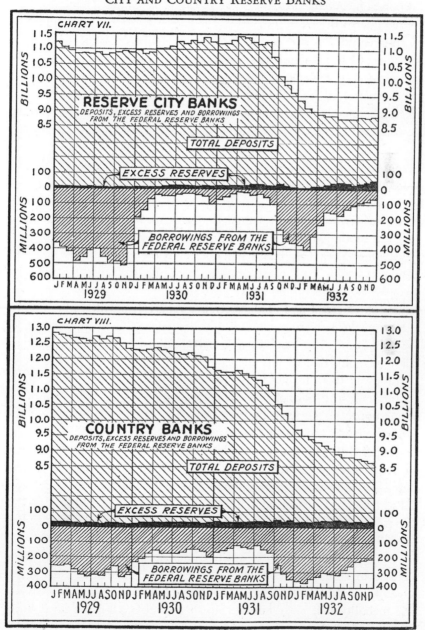

Reserve banks which went into the market and in a period of four months created a billion dollars of clear reserves and by the action of the federal government in creating the Reconstruction Finance Corporation. As the extensive open market operations began to add appreciably to the clear reserves in the banking system, the liquidation of the central Reserve city and Reserve city banks came to a quick halt (see Charts 31 and 32) while the liquidation of country banks continued at a slower rate. The New York and Chicago banks at once freed themselves from debt to the Reserve banks and began building up sizable amounts of clear reserves in excess of the legal requirements. By May 1932, the clear reserves of the New York banks exceeded by twenty per cent the total reserves required by law. This addition of clear reserves brought to a halt the liquidation of the New York banks. Moreover as their clear reserves were built up there came a parallel expansion in their loans and investments and in their deposits,— an expansion momentarily halted by the outflow of gold in May and June but continued after July and through the fall of 1932. By January, 1933, New York City banks had increased their deposits by over $1 billion, a major part of it coming from the making of loans and investments. The Chicago banks also built up excess reserves but their expansion of credit and of deposits was relatively small.

During the last six months of 1932, there was a steady increase in the volume of clear reserves in the banking system, mainly from an inflow of gold. Part of this went to the New York and Chicago banks and allowed them to build up clear reserves in amounts which would appear foolish in normal times but which, as we shall see, were by no means unreasonable from the point of view of the self interest of the particular banks concerned. In December, 1932, the New York banks as a group held clear reserves to the extent of 35 per cent more than the legal level, while the Chicago banks acquired and were hoarding clear reserves to an extent more than double the legal level.

For the reserve city banks, the effect of the open market operations was to gradually slow up their liquidation, which continued through June. Thereafter they showed neither expansion nor contraction until December, when liquidation again commenced. In spite of the large increase in clear reserves these banks had been unable to clear themselves from debt to the reserve banks and they were far from being able to build their clear reserves up to a level beyond the legal limit.

They were, however, able to build up their secondary reserves in other banks, mostly New York banks, practically to the level they had held in June of 1931.

The Plight of Country Banks

Though direct figures on the earning assets of country banks are not available for the last few months, it is apparent that they continued to liquidate throughout the whole of 1932, though in the later months at a very much slower rate. Only in small measure, did the clear reserves which came into the banking system percolate down to them. In December, 1932, more than half of their legal reserves as a group were borrowed and this was in spite of the fact that many of the stronger country banks held excess reserves in appreciable amounts. Neither were the country banks able to build up their secondary reserves in other banks to an appreciable extent.

Altogether, one can characterize the halting of the terrific liquidation of the fall of 1931 and the first two months of 1932 as one of the most spectacular successes of central banking policy this country has yet seen. It stopped the struggle for an inadequate supply of clear reserves by increasing the supply to such an extent that the stronger banks obtained a supply of clear reserves sufficient to more than satisfy their desire for extreme liquidity. They even expanded their portfolios to an important extent, an extent sufficient to suggest that if they had received additional clear reserves, they would have allowed them to be drawn off to other banks as a result of their own expansion.

The whole period of liquidation must necessarily have weakened all but the strongest banks by causing them to dispose of their more liquid assets under the most inauspicious conditions. Whether or not a further increase in clear reserves in the banking system would have reached them in sufficient volume to allow the repayment of their debt to the reserve banks and the building up of a fund of clear reserves in excess of the legal limits is a question which cannot be answered.

Liquidation Effects on Business

Before leaving this period of heavy bank liquidation, it is necessary to ask what it meant to our economy as a whole. In a period of eight months deposits amounting to approximately $10 billion disappeared from the active debt of banks. We have already indicated that $1,421 million of this loss came from bank suspensions, $559 million from net gold outflow and only $621 million from a net increase of currency in circulation. The remainder, or more than $7 billion of deposits, was destroyed by the liquidation process, thereby reducing the total money stock of the country by an equivalent amount. This would be a sufficiently heavy burden on any community to further sink the level of prices and of business and to cause untold hardship and misery.

The reality of the pressure on the community caused by this liquidation is apparent when we consider how this liquidation actually operated. During the eight-month period, the banks sold something like $2 billion worth of securities to investors and investment institutions, received their money in exchange for them and proceeded to destroy the money through the complex process of liquidation. In the same period they forced the repayment of over $2 billion worth of loans on securities, thereby forcing investors to come forward and invest this amount of money in securities,[26] an amount of money which was paid in to the bank and destroyed in the liquidation process. As a result the investing community must have purchased in total over $4 billion worth of securities, reducing their money holdings to that extent.

In the same eight months, the banks forced the repayment of commercial loans to the extent of approximately $3 billion. In order to repay these sums, business borrowers must have either reduced their holdings of money or else sold something in order to obtain the money to pay the bank.[27] Presumably, for the most part, business borrowers sold commodities to consumers and repaid their debt to the banks. If the whole of the commercial loans repaid were met by this process, the one by which commercial borrowings are supposed to be repaid according to traditional banking theory, it would mean that the consumers must have purchased $3 billion worth of commodities out of money which they already possessed. Presumably this would mean that consumers purchased $3 billion worth of goods more than their current income during this eight-month period. How much of this differential

26 Either the owner of the security who has borrowed must reduce his money holdings by investing them in the security (or sell something to someone else to get the money to repay—thereby reducing the money holdings of the second person) or he must sell part of his securities to a person with money holdings who thus invests this money in the security and reduces his money holdings.

27 Certain other courses are possible, such as (a) borrowing from other individuals, or (b) forcing other individuals to repay debts owed to the business man.

was brought about by forced and distressed selling of commodities and how much by a curtailment of income it is impossible to say.

What must be clear, however, is that if the banks destroyed over $7 billion of money by liquidation this must have come from somewhere—from the money holdings of business enterprises and from the money holdings of individuals. And, furthermore, the persons and enterprises which surrendered this money must for the most part have been persuaded to surrender this money by forcing them to increase their buying of securities and commodities or by curtailing their income while they continued to spend at something like their customary rate.

Causes of the Moratorium

It is too soon to trace with clarity the developments which led to the national moratorium. It is clear that the liquidation of the previous year had left the banking system in a seriously weakened condition. Whether the Michigan bank holiday directly resulted from current changes in the banking system or was a local reverberation of this earlier liquidation effecting an intrinsically weak group of banks cannot be as yet established. Presumably it was the latter. The banking figures of the weeks immediately preceding indicate a general increase in bank tension, particularly the important withdrawals of deposits in central reserve city banks by banks in other centers. Once the Michigan moratorium had been declared events followed swiftly to a climax.

Between February 15 and March 1 several major influences can be traced:—Withdrawals of gold for export and for internal hoarding to the extent of approximately $300 million and a further outflow of $200 million between March 1 and March 4, were coupled with an increase in currency in circulation of between $400 and $500 million to March 1 and approximately $500 million in the next three days.[28] These two influences combined reduced the debt of member banks to depositors by between $700 and $800 million to March 1st and $700 million from March 1 to March 4. The repercussions of these two sets of withdrawals combined with a shifting of deposits from bank to bank which it is difficult to trace, resulted in: (1) the reduction of clear reserves of member banks; (2) a further withdrawing of second-

---

[28] Both gold withdrawals and the increase in currency in circulation as reported by the Federal Reserve Board increased very much more than this but part of the increase was gold and currency in the hands of banks.

ary reserves from the banking centers, and (3) a destruction of deposits by the sale of securities and the calling of loans.

Clear reserves were reduced by withdrawals from the reserve banks to the extent of $700 million to March 1, with perhaps another $635 million decrease in the following three days. To stem this outflow of gold and currency, the reserve banks created $379 million of clear reserves with an additional $80 million between March 1 and March 4. The net effect of these forces, combined with other minor influences, was to reduce the clear reserves of member banks by $624 million by March 1 with a drop of $940 million in the following three days. This left the member banks with only $386 million of clear reserves on March 4, with the New York banks having a negative figure. The almost complete disappearance of clear reserves necessarily forced member banks to borrow extensively to meet the legal requirements. This they did to the amount of more than $1 billion between February 15 and March 4.

Inadequacy of Secondary Reserves in Other Banks

The withdrawal of secondary reserves from the banking centers was spectacular. Between February 1 and 15, reporting banks outside of New York had withdrawn from New York $364 million of deposits. Between February 15 and March 1, another $686 million was withdrawn, presumably with further extensive withdrawals in the succeeding three days. The withdrawals by non-reporting banks were of somewhat less magnitude, presumably because to an important extent they were composed of secondary reserves of savings banks which were not forced to draw upon them to an important extent. They declined $393 million in the month of February.

Liquidation can only be traced for the reporting banks. The New York banks which had been particularly affected by withdrawals of secondary reserves reduced their portfolios by $566 million in the two weeks from February 15 to March 1, while the other reporting banks decreased their portfolios by $182 million. It is clear that the banks outside of New York reacted to the loss of clear reserves by attempting to convert their secondary reserves into clear reserves, while the New York banks resisted this effort in part by liquidating their portfolios. By this action the banks outside of New York were prevented from converting their secondary into primary reserves such as would be available to meet currency demands. The secondary reserves thus proved in a crisis wholly inadequate as a form of reserve.

Since the reopening of banks, the return flow of hoarded gold and currency from circulation had increased the clear reserves of the system by March 22 to $1,247 million, though the return had not yet brought the clear reserves up to the volume which existed on March 1, or to much more than half of the amount existing during January.

The Responsibility of the Public

Hitherto we have discussed the liquidation in bank debt primarily in terms of the action of the banks which it reflected. Yet public attention has been primarily directed, especially by the Republican administration in 1931 and 1932, toward hoarding by individuals as the source of the banks' difficulties. What actual rôle has individual hoarding played?

During the period of heavy liquidation in the fall of 1931, hoarding was a very unimportant element in so far as its *direct* effect is concerned. The increase in the total money in circulation involved a shift of less than two per cent of the money of the community from deposits into currency. Only part of this increase, moreover, came from individual hoarding, for the need for an increased volume of currency to carry on business in communities whose banking facilities were suspended accounted for a proportion of this shift. Thus hoarding during this period was of negligible importance in its direct effect. Its important indirect effect, as it induced liquidation, would seem to reflect a weakness in the banking system rather than irresponsibility of action on the part of individual depositors.

During the period ending in the closing of all the banks on the other hand the conversion of deposits into currency was of greater direct importance. Once bank holidays had become epidemic, heavy withdrawals resulted partly from very greatly increased need for money in circulation as the banking facilities were closed in state after state, and partly from the very real and justifiable anxiety on the part of individuals with respect to the whole banking situation. Unquestionably the nation-wide bank holiday was directly precipitated by the withdrawals of depositors.

Because of the violent condemnation which has been heaped on "hoarding" by bankers and others a word on the matter seems called for. To cast aspersions on individuals who withdrew currency—except for those bankers who, already in positions of trust with respect to their depositors, took advantage of their inside knowledge to make personal withdrawals—is as unjustified as to condemn the big New York and Chicago banks for attempting to fortify their position by hoarding reserves. In each case the reaction was that which was to be expected in an individualistic system, and in each case the fault lies in the failure of the community either to organize a banking system so as to forestall the harmful effects of such natural and predictable action or to prevent its occurrence by more drastic means.

2. RECOMMENDATIONS

Banking policy and practice is undoubtedly the subject of more controversy than any other single phase of our economy. To make recommendations as to particular bank action is, therefore, to enter a field in which every suggestion should be supported by an extensive factual and analytical background. Only such recommendations are here given as grow fairly directly out of the material discussed, though they derive more fundamentally from a basic picture of the functioning of the banking system which it is impossible to present here and which, because of the diverse views of different writers, must necessarily differ from the basic picture held by many.

Federal Reserve Should Replenish Clear Reserves

The first recommendations have to do with the policy of the reserve banks. We have seen that the debacle of February and March, 1933, greatly depleted the clear reserves within the system. Since the reopening of banks, currency has been flowing back from circulation, but it seems unlikely that the inflow in the immediate future will fully counterbalance the previous outflow. Many communities have had to rely on currency to an increased extent as their medium of exchange, because of the reduced banking facilities left in the wake of the moratorium. An increased number of persons, with quite understandable fear, prefer to keep their money in the form of currency rather than as bank deposits. Both of these factors act to reduce the return flow of gold and other currency from circulation. As a result, the clear reserves of the system seem likely to remain at an insufficient level unless the Federal Reserve banks enter the open market and supply the deficiency.

It is of course possible that the closing of many weak banks will have restored the confidence of bankers and depositors to such an extent that the banks will be satisfied to rest with the existing volume of clear reserves. But since the clear reserves are so very much lower than they were before the moratorium period, if they are not replenished by open market operations, it seems likely that a renewed struggle for the existing clear reserves will take place with further bank liquidation and corresponding destruction of money. Such a development would be a national calamity, as it would further deplete the supply of money, already reduced from $50 billion in 1929 to something like $36 billion. To prevent such further liquidation, it is recommended that clear reserves be created by the reserve banks in sufficient quantity to make the amount of outstanding clear reserves at least equal to those in January, 1933.

Reserves Should be Expanded to Induce Bank Credit Expansion

The second recommendation has to do with steps to bring about an expansion of bank deposits and involves two elements; first, steps to increase the willingness of banks to make loans or investments, and, second, steps to increase the number of responsible borrowers. To increase the willingness of banks to lend, and in particular to induce them to lower the excessively high credit position which they now require of borrowers, it is presumably necessary to extend the creation of clear reserves beyond the point where there are enough reserves in the system to prevent further liquidation.

How far the open market operations of the reserve banks would have to go before this point was reached it is not possible to say before trial. It seems clear, however, if every bank in the country had clear reserves in an amount double the legal requirement, each would feel itself in a vastly more liquid position than if it had only the legal limit or somewhat less. Instead of frowning on prospective borrowers, the banks would be more aggressive in seeking them. Because of their heavy holdings of clear reserves, they would have less fear of bank runs and of adverse clearings. The great expansion in the portfolio and deposits of the New York City banks—over $1 billion [29]—in the fall of 1932 when their excess reserves were built up to a high level, tends to give support to this assumption. It is therefore recommended that the clear reserves in the banking system be increased to an important extent beyond that at which further liquidation is brought to a stop.

In considering this recommendation, it should be noted that, if the

[29] This expansion had little effect on our economy as a whole, presumably because a practically equivalent liquidation took place in banks outside of New York whose reserves were still deficient.

great increase in clear reserves does *not* result in any expansion of bank portfolios and deposits, it can have done no serious damage since its influence will have been entirely confined to the reserve banks and those whose bills or securities the reserve banks have purchased in the open market. If the increase in clear reserves *does* result in an expansion of portfolios and deposits of banks, it will have produced a result which seems essential as a step toward recovery—the replacement of part of the $14 billion of money destroyed in the last three years. Furthermore, such expansion would be *directly under the control of the Federal Reserve banks* since they could reduce the amount of clear reserves in the system at any time through reversing their previous open market operations.

It may be suggested that the open market operations in the spring of 1932 failed to bring bank expansion and that therefore open market operations are an ineffective instrument for the purpose suggested here. We have already produced enough evidence to show that the open market operations at that time were a spectacular success in halting bank liquidation, and that so far as the New York City banks which were able to build up heavy excess reserves were concerned, the open market operations resulted in a very great bank expansion.[30] We have also seen that the open market operations were insufficient to allow the reserve city and country banks to build up excess reserves or even to get clear of debt to the reserve banks and that, as was properly to be expected, these banks continued to liquidate. There is enough here to suggest that the failure of open market operations to induce a *net* expansion for the banking system as a whole was because they were only sufficient to stop net liquidation and not sufficient in amount to induce net expansion.

Steps to Increase the Effective Borrowers

The effect of increased clear reserves in inducing an expansion of bank portfolios and deposits could be greatly accelerated if means could be discovered of increasing the number of prospective borrowers who were safe risks. Here the federal and local governments could aid to an important extent if, in financing new construction and other projects, they employed a method comparable to that customary in private business. In ordinary times, when a private corporation arranges for a large construction project, the initial construction expenses are customarily paid

[30] A slight expansion also occurred in the case of the Chicago banks.

out of funds borrowed from the local banks, particularly when the construction is being done by a contractor who subsequently turns the completed property over to the corporation for which it is being built. As the construction is completed, the bank borrowings are repaid out of funds received from the issue of new securities to investors, the funds paid to the contractor, or other funds. Thus, construction carried on by private enterprise is customarily carried in its initial stages by bank borrowings and to that extent aids in maintaining the volume of money created by the banking system.

Reconstruction Finance Corporation Guarantee of Bank Loans

There would seem to be no reason why construction supported by the government—particularly that by the Reconstruction Finance Corporation—should not be financed *in its initial stages* in the same manner. Thus, if the Reconstruction Finance Corporation is proposing to finance a bridge, a tunnel, or a housing project for some local community, instead of supplying the funds, let the local authorities sponsoring the project borrow from the local banks for the expenses of construction, let the Reconstruction Finance Corporation guarantee the payment at the end of, let us say, six months, thereby not only making the borrower highly eligible to the banks but insuring a low rate of interest on the project. At the end of the borrowing period, the Reconstruction Finance Corporation would obtain the funds which it would otherwise have obtained at the outset and pay them to the local authorities who would in turn repay the bank borrowings. It should be noted, however, that to the extent that Reconstruction Finance Corporation funds would otherwise have been obtained from banks the only gain would be the more direct connection between the local construction project and the local banks.

In the end the Reconstruction Finance Corporation would pay out no more by this method than by the customary one, yet in the intervening period the construction projects could be the basis for the creation of an important volume of bank deposits and thereby add to the money of the country. It is also of considerable importance that this newly created money would be at once sent into circulation through the payment of wages and the purchase of supplies. The amount of construction work likely to be done by federal, state, and local governments in the near future which would not otherwise be financed by bank borrowing is enough to bring an appreciable, though not great, expansion of bank portfolios and would add one of the most desirable types of paper to the assets of banks.

Here, then, are two steps within the power of the banking and government authorities which would appear likely to aid in bringing recovery. It is not suggested that these steps contain the solution of the depression or of the major problem of debt, a problem which would itself be met to a very important extent by economic recovery. It does seem probable, however, that by their adoption the banking situation can be converted from one acting to further depress economic activity to one which is active in pushing in the direction of recovery. The banking situation can then be ruled out as an impediment to recovery.

Unified National Bank System Needed

It is not possible here to go into the more fundamental reorganization of our banking system, the necessity of which is so clearly indicated by the volume of bank failures and the bank liquidation already discussed. One recommendation can be made, however, which needs little more than the events of March, 1933, to give it support. It seems altogether clear that our banking system should be unified in the reserve system so that on the one hand the rules, regulations, and inspection will be uniform, and on the other hand, that the regulations can be made more stringent without fear of loss of banks to the system. This two-sided objective can probably be most effectively accomplished by forcing all commercial banks to take out national bank charters. All commercial banks would then be under a common inspection and would of necessity be members of the Federal Reserve System. In making this shift, however, care must be taken that the needs for clear reserves in the banking system are not suddenly increased by the change unless the reserve banks are in a position through open market operations to supply the added reserves.

Chapter Thirteen

GENERAL RECOMMENDATIONS [1]

IN the preceding chapters the volume of debt in the United States has been estimated, the size and incidence of the debt burden indicated, and more or less extensive proposals made for dealing with the debt problem in specific fields. In this final chapter it is proposed to deal with debts and the debt burden as they relate to our whole economy and to consider more general recommendations for action to meet the problems to which they give rise.

There is little disagreement as to the nature of the problem which debts create in our economy. Because of their inflexibility debts are, under certain conditions, the cause of serious economic dislocation and suffering. Debts are fixed contracts, usually money contracts, made on a basis of a given level of prices, of business activity, and of values. When there is a radical fall in prices, in business activity, or in a combination of the two, not only do the money incomes of debtors decline along with the money incomes of other parts of the community, but the values of their assets also tend to fall. Thus the only sources out of which debt and interest payments can be made undergo a shrinkage at the very time when creditors are more inclined to push their claims. Meanwhile the debtors' obligations to pay out specific sums of money remain unaltered.

The net effect on the debtor is to increase greatly the difficulty of meeting debt payments, either of principal or of interest. If the drop in prices and in business activity carries far enough, wholesale insolvencies result. These in turn beget other insolvencies as the forced liquidation of failing enterprises further depresses the level of money values and makes more difficult the payment of debt obligations by those enterprises still solvent. Debt defaults on an extensive scale cause

[1] This chapter is the joint product of all the contributors except Dr. Franklin W. Ryan. Two of the authors, however—Dr. Bauer and Dr. Eldred—have expressed certian reservations which are contained in Appendix III, p. 424.

debtors to lose properties at sacrifice values and often to suffer untold hardships. Even creditors lose, for in a period of drastic deflation in property values the legal remedy of foreclosure and resale affords only an uncertain and inadequate protection against loss. Thus debt defaults tend to disorganize a functioning economy, destroying values and paralyzing business activity with consequent loss to the whole population. Even if debtors remain solvent, the increased difficulty of making debt payments may cause dislocation and suffering almost as great as that involved in defaults and may have almost as great a disorganizing effect on the whole economy. Altogether, the effect of the fixed character of debt obligations is to introduce an inflexible element into an unstable economy, thereby adding further to its instability. The economic dislocation and the extensive suffering caused by this inflexibility make debt a major problem which becomes acute in times of depression.[2]

1. APPROACHES TO THE DEBT PROBLEM

The problem of debt subdivides into two separate, closely parallel problems: first, that presented by the existing disproportion between the burden of debt payments and the current levels of prices and business activity, and second, that more general problem presented by debt as an inflexible constituent of an unstable economy. These we will refer to as the immediate and the more permanent debt problems.

Practically all the suggestions for dealing with these two problems reflect one or the other of two directly opposing methods of approach —that which assumes the economy as given and seeks to solve the debt problem by adjustments on the side of debts, and that which accepts the debts as given and seeks to adjust the economy to their existence. So far as the immediate debt problem is concerned, the first of these schools would bring debt into line with prices and production by a downward adjustment of debts. The opposing school would bring them into line by lifting prices and production.

The first school of thought holds that only by a thorough clearing

---

[2] Rising prices and rising business activity do not affect debt relations in such a way as to cause important economic dislocation, or widespread suffering, while the impairment of creditors' real income through reduction in the purchasing power of fixed money payments is in part counterbalanced by the greater certainty of their payment. Rising prices and business activity do not produce such general economic disasters as wholesale bank failures. At the most they bring about a shift in real income and wealth between debtor and creditor.

out of all debts on which the contractual payments cannot be met at the present low levels of prices and business activity can a sound basis be laid for economic recovery. This school would meet the immediate debt problem either by rigorously enforcing the contractual obligations of debtors—forcing receivership, foreclosure, or bankruptcy where necessary—or by rewriting the debt contracts through voluntary or imposed agreement between debtor and creditor.

The opposing school of thought holds that to enforce the existing debt contracts to the point of wholesale bankruptcy would be further to disorganize the economy, thereby prolonging and deepening the depression. The representatives of this school would bolster up the existing debt structure by temporary adjustments, by moratoria, by the use of government credit and by other means until effective steps could be taken to raise both prices and business activity to such levels that the bulk of existing debts could be supported. The two schools of thought are thus, in general, directly opposed. The first group would adjust debts to the existing depressed state of the economy, while the second group would adjust the economy to support the bulk of the existing debts.[3]

This same opposition in approach appears also in discussions of the more permanent problem of debt, that concerned not with the current depression but with the preparation for future fluctuations. Some would take no action with respect to debts or would attempt to diminish the disorganizing influence of debts by limiting their volume and by making the burden of debts incurred in the future more flexible through the insertion of clauses in the debt contracts such that the money payments called for would reflect either changes in the price level or extremes of business activity.[4] Others would attempt to neutralize the inflexible character of debts by attempting to increase the stability of

[3] The opposition of these two schools seems to me overemphasized at this point. These two divergent theoretical assumptions undoubtedly exist and underlie differences in points of view. In framing practical policies, however, representatives of both schools can and do agree on a wide range of concrete proposals. For example, even the most ardent advocates of the economic stabilization theory among the contributors to this volume have favored adjustments of those existing debts which cannot be paid in full, even with some measure of general recovery. Furthermore, pending the successful application of an economic stabilization program, policies as to future debts must guard against future reductions in prices and business activity. EVANS CLARK.

[4] The more conservative minded would not approve either of the above suggestions for dealing with debts. Some believe that the best results in economic relations are to be had from a policy of untrammeled individual action; others are frankly skeptical of the results which they would expect to follow from the uncertainties implicit in any scheme for varying the dollar payments called for by debt contracts.

the economy. This position they take, not because they believe the economy ought to be operated in relation to debts, but because economic stability has itself become the key to many problems among which that of debts is only one. The stability of prices, with adjusted and controlled business activity, they maintain is essential to orderly economic development without regard to permanent debt policy. If this major objective, *economic stability,* could be attained, the inflexible character of debt would cease to have more than local importance. Thus, for meeting the more permanent problem of debts, as well as for meeting the immediate situation brought on by the current depression, the proposals divide between those aiming to adjust debts to an uncontrolled and unstable economy and those aiming to control the economy in such a manner as to make the debts no longer a serious problem. This divergence is essentially a phase of the opposition between the advocates of a policy of *laissez faire* in economic relations and the proponents of an economy in which planning plays a part.

In making general recommendations to meet both the immediate and the more permanent problem of debt, the authors of this report have adopted in general the second approach—namely, that the problem of debt should be met through the exercise of control over the economy rather than through the wholesale readjustment of the debt structure. For meeting the immediate debt problem this involves the use of temporary expedients to bolster up existing debt and action to raise the level of prices and production. For the more permanent problem it means the taking of active steps to stabilize the economy. Exceptions to this approach are, of course, made in particular situations but these in no way invalidate the underlying approach to the general problem.

2. MEASURES OF IMMEDIATE RELIEF

The general recommendations aimed to meet the immediate debt problem caused by the low level of prices and business activity rest on the conclusion that the bulk of existing debts could be supported under conditions of reasonable business activity at the present or somewhat higher price levels; that, while some debts must ultimately be written off and some enterprises must go through the receivership mill, it is not possible to determine which debts are essentially unsound [5]

[5] *I.e.,* could not be supported under conditions of prices and of business activity which might reasonably be expected to obtain in a country of the size and vitality of the United States.

(except in extreme cases) until a reasonable level of business activity has been established; and finally, that the economic disorganization and the destruction of values which would result, and in part have already resulted, from wholesale liquidation of debt constitute an injury to the people of the community so great that to the extent necessary to prevent the aggravation of this injury, but only to this extent, the rights of individuals must be held in temporary abeyance to the larger rights of the community.

(a) MEASURES RELATING TO EXISTING DEBTS

With these conclusions as a basis we make two general recommendations for immediate action:—first, action giving temporary support to the existing debt structure, and second, active measures to induce business recovery.

In the preceding chapters each author has dealt with his particular field, and in many instances the suggestions for relieving the pressure in that field apply there and nowhere else; it is therefore suggested that the reader refer to the individual chapters for detailed remedies applicable to any one field.

(1) *Individual Adjustment between Debtor and Creditor*

No single or broad plan for readjustment for all debtors [6] would seem to be expedient because, first, all debtors are not equally hard pressed, and second, because the type of remedy best for one case is often neither suitable nor effective for another. Thus, whether the debtor be an individual, a railroad, a corporation or a bank, each must be dealt with individually and a solution arrived at which will meet the needs of that particular case. To illustrate more clearly: the public utilities for the most part, with the exception of street railways, are able to meet their obligations without serious financial handicap, whereas a large proportion of the railroads would be facing receivership unless help had been administered to them in some form or other. Surely no one would argue that both of these industries should be treated alike.

Even in the same field different measures may be needed for the

---

[6] By "readjustment for all debtors" is meant readjustment of debt burdens, i.e., carrying charges, and of debts currently maturing. This does not include debts maturing in the future.

treatment of individual cases. Take, for example, the rural mortgage situation: while there are a large number of farmers who through no fault of their own but because of the fall in the prices of farm products are unable to meet their obligations, there are others more fortunate who can. In times of emergency like the present the adjustments have to be made where the pressure falls most heavily, even if the result seems to penalize in some cases good business management and judgment.

(2) *Establishment of an Administrative Mechanism in Each Particular Field*

It is obvious, human nature being what it is, that a great deal of difficulty may be encountered in securing a settlement between a debtor and a single creditor or a group of creditors. For instance, it would be almost impossible for a large railroad or industrial corporation to come to any voluntary adjustment between itself as debtor and its thousands of creditors.

Therefore, in order to facilitate adjustments between debtor and creditor it is recommended that an administrative mechanism be established in each field according to its particular needs. This body would function as an intermediary between debtor and creditor in cases where these two parties were unable to come to an agreement. In the case of the individual home owner a mechanism similar to the Joint Welfare Committee of the Philadelphia Real Estate Board could be established in the various parts of the country, with such changes in make-up as would be suitable for the particular geographical location. The railroad situation could be met through the new procedure provided under the revised bankruptcy act, the utilities through the state public utility commissions, the farm problem through the recently created Farm Credit Administration, and so on.

(3) *Reduction of Interest Rates*

A reduction of interest rates, in individual cases only, to levels comparable with the current earning capacity of the debtor is recommended. This suggestion has been one of the chief topics of discussion during the past few months, and is still a much debated one.

The advocates of a blanket reduction of all interest rates claim that to discriminate among debtors in regard to lower interest rates is to penalize good business judgment and management. We recognize the validity of this argument but, as has already been pointed out, in times of emergency relief must be given only where needed and not indiscriminately in all quarters whether needed or not. Furthermore, it would inflict a further hardship on many creditors such as life insurance companies, banks, institutions and so on, who would be forced in many cases to reduce interest rates, especially on real estate and mortgage loans, still further.

(4) Reduction or Waiving of Amortization Charges

It is further recommended that amortization charges be either reduced or waived, according to the necessity of each particular case, until the earning capacity of the property or industry is restored to levels justifying further payments of amortization. The same arguments as those presented for the reduction of interest rates are also applicable here and need not be repeated.

(5) Reasonable Extensions of Time for Maturing Obligations

Although there are no accurate data available which show the total amount of debts maturing this year, the figure would probably run into several billion dollars. In view of the reduced incomes which have made it impossible for many debtors to meet interest charges and amortization payments in full, it is obvious that these debtors will be unable to meet their respective maturing obligations. Furthermore, many debtors who have been and are able to meet fixed charges are not able to repay the principal of their maturing debts. To bring foreclosure proceedings against these debtors, who in normal times could have satisfied their creditors, would be an economic waste both from the viewpoint of the debtor and that of the creditor.

An example is that of the mortgage guaranty companies. In times of business activity the holder of a guaranteed mortgage was usually satisfied either to renew the mortgage or to purchase a similar security from the company when his holdings matured. Now, however, this same holder is asking for payment in full of the maturing mortgage. In a case like this where the record of the mortgage company has been entirely satisfactory during the past decade it would seem reasonable and equitable from the standpoint of both debtor and creditor to allow an extension of time for the maturing obligations rather than to foreclose and force a sale at a price far below the true value of the assets or property as the case may be.

(6) *Refunding and Refinancing Maturing Obligations*

Another way of meeting the maturity situation is to provide funds from public sources to refinance the maturing debt in instances where an extension of time is not expedient. As an example let us take the case of the railroads. Here the maturing obligations are ordinarily paid off by the creation of new debts, i.e., by "refunding," either on a short-term or a long-term basis. These new refunding issues are underwritten by banking syndicates and subsequently floated in the securities market. At the present time, however, due to the decline in railroad earnings and also to the general uncertainty prevailing as to the trend of business, the market for securities of this type has practically dried up so that it is almost impossible to raise new funds. A similar condition characterizes the farm mortgage situation with respect to extension of maturing obligations.

The question now naturally arises as to the source of the funds to refinance or refund the maturing debts. Generally speaking such funds would have to be provided in the majority of cases by the government. Steps in this direction have already been taken, as witnessed by the Reconstruction Finance Corporation, the Farm Credit Administration, and so on. For details as to the raising of these funds the reader is referred to the individual chapters.

(7) *Foreclosures*

Under present conditions we feel that receivership and foreclosure proceedings should not be permitted except as a last resort. The questions that immediately arise at this point are: first, what criteria should be established to determine whether or not a foreclosure is necessary, and second, who is to decide on the basis of these criteria which debtors should be given assistance and which should be forced into receivership. In regard to the former it is suggested that the criteria consist of the past-earnings record and future earning capacity of the mortgage property. In the latter case we recommend that the administrative mechanism, whose establishment has already been suggested, be given legislative authority to discriminate between competent and incompetent debtors on the basis of the criteria.

Our recommendation in regard to foreclosures may therefore be stated as follows: foreclosure proceedings should be avoided except in cases where misuse or neglect of the mortgaged property can be established, and even then only with the approval of the administrative mechanism in that particular field or locality.

The above recommendations are to be viewed as emergency relief measures only, and unless they are combined with a more comprehensive economic policy aimed at a general recovery of business activity, the problem will persist and further measures of a much more drastic nature may become necessary.

(b) MEASURES TO INDUCE RECOVERY

The recommendations so far made have been primarily concerned with bolstering up the existing debt structure until such time as economic recovery can be brought about. They rest on the assumption that active steps will be taken to induce such recovery. They therefore cover only one side of the program suggested for meeting the debt problem and must be supplemented by complementary recommendations which aim to lift the level of both prices and production.

(1) *Expansion of the Volume of Money*

The two steps to induce recovery most frequently discussed are: (1) the expansion of the volume of money and (2) extensive public works. The first is championed by advocates who maintain that an expansion of the volume of money, primarily bank deposits, would tend to increase prices and production. The opponents of money expansion usually take the position either that expansion of the volume of money would lead to uncontrolled inflation or that the expansion of the volume of money would have no effect on prices or production. The views of those who fear uncontrolled inflation are usually supported by the experiences with war or post-war inflation. The advocates of money expansion reply by pointing to the essential difference between inflation forced on a country which has exhausted its credit and its taxing power and money expansion directly chosen as an instrument of recovery by a country which has by no means exhausted its taxing power and has maintained its borrowing power at a high level.

In the first case the unbalanced relation between expenditure and income from taxes or borrowing forces the money expansion and, remaining unbalanced, continues the necessity for further emissions of money. In the second case the money expansion is undertaken by choice and is backed by extensive taxing and borrowing power so that not only can the expansion of money be brought to a halt but it can be reversed so as to reduce the volume of money outstanding. In the first case the very forces which bring about money expansion tend to prevent its control. In the second case the expansion is not forced and instruments are available for reversing it. To conclude that in the second case money expansion would be uncontrollable because experience shows that in the first case it could not be controlled is to reason by a false analogy.

Those who oppose money expansion on the ground that it would *not* raise prices and production usually maintain that money is a passive factor in the economy, that prices and production rise and fall with changes in the demand for goods, and that an increase in the volume of money will only result in a fall in the velocity of circulation of money without resulting in an increase in demand. In support of this view the post-war experiences in Europe are frequently cited: that on various occasions the causal relations in the inflation process involved first an increase in demand for goods, then an increase in prices, and finally an increase in money as the printing presses were set to work to meet the country's deficit which had been aggravated by the rise in prices.

Undoubtedly this has frequently been the causal sequence. Furthermore, few will deny that a change in demand or supply conditions is an essential to a change in prices or production. But the fact that on certain occasions the causal sequence has gone in one direction does not preclude the possibility that the sequence could sometimes run in the opposite direction, i.e. from money to demand to prices. There would seem to be much to indicate that sometimes the sequence runs from a change in money through a change in demand to a change in prices and production, while sometimes it runs from a change in demand to a change in prices with or without a subsequent change in the volume of money.[7] This conclusion is strongly supported by the very fact that

[7] It is difficult to imagine, for instance, that if the federal government printed $5 billion greenbacks and distributed them gratis to the unemployed, an increase in the volume of goods purchased by the unemployed would not result. Nor does there seem to be any reason why other persons would concurrently decrease their expenditures.

some acute observers fear uncontrolled inflation because they believe that the sequence runs from money through demand to prices, while other equally acute observers conclude that money expansion would be ineffective because they have found that the sequence in certain occasions has run the opposite way. Is it not probable that it runs sometimes one way and sometimes the other?

If, from a consideration of the claims of those who advocate or oppose the expansion of the volume of money, one concludes on the one hand that the expansion of the volume of money can be controlled and made reversible and on the other hand that it may under certain circumstances bring about an increase in the demand for goods and a corresponding increase in prices and production, then it becomes a possible instrument for aiding recovery.

(2) *Expansion of Public Works*

The second instrument for directly aiding recovery, the expansion of public works, needs no such lengthy discussion. By some writers public works are regarded as an ineffective instrument unless coupled with an expansion in the volume of money. By others they are regarded as likely to be effective not only in giving direct employment but in setting the wheels of industry in motion, whether or not the volume of money is expanded, except as it may expand as a result of the expansion of industry itself.

In considering these two possible steps aimed to further recovery, the expansion of money and public works, it must be kept in mind that one of the immediate objectives of action must be to repair the damage done to the country's economy by the bank liquidation of 1931-1932 and by the failure of some of the banks to be reopened after the bank holiday. In the drastic bank liquidation of 1931-1932 the money of the country, chiefly deposits in commercial banks, was reduced over $10 billion, though the supply of money necessary to maintain the then existing level of prices and production does not appear likely to have suffered any such tremendous decline. The money stock of the

---

Unless they did so, the net effect of the new money issue would be to increase demand to a very considerable extent, with a corresponding reaction on prices and production. Truly if the issue of new money will not affect prices and production, then the issue of new money would be a convenient and *costless* way to feed the unemployed. This note should suggest that at least *some* ways of increasing the volume of money would result in increased demand and increased prices and production.

country has been further reduced by several billion dollars as banks have remained closed after the bank holiday. Altogether the volume of money has thus been seriously contracted—presumably without any fully corresponding reduction in the country's money needs.[8]

To correct this inequality between the supply of money and the need for money if prices and production are to be supported on a reasonable basis, it would seem that either the supply must be increased or the need for money reduced (or a combination of both). The departure of this country from the gold standard and the extensive discussions of uncontrolled inflation have undoubtedly brought some reduction in the country's need for money as person after person has converted part of his money holdings into goods or securities. It is possible, though improbable, that further talk of inflation and the taking of initial steps to increase the volume of money may of themselves cause people to prefer to hold less money and thereby reduce the need for money to the point at which the supply is adequate to support a higher level of prices and production without further increase. Presumably an extensive decrease in the desire to hold money would result in additional expenditures on goods and securities, thereby bringing about an extensive rise

---

[8] "Money needs" is here used as a convenient term to refer to the amount of money which is needed to support a given level of prices and production. Presumably this amount fluctuates from a variety of causes as the desirability of holding wealth in the form of money rather than in the form of goods or securities fluctuates with changing conditions: more at Christmas time and in the crop-moving period, less as fears of inflation reduce the desirability of holding individual wealth in the form of money, more as interest rates drop and wealth in the form of securities becomes less advantageous, less as a rising interest rate shifts the relative advantage of holding wealth in the form of money and of holding wealth in the form of high yielding call loans or other safe assets in favor of the latter. It should be noted that the money needs of the country relate to a particular level of prices and production. It is assumed that if, with the level of prices and production remaining constant, a drop in the desirability of holding money at that level occurs—as for instance from an extensive fear of inflation—then, the effort will be made to convert part of the wealth held in the form of money into goods or securities thus tending to increase both prices in the areas where prices are highly flexible and the volume of production in the areas where prices tend to be inflexible. If the volume of money remains constant, prices and production presumably increase until a new relation between prices, production and income has been established such that the demand for wealth in the form of money is equal to the supply. In a similar manner, if the effective desire to hold wealth in the form of money were to remain constant over a period of time while the volume of money was markedly reduced, say by bank liquidation, and if, at the initial level of prices and production, there was a balanced adjustment between the advantages of holding wealth in the form of money and in the form of goods or securities, then with the reduction in the supply of money, the adjustment would be deranged and a balance would only be reestablished at a lower level of prices and production unless other influences intervened. It is assumed here that a balance must be maintained between the advantages of holding wealth in the form of money and holding it in any other form into which it can be converted at the *existing prices*.

in prices of those commodities and securities whose prices are highly flexible, with a general increase in business activity in the areas where prices are relatively inflexible.

More probably the talk of inflation will not reduce the country's need for money to a point low enough to induce an important measure of recovery, and the deficiency of money must be made good through the expansion of bank deposits or the issue of notes if extensive recovery is to be brought about. Action to increase the volume of money in the community is therefore recommended, but subject to reversal in case of an inordinately rapid rise in prices and business activity resulting from the mere discussion of inflation.

There are a variety of ways whereby the money stock of the country could be increased, certain of which have been mentioned in the chapter on bank debt. In selecting among them two objectives should be sought—first, that method should be employed which makes the newly created money most effective in reviving employment. To this end we recommend that the new money—whether created as a result of the extension of bank credit or through the limited operations of the printing press—be expended in the furtherance of public works or other projects aimed at unemployment relief. This would place much of the newly created money in the hands of individuals likely to spend it directly in the purchase of goods.

The second and perhaps equally important consideration in selecting the method of adding to the money stock of the country is that the process should be promptly reversible. In order to effect a controlled expansion it is essential that the government be able to bring about a withdrawal of money from circulation [9] if the changed business outlook should lead to an important expansion of bank credit (with the corresponding creation of money) quite apart from, or perhaps as a further product of, the government's action in adding to the money stock.

Just how extensive an increase in the volume of money is required to bring about a substantial recovery is a matter which can be determined only as the expansion process is set in motion. That such an expansion program is justified under the circumstances seems clear. Therefore, unless prices rise very much further and business activity

[9] Where the money has been put into circulation through government expenditure it should be withdrawn by sale of bonds to individuals and institutions other than banks or by the less flexible process of taxation.

greatly increases as a result of the fear of inflation, we recommend that the government take steps to increase the volume of money outstanding in a manner to place purchasing power in the hands of those able and willing to expend it and that this expansion of money be accomplished in a manner capable of immediate reversal, so as to maintain the fullest possible control in the hands of the government.

In addition to and coordinate with the program of money expansion we recommend an extensive program of public works. The cost of these should be met out of government borrowing, except to the extent that the program of money expansion calls for their payment out of newly created money.

In order that the steps here suggested should be permanently effective, it appears to be essential that a solution be found for the problems concerned in international debt, monetary, and trade relations. The elements concerned here are too complicated to warrant discussion in this volume. It may be pointed out, however, that insofar as the debt and price problems of American farmers are dependent upon the restoration of an adequate foreign market for the surplus of farm products beyond the capacity of the home market to absorb, the resumption of more normal relations in international trade is a *sine qua non* to the return of permanent prosperity to American agriculture.

3. MEASURES OF PERMANENT PROTECTION

The problem of debt is not alone a problem of the current depression. So long as we have a large body of debt and an unstable economy, debt will constitute a recurrent problem because of its inflexibility. In order to reduce or eliminate the harmful effects resulting from this inflexibility, four courses of action are open: (1) limit the volume of debt which can be incurred in the future to such a degree that it no longer constitutes a major problem; (2) increase the flexibility of debt by altering the character of debt which can be incurred in the future; (3) take steps to increase the stability of the economy; or (4) a combination of two or more of the above. Because of the seriously disorganizing effect of debts it seems essential that some one of these courses be taken.

In order to make recommendations for dealing with debt as an inflexible element in our economy, it is first necessary to have clearly in mind the function which debt performs. Most discussions of debt tend to be conducted almost entirely from the point of view of the creditor. Here we will adopt the point of view of the whole economy. Just what is the role of debt viewed from such a neutral position? Clearly it is twofold. On the one hand, evidences of debt in the form of bonds, notes, mortgages, etc., represent convenient and desirable forms in which individuals and organizations can invest part of their accumulated savings. On the other hand, this same debt represents a convenient and desirable arrangement whereby individuals and organizations can obtain part of the savings of others either for use in the form of capital or for immediate consumption. Since the bulk of debt is incurred in the process of obtaining capital goods, the double role of debt may be stated as the supplying of a convenient form of wealth for individuals or organizations to possess and the facilitating of the supplying of capital to the economy.

The Advantages of Debts

The role of debt as a common form of wealth [10] is immediately clear. If one asks an individual to list his wealth he will probably list money (mostly in bank debt in the form of bank deposits or bank notes), bonds, notes, mortgages and insurance (mostly debts of governments, corporations and individuals), stocks, other interests in business enterprises, real estate, and certain items of personal wealth. If we should add up the wealth of all the individuals in the country [11] we would find that something like half, measured in money terms, was in the form of debt. To a very great extent the savings of individuals have taken this form.

The advantages of debt as a form of wealth grow out of its relative safety, the lack of responsibility which it involves, and the ease with

---

[10] It should be noticed that the term "wealth" is used here from the point of view of the individual. It is well recognized that a debt instrument represents wealth to the creditor and that it represents negative wealth to the debtor. From the point of view of society the two counterbalance, so that debts may not involve social wealth. Stocks are also treated by individuals as things having exchange value and therefore as wealth to the individual—though perhaps not to society.

[11] This figure would of course differ from that for the wealth of individuals, corporations, and other organizations. Also, it would not represent the total national wealth since to an important extent debts cancel out.

which it can be converted into other forms of wealth. Because debts are usually backed by tangible wealth of one sort or another and are usually protected, at least when insured by an equity in the hands of the borrower, they tend to be a more certain claim on future services than do other forms of wealth in which individuals and institutions invest, though the risk of changes in the purchasing power of money is added [12] even while other risks are being reduced. This does not mean, of course, that every debt is a safer investment than every other form of wealth, but only that the range of bond safety tends to be higher than that of stocks or of other forms of wealth.

The second advantage of debt, the small responsibility it involves, makes it a highly desirable form of wealth to the individual or institution. The primary responsibility attached to debts is safe keeping, and registered bonds do not require even this minimum. In contrast, the possession of tangible wealth usually involves an active responsibility. The owner of tangible wealth is tied to it. As one financier put it, "If a horse lives the owner must feed it; if he lets it die he must at least bury it." Tangible wealth is therefore an unsatisfactory form of wealth for those who wish to save for the future but are not in a position to exercise responsibility over tangible property.

Finally, debt frequently has the added advantage that it can be readily converted into other forms of wealth through the market places. Debt acting as money (bank deposits and bank notes) is, par excellence, the form of wealth most readily exchanged for other forms of wealth or for services. Debt in the form of bonds is frequently more easily exchangeable than most types of wealth, exclusive of stocks, because a large number of essentially identical units make possible an almost continuous market. Other forms of debt are usually less easily converted into other types of wealth, but even for mortgages, insurance policies, and other loans, the ease of converting them into other forms of wealth compares favorably with most forms of tangible wealth.[13]

The major drawback to debts as a form in which to hold wealth grows out of the instability of prices. A marked rise in prices means that the man who receives interest or principal in a fixed number of dollars will receive a smaller purchasing power than would be the case

---

[12] Except, of course, where a debt is incurred in terms of purchasing power.

[13] It should be noted that most corporate stocks (excepting bank stocks) carry the same freedom from responsibility and ease of exchange that is carried by debt but tend to involve a higher element of general risk.

if prices had remained constant. Thus, the possessor of wealth in the form of debt incurs a risk of changing prices.[14] This risk is usually more than counterbalanced by the lower risks in other directions that are connected with debts though it makes debts a less satisfactory form of wealth than would otherwise be the case.

In spite of this drawback, debts, because of their relative safety, freedom from responsibility, and ready marketability constitute one of the most satisfactory forms in which individuals can hold a part of their savings. In a society in which the individual must rely so largely on past savings for security in times of distress and in old age, the provision of an adequate volume of this type of wealth appears to be highly desirable, at least from the point of view of those who have to save for the future and seek a form in which to hold their savings.

Debts as Savings Put to Use

From the point of view of those who can make use of the savings of others, the debt institution is likewise a desirable one. For governments, the outlay for capital equipment—schools, roads, post offices, water systems, etc.—must either be met out of current taxes or through borrowing. Incorporated business enterprises can either incur debt or sell stocks to add to their capital; therefore the institution of debt is not essential to their obtaining the use of the savings of others though it is a convenient method of obtaining a part of these savings, thereby increasing the element of risk and the prospect of profit attached to the junior securities. For individually owned enterprises, including farming, borrowing is almost the only method of extending the capital employed beyond the limits of the wealth of the owner. Finally, for the individual consumer, borrowing (whether through instalment credit or otherwise) makes possible the use of durable goods—sometimes called consumers' capital—too expensive to buy outright. The buyer is thus enabled to divide his payments for durable consumers' goods between present instalments paid from current income and future instalments to be met out of the income expected to accrue at the time the services are enjoyed.

In all these cases there is an approximate correspondence between wealth in the form of evidences of debt held by individuals who have

---

[14] Unless the payments contracted for are to vary with the price level.

invested their savings in such instruments, and the additions to the capital assets of governments, corporate enterprises or individual borrowers resulting from the use of their credit. The act of investment and the act of borrowing are simply different aspects of the same operation. The investment of saved money income thus makes possible the creation of new capital equipment for individual, corporate, or government use. The growth of savers' wealth is paralleled by the growth of social wealth. The bulk of all debts are of this character.

To a certain extent, however, savings are borrowed and employed in direct consumption. Government debts incurred for the prosecution of war, debts incurred to meet sickness or disaster, debts to support current consumption—these debts, while they represent wealth to the lender, do not result in a net addition to the wealth of the community. They may involve either a shift in the borrower's claims with respect to wealth he already possesses, as his wealth is pledged against the debt, or in a direct mortgage on the borrower's future earning capacity. In either case the debt arrangement serves to aid the borrower to emergency consumption or, to the extent allowed by lenders, to consumption of a non-emergency nature.

From the point of view of the whole economy, debt thus performs the function of supplying a highly desirable form of wealth in which those who wish to save for the future can place their savings and it facilitates the creation of economic capital and, to a less extent, supplies the means for emergency consumption. Its chief disadvantage, its inflexibility, has already been indicated. As a result of the unstable nature of our economy characterized by cycles of alternate prosperity and depression, the debt payments contracted for periodically become an aggravated burden and further disorganize the economy. Because of this seriously disorganizing effect of debts it seems essential that either (1) their volume and character be severely limited or (2) direct measures be taken to increase the stability of the economy. Both remedies could of course be developed.

(a) STEPS TOWARD ECONOMIC STABILITY

While making certain concrete recommendations with the aim of increasing the flexibility of debts to be incurred in the future and thereby reducing their disorganizing influence, the main recommendations which we make to meet the more general problem of debt follow the second course—namely, measures to increase the stability of the economy. In making such recommendations we recognize that they involve the entrance of the community into a more or less untried field, one in which no writer can afford to be dogmatic, and one in which the path of development can be clearly seen only as experience is built on experience. Despite the newness of the path, the uncertainties which it involves cannot be more fearsome than the almost complete certainty of a recurrence of depressions as devastating as the present one if no steps in the direction of stabilization are taken.

Just what are the causes of economic instability? No man is as yet able to say. But in recent economic writings, two *major* forces contributing to instability in the economy have been isolated,[15] first, a maladjustment between the volume of money, including deposits in commercial banks, and the community's need for money,[16] and second, a maladjustment between saving, the issuance of securities, and the creation of capital goods. It is with these two elements in the economy that our recommendations will deal, with the aim of meeting the more permanent problem of debt by increasing the stability of the economy.

(1) *The Control of Money*

As the economy now operates, the major part of the money of the community consists of deposits in commercial banks and is created by the banking system in the process of supplying credit to industry, either through making loans or purchasing securities. As the American banking system now operates this volume of bank money may fluctuate in relation to "banking" necessities rather than in relation to the fundamental monetary needs of the country—as the violent destruction of money through bank liquidation in 1931 and 1932 clearly suggests. An important step toward greater economic stability will have been taken if the banking system be reorganized in such a way as to place adequate control of the volume of money, including deposits in commercial banks, in the hands of some central authority, presumably an agency of the federal government.

We therefore recommend that such centralization be undertaken:

[15] See, for instance: J. M. Keynes, *A Treatise on Money* (2 vols.), N. Y., 1930; R. G. Hawtrey, *Currency and Credit*, London, 1923; D. H. Robertson, *Banking Policy and the Price Level*, London, 1926; F. A. Hayek, *Prices and Production*, London, 1931.
[16] For discussion of meaning of money needs, see footnote 8, page 390.

first, by requiring all commercial banks to become members of the Federal Reserve System, preferably by requiring that they take out national charters; second, by making large increases in the powers of the Federal Reserve Board with respect both to the rates and policies of the several Reserve Banks; third, by changing the reserve requirements so as to make bank debt in the form of bank deposits convertible into bank debt in the form of bank notes without dislocating repercussions on the banking system; and finally, by empowering the Federal Reserve Board, within broad limits, to control the character and volume of the loans and investments made by member banks.

To increase the safety of money (including deposits) created by banks, we further recommend that increased power of inspection and regulation over banking activity be placed in the hands of the federal authorities; that either the easy interconvertibility of time and demand deposits be reduced [17] or their respective reserve requirements be made equal; and that the Federal Reserve Board be empowered to set maximum rates of interest which could be paid on both demand and time deposits in order that the competition between banks should not force the payment of rates so high as to lead to unsound loans and investment policies.

If the steps indicated here do not give promise of a banking system in which the volume of money can be controlled according to the monetary needs of the country, we recommend the taking over of all commercial banks by the federal government. The justification for such a step is to be found in the fact that the banking system supplies the bulk of the money medium of the country. The extensive regulation of banking now practiced is a clear recognition that banking is an activity "affected with a public interest" and therefore in a broad and non-legal sense a public utility. Undoubtedly banking is the most important single public utility in our economy.[18] If in private hands it cannot operate to serve the public interest, its nationalization seems imperative.

[17] For instance, by placing a small tax on the withdrawal of time deposits when the stipulated 30 days (or more) notice is not given in advance.

[18] ". . . the public's concern about a particular business may be so pervasive and varied as to require constant detailed supervision and a very high degree of regulation. Where this is true, it is common to speak of the business as being a 'public' one, although it is privately owned. It is to such businesses that the designation 'public utility' is commonly applied; or they are spoken of as 'affected with a public interest.' " (From Justice Brandeis' dissent in New State Ice Co. v. Liebmann, 76 L. ed., Advance Opinions 479 (1931)).

(2) *Control of the Creation of Capital*

With respect to the maladjustments growing out of the process of saving and capital creation, very much less of a statistical nature is known than in the case of banking. In view of this lack of more detailed data it does not seem expedient to present detailed or specific recommendations in regard to the problem of control. Therefore the recommendations in this field are made with the aim of obtaining more exact current information in the expectation that in the presence of such information the maladjustments will be less extreme and that in the light of further knowledge more adequate steps may be taken to reduce the maladjustments if the necessity of such steps is indicated. With this in view, we recommend that a federal body be appointed or designated to compile a complete record of (1) all new capital outlays, both as to character and amount, industry by industry, (2) all security issues and retirements, and (3) other information necessary to give a comprehensive picture of the process of saving and capital accumulation as it develops. The information indicated above should be made public at frequent intervals—currently, if possible.

We further recommend that the material thus gathered be used as the basis for determining the necessity or desirability of establishing a more direct control over the process of saving and capital creation.

(b) INCREASING THE FLEXIBILITY OF NEW DEBTS

In addition to the direct attack on the problem of economic stability, steps could be taken to minimize the harmful effects of debt by reducing the volume and increasing the flexibility of debt incurred in the future. This could be accomplished in part by action along the following lines:

(1) *Volume of Debt*

By statute or a process of education the volume of new debt incurred could be reduced—particularly through the establishment of a maximum ratio of debt to assets which could be incurred by corporations in particular industries.

(2) *Duration of Debt*

By means similar to the above the duration of debt could be limited. Provisions for limiting the life of a debt to not more than the prospective life of the asset against which it is issued could be adopted in the corporate field.

(3) Flexible Debt Contracts

In future contracts, at least until means are found of controlling the price level, there could be a clause which would permit an automatic scaling down of interest rates and amortization requirements in times of severe economic depression, when the debtor's income, through no fault of his own but because of business inactivity, wage cuts or unemployment, is reduced to levels which make it impossible for him to meet current interest rates and charges. The time and amount of this scaling down should be determined in individual cases by an administrative agency in that particular field and locality.

(4) Recasting of Bankruptcy Laws

It would be expedient to recast the bankruptcy laws along the line of the revised railway reorganization procedure provided by the amended bankruptcy act of March 3, 1933, in order to prevent a single creditor or a small group from resisting an equitable adjustment of a debtor's burden. The question as to whether the adjustment was equitable or not would be decided by the administrative mechanism in that specific field. This would tend to simplify the reorganization process and would allow the mortgagor to function during the reorganization without the disrupting results of receivership.

(5) Permanent Bodies for Aiding Debt Adjustments

The permanent administrative mechanisms such as outlined in an earlier part of this chapter should be established on a permanent basis to aid in future debt adjustments.[19]

[19] See page 390.

APPENDICES

APPENDIX I

FARM LOANS AND MORTGAGE REFINANCING THROUGH THE FEDERAL LAND BANK SYSTEM [1]

By HENRY MORGENTHAU, JR.

Chairman Federal Farm Board and Designated to be Governor Farm Credit Administration

Title II [of the Farm Relief Act] which deals with farm credits . . . embodies the plan of the President and his advisors, and of Congress, for relieving the acute farm debt situation. It contains provisions through which excessive debts may be cut down, by which interest rates may be reduced and payments on principal postponed, and other provisions for direct loans to farmers for meeting urgent obligations and for redeeming land which has ' een taken from them by foreclosure.

All those farmers whose mortgages are held by any of the 12 Federal land banks will benefit directly under the new act. There are nearly 400,000 of these farmer-borrowers, and the amount of their loans aggregates more than $1,000,000,000. They are now paying rates of interest between 5 and 6 per cent, the average being about 5½ per cent. Sixty days after the approval of the act by the President, the interest rate on all of these mortgages in the continental United States will be reduced to 4½ per cent and it must remain at that rate for the next 5 years. The banks are enabled to make this immediate reduction in interest through authorization in the act of an appropriation of $15,000,000 to the banks for this purpose, to cover the interest lost to them in the first fiscal year, and such additional appropriations as may be necessary during the subsequent 4 years. Farmers whose mortgages are now held by the Federal land banks will save approximately $11,000,000 in interest payments a year, or $55,000,000 in the 5-year period. Any borrowers who receive loans from the Federal land bank through national farm-loan associations, during the next 2 years, will get the benefit of the same low rate of interest. This rate is materially lower than the average rate on farm mortgages throughout the country. The rates fixed by the Federal land banks have always had a strong influence in determining the rates charged by other lending agencies in the farm-mortgage field and it is anticipated that this reduction in land-bank rates will be followed by reductions by other mortgage holders.

[1] An address given over the National Broadcasting Company, May 12, 1933.

If all those who hold farm mortgages should reduce rates by as much as 1 per cent on the average, the saving to farmers in payments on the aggregate total farm-mortgage debt of $8,500,000,000 would be $85,000,000 annually.

The act provides additional benefits for those farmers whose mortgages are held by any one of the 12 Federal land banks. Federal land-bank mortgages provide for regular annual or semiannual payments by the borrower on the principal of the loan, in addition to the interest on the unpaid balance. The new act provides that for a period of 5 years these principal payments, called "amortization payments," shall not be required if the mortgage is otherwise kept in good standing. In addition, the land banks are given authority to permit borrowers to postpone such interest payments as they can show they are unable to meet. To make this possible, the Secretary of the Treasury is authorized to subscribe an additional $50,000,000 to the paid-in surplus of the Federal land banks.

These provisions which I have summarized are for the benefit of the nearly 400,000 farmers whose mortgages are now held by the Federal land banks. These, however, constitute only approximately one-eighth, in terms of the total debt, of the farm-mortgage debtors. To meet the needs of the larger class, whose mortgages are held by others, and especially to protect from the loss of their farms and homes those whose mortgages are in danger of foreclosure, the act supplies another means of financing. It authorizes the banks to issue $2,000,000,000 of a special type of bond on which the rate of interest may not be more than 4 per cent. To make these bonds readily marketable and thus to assure a great reservoir from which the land banks may make additional loans, interest payment on the bonds is guaranteed by the Federal Treasury, and the bonds have been made eligible as security for 15-day borrowings by member banks from the Federal Reserve banks. It is expected also that the bonds will be issued under a previous provision of the law by which all of the banks will be liable for all of the bonds issued and that they will be collectively secured by collateral kept separate and apart from the collateral securing bonds previously issued by the individual banks.

With the funds thus provided the Federal land banks are enabled to do two things. First, from proceeds of the sale of these bonds, the land banks may make new loans on the same liberal terms of payment as those granted to present borrowers. Second, they may exchange these bonds for farm mortgages. The terms of exchange are to be based on the value of the property covered by the mortgage. If the appraised value of the farm covered by a mortgage which is offered to the land banks for exchange is more than twice the amount of the mortgage, bonds may be issued in exchange for the balance of the unpaid principal of the mortgage. In no case, however, may the amount of bonds given in exchange for a mortgage exceed one-half the fair normal value of the land as appraised by land-bank appraisers plus 20 per cent of the value of permanent insured improvements on the land. The effect of this provision will be that in many cases those who hold mortgages in an excessive amount, based on inflated values, must consent to a scaling down of the amount of the principal in making the exchange for land-bank bonds. It is anticipated that mortgage holders in a great many cases will be quite willing to do this rather than take chances of ultimate collection of the principal of a mortgage which has not sufficient sound value behind it.

When mortgages are thus purchased by the land banks at a reduced figure the farmer borrower will immediately reap the benefit. He will be given the privilege of making a new mortgage to the Federal land bank for the amount the bank paid for the claim and will thus not only reduce his total obligation but will have the advantage of the low interest rate and liberal payment terms offered by the land banks.

Refinancing of mortgages by this process of exchange of bonds for mortgages requires not only the consent but the active interest of the person holding the mortgage. He must make application for the exchange to the land bank of the region in which the particular farm is situated. There are two other ways, however, by which farmers, whose mortgages are held by others than the land banks, may pay off the mortgages and obtain new loans from the land banks. In those cases where a mortgage has fallen due and is payable, or where the mortgage contains a provision that it may be paid off at any time, the farmer may make application to the Federal land bank for a new first-mortgage loan, with which to pay off the existing mortgage. If the holder of the existing mortgage is willing to accept the amount which the Federal land bank can lend on the property, the land bank has authority to make a loan for that purpose, and the farmer can then obtain the benefits of the low interest rates and favorable terms authorized by the refinancing act, in addition to any reduction in the principal of the loan which may result.

The new act, however, provides other means not only for paying off existing mortgages but for the redemption of land which has already been sold under foreclosure, for satisfying other than mortgage debts, and for obtaining funds with which to continue the operation of the farm. The act provides a fund of $200,000,000, which is to be used by the Farm Loan Commissioner in making direct loans to farmers for any of these purposes. Preference is to be given to the applications of those farmers who wish to borrow to save their land from foreclosure or to redeem land that has already been sold.

Acting through an agent in each one of the Federal land banks, the Farm Loan Commissioner is empowered to make individual loans in amounts not to exceed $5,000 in the case of any individual. These loans are to be for a period of 13 years and are to be paid off during the last 10 years of the term. For the first 3 years, nothing but interest payments, at the rate of 5 per cent, will be required. These loans may be made on the security of either first or second mortgages against not only the farm itself but any stock, machinery, or other farm property which the farmer possesses. The amount borrowed under this plan, together with the amount of all outstanding claims which take precedence, must not exceed 75 per cent of the value of all the farm property pledged for the loan. It is expected that loans under this provision of the act will permit many farmers to reduce their burdens of debt by coming to under-standings with their creditors.

Where farmers are totally unable to meet the claims against them, it is thought that in many cases creditors will be willing to pool their claims and accept a compromise settlement, for which the funds will be provided by the Farm Loan Commissioner through one of these direct loans. This could be done either by voluntary agreement of the creditors or through the action of a conciliation commissioner empowered by the Federal courts to make adjust-ments of this sort.

The act also contains special benefits for another class of farmers; those who own lands in special improvement districts, such as irrigation, drainage, and levee districts. The officers of these districts may apply to the Reconstruc-tion Finance Corporation for loans to refinance their projects by purchasing their depreciated securities outstanding. For this purpose the Reconstruction Finance Corporation is authorized to make loans in aggregate amounts not to exceed $50,000,000. In any case where the improvement district has reduced its indebtedness through this refinancing the benefits must be passed on pro rata to the farmer-borrowers in such areas.

All of the provisions of this farm debt refinancing section of the farm relief bill are to be administered by the Federal land banks and the office of the Farm Loan Commissioner, who exercises supervision in behalf of the Government of the United States over the Federal land bank system. It is important that farmers and the public generally should realize the distinction between the Federal land banks and the joint-stock land banks, which are also subject to limited supervision of the Farm Loan Commissioner. The Federal land banks are cooperative institutions controlled jointly by the United States Government and their farmer-borrowers, who are members of local organizations known as national farm loan associations. The joint-stock land banks, on the other hand, are separate private enterprises whose records are open to the inspection of the Farm Loan Commissioner and which have had heretofore the privilege of issuing tax-exempt bonds to refinance farm mortgages. The joint-stock land banks have not been subject to the same re-strictions in making loans as the Federal land banks and their business opera-tions have been far less successful, so that their bonds in many instances are selling at a minor fraction of their face value.

The new refinancing act provides for the liquidation of these joint-stock land banks; their privilege of issuing tax-exempt bonds is withdrawn and they are not to be permitted to make any more new mortgage loans. For the purpose of permitting them to liquidate their business in an orderly fashion a fund of $100,000,000 is provided from which the joint-stock land banks may borrow, on the security of mortgages held by them, up to 60 per cent of the normal value of the land pledged, but to obtain these loans the joint-stock land banks must agree to reduce their interest rate on mortgages to 5 per cent and must agree not to institute any foreclosure actions for the next 2 years, except with the express permission of the Farm Loan Commissioner.

The liquidation of these banks will result in many of their mortgages being refinanced through the Federal land banks. In most cases this will result in a scaling down of principal of their mortgages as well as reduction of interest.

The general purposes of the mortgage refinancing portion of the farm relief bill are two:

The first is to reduce the debt burden now carried by farmers of the Nation and to provide terms on which they may have hope of working out of their debt difficulties.

The second is to provide better means, on a permanent basis, for meeting the farmers' land-loan needs.

The policy adopted for accomplishing this second purpose is to put land credit, so far as possible, on a cooperative footing. Encouragement is given in the bill to the method of borrowing through National farm-loan associations. These are strictly cooperative associations of farmer-borrowers, who assume mutual responsibility for their loans and underwrite all these loans within specific limits. These local associations are partners with the Government in the ownership of the capital stock of the Federal land banks and share the responsibility for Federal land-bank management. In the 16 years that the Federal land-bank system has been functioning, these farm-loan associations have had an extraordinary record of safe operation and have proved the worth of the cooperative principle as applied to farm finance. The manner in which these associations, and the land banks themselves, have weathered the financial storm of the last few years and the calamitous fall in farm-land values, is the most striking testimony possible to the soundness of this form of organization.

Within a month from today the office of the Farm Loan Commissioner, supervising authority over the Federal land banks, will become a part of the Farm Credit Administration, a new agency of the Government which will have the responsibility for all the various classes of loans and credit supervision which the Federal Government administers. As the person designated by the President to be the head of the Farm Credit Administration, I am especially anxious that the terms of the mortgage refinancing section of the farm relief bill shall be administered in such a manner as to do the greatest possible good to farm borrowers and farm investors and to put an end to the present chaotic conditions in farm credits and farm investments.

Applicants for loans and those who have mortgages which they wish to exchange for interest-guaranteed land-bank bonds, should note, however, that their applications must be dealt with by officers who will be stationed in the land banks in each of the 12 regions into which the United States is divided. These land banks and the States over which they have jurisdiction are as follows:

District No. 1: Federal Land Bank of Springfield, Mass.; Maine, New Hampshire, Vermont, Massachusetts, Rhode Island, Connecticut, New York, and New Jersey.

District No. 2: Federal Land Bank of Baltimore, Md.; Pennsylvania, Delaware, Maryland, Virginia, West Virginia, and the District of Columbia.

District No. 3: Federal Land Bank of Columbia, S. C.; North Carolina, South Carolina, Georgia, and Florida.

District No. 4: Federal Land Bank of Louisville, Ky.; Ohio, Indiana, Kentucky, and Tennessee.

District No. 5: Federal Land Bank of New Orleans, La.; Alabama, Mississippi, and Louisiana.

District No. 6: Federal Land Bank of St. Louis, Mo.; Illinois, Missouri, and Arkansas.

District No. 7: Federal Land Bank of St. Paul, Minn.; Michigan, Wisconsin, Minnesota, and North Dakota.

District No. 8: Federal Land Bank of Omaha, Nebr.; Iowa, Nebraska, South Dakota, and Wyoming.

District No. 9: Federal Land Bank of Wichita, Kans.; Oklahoma, Kansas, Colorado, and New Mexico.

District No. 10: Federal Land Bank of Houston, Tex.; Texas.

District No. 11: Federal Land Bank of Berkeley, Calif.; California, Nevada, Utah, and Arizona.

District No. 12: Federal Land Bank of Spokane, Wash.; Washington, Oregon, Montana, and Idaho.

Applicants for the Farm Loan Commissioner's loans, the direct loans, should write to the agent of the Farm Loan Commissioner in care of the Federal land bank in the region in which the farm is situated. Applicants for first-mortgage loans, or for the refinancing of first mortgages, should write to the Federal land bank in their region.

The administration of the new law imposes an extremely heavy task on the office of the Farm Loan Commissioner and on each of the 12 Federal land banks. I know that it is the ambition and hope of Mr. Paul Bestor, the Farm Loan Commissioner, and of each one of the presidents of the land banks, to give as full and as prompt consideration as is possible to every application presented. On their behalf and my own, I ask the cooperation of every land-bank borrower and applicant in expediting the work and in furnishing accurate and complete information to the land-bank officers and their agents. We believe that the law has been wisely drawn and we hope with your help to make of it a real boon to agriculture.

APPENDIX II

SOURCES OF DATA ON PUBLIC UTILITIES

The sources of the underlying data for the public utility chapter were as follows:

1. U. S. Dept. of Commerce, Bureau of the Census, *Census of the Electrical Industries: Telephones, Telegraph, Central Electric Light and Power Stations, and Electrical Railways*
2. *Statistics of Railways,* Interstate Commerce Commission
3. *Statistical Abstract of the U. S.* 1932
4. Publications and special figures supplied by:
   American Gas Association
   American Electric Railway Association, now Transit Association
   National Electric Light Association, now Edison Electric Institute
5. *Standard Bond Investments,* Bond Values Edition, December 31, 1932, published by Standard Statistics Company (N. Y).
6. Latest figures of earnings appearing in the press and *New York Stock Exchange Bulletin.*

Telephones

The *Statistical Abstract of the U. S.* sets forth a summary of physical data, plant investment, capitalization, earnings, etc., for the telephone companies in the Bell system. This accounts for approximately 80 per cent of the entire telephone industry in the United States. The physical items are also shown for telephone companies outside the Bell System; but no financial data.

The I. C. C. reports furnish similar figures for companies having interstate connections, and thus reporting to the Commission.

From these various figures, approximate data for the entire telephone industry were developed.

Electric Light and Power

The data for the years 1912 and 1922 were taken from the Census reports while those for the later years were derived from figures based on the 1927 Census, supplemented by the National Electric Light Association.

Since there are frequently close affiliations between this utility and others, such as street railways, gas, etc., the reports out of which the figures have been compounded are based upon allocations which may be rather arbitrary. In some cases the investment and activities of affiliated utility services are included in the figures for 1912 and 1922. But inasmuch as there were no means by which to effect a complete segregation, the reports were taken as the Census published them.

Manufactured Gas

It was deemed advisable to exclude natural gas from this study, partly because it has been found difficult to obtain data, since the Gas Association confined itself to companies engaged in gas manufacture and its distribution, and partly because the natural gas industry involves special problems, such as pipe line connections and depletion reserves.

The dividing line, however, between the two industries is not, and cannot be, sharply drawn. While the tabulation excludes companies distributing natural gas exclusively, they include some that distribute a mixture of both manufactured and natural gas. In the text, however, we have included the long term debt for all gas distributing companies by adding 25 per cent to the figures given in Table 38. This additional 25 per cent is based upon analysis of data published by the American Gas Association.

Figures of capitalization and other financial data for the earlier years have not been compiled, and hence had to be omitted. The manufactured gas industry, however, had been relatively much further developed in 1912 than the electric or the telephone industry, compared with recent years. The manufactured gas distribution systems, except for extensions and improvements, date back to the latter part of the 19th century, and the capital structure and earnings have not been changed nearly as much as is the case in the other utilities.

Electric Railways

The data for the electric railway industry were derived from the special Census reports in the years 1912 and 1922, while the figures for 1929 and 1931 were obtained from reports of the Transit Association. At present 80 per cent of the investment is in city transportation, and 20 per cent in interurban service.

Many electric railway systems have been engaging increasingly in recent years in affiliated motor transportation services. Where separate corporate entities have been formed to carry on this business, the investment and earnings therefrom were not included in the street railway tabulations. Where, however, the affiliated motor services were comparatively small and incidental, the net earnings and interest requirements of these were apparently included, although it is doubtful whether the investments in facilities were likewise included.

Telegraph and Water Companies

While telegraphs are considered to be common carriers, insofar as discrimination in service and rates is not permitted, their rates are largely uncontrolled, and they, therefore, cannot be considered full fledged public utilities.

As to water, by far the major part of the population is served by publicly owned and operated water systems, or by individual wells and springs. The position of water service is therefore relatively of minor importance in the utility field.

In neither case, however, were data available for the industry as a whole. The investment, total capitalization, and funded debt figures given in the text, were approximated from various bond lists, financial reports, etc.

Holding Companies

The detailed figures shown in the tabulations were confined to operating utility companies. They do not include purely holding companies. Exact figures of capitalization for the latter were not available, and even approximate earnings could not be ascertained.

A tabulation of holding company active bonds, however, indicates that the total outstanding aggregates approximately two and one-half billion dollars. This debt is in addition to that of the operating companies, except in the relatively rare instances where the bonds of the operating unit were employed as collateral in the issue of the long term debt by the parent holding company.

Capitalization and Funded Debt

Wherever in a tabulation for an entire utility industry specific figures were shown as to the amount of outstanding securities held within the industry itself, that amount was deducted from the total issued. Likewise, securities held in the treasury of the issuers were excluded. In case of the telephone, of which approximately 80 per cent consists of Bell Companies, all intercompany holdings had been eliminated from the tabulations available. Otherwise, however, no distinctions as to holdings were made.

But inasmuch as intercompany holdings are more commonly found in capital stock, the aggregate funded debt shown in the tabulations may be considered as practically all held by the public.

The term funded debt, or long-term debt, is not uniform throughout all public utility industries, or within the companies in the same industry. Thus, some confine the term to bonds, excluding real estate mortgages and notes, while others include the latter two categories. No attempt has been made to distinguish between the various types of debt. The figures were taken as given in the reports at hand.

Security of Debts

The available information on the aggregate investment, capitalization and earnings of public utility industries can indicate the security of utility bonds only in a most general way. For a clearer picture, consideration of the position of individual bond issues is necessary. A tabulation of utility bonds by yield accordingly has been made from data taken, primarily, from a publication of Standard Statistics Company, *Standard Bond Investments* (N. Y. December

31, 1932). That compilation presents prices, yields, amounts outstanding, etc., as they existed near the end of the year. Prices and yields are not all of a specific date, but few or none are earlier than December 15, 1932.

Not all outstanding bonds are covered in this source, nor in the tabulations made from it for this study. The total bond capitalization of utility companies, excluding electric and gas holding companies, tabulated for analysis aggregates $9,304 million, which is 83 per cent of the total outstanding bond capitalization of all operating utility companies, as estimated for the individual industries, and shown in the text.

The individual bond issues were classified into five groups—those of operating companies providing principally electric and gas service, those of electric and gas holding companies, of telephone and telegraph companies, of water companies, and of traction companies. The electric and gas operating group comprises those companies which derive the major portion of their operating revenue from the sale of electricity and/or manufactured gas. They may, however, act also in part as holding companies and provide other utility

TABLE 97

DISTRIBUTION OF UTILITY BOND CAPITALIZATION BY YIELD AT THE END OF 1932

Yield to Maturity	All Companies		Operating Companies, Mainly Gas & Electric		Gas & Electric Holding Companies	
	Millions of Dollars	Per Cent of Total	Millions of Dollars	Per Cent of Operating Total	Millions of Dollars	Per Cent of Holding Company Total
Under 5.00%..	$3,966.5	34.4	$2,971.5	44.7	$ 7.5	0.3
5.00–5.99.....	1,358.6	11.8	1,205.6	18.1	74.5	3.3
6.00–6.99.....	1,368.6	11.9	927.6	14.0	246.3	11.1
7.00–7.99.....	550.0	4.8	424.4	6.4	27.7	1.2
8.00–8.99.....	582.2	5.0	390.7	5.9	143.9	6.5
9.00–9.99.....	435.0	3.8	269.1	4.0	122.0	5.5
10–plus......	2,628.2	22.8	428.6	6.4	1,363.1	61.2
Default.......	642.1	5.5	31.3	0.5	242.4	10.9
Total.......	$11,531.2	100.0	$6,648.8	100.0	$2,227.4	100.0

Yield to Maturity	Telephone & Telegraph		Water Companies		Traction Companies	
	Millions of Dollars	Per Cent of T. & T. Total	Millions of Dollars	Per Cent of Water Company Total	Millions of Dollars	Per Cent of Traction Companies Total
Under 5.00%..	$941.0	77.2	$ 36.6	15.4	$ 9.9	0.8
5.00–5.99.....	11.7	1.0	64.3	27.0	2.5	0.2
6.00–6.99.....	14.8	1.2	32.7	13.7	147.2	12.3
7.00–7.99.....	2.5	0.2	53.2	22.3	42.2	3.5
8.00–8.99.....	14.3	1.2	24.2	10.2	9.1	0.8
9.00–9.99.....	25.8	2.1	9.3	3.9	8.8	0.7
10–plus......	208.6	17.1	17.8	7.5	610.1	50.9
Default.......	....	.....	.....	.....	368.4	30.8
Total.......	$1,218.7	100.0	$238.1	100.0	$1,198.2	100.0

services such as electric railway transportation, steam heat, ice, etc. Electric and gas holding companies are those whose subsidiaries are engaged in providing gas or electricity, though not necessarily exclusively or even primarily, but there are only one or two instances in which other utility services predominate. Companies classified in the telephone and telegraph, water, or traction group operate primarily in the one of these fields in which they are classified. Holding companies in these groups are not segregated from operating companies in the following tabulations. They form a much smaller percentage of the total capitalization and are not of sufficient importance to merit separate treatment.

Issues of companies whose operations are primarily outside the continental United States were excluded. So also were those of companies, sometimes classified as utilities, primarily engaged in providing such services as urban and interurban motor transportation, natural gas, ice and steam heat. (See Table 97.)

A further classification of operating companies mainly gas and electric was made, distinguishing those companies which were exclusively gas or exclusively electric from those not exclusively either. Operating subsidiaries of mixed systems were classified as exclusively gas or exclusively electric when information available on the company as an individual unit so indicated. (See Table 98.)

TABLE 98

DISTRIBUTION OF BOND CAPITALIZATION OF OPERATING COMPANIES, MAINLY GAS AND ELECTRIC BY YIELD AT THE END OF 1932

Yield to Maturity Per Cent	All Electric and Gas Operating Companies		Exclusively Gas		Exclusively Electric		Neither Exclusively Gas nor Electric	
	Millions of Dollars	Per Cent of Total	Millions of Dollars	Per Cent of Total	Millions of Dollars	Per Cent of Total	Millions of Dollars	Per Cent of Total
Under 5.00	$2,971.5	44.7	$175.0	49.0	$ 964.1	53.7	$1,832.4	40.7
5.00–5.99	1,205.6	18.1	68.8	19.3	354.5	19.8	782.3	17.4
6.00–6.99	927.6	14.0	47.3	13.3	198.5	11.1	681.8	15.1
7.00–7.99	424.4	6.4	1.4	0.4	66.7	3.7	356.3	7.9
8.00–8.99	390.7	5.9	......	......	125.8	7.0	264.9	5.9
9.00–9.99	269.1	4.0	23.0	6.4	7.5	0.4	238.6	5.3
10.00-plus	428.6	6.4	36.7	10.3	74.7	4.2	317.2	7.1
Defaulted.	31.3	0.5	4.7	1.3	1.1	0.1	25.5	0.6
Total...	$6,648.8	100.0	$356.9	100.0	$1,792.9	100.0	$4,499.0	100.0

The telephone and telegraph classification includes three distinct groups of companies, the telegraph, the Bell-system telephone, and the non-Bell telephone companies. These are separately tabulated in Table 99.

TABLE 99

DISTRIBUTION OF TELEPHONE AND TELEGRAPH BOND CAPITALIZATION BY YIELD AT END OF 1932

	Under 5.00%		5.00–5.99%		6.00–6.99%		7.00–7.99%		8.00–8.99%		9.00–9.99%		10.00% plus		Defaulted		Total	Per Cent
	Millions of Dollars	Per Cent	Millions of Dollars	Per Cent	Millions of Dollars	Per Cent	Millions of Dollars	Per Cent	Millions of Dollars	Per Cent	Millions of Dollars	Per Cent	Millions of Dollars	Per Cent		Per Cent		
Telegraph...	$.....	....	$1.9	1.2	$.....	....	$.....	....	$.....	....	$20.0	12.7	$135.9	86.1	....	....	157.8	100.0
Telephone, Bell System	927.4	100.0	.....	....	.....	....	.....	....	.....	....	.....	....	.....	....	....	....	927.4	100.0
Telephone, Non-Bell..	13.6	10.2	9.8	7.3	14.8	11.1	2.5	1.9	14.3	10.7	5.8	4.3	72.7	54.5	....	....	133.5	100.0
Total...	$941.0	77.2	$11.7	1.0	$14.8	1.2	$2.5	0.2	$14.3	1.2	$25.8	2.1	$208.6	17.1	....	....	1,218.7	100.0

Prices and Yields

The time to which the prices and yields used in these studies apply—the latter part of December, 1932—was one of relative stability in the utility bond market. The demoralization of the early summer and the enthusiasm of the subsequent recovery had both passed. Utility securities had had time to become adjusted to the lower level of earnings which first became pronounced in the latter half of the year. On the whole, the period was as favorable a one for the accurate reflection of the then current security of utility bonds, as determined by earnings under existing rates, cash position, etc., as has existed in recent months.

In an effort to determine what a utility bond yield signified in terms of other indices of security, the yield was compared with the number of times 1932 earnings are estimated to have covered fixed charges. The estimates were made by Standard Statistics Company on the basis of interim reports and, judging from the scattering of actual statements which have been already published, are sufficiently accurate for the purposes of this study. It must be emphasized that a figure showing the number of times fixed charges were earned does not accurately indicate the number of times the interest on any particular issue is earned. If an issue is a small prior lien protected by the large junior issues, the true situation may be vastly understated.

For what the figures are worth, however, the following distribution of utility bond yields by number of times fixed charges were estimated to have been earned in 1932 is given. The averages are unweighted by size of issue. All issues are included for which earnings estimates were published except those maturing in less than six years and thus influenced by short term money rates. (See Table 100.)

There are, of course, many other factors which influence the security of a bond issue besides earnings, but limitations of time prevent a deeper investigation in this study. Neglecting these other factors, and attempting to read back from the yields to the number of times fixed charges were earned, among electric and gas operating companies an issue yielding 8.0 per cent would appear to belong to a company earning its fixed charges at least 1.25 times. Because prior liens must make the yield of the 1.25–1.50 times earnings group considerably lower than it would be were only junior issues considered, it is probable that, on the whole, issues yielding up to 9 per cent are supported by an earnings margin of at least 25 per cent. Similarly, most issues yielding less than 7 per cent probably have a margin of at least 50 per cent of their 1932 interest requirements. Issues yielding less than 5 per cent are probably protected by at least a 100 per cent margin of earnings.

Electric and gas holding company issues yield more, in comparison with earnings than the issues of operating companies, but the discrepancy is not much larger than would be expected, considering the much larger shrinkage of earnings that holding companies will experience in 1933, provided there is no recovery from the current low level of earnings. There seems to be little

TABLE 100

DISTRIBUTION OF UTILITY COMPANY BONDS BY YIELD AND NUMBER OF TIMES FIXED CHARGES ARE ESTIMATED AS EARNED IN 1932

No. Times in 1932 Fixed Charges Earned	Electric and Gas Operating			Electric and Gas Holding			Telephone & Telegraph			Water			Figures Computed by Dr. G. W. Edwards(a)	
	No. of Issues	No. Issues Yielding Over 10%	Average Yield of Other Issues	No. of Issues	No. Issues Yielding Over 10%	Average Yield of Other Issues	No. of Issues	No. Issues Yielding Over 10%	Average Yield of Other Issues	No. of Issues	No. Issues Yielding Over 10%	Average Yield of Other Issues	No. of Issues	Average Yield
Under 1.00...	5	5	....	....	....	....	6	4	7.57	....	....	....	21	10.60
1.00–1.24....	9	8	6.65	21	19	9.38	7	7	....	1	1	....	112	} 8.92
1.25–1.49....	22	5	8.07	20	13	7.84	1	0	8.68	9	0	7.69	211	7.10
1.50–1.99....	55	3	6.53	15	8	7.63	3	0	7.80	22	0	7.03	245	6.53
2.00–2.49....	34	0	5.72	3	0	6.46	8	0	4.69	8	0	5.05	219	5.83
2.50–2.99....	37	0	5.02	1	0	5.00	4	0	4.59	3	0	4.98	176	5.51
3.00–3.99....	38	0	4.67	....	....	....	5	0	4.65	....	....	....	115	5.05–5.11
4.00–plus....	12	0	4.52	....	....	....	7	0	4.50	....	....	....		

(a) See accompanying text for explanation.

discrimination against holding company bonds merely because they are such issues. The telephone and telegraph group is not sufficiently uniform in its constituents to compare with either of these other classes. Water company bonds apparently rate much in line with electric light and gas issues protected by similar earnings margins.

At the right of Table 100 is given a somewhat similar compilation of utility bond yields made by Dr. George W. Edwards and published in the *American Bankers' Journal* for February 1933, p. 28.

His prices and yields were taken near the bottom of bond prices in the summer of 1932 and the earnings are those of 1931.

The higher yields existing at that time place all his average yields for earnings groups on a higher plane than that obtained in the compilation from December yields, but the increase in yield from class to class as the margin of safety in earnings declines is much the same.

Figures in the aggregate earnings available to meet the interest charges of the utility groups here studied have not as yet been compiled for 1932. Some idea of the extent of the decline from 1931 can be obtained by comparing the number of times fixed charges were estimated as earned in 1932 by the companies for which Standard Statistics Company has made an estimate, with the corresponding 1931 figures. An unweighted average of the percentage changes in the "operating company mainly gas and electric" group indicates a decline of 12.9 per cent. An average weighted by amount of bond capitalization involved would not differ materially from this figure. The corresponding average decline in times fixed charges were earned in the electric and gas holding company group approximates 15.5 per cent.

APPENDIX III

RESERVATIONS BY AUTHORS OF CHAPTER THIRTEEN

1. BY JOHN BAUER

I agree substantially with the analysis presented in this chapter, especially with the general recommendations of coordinated public works and money expansion. My divergence, if any, is a matter of special emphasis and procedure.

The basic conception of the chapter is that reasonable continuance of an extensive debt structure in our economic system requires permanent stabilization of basic industrial factors, especially money and business activity; with this view, I am in full accord. The question is how such stabilization may be best brought about.

As to business activity, stabilization requires not only maintenance and steady increase in volume of production, but also full employment in work that is socially useful at wages that conform to high and steadily rising standards of living. This means primarily stabilization of employment. To bring about such stability requires an extensive program of public works to supplement the activities of private business, not only as a necessary measure of recovery from the present depression, but also as a continuous part of a stable economy to offset the fluctuations of activity and employment in private business. Comprehensive planning can be systematically established with respect to public activity, but cannot be effectively applied to private business. Success of stabilization, therefore, depends almost entirely upon a continuous program of public activities, properly coordinated as between federal, state and local government.

As to money expansion, enough new money must be made available to finance systematically a program of public works for the establishment and maintenance of full employment upon reasonably determined price level. For this purpose, we need more direct and complete public control of money than is attainable under our present banking system.

Probably the chief element of instability has been our bank money which at one time is expanded without regard to basic money needs, and at another is pulled down, notwithstanding the continued need of a volume once created. Such instability is virtually inevitable when the great bulk of active money is created by banks organized as private profit-making competitive business.

As new money is needed with the expansion of business activity, it may be issued by the government for the support of the public works program, without banking intermediaries, provided that it is controlled through taxation, or otherwise on the basis of an established price level. In such direct form, the new money when once issued is not subject to uncontrolled contraction as are bank deposits, and can be directly expanded with growth of business activity.

For the desired stability in the future, the federal government must assume full control of new money issuance. The extent of bank money should, in any case, be greatly reduced. Its proper function is to furnish seasonal or other cyclical variations in the need of money. The gradual expansion of money to meet the requirements of increasing activity at stable prices should be provided directly by the government. This function does not reasonably belong to the banks, and particularly not to banks conducted as private business. As long as we rely for our expanding money needs chiefly upon banking processes, we shall probably not be able to attain monetary stability and shall render largely ineffectual any program of public works established for the purposes of stabilization.

Complete government control of money, coupled with comprehensive planning of coordinated public activities, furnishes a reasonably certain and simple plan for a permanently stable economy. This is necessary for a decent civilization, to free the individuals from the demoralization of unemployment, to make universally attainable an advancing standard of living, to prevent repeated depressions, and to preserve an economy under which a large volume of debt is not an added factor of disorganization.

2. By Wilfred Eldred

(a) Monetary Expansion

A policy of monetary expansion undertaken *in order to bring about a general rise in prices* and thus stimulate business recovery cannot be given unqualified indorsement. It is not primarily a general rise in prices that is needed to induce business recovery but a correction of the unbalanced relation of prices to each other within the general price structure. This correction can only be brought about by removing or reducing the obstacles which impede the free flow of goods and services both nationally and internationally.

To the extent that the deflation in purchasing power resulting from the bank liquidations of 1931–32 and the failure of many banks to reopen after the "holiday" of March, 1933, can be made good, some increase in the volume of money (including bank deposits) may be in order. This increase must be applied, however, in the particular localities and to the particular individuals—the bank depositors—immediately concerned; it cannot be a general increase.

The obvious difficulty about a policy of general monetary expansion is that it is not sufficiently discriminating and fails to apply remedies at the particular points where needed. It is, moreover, likely to be uneven in its incidence and to cut athwart many of the adjustments already made, as those between debtors and creditors, between employers and wage earners, etc. To be effective in promoting general business recovery such a policy would have to be combined with a vigorous attack upon some of the non-monetary influences which have contributed, perhaps even more than purely monetary factors, in causing the world-wide business depression.

(b) *Adjustments of Principal and Interest*

Reductions in interest rates (and adjustments in principal and/or amortization arrangements) should, as far as possible, be made on the basis of some principle having a general economic validity rather than left to the uncertain and uneven results of individual "catch as catch can" bargaining. Where the causes of inability to pay are general in nature, rather than purely local or individual, the remedies should be equally general in their application. For example it is suggested that all farm mortgagors in a given economic area whose mortgages were contracted on the basis of a given agricultural price level should be treated alike if their distress arises primarily because of a marked divergence between that price level and the existing one.

Such a general plan of adjustment is believed to be especially suitable for the treatment of debt in such fields as farm and urban mortgages (not, however, for the case of real estate mortgage bonds, which present a more complex problem) where the debtors are numerous and unorganized and the creditors relatively few (e.g., insurance and savings institutions). The periodic adjustment in interest paid to savings bank depositors and in "dividends" to life insurance policy holders is a suggestive analogy. In fields where the debtors are relatively few in number and represent large economic units, e.g., railroads, public utilities, industrial concerns, office buildings, etc., and the creditors likely to be more numerous and widely scattered, individual adjustments in respect both of current interest and of permanent capital structure may well be the more appropriate procedure.

INDEX

Adjustment, individual between debtor and creditor, xviii, 389
of amortization and interest charges, 86–87
of utility debts, 166–168
of debt principal, 273–274
an administrative mechanism to facilitate debt, 390, 406
Amortizations, of utility debts, 168–170
reduction or waiving of charges for, 391
Assets *vs.* debts, of industrial corporations, 180–183, 186–195
of banks, 345–346
Axias, 316

Bankruptcy, recasting of laws of, 406
Banks, debts of, 23, 326–384
in urban mortgage field, 69–73, 79–81
short-term debts of, 297
Blanket remedies, ill-advised, xviii, 4, 87–88
Bonds, railroad, 95, 133–135
industrial, prices, 200–202
U. S. government, 229–234
Borrowers, effective, steps to increase, 382–383
Borrowing, for emergency relief, 248, 250
illicit, 288
Brokers, loans by, 298–299
Budget, national, balancing, 237, 238–246
local, 288
Building, activity in, 65–68
financing of, 68
credit position of industry, 190
Building and loan associations, 69, 79–82
Business, effects of bank liquidation on, 375
Business cycle, 322
Buying, change in habits of, 321–322

Capital, control of creation of, 405
Cities, floating debts of, 22, 23
economies by, as price for loans, 240

Commercial banks, growth of, 336, 338–342
Competition, in transportation, 123–127, 128, 129, 153
Consolidations, railway, 137
Corporations, debt position of, xviii, 20–21
debt expansion by, 17–18
debts of industrial, 171–203
debts of financial, 204–210
Country banks, plight of, 375
Credit, railway, recovery of, 122–130
position of industrial corporations, 180–183, 186–195
limitations on government, 239
debt and, 292–294
retail sales on, 306–308, 321–322
expansion of bank, steps toward, 381
Credit unions, 316
Creditors, not separate from debtors, 3–4
farmers', 39–41
Currency, inflation of, 248, 250–252
devaluation of, 252–253
as money, 350–352

Debt adjustment counselors, 57, 59
Debt service, cost of, 269–270
Debtors, not separate from creditors, 3–4
policies toward delinquent, 41
Debts, fixed, and reduced incomes, xv–xvi
character of this study of, xvi–xvii
conclusions on, xvii–xx, 4
classified, 3, 6
as credits, 3–4
sum total of, 4–5
growth of, 5–7, 8
vs. assets and income, 7–13
pre-war and post-war, 13–16
expansion of, 1921–1929, 16–18
boom-time policies on, 18–19
varying strains of, 19–23
farm mortgage, summary of, 24–26
farm mortgage, present situation of, 27–45

Debts—(*Continued*)
farm mortgage, recommendations as to, 45–61
urban mortgage, summary of, 63–64
urban mortgage, present situation of, 65–86
urban mortgage, recommendations as to, 86–91
railroad, summary of, 92–94
railroad, present situation of, 95-130
railroad, recommendations as to, 130–139
public utility, summary of, 140–142
public utility, present status of, 142–165
public utility, recommendations as to, 165–170
industrial, summary of, 171–173
industrial, present status of, 173–202
industrial, recommendations on, 202–203
of financial corporations, 204–210
of U. S. Government, 211–253
of state and local governments, 254–290
short-term business, 291–301
short-term personal and household, 302–325
bank, 326–384
approaches to problem of, 386–388
relief of immediate problem of, 388–398
permanent protection against disorganizing effects of, 398–406
Defaults, by local governments, 270–272
Deficit, federal treasury's treatment of, 234–237
Deflation, of short-term debts, 22
Delinquent payments, on farm mortgages, 35–37
of taxes, and credit, 267–268
of taxes, and debts, 268
Demand deposits, 341
Depositors, demands of, 350
Deposits, bank, 328–345
as money, 350–352
creation and destruction of, 352–355

Earning power, of urban property, 82–84, 86
Economies, by railroads, 126–130
bankers' insistence on, by cities, 240
Employees loan plans, 318
Europe, its banking difficulties, 365–368
Expansion, of 1921–1929, 16–18

Failures, commercial, 195–200
bank, 346–349
Farmers, debt position of, xviii, 19–20
as creditors, 4
debt expansion by, 18, 29
resist foreclosures, 27
Farms, loans on, through Federal Land Banks, 409–414
Federal Farm Loan Act, amendments to, 47–50, 52
Federal Government, credit of, 20
aid by, to railroads, 135–138
debt of, 211–253
Federal Land Banks, loans by, 40
foreclosure policy of, 41–45
extension of, 47–50
increased resources needed by, 50–52
and farm loans and mortgage refinancing, 409–414
Federal Reserve banks, in the great liquidation, 371–375
policy toward reserves, 380–382
Finance, debt in railway, 109–122
Federal Government and railway, 135–138
Fletcher bankruptcy bill, 282, 283
Flexibility, steps toward, in new debts, 405–406
Florida, authorizes refunding of local debts, 280
local bonds scaled down, 282, 284
Foreclosures, farm, 27, 35
policies on farm, 41–45
measures against, 52–54
on urban real estate, 84–85
avoidance of, 392–393

Gold clause, 252–253

Hebrew free loan societies, 318
"Hoarding," condemnation of, 379
Holding companies, in public utility field, 142
debts of, 143, 156–158, 204, 210

Income, *vs.* debt on farms, 30–32
vs. debt, of industrial corporations, 177, 178
national wealth and, *vs.* federal debt, 215, 227
relation of, to debts, 262–265
Inflation, and mortgage debts, 60–61
currency, 248, 250–252
and local debts, 284
Instalment buying, 320, 322

Interest rates, reduction of, 87–88, 117–122, 274–276, 390
Interstate Commerce Commission, authorizes higher railroad rates, 103
  and railroad loans, 105, 112–113
  and railway reorganization, 120–121
  on competition in transportation, 123–125, 126
Investment, public utilities debt and, 148–152, 154–158
Investment trusts, debt of, 207–208

Joint Stock Land Banks, loans by, 40
  foreclosure policy of, 41–44

Legislation, mortgage relief, 47–50
Lenders, unlawful, 317
Liabilities, current business, 300
Liberty bonds, retirement of, 223–224
  conversion of, 247–248
Life insurance companies, in farm mortgage field, 25, 41
  in urban mortgage field, 69–70, 79–81
  debt of, 206
Liquidation, of banks, 349, 352
  pressure for, 355
  simultaneous, 360–363
  the great, 370–377
Loans, for farm interest and taxes, 54–55
  on life insurance policies, 308
  government, 309
  short-term cash, 310, 320
  R. F. C. guarantee of bank, 383

McLeod bankruptcy bill, 282–283
Michigan, controls local bond refunding, 280–281
Money, as debt, 295–297
  currency and deposits as, 350–352
  expansion of volume of, 393–395
  control of, 403
Moratoriums, on farm mortgage interest, 52–54
  causes of national, 377–378
Mortgage guarantee companies, 74–76, 79–81
Mortgages, held by farmers, 4
  urban, growth of, 7
  farm, present situation of, 27–45
  recommendations as to farm, 45–61
  on dwellings, 319
Mortgagors, farm, classified, 46
Motor truck, competes with railroads, 123–125, 126

Municipalities, defaulting, 270
  receiverships of bankrupt, 277–280, 282–284

National banks, decline in, 336
  time deposits in, 341
  earning assets of, 347
  unified system of, needed, 384
National wealth, debts compared with, 7, 9–13
North Carolina, controls local borrowing, 280
Notes, premium, 308

Operating costs, of urban property, 84
  of railroads, 108–109, 118

Pawnbroking, 311–316
Personal finance companies, 310
Population, compared with debts, 228, 260
Prices, for farmers, 33, 38–39
  commodity, compared with federal debt, 228
  effect of, on debt burden, 261
Prosperity, personal debts and, 322
  prolonged, 324
Protection, measures of permanent, 398–406
Public, responsibility of, in liquidation, 379
Public finance, and debt increase, 16
Public utilities, debt position of, xviii, 19
  debt expansion by, 18
  debts of, 140–170
  sources of data on, 415–423
Public works, expansion of, 395–398

Railroad Credit Corporation, creation of, 97, 102, 103–104, 105
  loans by, 130–131, 132
Railroads, debt position of, xviii, 20
  debt expansion by, 18
  debts of, 92–139
Rates, public utility, 158–165
Real estate, urban, expansion in, 16–17, 20
  bond houses, 73–74
  urban, lightening taxes on, 88–89
  urban, central offices to relieve, 90
  companies, debt of, 207
Realty market, analysis of, 68–86
Receivership, railroads in, 101–102, 120, 132–133
  reorganization without, 121, 131

Receivership—(*Continued*)
  public utilities in, 154, 166–168
  of bankrupt municipalities, 277–280, 282–284
Recommendations, on farm mortgage debts, 25–26, 45–61
  on urban mortgage debts, 64, 86–91
  on railroad debts, 93–94, 130–139
  on public utility debts, 142, 165–170
  on industrial debts, 173, 202–203
  on government debt, 212, 237–253
  on state and local debts, 255, 272–290
  on bank debts, 327, 380–384
  general, 385–406
Reconstruction Finance Corporation, and railroads, 97, 102, 104–106, 130–131, 132
  loans by, 299
  creation of, 374
  guarantee by, of bank loans, 383
Recovery, measures to induce, 393–398
Refunding, xix, 55–57
  federal debt, 246
  of local debts, 280, 285, 287
  of maturing debts, 392
Relief, measures of immediate, 388–398
Remedial loan societies, 317
Reserves, banks' struggle for, 355
  "borrowed," 357
  clear, 358–370
  inadequacy of secondary, 378
  replenishing and expansion of, 380–382
Retail sales finance companies, 209

Revenues, decline in railroad, 102, 106–108, 131
  reallocation of, to redeem debts, 276
Review, state debt, 285-288

Sales, retail, 305–306, 321, 322
Savings, accumulation of, 323–325
  debts as, put to use, 401
Savings banks, deposits, 336, 338
Scaling down, of local debts, 282
Settlements, debt, two types of, 57–58
  case for voluntary, 58–59
Stability, steps toward economic, 402–406
Street railways, retrogression of, 152–154
Suspensions, bank, 346–349

Tax-exemption, elimination of, 248–250
Taxes, farm, 38–39
  relation of, to debts, 265–266
Time deposits, growth of, 341–342
Title guarantee companies, 74–76, 79–81
Twentieth Century Fund, this study of indebtedness by, xvi–xvii

Valuation, public utility, 159–162
Values, farm, *vs.* debts, 32–35
Victory notes, retirement of, 223

Wages, railway, 127–128
Wealth, national, compared with national debt, 227
  relation of state and local debts to, 262–265
Wilcox bankruptcy bill, 282, 283, 284